The Construction of Social Judgments

**Publications of the University of Georgia
Institute of Behavioral Research:**

Schwanenflugel • The Psychology of Word Meanings

Britton/Pellegrini • Narrative Thought and Narrative Language

Martin/Tesser • The Construction of Social Judgments

The Construction of Social Judgments

Edited by

Leonard L. Martin
Abraham Tesser
University of Georgia

LEA LAWRENCE ERLBAUM ASSOCIATES, PUBLISHERS
1992 Hillsdale, New Jersey   Hove and London

Lawrence Erlbaum Associates, Inc., Publishers
365 Broadway
Hillsdale, New Jersey 07642

Library of Congress Cataloging-in-Publication Data

The Construction of social judgments / edited by Leonard L. Martin,
    Abraham Tesser.
        p.   cm.
    Includes bibliographical references and index.
    ISBN 0-8058-1149-4
    1. Social perception. 2. Judgment. I. Martin, Leonard L.
    II. Tesser, Abraham.
    HM132.C6265 1992
    302'.12--dc 20   91-45882
                                                                 CIP

Printed in the United States of America
10 9 8 7 6 5 4 3 2 1

Contents

Preface

About 30 years ago, psychology underwent a revolution. The methods, concepts, and research strategies changed from largely behavioristic to largely cognitive. Whereas models employing hypothetical mental processes were once out of fashion, they are now the mode. Social psychology, however, did not experience the cognitive revolution in quite the same way as did the rest of psychology. In a sense, social psychology has always been cognitive. Since the time of Bartlett (1932),[1] social psychologists have studied covert mental phenomena such as schemas and attitudes. What the cognitive revolution has done within social psychology is to move us toward a more detailed account of process. Our models of impression formation, attitude change, and the like have become more sophisticated and more process oriented. In addition, the introduction of new procedures has allowed us to test our models with more precision than was previously possible.

There has been a downside to this concentration on process, however. In trying to gain a more complete understanding of underlying processes, researchers have sometimes stayed within the narrow confines of the experimental paradigms within which the target phenomenon was initially demonstrated. In fact, several research programs seem to have grown up around very specific stimulus materials and procedures. Recently, there have been moves to expand some research programs by using different methods in different contexts. Interestingly, when we have done this, we have found that the initial models sometimes came up short. It was a concern with the paradigm boundedness of some social judgment research that prompted this volume. Our current models

---

[1]Bartlett, F. C. (1932). *Remembering*. Cambridge, England: Cambridge University Press.

do a good job of predicting behavior within their traditional paradigms but frequently do less well in new situations. If we approach these "failures" with a productive attitude, then we may be able to learn things that will help to increase the generality and power of our models.

We entitled the book *The Construction of Social Judgments* for two reasons. First, we hope that the research presented in the book is constructive in showing us not only where the traditional models fall short but also in pointing the direction toward more complete models. Second, the research reported in the book suggests that perceivers are more sophisticated than they have been depicted by previous models of social judgment. People appear to have a number of different types of information available to them (e.g., feelings, concepts, procedures, episodic memories), and they combine and integrate these different types of knowledge in different ways to create or construct their judgments.

This book grew out of a conference at the University of Georgia in the Spring of 1990 and was sponsored by the university's Institute of Behavioral Research. In attendance were Leonard Martin, Abraham Tesser, Tory Higgins, Tim Wilson, and Bob Wyer. A provocative set of papers was presented (edited versions of these are presented herein), and fruitful discussion ensued. We then solicited contributions from other researchers whose work we felt also presented challenges to the "traditional" ways of thinking about social judgment.

AN OVERVIEW OF THE VOLUME

The chapters in the first part of the book lay out some of the emerging problems in social judgment research. The chapter by Wyer, Lambert, Budesheim, and Gruenfeld reviews research on one of the most productive theoretical orientations in the area of person perception, the person memory model. This model has received a great deal of support, but as Wyer et al. point out, the model has sometimes fallen short as the research paradigm has expanded. This does not lead the authors to a nihilistic or destructive conclusion, however; rather, they convincingly argue that such failures often point the way to the development of even more sophisticated models.

The chapter by Wilson and Hodge addresses two basic issues in social psychology: the stability of attitudes and the nature of self-reports. In a series of experiments, Wilson and his colleagues have asked people to explain why they hold the attitudes they do. The surprising result is that attitudes measured subsequent to this self-analysis are less useful predictors of subsequent behavior, and choices made following this self-analysis tend to be poorer choices. Such findings suggest that attitudes (at least some) are not stable, ready-made evaluations, but rather are evaluations constructed by people on the basis of whatever considerations happen to be salient to them at the time they are reporting their attitudes.

Higgins and Bargh take on the general question of consciousness. The traditional assumption is that unconsciousness is "bad," whereas consciousness is "good." In fact, this assumption has been the cornerstone of a number of therapies. Presumably, the unconscious gives rise to undesirable "habits" that people overcome only by becoming aware of these habits. Higgins and Bargh present research that suggests that things are not quite that simple. Rather, it appears that automatic processes are sometimes useful and sometimes not, and that controlled processes are sometimes useful and sometimes not. Some conditions when each of these possibilities occur are discussed.

The second set of chapters also challenges some existing theories and assumptions in social judgment. They do so, however, not by analyzing these theories and assumptions directly but by presenting research supporting new assumptions. Smith, for example, challenges the generality of schemata in information processing. He persuasively argues that people often make judgments using particular instances (i.e., exemplars) rather than prototypic or schematic categories. He then shows how a number of basic social psychological phenomena (e.g., stereotyping) can be understood in terms of the effects of exemplars.

The chapter by Clore raises questions about the kind of information people use when making judgments. He argues that in many cases people use bodily sensations, such as moods and feelings of familiarity, in place of or in addition to semantic knowledge. He argues further that people's use of their sensations can be determined by their meta-knowledge. His assumptions allow us to place a range of seemingly disparate phenomena into a common framework.

Sinclair and Mark examine the way in which the mood people are in can change the way people process information. They argue that being in a negative mood causes people to categorize information into a number of narrow categories, whereas being in a positive mood causes people to categorize information into fewer, broader categories. The authors present evidence that is consistent with this hypothesis and also demonstrate that these differences in categorization can produce differences in judgments.

The Martin and Achee chapter questions the generality of the accessibility assumption. A great deal of recent research has been guided by the assumption that people use the information they most easily retrieve. Martin and Achee present evidence that people's judgments are guided by their processing objectives, and that these objectives sometimes tell people to use information other than that which is most accessible. More specifically, Martin and Achee interpret the effects of concept priming (i.e., assimilation and contrast) in terms of people's attempts to satisfy their processing objectives.

Schwarz and Bless also discuss assimilation and contrast effects in judgment. However, they emphasize categorization processes rather than processing objectives. They present evidence that assimilation is most likely to occur when people judge the context and the target stimulus to be members of the same category, whereas contrast occurs when people judge these stimuli to be members of different categories.

The chapters in the third section of the book not only discuss the role of different types of knowledge in judgments but also spell out the structure of this information and/or how different types of information interact. Strack, for example, argues (as did Clore) that people use bodily sensations, episodic memories, and stimulus information in making judgments. He goes a little further, however, in suggesting specific ways in which different kinds of knowledge interact. One of the main explanatory constructs in his model is representativeness. According to Strack, people use information in their judgments if this information is either related to or seems to have arisen from the target stimulus.

In their chapter, Millar and Tesser discuss the role that self-examination of feelings or beliefs has on the attitude–behavior link. They propose a match/mismatch model that predicts greater attitude–behavior consistency when the content that is most accessible when people report their attitudes (beliefs vs. feelings) is the same as that which is driving their behavior. Millar and Tesser present evidence that is consistent with their model, and then describe ways in which the model relates feelings, beliefs, and behavior in a variety of social psychology domains (e.g., helping).

Perhaps the most comprehensive model is that proposed by Carlston. Not only does Carlston delineate the kinds of information people use in making social judgments and engaging in social behavior, but he also shows the structure of that information, and the manner in which people move around that structure when making different types of judgments. He reviews an extremely wide range of phenomena and indicates how these phenomena can be accommodated within his model.

We began this project with the belief that it was time to reexamine some of the assumptions that have been guiding the general area of social judgment. It was becoming increasingly clear that many of the initial models of social judgment were incomplete. Each of the chapters in this volume has highlighted some of the shortcomings of our established models and has made some suggestions about the direction in which we need to head in order to make our models more complete. The process of editing these chapters has convinced us that we are indeed at a turning point in social judgment research. We have been able to identify deficiencies in our models and have developed ways to deal with those deficiencies. Social judgment research appears to be making some interesting and important moves forward, and it is an exciting time to be involved in this enterprise.

Leonard L. Martin
Abraham Tesser

I

*Emerging Problems in
Social Judgment Research*

Theory and Research on Person Impression Formation: A Look to the Future

Robert S. Wyer, Jr.
Alan J. Lambert
Thomas Lee Budesheim
Deborah H Gruenfeld
University of Illinois at Urbana-Champaign

A general understanding of social phenomena requires a theoretical framework within which both old and new empirical findings can be conceptualized. To be useful, the theory must have both specificity and generality. That is, the assumptions of the theory must be clearly stated, empirically verifiable and, in various combinations, able to generate testable hypotheses. At the same time, the theory must be sufficiently general that newly discovered and unexpected phenomena can be interpreted in terms of its assumptions.

These remarks almost go without saying. However, there is another side of the coin. That is, a theory can sometimes *interfere* with understanding, by retarding the acquisition of knowledge that is necessary to gain insight into the phenomena to which the theory is supposed to apply. The reason for this may again be obvious. A precise theoretical formulation of social judgment and behavior can only be developed and validated through rigidly controlled experiments that employ well-specified types of stimulus materials, and that restrict subjects' responses to a relatively small range of alternatives. In short, the validation of a theory often requires a well-developed research paradigm within which the relevant variables can be easily manipulated and their effects can be clearly interpreted.

Problems can arise, however, when a theory is applied and evaluated only within a given paradigm.[1] First, the use of a single research paradigm can limit

---

[1]By *paradigm*, we refer to the set of procedures that are used to collect and analyze data along with the implicit or explicit assumptions that surround the operationalization of independent and dependent variables.

greatly the theoretical and empirical questions that can be asked about the phenomena being investigated. Second, it is unclear whether the theory, whatever its success in accounting for phenomena that are identified using the paradigm, has implications that extend beyond the procedures that have been used to evaluate it. In the extreme case, a theory can concern processes that are *created* by the paradigm itself and seldom if ever occur under conditions that differ even slightly from those in which the theory is tested.

Theories that have been developed to account for person perception and impression formation exemplify these problems. The predominant theory of impression formation to emerge in the early 1970s was developed by Norman Anderson (1971, 1981). His information-integration formulation provided precise theoretical statements of the manner in which the evaluative implications of different pieces of information about a person were combined subjectively to form an overall impression of how much the person was liked. The formulation could only be rigorously tested, however, under conditions that bear little resemblance to those one might encounter in everyday life. Specifically, subjects were required to judge their liking for a large number of persons, each described by a different set of randomly selected stimulus adjectives. These adjectives were usually presented in all possible combinations. As a result, many adjective sets provided very unlikely and often quite implausible descriptions of the sorts of people one would be likely to meet or even imagine to exist. The information-integration model accounted very successfully for the pattern of judgments that subjects reported under these conditions (for a summary, see Anderson, 1981). It is nevertheless questionable whether the integration processes that were inferred from these data typically occur when people form an impression of a single individual on the basis of more plausible configurations of stimulus information that are presented in a more meaningful social context. (For a more detailed analysis of the information-integration paradigm and its possible effects on the processing of information, see Wyer & Carlston, 1979.)

Indeed, it was partly in reaction to the obvious artificiality of the information-integration paradigm that many impression-formation researchers turned their attention to the mental representations that people formed from the information they acquired about a person, and how they later used these representations both to recall this information and to judge the person it describes. The theoretical formulations that were initially brought to bear on these matters (for a sample of several such formulations, see Hastie et al., 1980), and the research that was generated by them, promised to answer fundamental questions about the way information about an individual is encoded and organized in memory and the processes that underlie its later retrieval and use.

Perhaps the most influential of these early formulations was a model of person memory proposed by Hastie (1980). The model was initially developed to account for a particular phenomenon (i.e., the relatively better recall of behaviors that are inconsistent with a trait-based expectation for what the actor is like).

However, it has been continually modified, refined, and extended over the decade since its inception (cf. Srull, 1981; Srull, Lichtenstein, & Rothbart, 1985; Wyer, Bodenhausen, & Srull, 1984; Wyer & Gordon, 1982, 1984; Wyer & Martin, 1986; Wyer & Unverzagt, 1985). The most recent version (Srull & Wyer, 1989; Wyer & Srull, 1989), to be referred to hereafter as the *Person Memory* model, can be used to conceptualize a wide variety of phenomena including (a) differences in the processes of forming impressions of a single person and those involved in forming impressions of a group (Wyer, Bodenhausen, & Srull, 1984), (b) the impressions that are formed of persons whose personality trait descriptions conflict with the implications of a stereotyped social group to which they belong (Wyer & Martin, 1986), (c) the effects of on-line and post-information processing time on the type of information recalled (Srull, 1981; Wyer, Budesheim, Lambert, & Martin, 1989; Wyer & Martin, 1986), and (d) the effects of instructions to disregard information on trait judgments and its effects on evaluative judgments (Wyer & Budesheim, 1987; Wyer, Srull, & Gordon, 1984). More generally, the model can account for differences in both judgments and recall even under conditions in which the correlation between judgments and the implications of recalled information is negligible (Lichtenstein & Srull, 1987; Srull & Wyer, 1989; Wyer & Unverzagt, 1985).

Because of the diversity of its implications, it is tempting to view the theory as a comprehensive formulation of person impression formation. However, although the model is clearly superior to information-integration theory in terms of the range of phenomena for which it has potential implications, it has nevertheless inherited problems similar to those of its predecessor. The Person Memory model has been rigorously tested under very circumscribed instructional and information-presentation conditions. In particular, subjects are usually told to form an impression of how well they would like someone on the basis of a series of randomly ordered behavior descriptions that vary in their trait and evaluative implications. In many instances, the behaviors are preceded by a set of trait adjectives with which some of the presented behaviors are consistent and others are inconsistent. After receiving this information, subjects are asked to report their judgments of the person and then to recall the behaviors that were presented. The model postulates the cognitive activities that are involved in informing an impression of the person on the basis of such information, the cognitive representations that are constructed as a result of these activities, and the way that these representations are used both to recall the information and to judge the person to whom they refer.

The Person Memory model has had considerable success in accounting for the phenomena identified under the conditions described earlier (see Srull & Wyer, 1989). On the other hand, one can easily question the extent to which the impression-formation processes that occur under these conditions resemble those that occur in other situations in which people receive information about persons. For one thing, much of the information we receive about a person is conveyed in a social context. We personally observe the person's behaviors, or learn about them in a book, a movie, or an informational conversation. Moreover, the behaviors we learn about a person are seldom unrelated to one another. Rather, they compose a temporally or causally related sequence of acts that are often directed toward a particular goal.

In addition, we do not always receive information about people and their behavior for the purpose of evaluating them. In many instances, for example, we may simply be interested in understanding the nature of the events that are being described, or in imagining how we might personally act in similar situations. When we do have a judgmental objective in mind, it is often more specific than simply that of forming a general impression. We may wish to decide whether to hire the person for a job, to go out on a date with the person, or to loan the person money. It is not at all clear that the cognitive representations of individuals that are formed in any of these conditions are similar to those that the Person Memory model postulates. Indeed, many of the processes the model assumes could easily be specific to the paradigm that is used to investigate them. In other words, this model, like the Anderson model, could be a theory of the research paradigm and not of person impression formation in general.

Finally, the interpretation of information that is conveyed in a social context may often require a consideration of its pragmatic implications as well as its semantic implications. That is, one must take into account the reasons why the information was conveyed. People who describe an acquaintance as stupid, or who tell anecdotes about another's social ineptness, often convey information about themselves as well as the person they are describing. That is, their statements constitute speech acts that might be interpreted as obnoxious or insensitive and, therefore, create dislike for the speakers themselves as well as the individual being described. These considerations do not come into play under conditions in which the Person Memory model has typically been applied.

These considerations combine to suggest that the processes postulated by the Person Memory model (like Anderson's information-integration formulation) could be specific to the research paradigm that has been used to investigate them. That is, the model does not provide a valid characterization of impression formation processes in general. This is not an argument, however, that the theory should be discarded. As McGuire (1972) pointed out, a theory does not need to be correct in order to be useful. Indeed, an invalid theory can often be extremely valuable in understanding phenomena that occur in domains in which it is, in fact, inapplicable. If the implications of a theory are sufficiently well specified, a failure for the theory's predictions to be supported can be attributed to certain specific assumptions on which these predictions are based. Likewise, the failure of an empirical phenomenon to generalize beyond the paradigm in which it was originally observed can be traceable to specific assumptions of the theory that are valid in one situation but not in the other. Indeed, the assertion that the results obtained in one situation do not generalize to other situations is vacuous unless one can state precisely what differences exist between the situations and what specific effects these differences are likely to have. But such precise statements can usually be made only if a well-elaborated theoretical formulation has been developed and validated within at least one of the situations being compared.

In the remainder of this chapter, we provide examples in support of these arguments. As a framework for our discussion, we first review briefly several assumptions of the Person Memory model that have received empirical support within the paradigm in which the theory is traditionally tested. Then, we discuss research performed in both similar and different paradigms, the results of which differ in important respects from those that are usually obtained. In each case, the research we describe places constraints on the generalizability of the model's assumptions. At the same time, a consideration of the results of this research from the perspective of our Person Memory formulation demonstrates the theory's value in conceptualizing phenomena even in situations to which it is inapplicable and, therefore, in extending our general understanding of person impression formation.

STATEMENT OF THEORY

The Person Memory model is described in detail elsewhere (Srull & Wyer, 1989; Wyer & Srull, 1989). Here, we only summarize those features that are of primary relevance to the discussion to follow.

The theory has three components, each of which pertains to a different phase of information processing. The first, *representational* component concerns the processes that occur in the course of forming a general impression of someone on the basis of information about the person's traits and behaviors, the associations that are formed among the various pieces of information as a result of this cognitive activity, and the types of representations of the person that are constructed as a result of these associations. The second, *recall* component specifies the manner in which information is extracted from these representations when a subject is later asked to recall it. The third, *judgment* component pertains to the way these same representations are used to compute a judgment of the person to whom they refer. The three components of the theory are conceptually independent. Thus, an incorrect assumption pertaining to one component does not necessarily affect the validity of the other components. At the same time, because the representational component of the theory is typically verified on the basis of judgment and recall data, there is an inherent indeterminacy of the model that may be unavoidable (see J. Anderson, 1976).

In most applications of the model, subjects with instructions to form an impression of how well they would like a target person receive information consisting of a series of behaviors, some of which are favorable and others of which are unfavorable. In some instances, these behaviors are preceded by a more general description of the target's traits, which are also either favorable or unfavorable. In such cases, the behaviors that follow are (a) either evaluatively consistent or evaluatively inconsistent with the trait descriptors, and (b) imply values along either the same trait dimensions to which the initial adjectives refer or different, descriptively unrelated dimensions. The cognitive activity that theoretically surrounds subjects' responses to this information, and that underlies the later recall of the information and judgments based on it, are summarized in Table 1.1 in a series of seven postulates (for a more detailed explication of the overall model, see Srull & Wyer, 1989; Wyer & Srull, 1989). Elaborations of these postulates and their implications follow.

Representational Processes

Postulate 1 (Trait Encoding and Organization).   Subjects interpret the behaviors the target has performed in terms of trait concepts that they exemplify.

   a. If initial trait descriptions of the target have not been provided, subjects encode each behavior in terms of the first applicable trait concept that comes to mind.
   b. If initial trait descriptions of the target have been provided, only these traits are used to encode the behaviors presented. That is, behaviors that do not exemplify any of the initial traits are not encoded in trait terms.
   c. The encoding of a behavior in terms of a trait concept leads an association to be formed between the behavior and the concept. If more than one behavior becomes associated with the same concept, a trait-behavior cluster is formed (of a sort to be indicated presently).

   To give an example, suppose subjects receive a series of behaviors that could be interpreted as hostile, kind, and intelligent. If no initial trait description of the target is provided, subjects presumably encode all of these behaviors in terms of the traits they exemplify. This would lead to the formation of three trait-behavior clusters. However, suppose the initial trait information about the person describes him[2] as hostile but does not mention other attributes. Then, according to Postulate 1b, only the behaviors that exemplify hostility would be encoded in terms of a trait, and only one trait-behavior cluster would be formed.

Postulate 2 (Evaluative Concept Formation).   Subjects attempt to extract a general concept of the target as likeable or dislikeable. If the first several pieces of information presented about the target are evaluatively consistent

---

[2]For reasons that are not entirely clear, the stimulus persons used in this research have almost invariably been male.

TABLE 1.1
Summary of Postulates of the Person Memory Model

Postulates

1. (Trait encoding and organization) Subjects interpret the behaviors the target has performed in terms of trait concepts they exemplify.
   a. If initial trait descriptions of the target have not been provided, subjects encode each behavior in terms of the first applicable trait concept that comes to mind.
   b. If initial trait descriptions of the target have been provided, only these traits are used to encode the behaviors. That is, behaviors that do not exemplify any of the initial traits are not encoded in trait terms.
   c. The encoding of behavior in terms of a trait concept leads an association to be formed between the behavior and the concept. If more than one behavior becomes associated with the same concept, a trait-behavior cluster is formed.

2. (Evaluative concept formation) Subjects attempt to extract a general concept of the target as likeable or dislikeable. If the first several pieces of information about the target are evaluatively consistent, this initial information will be used as a basis for the concept. Once an evaluative person concept is formed, subsequent descriptions of the target's behavior are encoded evaluatively (as favorable or unfavorable) and are thought about in relation to the concept. This leads the behaviors to become associated with the person concept.

3. (Inconsistency resolution) Subjects who encounter a behavior that is evaluatively inconsistent with their concept of a person attempt to understand why the behavior might have occurred (why a likeable person might do a bad thing, or why a dislikeable person might behave favorably). In doing so, they think about the inconsistent behavior in relation to other behaviors the person has performed, leading associations to be formed between these behaviors.

4. (Bolstering) Subjects who encounter a behavior that is evaluatively inconsistent with their concept of a person attempt to reconfirm the validity of this concept. Therefore, they mentally review behaviors of the target that are evaluatively consistent with the concept. This activity strengthens the association between these behaviors and the concept.

5. (Storage) The trait-behavior clusters and evaluative person representation that are formed from the above activities are stored independently of one another at a memory location that pertains to the person being described.

6. (Judgment) Subjects who are asked to make a judgment of the target search memory for a representation whose central concept has direct implications for the judgment. If such a representation is found, subjects use its central concept as a basis for their judgment without consulting the contents of the representation itself.

7. (Judgment) If a representation whose central concept has direct implications for the judgment cannot be identified, subjects base their judgment on both (a) the evaluative implications of the concept defining the person representation, and (b) the descriptive implications of behaviors they identify in a partial review of those that are contained in this representation.

(either all favorable or all unfavorable), this initial information will be used as a basis for the concept. Once an evaluative person concept is formed, subsequent descriptions of the target's behavior are encoded evaluatively (as favorable or unfavorable) and are thought about in relation to the concept. This leads the behaviors to become associated with the person concept.

Note that as a result of this activity, a representation is formed that is separate from the trait-behavior clusters implied by Postulate 1. This implies that behaviors are often contained in two different representations: a trait-behavior cluster and the representation that is defined by the evaluative person concept.

The behaviors that are considered with reference to the evaluative person concept are sometimes evaluatively inconsistent with this concept. In such cases, subjects theoretically respond in two possible ways:

Postulate 3 (Inconsistency Resolution). Subjects who encounter a behavior that is evaluatively inconsistent with their concept of a person attempt to understand why the behavior might have occurred (i.e., why a likeable person might do a bad thing, or why a dislikeable person might behave favorably). In doing so, they think about the inconsistent behavior in relation to other behaviors the person has performed, leading associations to be formed between the inconsistent behavior and the others.

Postulate 4 (Bolstering). Subjects who encounter a behavior that is evaluatively inconsistent with their concept of a person attempt to reconfirm the validity of this concept. Therefore, they mentally review behaviors of the target that are evaluatively consistent with this concept. This activity strengthens the association between these behaviors and the concept.[3]

Postulate 5 (Storage). The trait-behavior clusters and evaluative person representations that are formed from the above activities are stored independently of one another at a memory location that pertains to the person being described.

To see the implications of these postulates, suppose subjects receive information about a person P that consists of two favorable trait descriptors, T_A and T_B, followed by a series of behaviors that exemplify these traits and are either favorable or unfavorable ($b_{A,+}$, $b_{A,-}$, $b_{B,+}$, and $b_{B,-}$). Subjects should theoretically encode the behaviors that exemplify T_A and T_B in terms of these traits, forming two trait-behavior clusters. These clusters would resemble those shown on the left side of Fig. 1.1, associations between the behaviors and concepts they connect.

In addition, subjects should form a favorable concept of the target on the

---

[3]In the complete model, inconsistency resolution and bolstering are both more likely to occur if the inconsistent behavior is descriptively related to the initial trait description than if it is unrelated. For purposes of our present discussion, however, this distinction is ignored.

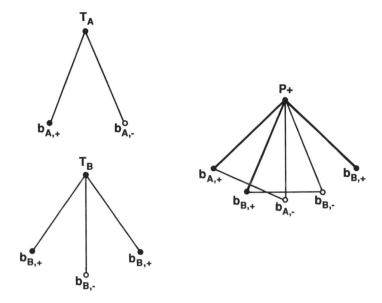

FIG. 1.1. Trait-behavior clusters and evaluative person representations formed from information consisting of two favorable trait descriptions, T_A and T_B, one favorable and one unfavorable behavior that exemplifies T_A ($b_{A,+}$ and $b_{A,-}$), and two favorable and one unfavorable behavior that exemplify T_B ($b_{B,+}$ and $b_{B,-}$). P+ denotes the favorable evaluative person concept that is formed on the basis of the trait information. Evaluatively inconsistent behaviors in the evaluative person representation are assumed to form associations with the two behaviors that immediately precede them in representation.

basis of the trait descriptors, and should think about the behaviors with reference to this person concept as well, forming associations of the behavior with this concept. If a behavior is unfavorable, and therefore is evaluatively inconsistent with the person concept, subjects think about it in relation to other behaviors. This leads associations to be formed between the inconsistent behavior and the others (Postulate 3). In addition, the inconsistent behavior can stimulate bolstering, which strengthens the associations of favorable (consistent) behaviors with P+ (Postulate 4). The representation that is formed as a result of these activities would resemble that shown on the right side of Fig. 1.1. This representation and the two trait-behavior clusters are then stored independently of one another in a memory location pertaining to the target (e.g., a "referent bin"; see Wyer & Srull, 1989).

Retrieval Processes

Suppose that some time after the information about the target has been presented, subjects are asked to recall the information they have received. They first identify the memory location at which the information is stored and retrieve one of the representations that is contained there (i.e., whichever one happens to be most accessible). They then report the contents of this representation. To do so, subjects theoretically begin their search from the central concept node, progress along a pathway to a behavior node, and report this behavior. They then traverse a pathway (if any) that connects this node to a second behavior node, report this behavior, and so on, returning to the central concept node and reinitiating the search whenever they reach a dead end (a node that is not linked to any other behavior). If more than one pathway from a node exists, pathways that denote stronger associations are relatively more likely to be selected. When no new behaviors within a given representation can be identified, a second representation is drawn from the location and the process is repeated.[4]

There are two implications of these assumptions. First, if subjects happen to retrieve a trait-behavior cluster to use as a basis for recall, they will report the behaviors contained in this cluster before behaviors in a different cluster. This means that the recalled behaviors will often be clustered in terms of the trait concepts they exemplify.

Second, suppose subjects retrieve the evaluative person representation to use as a basis for recall. The likelihood of identifying a particular behavior in this representation depends on two factors. Evaluatively consistent behaviors become more strongly associated with the central concept as a result of bolstering. Therefore, these behaviors should be relatively more easily identified on the basis of a search that initiates at this concept. However, evaluatively inconsistent behaviors become associated with a greater number of other behaviors than do consistent behaviors as a result of inconsistency resolution. Consequently, these behaviors are more likely to be accessed on the basis of a search from a behavior node. The relative likelihood with which inconsistent behaviors and consistent behaviors are recalled theoretically depends on which process (inconsistency resolution or bolstering) predominates under the conditions being investigated. In most of the research that has been performed to evaluate the model, inconsistent behaviors have a recall advantage, indicating that inconsistency resolution processes initially take priority over bolstering. When subjects have ample opportunity to think about the information they receive, however (either at the time it is presented or subsequently), consistent behaviors gain a recall advantage. This suggests that bolstering ultimately predominates if subjects have sufficient time to engage in it (Wyer, Budesheim, Lambert, & Martin, 1989; Wyer & Martin, 1986).

Judgment Processes

Postulate 6. Subjects who are asked to make a judgment of the target search memory for a representation whose central concept has direct implications for the judgment. If such a representation is found, subjects use its

---

[4]All of the behaviors contained in a representation are usually not recalled; for an explication of the "stopping" rule, see Srull and Wyer (1989).

central concept as a basis for their judgment without consulting the contents of the representation itself.

Postulate 7. If a representation whose central concept has direct implications for the judgment cannot be identified, subjects base their judgment on both (a) the evaluative implications of the concept defining the person representation, and (b) the descriptive implications of behaviors they identify in a partial review of those that are contained in this representation.

Although these two judgment postulates are somewhat oversimplified (cf. Wyer & Budesheim, 1987), they have interesting implications. For example, they imply that the traits specified by the initial trait adjective descriptions of the target are judged on the basis of these descriptions alone. (More specifically, the judgments are based on the concepts that define the trait-behavior clusters formed as a result of these descriptions.) Similarly, evaluative judgments of the target are based solely on the concept that defines the evaluative person representation without consulting the behaviors contained in it. In other words, specific behaviors only enter into judgments of traits for which no trait-behavior cluster has been formed. Consequently, there is often very little relation between the judgments that are made of a person and the implications of the person's behaviors that subjects are able to recall (Dreben, Fiske, & Hastie, 1979; Hastie & Park, 1986; Lichtenstein & Srull, 1987).

The postulates outlined have received substantial support within the paradigm in which the Person Memory model is usually tested. This support is well documented (Srull & Wyer, 1989; Wyer & Srull, 1989) and is not elaborated here. Rather, we devote the remaining discussion to research that both we and others have performed that raise questions about the generalizability of the theory's assumptions. The first two sections focus on the encoding of behaviors in terms of trait and evaluative concepts and the conditions in which this encoding occurs. The last two sections focus more generally on the cognitive representations that are formed from different types of information when the information is presented in ways that differ from that employed in the usual person memory paradigm. These latter data indicate that impression formation processes are often quite different from those the model assumes. At the same time, the research calls attention to the value of the model, albeit incorrect, in conceptualizing the phenomena investigated.

THE ROLE OF TRAIT CONCEPTS IN THE PROCESSING OF BEHAVIORAL INFORMATION

Effects of Trait Concepts On the Interpretation of Individual Behaviors

The trait-encoding postulate (see Table 1.1) implies that when a target is initially described by a set of trait concepts, these concepts are used to encode the target's behaviors. If, on the other hand, an initial trait description of the target is not provided, the target's behaviors are encoded in terms of whatever applicable trait concepts come to mind most easily. As a result, the target is typically judged to have the traits implied by these concepts.

The effects of concept accessibility on the interpretation of behaviors were initially identified by Higgins, Rholes, and Jones (1977) and by Srull and Wyer (1979, 1980). (For a summary of this work, see Higgins & King, 1981; Wyer & Srull, 1981, 1989.) This research suggested, for example, that activating a concept of hostility increases the likelihood that an ambiguous target behavior (e.g., refusal to pay the rent until the landlord paints his apartment) will be interpreted as hostile and, therefore, will lead the target himself to be judged as more hostile than he would if the concept had not been activated. More recent research, however, has placed qualifications on the conditions in which these effects occur. In some instances, for example, subjects believe that the trait concept that first occurs to them when they consider a behavior has come to mind for reasons that are unrelated to either the behavior or the person being described. Then, they are likely to avoid use of this concept, and interpret the behavior in terms of a different concept than the one they first considered (Martin, 1986; for a related conceptualization, see Lombardi, Higgins, & Bargh, 1987).

Moreover, other studies (Herr, 1986; Manis, Nelson, & Shedler, 1988), suggested that although activating a trait concept has a positive, assimilation effect on the interpretation of behaviors whose features are generally similar to those of the concept, it has a negative, contrast effect on the interpretation of behaviors whose features are generally opposite to those of the concept. (Thus, for example, activating the concept *hostile* leads moderately hostile behaviors to be encoded as more hostile, but moderately kind behaviors to be interpreted as more kind, than they otherwise would.)

Although several explanations of these contrast effects are possible, none of them is implied by the Person Memory model in its present form. In particular, the trait-encoding postulate makes no provision whatsoever for the encoding of behaviors in terms of traits that are diametrically opposite to those that have been activated. Some more subtle challenges to the Person Memory model are also provided by these effects. According to the second part of the trait-encoding postulate (see Table 1.1), the trait-behavior clusters that are formed should pertain only to attributes that are explicitly mentioned in the initial trait information presented. Thus, as in our example, an initial description of a target as *hostile* should lead behaviors that exemplify hostility to be encoded and organized in terms of this trait. However, behaviors that are interpretable as kind should not be encoded in trait terms at all.[5] The contrast effects obtained

---

[5]This assumption of the model is supported by evidence that when the evaluative implications of the target's behaviors are controlled, behaviors are recalled better if they exemplify the traits contained in an initial description of the target than if they exemplify the bipolar opposites of these traits (Wyer & Gordon, 1982). Moreover, the presented trait adjectives appear to cue the recall only of behaviors that exemplify them and not behaviors that exemplify the bipolar opposite traits.

in category accessibility research, on the other hand (cf. Manis et al., 1988), suggest that these encodings do indeed occur. The research paradigms in which assimilation and contrast effects have been observed are, of course, quite different from those used in person memory research. Nevertheless, a consideration of these effects in the context of the Person Memory model indicates a need to circumscribe more clearly the conditions in which its trait encoding assumptions are applicable.

Effects of Trait Concepts On the Organization of Behaviors

A second body of research, which has been performed in a paradigm very similar to that in which the model is usually applied, bears more directly on the model's assumption concerning the organization of behaviors into trait-behavior clusters. The third part (c) of the trait-encoding postulate, in combination with the retrieval processes assumed by the theory, implies that if subjects encode and organize behaviors in terms of trait concepts at the time the behaviors are learned, the order of the behaviors they later recall should reflect this organization. That is, behaviors should be clustered in terms of the trait concepts they exemplify. Support for this hypothesis was first reported by Hamilton, Katz, and Leirer (1980). Specifically, subjects had better recall of behaviors overall, and the recalled behaviors were more likely to be clustered in terms of the trait concepts they exemplified, when subjects had read the information for the purpose of forming an impression of the person it described than when they were explicitly told to remember this information.[6]

Gordon and Wyer (1987) confirmed these conclusions using different criteria. In their study, subjects were asked to form an impression of someone on the basis of 18 behaviors, of which 3 exemplified one trait, 6 exemplified a second trait, and 9 exemplified a third. Some subjects were told at the outset that the target person possessed the three traits, whereas other subjects were not given this information. In both conditions, however, the likelihood that subjects recalled a given behavior decreased as the number of behaviors exemplifying the same trait increased. In other words, a category set size effect occurred of a sort that is typically assumed to reflect the organization of information into categories (Rundus, 1971; for a conceptualization of set size effects in terms of the Person Memory model, see Srull & Wyer, 1989). These differences should

---

[6]Hamilton, Katz, and Leirer (1980) attributed subjects' generally better recall of behaviors under impression formation conditions than under memory conditions to subjects' organization of the behaviors into trait categories in the former condition. According to the Person Memory model, however, the better recall of behaviors under impression formation conditions could also result from the organization of the behaviors around the evaluative person concept. Thus, according to this theory, the two results reported by Hamilton et al. do not necessarily reflect the same underlying process.

not occur if the behaviors were encoded separately in memory, or alternatively, were organized around a single concept. In such cases, each behavior would have an equal likelihood of being recalled, regardless of the trait it exemplified.

More recent research by Klein and Loftus (1990) created problems for this conclusion. In one study, subjects were given a series of behaviors that exemplified different traits with instructions either to form an impression of the person they described (impression formation conditions), to remember the behaviors (memory conditions), or to encode each behavior in terms of a trait concept (explicit trait-encoding conditions). Later, they were asked to recall the behaviors. The degree of clustering of recalled behaviors by trait category was much lower in impression formation conditions than in explicit trait-encoding conditions even though the ease of recalling the behaviors was the same. Moreover, clustering was not appreciably greater in impression formation conditions than in memory conditions.[7]

In a second study, subjects were again given a series of behaviors, but in this case, each behavior exemplified a different trait concept. Consequently, the behaviors were impossible to organize by trait category. Or, in terms of the Person Memory formulation, each "trait-behavior cluster" contained only a single behavior. Nonetheless, subjects recalled a greater proportion of behaviors under both impression set conditions (M = .62) and explicit trait-encoding conditions (M = .58) than they did under memory conditions (M = .40). These data indicate that although the encoding of behaviors in terms of trait concepts facilitates their later recall, this is not because the behaviors are subjectively organized into trait categories (see Footnote 6).

In summary, Klein and Loftus' findings call into question the assumption that the encoding of behaviors in terms of trait concepts leads these behaviors to be organized into trait-behavior clusters, and that this organization facilitates the recall of the behaviors later. But how can these findings be reconciled with Gordon and Wyer's? One possibility is that the effects obtained by Gordon and Wyer also do not reflect the organization of the behaviors into trait categories. Rather, they reflect a retrieval strategy that subjects used to access the behaviors at the time of recall. Suppose subjects who have encoded behaviors in terms of traits store them independently of one another in memory as trait-behavior pairings. Suppose further that when subjects are later asked to recall the information they received, they have better memory for the traits than for the behaviors that are paired with them (Carlston, 1980). Then, subjects might intentionally recall and review the trait concepts they had applied in the hope that some of them will cue a behavior that was associated with it. Such a strategy

---

[7]This finding, which appears to contradict Hamilton, Katz, and Leirer's (1980) results, may reflect the fact that the index of clustering used by Klein and Loftus, unlike that used by Hamilton, Katz, and Leirer, corrects for differences in the total amount of information recalled. To this extent, Klein and Loftus' conclusion seems more likely to be valid.

would often be effective. However, subjects who are successful in identifying a trait that cues the recall of a behavior might not continue thinking about this trait but rather might go on to a different one. Consequently, other behaviors that are associated with this same trait would often be missed. If this is so, the proportion of recalled behaviors that exemplify a given trait would decrease as the total number of trait-behavior pairs that exist in memory increases. This could account for Gordon and Wyer's (1987) findings without the need to postulate the existence of trait-behavior clusters.

In summary, Klein and Loftus' data call into question the postulate that the encoding of the behaviors in terms of trait concepts leads to the construction of trait-behavior clusters. Moreover, our reinterpretation of Gordon and Wyer's (1987) data suggests a need to modify the model's retrieval assumptions as well.

EFFECTS OF CONCEPT ACTIVATION ON THE EVALUATIVE ENCODING OF BEHAVIOR

A further challenge to the assumptions of the Person Memory model is provided by the results of a study by Hong and Wyer (1990) in a different content domain. This study concerned the effects of a product's country of origin on the processing of other, more specific product attribute information. This study showed that concepts activated by the country of origin affected the *evaluative* encoding of specific attribute information. When the attribute information was evaluatively ambiguous, it was interpreted more favorably when the product's country of origin had a reputation for manufacturing high quality merchandise than when it had a reputation for low quality merchandise. When the attribute information was either moderately favorable or moderately unfavorable, concepts activated by the country of origin had both assimilation and contrast effects on subjects' interpretations of this information.[8]

Perhaps more important was the finding that these evaluative encoding effects occurred only when the product's country of origin was conveyed 24 hours before the attribute information was presented. When the product's country of origin was activated immediately before the other product information, it functioned simply as another characteristic of the object that influenced judgments in much the same way as other attribute descriptions. Hong and Wyer concluded that in order for the product's country of origin to affect the interpretation

---

[8]More specifically, a favorable country of origin led the attributes described by moderately favorable information to be perceived as more favorable (assimilated) and the attributes described by moderately unfavorable information to be perceived as more unfavorable (contrasted). An unfavorable country of origin led the attributes described by moderately favorable information to be interpreted as more favorable (contrasted) and those described by moderately unfavorable information to be interpreted as less favorable (assimilated). Therefore, these attributes, and consequently the product itself, were judged more extremely when concepts associated with the product's country of origin had been activated than when they had not.

of other information presented, it had to be conveyed a sufficient length of time before this information to lead subjects to form a separate concept of the product on the basis of country of origin alone.

To the extent that the processes that underlie the formation of impressions about commercial products are comparable to those that underlie the formation of person impressions, the phenomena identified in 1990 by Hong and Wyer suggest two deficiencies of the Person Memory model in its present form. Specifically, the model's evaluative-concept-formation postulate (see Table 1.1) asserts that an evaluative concept of the target is typically formed on the basis of the initial information about it, and that the later information about the target is evaluatively encoded in terms of this concept. For at least two reasons, however, this postulate is insufficient to capture the findings reported by Hong and Wyer.

First, the evaluative encoding of behaviors with reference to a general person concept is likely to be more elaborate than the above postulate implies. That is, the evaluative person concept with which the target's behavior becomes associated can also affect the interpretation of this behavior, leading the behavior to be seen as either more evaluatively consistent with the concept than it might otherwise be regarded (i.e., assimilated) or as more inconsistent with the concept than it would otherwise be seen (contrasted). These evaluative encoding effects may precede the responses to inconsistency implied by the inconsistency-resolution and bolstering postulates.

Second, the initial information presented about a target does not always lead a general evaluative concept of the target to be formed. In person impression formation, for example, the initial trait descriptions of a target can sometimes function simply as favorable or unfavorable pieces of information that are not distinguished from the person's behaviors in terms of their effect on subjects' overall impression. To the extent this occurs, it would also challenge the evaluative-concept-formation postulate.

On the other hand, results obtained in the usual person memory paradigm indicate that the initial descriptions of a target *are* often used to form an evaluative concept of him or her (for a review of this research, see Srull & Wyer, 1989). What accounts for the difference between these results and Hong and Wyer's? The answer to this question could lie in the way the initial information is presented. In Hong and Wyer's (1990) study, the country of origin was conveyed in the context of other product information. Although the context information was evaluatively neutral and therefore unimportant for evaluating the product, this was not stated explicitly. Moreover, subjects were not given any indication that they should pay particular attention to the product's country of origin or should give it special status relative to the information that accompanied it. In the person memory paradigm, however, the initial trait adjectives are explicitly called to subjects' attention by the experimenter, and are often presented in a way that distinguishes them from the list of behaviors that follow (for an exception, see Wyer & Gordon, 1982). If the trait descriptions of a target person are not presented in a way that appears to give them special importance, a delay between the presentation of these descriptions and the behavior information might be necessary to obtain the effects that are typically observed in the person impression paradigm.

IMPRESSIONS FORMED ON THE BASIS OF INFORMATION CONVEYED IN CONVERSATIONS

Much of the information we acquire about people is conveyed in the context of a conversation. That is, we hear others exchange opinions about what a person is like or give anecdotal accounts of the person's behavior. There is an important difference between this impression formation situation and those that are typically investigated using the person memory paradigm described earlier. Specifically, people who listen to a conversation may not only form impressions of the person being discussed. In addition, they may form impressions of the speakers themselves, based on the comments they make about the target.

Conversations About a Third Party

Wyer, Budesheim, and Lambert (1990) asked subjects to listen to a taped conversation between a male and a female college student about a mutual (male) acquaintance. Before engaging in the conversation, each speaker ostensibly wrote down three adjectives that described the person they had chosen to discuss. These written descriptions, which were either favorable or unfavorable, were given to the subjects. The speakers then exchanged anecdotes about the target's behavior. In fact, the behaviors they mentioned were very similar to those used in previous studies of person memory (e.g., Wyer & Martin, 1986). That is, they varied in favorableness and, therefore, in their evaluative consistency with both the trait description of the target by the speaker who mentioned them and the trait description provided by the other speaker. Subjects listened to the conversation with the objective of either forming an impression of the target or of forming an impression of the speakers. Later, they reported their liking for both the target and the speakers, inferred the speakers' liking for the target, and recalled the behaviors that were mentioned.

Judgments. First, consider the speaker-impression condition. In this condition, the favorableness of each speaker's trait description of the target had a positive effect on subjects' beliefs that the speaker liked the target, and on subjects' own liking for the speaker. However, it had a slight contrast effect on subjects' liking for the target himself. That is, subjects evaluated the target more favorably when the speakers' trait descriptions of him were unfavorable than when they were favorable. These data suggest that subjects used the speakers' characterizations of the target to infer whether the speakers were either friendly or unfriendly, and, therefore, to form concepts of them as likeable or dislikeable. Having done this, they apparently used these concepts as standards of comparison in evaluating the target at the time of judgment.

These conclusions seem quite plausible when a subject's explicit objective in listening to the conversation is to form impressions of the speakers. Indeed, they support the evaluative concept formation postulate, that subjects use the initial information they receive about individuals to form evaluative concepts of them. However, the same pattern of judgments also occurred when subjects were told to form an impression of the *target*. In other words, even under these conditions, subjects did not use the information presented to form an impression of the target person himself. Rather, they spontaneously formed concepts of the speakers as likeable or dislikeable on the basis of their descriptions of the target, just as they did under speaker-impression conditions, and then used these concepts as standards of comparison in evaluating the target when they were later asked to do so.

The results, therefore, clearly contradict the evaluative concept formation postulate (at least insofar as it pertains to the target person and not to the speakers). Moreover, they are contrary to the results typically obtained in person memory research in which initial information about a target *does* have a major positive effect on judgments of this target. What is the reason for this discrepancy?

In retrospect, it seems reasonable to attribute the persisting effect of the initial trait information that is observed in the usual research paradigm to the conditions that surround the presentation of this information. In this paradigm, subjects are often told simply that the person possesses the traits being described without being given any indication that the description might not be accurate (cf. Srull, 1981; Wyer & Gordon, 1982). In other cases (cf. Wyer, Bodenhausen, & Srull, 1984; Wyer & Martin, 1986), they are told that the target is a character in a novel and that the trait adjectives were used by the author to describe this character. In both cases, therefore, subjects are effectively told by the experimenter to assume a priori that the trait descriptions are indeed valid characterizations of the target's personality and that there is no reason to question them.

In contrast, subjects are more likely to consider an acquaintance's description of a person in the course of a conversation to be a matter of opinion that does not necessarily convey what the target person is actually like. Indeed, such descriptions may convey as much about the speaker as about the person being described. The results obtained by Wyer, Budesheim, and Lambert (1990) would be consistent with this conjecture. In any event, the data call into question the generality of the assumption that subjects' impressions of a person are based largely on the initial information that is conveyed about the person. When this information is conveyed in a social context, this is clearly not always the case.

Recall. The judgment data suggest that subjects organized the information in the conversation around concepts of the speakers rather than of the target. The content and structure of these representations should be reflected in the type of information that subjects recalled. Under speaker-impression conditions, subjects had better recall of behaviors a speaker mentioned that were evaluatively inconsistent with the *other* speaker's trait description of the target. (Thus, subjects had better recall of behaviors the male speaker mentioned that were inconsistent with the female's description.)

At first glance, this finding is curious. When considered in the context of the judgment data, however, it has a plausible explanation. Specifically, although subjects used the speakers' trait descriptions of the target to form impressions of the speakers, they may not have been completely confident of their assumption that the descriptions did, in fact, reflect characteristics of these speakers rather than of the person being described. Consequently, they paid particular attention to statements made in the conversation that confirmed this assumption. When the behaviors mentioned by one speaker are inconsistent with the second speaker's trait description, they suggest that this trait description is not a valid characterization of the target but rather reflects the likeableness of the speaker instead. Subjects may therefore have thought about such behaviors more extensively in relation to their concept of the second speaker in the course of confirming the validity of this concept, thereby establishing associations between the behaviors and the concept. These associations facilitated the recall of the behaviors later. To the extent that this reasoning is correct, the representation that was formed under conditions in which the two speakers' trait descriptions of the target evaluatively differs would resemble that shown in Fig. 1.2a.

Considered from this perspective, the representation that was constructed when subjects were told to form an impression of the target can also be understood. Judgment data indicated that subjects formed equally strong impressions of the two speakers in this condition. However, their recall of the behaviors mentioned in the conversation was affected only by their consistency with the target description provided by the female. That is, subjects had better recall of behaviors mentioned by the male if they were inconsistent with the female's description of the target (thus replicating the results obtained under speaker-impression conditions). However, they also had better recall of behaviors that the female herself mentioned that were inconsistent with her description of the target.

These data suggest that if subjects were not explicitly told to form an impression of both speakers, they did not listen to the conversation from a disinterested perspective. Rather, they focused their attention on only one of the speakers, specifically, the female.[9] In doing so, they considered more carefully

---

[9]The target person was male. It is therefore conceivable that subjects were more intrinsically interested in the comments about the target by a person of the opposite sex than by a person of the same sex. This, of course, is pure speculation.

a. Speaker-impression Conditions

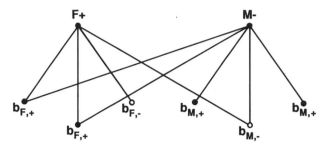

b. Target-impression Conditions

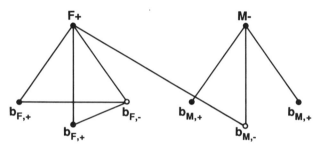

FIG. 1.2. Speaker-based representations formed from information in a conversation when subjects have the objective of (a) forming an impression of the speakers and (b) forming an impression of the target. F + and M – denote favorable and unfavorable concepts of the female and male speakers respectively, based on their trait descriptions of the target; $b_{F,+}$ and $b_{F,-}$ denote favorable and unfavorable behaviors mentioned by the female speaker; and $b_{M,+}$ and $b_{M,-}$ denote favorable and unfavorable behaviors mentioned by the female.

behaviors the male mentioned that confirmed their concept of her (i.e., behaviors that suggested that her trait description of the target did not reflect attributes of the target). In addition, they engaged in inconsistency-resolution processes similar to those assumed by the Person Memory model (Postulate 3). That is, they thought about behaviors the female mentioned that were evaluatively inconsistent with their concept of her in relation to other behaviors she had mentioned in order to understand why the statements might have been made (i.e., why a likeable person would mention an undesirable thing about the target, or why a dislikeable person would bother to mention something nice). To the extent these cognitive processes led associations to be formed among the behaviors and concepts involved, the resulting representation would resemble that shown in Fig. 1.2b.

Conversations About One of the Speakers

The aforementioned studies point out that people's statements in a conversation are often interpreted as communicative acts. That is, they constitute behaviors of the speakers that have implications for attributes of the speakers themselves. When this is the case, additional considerations can arise. That is, speakers' statements can often vary in their consistency not only with evaluative concepts that subjects have formed of these particular speakers but also with more generalized expectations for the things that people are likely to say in conversations and the meaning that is attributed to them (Grice, 1975; Higgins, 1981; Kraut & Higgins, 1984). A rather obvious norm is politeness. That is, people usually communicate to others in a way that will not unduly offend the person with whom they are speaking or others who might be listening. These normative expectations may be applied to people in general, regardless of their underlying personality dispositions.

In the studies described here, the speakers ostensibly talked to one another about a mutual acquaintance who was unknown to both the experimenter and the potential listeners. In this situation, speakers' descriptions of socially undesirable acts the target performed are unlikely to be considered impolite. Indeed, because such acts usually occur less frequently than desirable ones, they may be more interesting to talk about, and consequently, they may be often mentioned. Suppose, however, that the person being discussed is one of the speakers. The social appropriateness of mentioning things one has personally done may not vary systematically with the favorableness of the actions. (The mention of unfavorable behaviors, for example, is often an indication of modesty, whereas the mention of favorable acts can sometimes be self-serving.) In contrast, calling attention to an unfavorable thing that the other has done, particularly in front of the experimenter, is likely to embarrass or offend the actor and, therefore, to be counternormative. Subjects may therefore think more extensively about such statements in an attempt to reconcile their occurrence, and this may occur independently of more speaker-specific expectations that subjects have formed on the basis of the speaker's trait description.

A later study by Wyer, Budesheim, and Lambert (1991) provided some evidence for this. The stimulus materials were similar to those used in the first conversation studies except that in this case, the conversation was between two male speakers, P and O, and the target was one of the speakers, P. Thus, Speaker O first wrote down a favorable or unfavorable trait description of Speaker P, and Speaker P wrote down a favorable or unfavorable description of himself. These descriptions were conveyed to the subjects. Then, Speakers P and O exchanged anecdotes about favorable and unfavorable behaviors that Speaker P had performed in various situations. Subjects listened to the conversation with instructions either to form an impression of Speaker P or to form an impression of Speaker O. Later, they rated both speakers and recalled the behaviors.

Data were generally similar under both instructional conditions. Judgment data indicated that the favorableness of Speaker O's description of Speaker P had a positive effect on subjects' liking for Speaker O, but had no influence on their liking for Speaker P himself. The favorableness of Speaker P's self-description had no effect on ratings of either speaker. Thus, in no case did the initial trait descriptions of the target affect subjects' evaluations of him.

The recall data of primary interest are shown in Table 1.2. Subjects had better recall of behaviors Speaker P mentioned that were inconsistent with Speaker O's trait description of Speaker P. This result provides a conceptual replication of the earlier studies. That is, subjects thought more extensively about behaviors Speaker P had mentioned that confirmed their assumption that Speaker O's trait description of the target was a reflection of Speaker O's general likeableness rather than characteristics of the target himself. In contrast, behaviors Speaker O mentioned were recalled better if they were unfavorable, and therefore deviated from normative expectations for Speaker O to be polite. This was true regardless of the behaviors' consistency with either Speaker O's description of Speaker P or Speaker P's self description.

The interpretation of these data is reasonably straightforward. A consideration of their implications within the framework of the Person Memory model, however, raises an important theoretical issue. The storage postulate (Postulate 5, see Table 1.1) implies that the representations that are formed are stored in memory as independent entities and are not connected either to one another or to more general knowledge that people have acquired. The results of the present study, however, indicate that behaviors were also thought about in relation to more general norms and concepts that compose one's general world knowledge. To this extent, the representation that was formed was not independent, but rather, was associatively linked to subjects' semantic or episodic knowledge.

Summary

The series of aforementioned studies indicate that the information about persons is processed quite differently when it is presented in the context of a conversation than when it is conveyed as a list of trait descriptions and behaviors

TABLE 1.2
Proportion of Behaviors Recalled as a Function of their Favorableness,
Which Speaker Mentioned the Behaviors, and the Favorableness of
Speaker O's Trait Description of Speaker P

O's Trait Description of P	Behaviors Reported by P		Behaviors Reported by O	
	Favorable	Unfavorable	Favorable	Unfavorable
Favorable	.375	.401	.323	.430
Unfavorable	.385	.336	.307	.446

out of any social context. These differences call into question several postulates of the Person Memory model as described in Table 1.1.

First, in contradiction to the evaluative concept formation postulate, subjects' impressions of the person to whom the information pertains were not formed from the initial information presented about these persons. Rather, subjects used the initial information to form concepts of the speakers who provided this information. Subjects' judgments of the target may have been computed at the time they were requested, using previously formed concepts of the speakers as standards of comparison.

Second, when subjects listen to conversations about someone, they do not typically respond to behaviors that are mentioned in the manner implied by the inconsistency-resolution or bolstering postulates. Rather, they try to confirm their impressions of the speakers, based on what they say about the person being discussed. Thus, they think more extensively about the behaviors a speaker mentions that confirm the validity of the general concept they have formed of the *other* speaker (i.e., behaviors that are evaluatively inconsistent with the second speaker's trait description of the target, and therefore, imply that this description reflects attributes of the speaker and not the target himself).

Third, in contradiction to the storage postulate, the behaviors that speakers mention in a conversation can often become associated with concepts that compose subjects' general knowledge as well as concepts that are specific to the persons who are involved in the conversation. Put another way, people engage in elaborative processes as well as organizational processes (Klein & Loftus, 1990).

Thus, many assumptions underlying the representational component of the Srull and Wyer model are inapplicable for conceptualizing the processing of information acquired in a social context. At the same time, it is clear that without the model and the processes it implies to use as a comparative standard, it would have been much more difficult to conceptualize the processes that did in fact occur. In this regard, we have assumed that the failure of the Person Memory model to account for our results reflects errors in the representational component of the model rather than in its judgment and retrieval components. In fact, it was necessary to assume the validity of Postulate 6 (that subjects base their judgments on the central concept of a representation they form rather than the target's behavior) in order to infer from the judgment data that the behaviors were organized around concepts of the speakers rather than of the target. Moreover, the retrieval assumptions were necessary to conceptualize the representations that were formed and the processes that led to their construction. Without these aspects of the theory to draw upon, our conclusions concerning the processing of the information would be much more imprecise.

Whether the model will continue to be useful in conceptualizing the formation of impressions in conversations is of course unclear. In our current work, subjects themselves participate in get-acquainted conversations, and the impressions they form and the type of information they remember are evaluated under much less constrained conditions. The cognitive dynamics that underlie the formation of impressions in conversations of this sort are not at all obvious. Thus, the work described here is only a preliminary step in understanding the dynamics of impression formation in social context, based on information of the sort people are likely to acquire outside the laboratory.

Some of the factors that will ultimately need to be taken into account are suggested by the studies described and noted earlier in this chapter. That is, when information is conveyed in a social context, its pragmatic implications may often be as important a determinant of people's reactions to it as its semantic implications. In conversations, for example, people are likely to consider why a statement was made as well as its literal meaning, and these considerations may have indirect effects on the impressions they form of both the referent and the speaker. The evidence in Wyer, Budesheim, and Lambert's (1990, 1991) studies, that subjects attributed speakers' trait descriptions of the target to characteristics of the speakers rather than the person they describe, is one reflection of this tendency. Statements that violate conversational norms to be informative, accurate or polite (cf. Grice, 1975; Higgins, 1981) can sometimes indicate that the speaker does not expect them to be taken literally. The processes of identifying the intended meaning of such statements underlie the appreciation of witticisms (Wyer & Collins, 1990) but are also important factors in the communication of emotion (for an elaboration of this possibility, see Scott, Fuhrman, & Wyer, 1991; Wyer, in press). Whether a reviewed version of the Person Memory model will be able to take into account these factors and the processes that underlie their effects remains to be seen.

However, just as the original model has been a valuable conceptual tool in understanding information processing in the studies by Wyer et al. described previously, it should provide a preliminary framework for understanding the dynamics of more natural conversations and the representations that are formed from them.

THE PROCESSING OF PERSONALLY RELEVANT INFORMATION

In the studies described in the last section, the traits and behaviors we presented were identical to those used in previous studies of person memory and judgment but the manner of conveying them to subjects differed. In a second series of studies (Wyer, Lambert, Gruenfeld, & Budesheim, 1990), we returned to the information presentation procedure used in the traditional research paradigm but varied the type of information presented and the type of person to whom it referred. These factors also had substantial effects on the way the information was processed and the representations that were formed from it.

The Processing of Personal Opinions

Experiment 1.   In an initial study, subjects were asked to form an impression of a political candidate. An initial description of the target portrayed him as having either a liberal or a conservative political ideology. This description was followed by indications of his opinions on several issues, some of which reflected a liberal point of view and others a conservative orientation. After receiving this information and judging the candidate, subjects recalled the information.

Subjects' post-experiment ratings indicated that they were quite aware of both the candidate's ideology and the ideological implications of his opinions. One might expect, therefore, that the processing of this information would resemble that observed in other person memory studies. That is, subjects should form a concept of the target on the basis of the initial description of his ideology, and should respond to opinion statements (behaviors) that are inconsistent with this concept in the way implied by the inconsistency-resolution and bolstering postulates. Thus, they should have better recall of opinions that are ideologically inconsistent with the target's ideology than opinions that are consistent with it.

There was no evidence, however, that this was the case. Rather, subjects recalled those opinions with which they personally disagreed better than those with which they agreed, and this was true regardless of either the ideological implications of these opinions or the target's ideology. In other words, subjects apparently thought about the target's opinion statements with reference to themselves, and the knowledge on which their own opinions were based, without considering the consistency of these statements with their concept of the target's ideology.

Experiment 2.   It was unclear from Experiment 1 whether the failure to obtain results similar to those obtained in other person memory studies reflected a difference in the type of target that subjects considered (a political candidate rather than a person who was unspecified as to background or vocation), or in the type of information that was presented (opinion statements vs. overt behavior descriptions). To clarify this, we performed a second study in which these factors were systematically varied.

Specifically, subjects under *politician-impression* conditions, like subjects in Experiment 1, were told to form an impression of a political candidate. In contrast, subjects under *general-impression* conditions were given instructions comparable to those used in the traditional person memory paradigm. That is, they were simply told to form an impression of the target without further elaboration. In each case, the initial information about the target consisted of (a) either favorable or unfavorable personality trait adjectives, and (b) a description of the target's political ideology (either a conservative Republican or a liberal Democrat). Finally, the information that followed included descriptions of both favorable and unfavorable overt behaviors and conservative and liberal opinion statements. As usual, subjects made evaluations of the target and then recalled the information they had received.

Both the target's trait description and the indication of his ideology influenced subjects' overall evaluations of him. When the two sets of descriptions had evaluatively similar implications, thus permitting an evaluative concept to be formed on the basis of this initial information, subjects in both instructional conditions had better recall of overt behaviors that were evaluatively inconsistent with this concept than behaviors that were evaluatively consistent with it. This result replicates the recall advantage of inconsistent behaviors obtained in many other studies of person memory. However, subjects' recall of the target's opinion statements was governed by other factors, the nature of which depended on the type of target they were asked to judge:

First, subjects under politician-impression conditions had better recall of opinion statements with which they disagreed than of those with which they agreed, replicating the results obtained in the first experiment. In contrast, subjects under general-impression conditions had better recall of opinions that were evaluatively inconsistent with the target's personality trait description. (That is, they had better recall of opinions with which they disagreed when the target's traits were favorable, but better recall of opinions with which they agreed when the target's traits were unfavorable.)

Second, when the target's personality trait description was favorable, the recall of his opinions was not affected by his ideology, replicating the results of Experiment 1. When the target's personality traits were unfavorable, however, opinion statements had a recall advantage if they were ideologically inconsistent with the target's political orientation.

The evidence that the effect of the ideological consistency of opinion statements on their recall depended on the nature of the target's personality trait description might seem a bit odd. However, it has a quite plausible explanation. One of the unfavorable personality traits we used was *insincere*. Conceivably, this attribute stimulated subjects to think more extensively about opinion statements that potentially confirmed this insincerity (that is, statements that were inconsistent with the target's general ideology and, therefore, suggested that he might not believe what he was saying). In the absence of an explicit indication of the target's insincerity, however, subjects may take the target's expression of opinion at face value, and not think of their consistency with the target's ideology.

The effects of task objectives on the recall of opinion statements are also readily explainable. Subjects in both conditions apparently encoded the opinion statements as either favorable or unfavorable, depending on whether they agreed or disagreed with them. When the target was someone whose social role and relationship to the subject was not stated, however, subjects may have considered the validity of his opinions to be of little importance. Therefore, they did not attempt to assess the validity of these opinions. Rather, they thought about the evaluative implications of those opinions with reference to the target's more general personality. In doing so, they responded to evaluative inconsistencies between these opinions and the target's personality traits in a manner analogous to that implied by the inconsistency-resolution postulate, and this activity resulted in a recall advantage of these evaluatively inconsistent opinions later.

The opinions of a politician, however, can have personal and social consequences, and so their validity is important. In evaluating a politician, therefore, subjects thought particularly carefully about the opinions with which they disagreed and evaluated their validity with reference to their personal beliefs about the issues of concern. Consequently, the opinions with which the subjects disagreed were processed more extensively than opinions with which subjects agreed regardless of the target's ideology and general personality. As a result, the former opinions were better recalled later on.

The cognitive representations that are suggested by these conclusions have several components. Consider conditions in which the trait descriptions and the target's ideology are both considered to be unfavorable. Concepts based on these descriptions (denoted T- and Ideology, respectively) presumably combine to produce an unfavorable person concept, P-, around which the target's overt behaviors are organized in the manner implied by the Person Memory model. This activity results in a representation that is similar under both instructional conditions and is of the type shown on the left side of Figs. 1.3a and 1.3b.

The opinion statements, however, are not considered with reference to the overall concept of the person (P-). Specifically, they are encoded both descriptively (in terms of their ideological implications) and evaluatively (based on subjects' agreement with them). Subjects think about the descriptive implications of the opinions with reference to their concept of the target's ideology. Moreover, if subjects have reason to believe that the target is insincere, they think about opinions that are descriptively inconsistent with this concept in relation to other opinions the target has expressed in an attempt to evaluate their sincerity, producing inter-item associations.

The evaluative encodings of the target's opinion appear to be processed differently, depending on the importance of these opinions. Under general-impression conditions, the validity of the target's opinion is of little importance. In this case, subjects think about these opinions with reference to the (unfavorable) trait concept of the target and attempt to reconcile those opinions that are evaluatively inconsistent with this concept. This activity leads inter-item associations to be formed of the sort shown in Fig. 1.3a. Under politician-impression conditions, however, subjects think about the target's opinions with reference to general issue-relevant knowledge they have acquired in an attempt to assess their validity. This cognitive activity, which is more extensive when subjects disagree with the opinions than when they agree with them, produces associations be-

a. General-Impression Objective

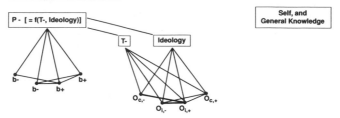

b. Politician-Impression Objective

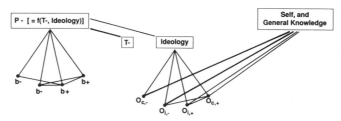

c. Representative-Judgment Objective

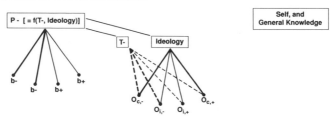

FIG. 1.3.   Hypothetical representations formed under (a) general-impression conditions, (b) politician-impression conditions, and (c) conditions in which subjects are told to make a specific judgment of the target, P. In each representation, P-, T-, and Ideology denote person, trait, and ideological concepts of the target formed from an initial description of him; b + and b − denote favorable and unfavorable behaviors; $o_{c,-}$ and $o_{i,-}$ denote unfavorable opinion statements that are ideologically consistent and inconsistent, respectively, with the target's ideology. Wider pathways denote stronger associations with the items they connect. Items that are inconsistent with the concept with which they are connected are assumed to become associated through inconsistency resolution with the two items that immediately precede them in the set of those that are connected to this concept.

tween the opinion statements and features of this general knowledge. Consequently, the representations that are formed would resemble those shown on the right side of Fig. 1.3b.

Effects of Target Relevance On Information Processing

In the two conditions just described, subjects were asked to form a global impression of the target who was of little personal relevance to them. Their cognitive responses to information are likely to differ when they have a more specific judgmental objective in mind that makes the validity of the concepts they form of the target more important. In a third (*representative-judgment*) condition of Experiment 2, subjects were told to decide if the target was the sort of person they would like to have accompany them to an important social gathering at which the impression the people formed of them personally was likely to depend in part on the sort of person they were with. This condition differs from the other two in that the target's behavior and expressions of opinion have potential implications for the subjects themselves. Therefore, subjects are likely to consider it more important to form valid concepts of the target than they do under the other two task objective conditions. Consequently, they might devote more effort to confirming the validity of the concepts they form.

The results we obtained under representative-judgment conditions are consistent with these speculations. The factors that affected the recall of information in these conditions were the same as those that affected its recall in general-impression conditions. However, the effects of these factors were opposite in direction. That is, subjects had better recall of overt behaviors that were consistent rather than inconsistent with the general person concept they had formed from the initial information. Moreover, under conditions in which the trait description of the target was unfavorable, they had better recall of opinion statements that were ideologically consistent rather than inconsistent with the target's political orientation, and nonsignificantly better recall of opinion statements that were evaluatively consistent with the target's trait description. These results suggest that subjects in this condition generally did not attempt to reconcile the inconsistencies of individual items with their concepts of the target, contrary to the implications of Postulate 3. Rather, they responded to inconsistencies by reviewing information that confirmed the validity of these concepts, as implied by Postulate 4. The representation suggested by the data obtained in this condition, therefore, resembles that shown in Fig. 1.3c.

Summary

Subjects clearly engage in different cognitive processing of the opinions a person expresses than of overt behaviors the person performs. Moreover, the way these opinions are processed depends on both the type of person who expresses them and the implications of other information about the person. The more specific implications of our findings are difficult to assimilate. However, although our results are not always of the sort implied by Person Memory theory, a consideration of these results in terms of the constructs of this theory permit some reasonable conclusions to be drawn.

First, the processes implied by the inconsistency-resolution postulate appear to occur only when subjects have the objective of forming an overall impression of a person with whom they are unlikely to be identified and, therefore, is not personally important to them. When the target is someone about whom it is important to have an accurate impression, subjects may give more priority to bolstering in order to confirm the validity of the concepts they have formed of the target rather than attempting to reconcile the inconsistency of individual items of information with these concepts.

Second, subjects encode a person's opinion statements both descriptively (in terms of the ideology they convey) and evaluatively (in terms of their favorableness). However, the effects of these encodings on subjects' later processing of the statements depend on the importance that subjects attach to the validity of the target's opinions. If the target's opinions are of little consequence, subjects think about them in relation to the target's personality trait description, and respond to evaluative inconsistencies that exist in much the same way they respond to inconsistencies between the target's overt behavior and their general evaluative concepts of him. If the validity of the target's opinions is important, however (e.g., if the target is someone whose opinions have social consequences), subjects may evaluate these opinions with reference to their general knowledge about the issues at hand, thinking more extensively about opinions with which they disagree than those with which they agree.

Our conceptualization of the processes that occurred in the present studies is obviously quite tentative. However, the thrust of our present discussions is twofold. First, it is obvious that the representational component of the Person Memory model as it is now stated cannot account for the entire pattern of results we have obtained. To recognize this limitation, however, it was necessary to move away from the stimulus materials and instructional conditions in which the model has typically been tested. At the same time, the phenomena we have uncovered in this research would probably not even have been investigated except for the existence of the Person Memory model and of the paradigm in which it is usually applied. It was only within the framework provided by the theory that general questions arose that led our research to be conducted in the first place.

Second, the interpretation of our data, complex though it may be, would be even more difficult without reference to the constructs and processes that the theory postulates. Thus, although the theory as stated is inapplicable under the conditions we investigated, a conceptualization of our results in terms of the theory's constructs calls attention to specific assumptions that may not be valid under these conditions, and permits the development of more specific hypotheses concerning the processes that do in fact occur.

CONCLUDING REMARKS

In this chapter, we have called attention to two consequences of theory development using our own theory of person memory and judgment as an example. First, the more precisely the assumptions of a theory and their implications are specified, the more likely it is that rigorous tests of the theory will require the development of a restricted research paradigm within which theory-relevant variables can be manipulated and their effects on specific responses can be measured. There is a danger, therefore, that the paradigm developed for such purposes *creates* the phenomena that are observed rather than capturing more general phenomena that exist outside the conditions in which the theory is applied.

At the same time, we have argued that if a theory is well-specified and its assumptions have been empirically validated within the paradigm that has been used to evaluate it, it can be a valuable tool in conceptualizing phenomena identified in other situations in which it is actually invalid. That is, differences between these phenomena and those observed within the paradigm in which the model has been tested can often be traced to specific sets of assumptions that do not generalize over the conditions being compared. Consequently, an incorrect theory is not necessarily a poor one but, to the contrary, may be very valuable.

This point has also been made, far more eloquently than we can express it, by William McGuire (1972). We close this chapter with his words, which have had a profound impact on our own theoretical and empirical work since they were written two decades ago:

> The danger of a paradigm lies not so much in its persisting in the face of some contradictory evidence as in the possibility that it will blind workers in the field to the implications and even existence of discordant evidence . . . A researcher . . . should learn any one paradigm thoroughly and master it so that he can use it creatively, but not think of it in such exclusive terms that it blinds him to the usefulness of the other paradigms. . . .
>
> When there is not exclusive preoccupation with one paradigm that blinds the researcher to the contrary evidence and creative value of the other approaches, we see no danger in continuing to use it for the derivation of predictions and the understanding of findings, even though it has numerous shortcomings. . . . We feel that an appropriate analogy for the use of an imperfect paradigm can be found in the image of a Boy Scout lost in the woods. If the boy strikes out in any one direction and keeps making progress in that direction, it is likely that he will eventually find his way out of the woods. It might be that if he had pursued a different line of progress he would have gotten out even sooner, but almost any line of advance will suffice if pursued sufficiently long. The only real danger is that one will not persist in any one direction but will wander around at random and never get out of the woods. Analogously, if the empirical scientist is lost in a complex area, his pursuing the implications of any reasonable paradigm in a steady direction will probably lead him to some ultimate clarification of the area. If instead he drops each theory as soon as the slightest negative evidence crops up, there results the danger that he will wander around in circles and not obtain any clarification. The researcher who keeps the faith and pursues his paradigm to ultimate enlightenment may find that there is a much better theory he could have chosen initially. But his persistence will also have demonstrated the truth of Blake's proverb that "if the fool would persist in his folly, he would become wise." (McGuire, 1972, pp. 137–138)

ACKNOWLEDGMENTS

The writing of this chapter and much of the research reported herein was supported by grant MH 3-8585 from the National Institute of Mental Health. Appreciation is extended to the University of Illinois Social Cognition Group for their comments and suggestions on both the theoretical ideas conveyed in the article and comments and advice on many of the experiments cited.

REFERENCES

Anderson, J. R. (1976). *Language, memory, and thought.* Hillsdale, NJ: Lawrence Erlbaum Associates.

Anderson, N. H. (1971). Integration theory and attitude change. *Psychological Review, 78,* 171–206.

Anderson, N. H. (1981). *Foundations of information integration theory.* New York: Academic.

Carlston, D. E. (1980). Events, inferences, and impression formation. In R. Hastie, T. Ostrom, E. Ebbesen, R. Wyer, D. Hamilton, & D. Carlston (Eds.), *Person memory: The cognitive basis of social perception* (pp. 89–119). Hillsdale, NJ: Lawrence Erlbaum Associates.

Dreben, E. K., Fiske, S. T., & Hastie, R. (1979). The independence of item and evaluative information: Impression and recall order effects in behavior-based impression formation. *Journal of Personality and Social Psychology, 37,* 1758–1768.

Gordon, S. E., & Wyer, R. S. (1987). Person memory: Category set-size effects on the recall of a person's behaviors. *Journal of Personality and Social Psychology, 53,* 648–662.

Grice, H. (1975). Logic and conversation. In P. Cole & J. Morgan (Eds.), *Syntax and semantics: Vol. 3. Speech acts* (pp. 68–134). New York: Academic.

Hamilton, D. L., Katz, L. B., & Leirer, V. O. (1980). Cognitive representation of personality impressions: Organizational processes in first impression formation. *Journal of Personality and Social Psychology, 39,* 1050–1063.

Hastie, R. (1980). Memory for behavioral information that confirms or contradicts a personality impression. In R. Hastie, T. Ostrom, E. Ebbesen, R. Wyer, D. Hamilton, & D. Carlston (Eds.), *Person memory: The cognitive basis of social perception* (pp. 155–177). Hillsdale, NJ: Lawrence Erlbaum Associates.

Hastie, R., Ostrom, T. M., Ebbesen, E. B., Wyer, R. S., Hamilton, D. L., & Carlston, D. E. (Eds.). (1980). *Person memory: The cognitive basis of social perception.* Hillsdale, NJ: Lawrence Erlbaum Associates.

Hastie, R., & Park, B. (1986). The relationship between memory and judgment depends on whether the judgment task is memory-based or on-line. *Psychological Review, 93,* 258–268.

Herr, P. (1986). Consequences of priming: Judgment and behavior. *Journal of Personality and Social Psychology, 51,* 1106–1115.

Higgins, E. T. (1981). The "communication game": Implications for social cognition and persuasion. In E. T. Higgins, C. P. Herman, & M. P. Zanna (Eds.), *Social cognition: The Ontario Symposium* (Vol. 1, pp. 343–392). Hillsdale, NJ: Lawrence Erlbaum Associates.

Higgins, E. T., & King, G. (1981). Accessibility of social constructs: Information processing consequences of individual and contextual variability. In N. Cantor & J. F. Kihlstrom (Eds.), *Personality, cognition, and social interaction* (pp. 69–121). Hillsdale, NJ: Lawrence Erlbaum Associates.

Higgins, E. T., Rholes, W. S., & Jones, C. R. (1977). Category accessibility and impression formation. *Journal of Experimental Social Psychology, 13,* 141–154.

Hong, S. T., & Wyer, R. S. (1990). Determinants of product evaluation: Country of origin, intrinsic attributes, and time delay between information presentation and judgment. *Journal of Consumer Research, 17,* 277–288.

Klein, S. B., & Loftus, J. (1990). Rethinking the role of organization in person memory: An independent trace storage model. *Journal of Personality and Social Psychology, 59,* 400–410.

Kraut, R. E., & Higgins, E. T. (1984). Communication and social cognition. In R. S. Wyer & T. K. Srull (Eds.), *Handbook of social cognition* (Vol. 3, pp. 87–127). Hillsdale, NJ: Lawrence Erlbaum Associates.

Lichtenstein, M., & Srull, T. K. (1987). Processing objectives as a determinant of the relationship between recall and judgment. *Journal of Experimental Social Psychology, 23,* 93–118.

Lombardi, W. J., Higgins, E. T., & Bargh, J. A. (1987). The role of consciousness in priming effects on categorization. *Personality and Social Psychology Bulletin, 13,* 411–429.

Manis, M., Nelson, T. E., & Shedler, J. (1988). Stereotypes and social judgment: Extremity, assimilation, and contrast. *Journal of Personality and Social Psychology, 55,* 28–36.

Martin, L. L. (1986). Set/Reset: The use and disuse of concepts in impression formation. *Journal of Personality and Social Psychology, 51,* 493–504.

McGuire, W. J. (1972). Attitude change: An information processing paradigm. In C. G. McClintock (Ed.), *Experimental social psychology.* New York: Holt, Rinehart & Winston.

Rundus, D. (1971). Analysis of rehearsal processes in free recall. *Journal of Experimental Psychology, 89,* 63–77.

Scott, C. K., Fuhrman, R. W., & Wyer, R. S. (1991). Information processing in close relationships. In G. Fletcher & F. Fincham (Eds.), *Cognition in close relationships* (pp. 37–68). Hillsdale, NJ: Lawrence Erlbaum Associates.

Srull, T. K. (1981). Person memory: Some tests of associative storage and retrieval models. *Journal of Experimental Psychology: Human Learning and Memory, 7,* 440–463.

Srull, T. K., Lichtenstein, M., & Rothbart, M. (1985). Associative storage and retrieval processes in person memory. *Journal of Experimental Psychology: Learning, Memory, and Cognition, 11,* 316–345.

Srull, T. K., & Wyer, R. S. (1979). The role of category accessibility in the interpretation of information about persons: Some determinants and implications. *Journal of Personality and Social Psychology, 37,* 1660–1672.

Srull, T. K., & Wyer, R. S. (1980). Category accessibility and social perception. Some implications for the study of person memory and interpersonal judgment. *Journal of Personality and Social Psychology, 38,* 841–856.

Srull, T. K., & Wyer, R. S. (1989). Person memory and judgment. *Psychological Review, 96,* 58–83.

Wyer, R. S. (in press). Information processing in interpersonal communication. In D. E. Hewes (Ed.), *The cognitive bases of interpersonal communication.* Hillsdale, NJ: Lawrence Erlbaum Associates.

Wyer, R. S., Bodenhausen, G. V., & Srull, T. K. (1984). The cognitive representation of persons and groups and its effect on recall and recognition memory. *Journal of Experimental Social Psychology, 20,* 445–469.

Wyer, R. S., & Budesheim, T. L. (1987). Person memory and judgments: The impact of information that one is told to disregard. *Journal of Personality and Social Psychology, 53,* 14–29.

Wyer, R. S., Budesheim, T. L., & Lambert, A. J. (1990). Cognitive representation of conversations about persons. *Journal of Personality and Social Psychology, 58,* 218–238.

Wyer, R. S., Budesheim, T. L., & Lambert, A. J. (1991). *Memory and impression formation in conversations about persons: The effects of information about a person who is either a source or recipient of this information.* Unpublished manuscript, University of Illinois at Urbana-Champaign.

Wyer, R. S., Budesheim, T. L., Lambert, A. J., & Martin, L. L. (1989). *Person memory: The cognitive activities involved in person impression formation.* Unpublished manuscript, University of Illinois at Urbana-Champaign.

Wyer, R. S., & Carlston, D. E. (1979). *Social cognition, inference, and attribution.* Hillsdale, NJ: Lawrence Erlbaum Associates.

Wyer, R. S., & Collins, J. E. (1990). *A comprehension-elaboration theory of humor elicitation.* Unpublished manuscript, University of Illinois at Urbana-Champaign.

Wyer, R. S., & Gordon, S. E. (1982). The recall of information about persons and groups. *Journal of Experimental Social Psychology, 18,* 128–164.

Wyer, R. S., & Gordon, S. E. (1984). The cognitive representation of social information. In R. S. Wyer & T. K. Srull (Eds.), *Handbook of social cognition* (Vol. 2, pp. 73–150). Hillsdale, NJ: Lawrence Erlbaum Associates.

Wyer, R. S., Lambert, A. J., Gruenfeld, D., & Budesheim, T. L. (1990). *Politicians, strangers, and social representatives: The influence of information-processing goals on the recall of a person's opinion statements and overt behaviors.* Unpublished manuscript, University of Illinois at Urbana-Champaign.

Wyer, R. S., & Martin, L. L. (1986). Person memory: The role of traits, group stereotypes, and specific behaviors in the cognitive representation of persons. *Journal of Personality and Social Psychology, 50,* 661–675.

Wyer, R. S., & Srull, T. K. (1981). Category accessibility: Some theoretical and empirical issues concerning the processing of social stimulus information. In E. T. Higgins, C. P. Herman, & M. P. Zanna (Eds.), *Social cognition: The Ontario Symposium* (pp. 161–197). Hillsdale, NJ: Lawrence Erlbaum Associates.

Wyer, R. S., & Srull, T. K. (1989). *Memory and cognition in its social context.* Hillsdale, NJ: Lawrence Erlbaum Associates.

Wyer, R. S., Srull, T. K., & Gordon, S. E. (1984). The effects of predicting a person's behavior on subsequent trait judgments. *Journal of Experimental Social Psychology, 20,* 29–46.

Wyer, R. S., & Unverzagt, W. (1985). The effects of instructions to disregard information on its subsequent recall and use in making judgments. *Journal of Personality and Social Psychology, 48,* 533–549.

Attitudes as Temporary Constructions

Timothy D. Wilson
Sara D. Hodges
University of Virginia

For the past several years we have investigated the effects of introspection on attitude change. We have found that when people are asked to think about why they feel the way they do about something, they often change their minds about how they feel. People who analyze their reasons have been found to change their attitudes toward such diverse things as political candidates (Wilson, Kraft, & Dunn, 1989), dating partners (Wilson, Dunn, Bybee, Hyman, & Rotondo, 1984), art posters (Wilson, Lisle, & Schooler, 1990), food items (Wilson & Schooler, 1991), vacation pictures (Wilson et al., 1984), and puzzles (Wilson & Dunn, 1986; for reviews, see Wilson, Dunn, Kraft, & Lisle, 1989 and Wilson, 1990).

We have been struck by how easy it has been to get people to change their attitudes, in marked contrast to how unyielding people are in other kinds of social psychological studies. Our findings seem inconsistent with the vast literature on attitude change, which has found that you have to go to some length to change people's views. Consider research on persuasive communications. Only after listening to carefully crafted speeches that contain powerful arguments, or are delivered by attractive, expert sources, or both, do subjects change their attitudes (Eagly & Chaiken, 1984; Petty & Cacioppo, 1986). In our studies all we ask people to do is to think, privately and anonymously, about why they feel the way they do—and they change their minds about how they feel.

The ease with which people adopt new attitudes has caused us, along with some other recent theorists, to question the view that people hold stable attitudes. In this chapter we review evidence contrary to this traditional viewpoint.

To preview, we suggest that people often have a large, conflicting "data base" relevant to their attitudes on any given topic, and the attitude they have at any given time depends on the subset of these data to which they attend. We review evidence showing that the data people use are influenced by both contextual factors and the kind of thought in which they engage. Finally, we argue that the attitude change resulting from these contextual and thought processes is sometimes detrimental, leading to nonoptimal preferences and decisions.

Our characterization of attitudes as temporarily constructed judgments is quite consistent with the overall theme of this book concerning the construction of social judgment. It has become clear that many different kinds of judgments and impressions are influenced by the context in which they are formed. Most models of social construction, however, are concerned with situations in which people judge stimuli that are ambiguous or about which they know little (such as the priming literature, in which people form impressions of a person they know only from a brief, ambiguous paragraph describing his or her behavior). Attitudes have traditionally been viewed as more immune to changes in context, because they have been thought to be enduring predispositions that do not change from one situation to the next. In this chapter we extend models of social construction to the area of attitudes, arguing that attitudes can be profitably viewed as temporary constructions from whatever data are most accessible to people.

THE TRADITIONAL VIEW OF ATTITUDE STABILITY

Historically, attitudes have been defined as evaluations that are stable over time (Cook & Flay, 1978). Allport (1935) noted that attitudes "often persist throughout life in the way in which they were fixed in childhood or in youth" (p. 814), whereas M. Sherif and Cantril (1947) suggested that "attitudes, once formed, are more or less enduring states of readiness" (p. 22). Petty and Cacioppo (1981) defined an attitude as an "enduring positive or negative feeling about some person, object, or issue" (p. 7). In Wilson, Lisle, and Kraft (1990), we referred to this as the file drawer analogy of attitudes: When people are asked how they feel about something, such as legalized abortion, their Uncle Harry, or anchovies on a pizza, presumably they consult a mental file containing their evaluation. They look for the file marked *abortion, Uncle Harry,* or *anchovies,* and report the evaluation it contains. The contents of these "files" may be changed by personal experiences, persuasive messages, and the like, but for the most part they are enduring evaluations that remain unchanged.

We acknowledge that this file drawer analogy is simplistic, and underestimates the complexity of models of attitude structure. The exact nature of attitudes continues to generate considerable debate (see Pratkanis, Breckler, & Greenwald, 1989; Tesser & Shaffer, 1990; Zanna & Rempel, 1988 for reviews).

Despite the disagreements between different models of attitude structure, however, many of them assume that attitudes are stable, unchanging entities. That is, whatever the underlying structure of an attitude may be, the resulting evaluation is thought to remain relatively constant. People simply do not hate anchovies one day, only to spread them liberally on their pizza the next. A number of studies support this view, including many in the political domain that find considerable stability in people's political attitudes (e.g., Bennett, 1975; G. D. Bishop, Hamilton, & McConahay, 1980; Brown, 1970). For example, Marwell, Aiken, and Demerath (1987) found that the political attitudes of civil rights workers changed little over the course of 20 years. Other kinds of attitudes are also notorious for their resistance to change, such as prejudiced and racist opinions of minority groups.

ATTITUDES AS CONSTRUCTIONS

Despite this support for the idea that attitudes are stable constructs, there is another position gaining in popularity. According to this view there are no "true" attitudes. How people feel may depend on how they are asked and what they are thinking about at the time. Consider, for example, this statement by Abraham Tesser (1978): "an attitude at a particular point in time is the result of a constructive process. . . . *there is not a single attitude toward an object* but, rather, any number of attitudes depending on the number of schemas available for thinking about the objects" (pp. 297–298, emphasis in original). Other theorists have echoed and elaborated on Tesser's views (Schwartz, 1978; Schwarz & Strack, 1985; Tourangeau & Rasinski, 1988; Wyer & Hartwick, 1980; Zanna, 1990; Zanna & Rempel, 1988). Zanna and his colleagues, for example, argued that attitudes can be based on either affective, cognitive, or behavioral information, and vary depending on which of these three kinds of information is salient to people. Thus, it may not be very meaningful to ask how people feel about such issues as the welfare system or the death penalty. How they feel may depend on what kind of information they are currently using to construct an evaluation.

Our position is similar to these recent conceptions of attitudes. We argue that:

1. People often construct their attitudes, rather than simply reporting the contents of a mental file.
2. When people construct their attitudes they have a large data base to draw from, including their behavior, their moods, and a multitude of (often contradictory) beliefs about the attitude object.
3. People rarely use the entire data base, instead constructing their attitude from a subset of these data.

4. The data people use are influenced by both the social context and the kind of introspection in which they engage. As a result, many attitudes are unstable, depending on the context and what people are thinking about.

5. The context and the content of people's introspections can lead to consequential changes in attitudes, changes that are sometimes nonoptimal.

The careful reader will have noted a hedge in our argument, namely the statement that people "often" construct their attitudes. Although we argue that attitudes are often temporary constructions, we acknowledge that under some conditions people do have pre-packaged attitudes that do not have to be generated on the spot. We postpone a discussion of when this is likely to be the case. For now we examine the evidence for the position that attitudes are constructions, and as a result, can vary depending on the kind of data people use as building materials.

CONTEXTUAL INFLUENCES ON THE DATA PEOPLE USE TO CONSTRUCT THEIR ATTITUDES

Inferring Attitudes from One's Own Behavior

Sometimes people find themselves behaving in a way that is inconsistent with a prior attitude. As a result, they change their attitudes to match their behavior. We refer, of course, to research on dissonance and self-perception processes (Bem, 1972; Festinger, 1957). Subjects in an experiment by Cohen (1962), for example, were quite upset about how violently the police had behaved during a recent confrontation with students. After the experimenter asked the subjects to write an essay in support of the police for low external justification (i.e., little money), subjects moderated their views. This finding—one of the most replicated in social psychology—suggests that attitudes are, under some conditions, quite malleable. Despite the fact that people might have felt differently in the past, the datum they see as most relevant to how they feel now is often their own behavior, even when their behavior is caused by an external agent.

Context Effects in Survey Research

A common finding in survey research is that seemingly minor changes in wording or question order have large effects on people's responses to attitude questions (e.g., G. F. Bishop, 1987; Feldman & Lynch, 1988; Fischhoff, Slovic, & Lichtenstein, 1980; Hippler, Schwarz, & Sudman, 1987; Hogarth, 1982; Ottati, Riggle, Wyer, Schwarz, & Kuklinski, 1989; Schuman & Kalton, 1985; Schuman & Presser, 1981; T. Smith, 1987; Strack & L. Martin, 1987; Tourangeau

& Rasinski, 1988; Turner & E. Martin, 1984). The way in which questions are asked can influence how people interpret which attitude the researcher wants to know, what information is relevant to that attitude, the standards of comparison people use, and how they choose to report their attitude. (See Strack & Martin, 1987, and Tourangeau & Rasinski, 1988 for excellent reviews of this literature.)

Sometimes the way in which a question is asked influences the attitude people report, but not how they actually feel. Research on self-presentation has documented the powerful effects of situational variables on people's public reports of their feelings. A striking example of this was found in the 1989 gubernatorial race in Virginia, where many White voters were reluctant to tell pollsters that they favored Marshall Coleman, a White candidate, over Douglas Wilder, a Black candidate. The election day exit polls indicated that Wilder was ahead by 10 percentage points. He ended up winning by less than half a percentage point. White voters who were questioned by Black interviewers were especially reluctant to admit their support for Coleman (Shapiro, 1989).

Such effects, while interesting in their own right, do not challenge the traditional view that attitudes are stable. Presumably, people's attitudes toward Coleman did not change; all that varied—from their responses to pollsters to their actions in the voting booth—was the attitude they chose to express. The important question for our purposes is whether the way in which survey questions are asked can influence how people actually feel. Though this is not a distinction that survey researchers have addressed very often, it is relatively clear that some kinds of context effects cause genuine attitude change. Tourangeau, Rasinski, Bradburn, and D'Andrade (1989a), for example, suggested that many people have contradictory beliefs about an issue such as welfare. Most people agree that the federal government has the responsibility to help needy people, but also that it is possible to succeed in America with determination and hard work. Tourangeau et al. hypothesized that people's attitude toward welfare would depend on which of these beliefs was most accessible. Consistent with this prediction, people who first answered questions about the government's obligation to the needy expressed much more support for welfare than did those who first answered questions about individual determination (see also Judd, Drake, Downing, & Krosnick, 1991).

Accessibility and Impression Formation

The Tourangeau et al. (1989a) study is reminiscent of another large literature, namely that on accessibility and impression formation. According to this literature, it is often difficult to form impressions of other people because their behavior can be interpreted in different ways. Does the fact that John says little at the dinner party mean that he is shy? Depressed? Under the weather? Angry at the host? People's impressions of John will depend in part on which of these categorizations are most accessible. Whether a particular concept is accessible depends on many things, such as how frequently a category has been used in the past (Higgins & King, 1981). Most relevant to our concern are times when a category is primed, temporarily and arbitrarily, by the context people are in, thereby causing people's impressions to vary from one context to the next. For example, if we had seen a television program about depression right before encountering John at the dinner party the construct of depression would be accessible, increasing the likelihood that we would think John is quiet because he is depressed (Higgins, Rholes, & Jones, 1977; Srull & Wyer, 1979). Models of accessibility have been concerned primarily with people's impressions of other people they have never met before (Higgins, 1989; Higgins & King, 1981; Wyer & Srull, 1980, 1989). It is important to note, however, that these models can be applied more generally to attitudes, be they about other people, physical objects, or social issues, as argued by Wyer and Srull (1989).

Inferring Attitudes About Oneself
from What is Distinctive

There is one class of attitudes that is thought by many to be especially immutable: people's attitudes about themselves. Throughout the history of psychology a prominent view has been that the self-concept is a unitary, stable, construct (e.g., Allport, 1937; Greenwald, 1980; Rogers, 1951; Swann, 1990). Others have suggested, however, that the self-concept is very much a social phenomenon, and varies according to the situation people are in (e.g., H. Markus & Kunda, 1986; Martindale, 1980; McGuire & Padawer-Singer, 1976; Mead, 1934; Sidis & Goodhart, 1904). James (1910), for example, suggested that a person has "as many different social selves as there are distinct groups of persons about whose opinion he cares" (p. 294). Recent experimental work has corroborated this claim. McGuire and Padawer-Singer found that people were likely to describe themselves in ways that were distinctive, as compared to their current social group. For example, when people who live in New York City are visiting Seattle, the fact that they are New Yorkers is distinctive, and thus is likely to be part of their self-concept. When back at home this fact is not at all distinctive, and thus will not be part of their self-concept. The fact that they live in Greenwich Village or Harlem or Staten Island sets them apart from most other New Yorkers, and thus is more likely to be part of the way they view themselves. In short, even our most important, basic attitude—our self-concept—depends on the data we use to construct it at any given point in time, and these data have been found to vary according to the context we are in.

Inferring Attitudes from One's Mood

Another kind of datum people use to infer their attitudes is their current mood. Several studies have found that when people assess their overall satisfaction with their lives, they are particularly influenced by their current mood states (e.g., Schwarz, Strack, Kommer, & Wagner, 1987). The better their mood the greater their reported satisfaction with their lives, even though people know that moods vary from time to time. There are limits to these effects. If it is obvious to people that their mood is influenced by some arbitrary factor—such as the weather—they ignore their mood when reporting their overall life satisfaction (Schwarz & Clore, 1983).

Summary

Each of the literatures we have reviewed calls into question the assumption that attitudes are stable constructs. Each suggests that attitudes vary depending on the data people use to construct their attitude. Depending on the context, people have been shown to base their attitudes on their behavior, their mood, or a subset of their beliefs about the attitude object. What determines what kind of information people will use? Interestingly, each literature we have reviewed suggests that this depends on external, environmental events, such as someone inducing us to behave contrary to our beliefs, being in Seattle when describing oneself, or being asked about the government's obligation to the needy right before being asked about the welfare system. The implication is that if we were a hermit living in a cave our attitudes would remain stable. Because the social context would remain the same, so would our attitudes.

EFFECTS OF THOUGHT ON ATTITUDES

We suggest that not even hermits have stable attitudes. Simply ruminating about one's attitudes and their causes can change the data people use to construct them. As we see in the following sections, two different kinds of thought have been found to lead to two different kinds of attitude change.

Thinking About the Attitude Object

Sometimes people ruminate about an attitude object, be it a social issue, a troublesome employee, or one's favorite baseball team. Research by Tesser and others has shown that such "mere" thought can lead to attitude change. Under some conditions thought leads to polarization, where people with a favorable attitude become even more favorable, and people with an unfavorable attitude become even more unfavorable. Polarization is likely to occur when people's beliefs are evaluatively consistent (i.e., all implying a pro or a con position). Thought highlights these beliefs, making the attitude more extreme (Chaiken & Yates, 1985; Judd & Lusk, 1984; Millar & Tesser, 1986b; Tesser, 1978). When people have several thoughts that are inconsistent with each other, thought leads to moderation (Linville, 1982; Millar & Tesser, 1986b). The important point for our purposes is that mere thought changes attitudes by changing the salience of the data people use to construct their attitude.

Explaining the Reasons for One's Attitudes

We have investigated a kind of thought that can also produce attitude change, but in a different way than merely thinking about the attitude object. In our studies, people think about *why* they feel the way they do about something. As mentioned at the beginning of this chapter, we have found that introspecting about reasons often causes people to change their minds about how they feel. We now discuss the processes thought to be responsible for this effect, to show that it is consistent with the view that attitudes are constructions based on a subset of a large data base.

People Are Often Unaware of Exactly Why They Feel the Way They Do.   The reasons people give for their attitudes are often incomplete or incorrect (Nisbett & Wilson, 1977; Wilson & Stone, 1985). Although some have found this conclusion to be too extreme (e.g., Ericsson & Simon, 1980; E. Smith & Miller, 1978), few would dispute the claim that people sometimes have difficulty knowing the exact determinants of their feelings. This is particularly true of our reactions to complex, multidimensional stimuli. For example, it is doubtful that we can explain exactly why we feel the way we do about other people. We have never heard anyone say, "I like Jane because I see her a lot," even though the effect of repeated exposure on people's attitudes is well established (Zajonc, 1968). Nor have we ever heard anyone say, "Because hostility is a category that is chronically accessible to me, I think John is a hostile person," even though the effects of chronic accessibility are also well documented (e.g., Bargh, Bond, Lombardi, & Tota, 1986). Wilson (1990) discussed several other influences on attitudes that people tend to overlook.

The Reasons People Bring to Mind Can Imply a Somewhat Different Attitude.   If people are unaware of exactly why they feel the way they do, what kinds of reasons do they bring to mind? One possibility is that people first access how they feel, and then bring to mind only those reasons that are consistent with their feelings. We suggest that this is most likely to occur when people have strong, accessible feelings. Many times, however, people's attitudes are not very accessible, and their search for reasons may be guided by a different search strategy. They may focus on those reasons that are accessible and plausible, regardless of whether they are consistent with their initial attitude. If a potential cause is plausible—that is, if it fits into people's causal theories about why they would like or dislike the attitude object—and if it is accessible in their memories, then they are likely to cite it as a reason. Attributes are also likely to be cited as reasons if they are easy to verbalize or flattering to oneself.

We should note that this view is compatible with some current models of person memory that suggest people use different kinds of memory searches when forming impressions (e.g., Carlston & Skowronski, 1986; Lingle & Ostrom, 1981). Carlston and Skowronski, for example, argued that people's impressions of others can be based on either their recall of prior impressions or recall of the person's specific behaviors. Similarly, we suggest that people use different strategies when thinking about why they feel the way they do. Sometimes their search for reasons will be guided by their past attitudes, particularly if these attitudes are highly accessible. Other times people are guided more by the plausibility and salience of different reasons, even if such reasons are not entirely consistent with their prior attitude. That is, if people's attitudes are not very accessible, they might focus on reasons that seem plausible but which imply a somewhat different attitude than they held before.

Unaware That Their Reasons Are Biased, People Adopt the Attitude Implied by Their Reasons. Because people are often unaware that the reasons they bring to mind are incomplete or biased, they assume that these reasons reflect how they feel. Earlier we argued that people have a large data base from which to construct their attitudes, but often use only a subset of these data. After thinking about why they feel the way they do, the data people appear to use are the reasons that come to mind. In our studies we examine people's reasons, and code them according to the attitude they imply. The correlation between this index and the attitude people report after analyzing reasons is usually very high. For example, it was .92 in a study by Wilson and Schooler (1991).

There are several possible explanations for why we have found such high correlations between people's reasons and their subsequent attitudes. One not very interesting possibility is that people are fully aware of why they feel the way they do, and thus report reasons that are consistent with their prior feelings. The attitude they report after giving reasons is thus the same as they held before. Another possibility, as we have seen, is that people are not fully aware of the reasons for their attitude, but the reasons they call upon are still consistent with their feelings. For example, suppose people do not realize that they like a presidential candidate because of mere exposure (e.g., they have seen the candidate on television many times). When asked why they feel the way they do, they say it is because he or she is trustworthy. Even if they are wrong about the role of the candidate's trustworthiness, focusing on this attribute implies the same, favorable attitude, and no attitude change results. The most interesting case occurs when people bring to mind one or more reasons that are evaluatively *in*consistent with their prior attitude. As mentioned earlier, sometimes the reasons that are most plausible and accessible imply a new position. Suppose that when explaining their attitude people focus on the fact that, now that they think about it, the candidate looks rather *untrustworthy* and excitable. We have found repeatedly that when this happens, people adopt the attitude implied by their reasons, resulting in attitude change.

For example, Wilson, Kraft, and Dunn (1989) surveyed introductory psychology students' attitudes toward several possible Democratic and Republican presidential candidates in the spring of 1987. Several weeks later students came to the laboratory to participate in an ostensibly unrelated study. We asked half of them to write down why they felt the way they did about six of the candidates. As in most of our studies we told them that the purpose of this was to organize their thoughts, and that they would not be asked to hand in their reasons. To minimize self-presentational concerns even more, when the participants had completed the reasons questionnaire the experimenter said it would not be needed anymore, and deposited it in a trash can. People in a control condition completed a filler task of similar length. All subjects then rated their attitudes toward each of the candidates.

The first question of interest is whether the reasons people brought to mind were consistent with their initial attitude. It turns out that they were, at least to some extent: The mean, within-subject correlation between the attitudes toward the candidates people expressed in their reasons and the attitudes they reported at the beginning of the semester was .71. Note, however, that this is not perfect consistency; in fact, the attitude expressed in people's reasons shared only half the variance of the attitudes reported earlier. In other words, there was some slippage between their prior attitude and their reasons. What about the attitudes toward the six candidates they reported right after listing reasons? One possibility is that people recognized that their reasons were biased or incomplete. If so, they might have disregarded the attitude implied by their reasons, reporting the same attitude as they had earlier. Our hypothesis was that people would fail to recognize that their reasons were biased or incomplete, and would use these reasons as the data to infer how they felt. Consistent with this hypothesis, the mean, within-subject correlation between the attitudes people expressed in their reasons and their subsequent attitudes was very high, $M = .88$. The difference between this mean and the one between attitudes expressed in reasons and Time 1 attitudes was nearly significant, $p = .06$.

These results, although consistent with our hypotheses, do not address directly whether attitude change occurred as a result of analyzing reasons. Before reporting these results, we need to digress a moment to discuss the kind of attitude change we would expect to occur. We have argued that people often bring to mind reasons that are (at least somewhat) inconsistent with their initial attitudes, and adopt the position implied by these reasons. But in what direction will this change be? Will the change be in a common direction, such that everyone becomes more positive or more negative, or will different people shift in different directions? Our position is that it depends on the kinds of reasons that come to mind. In some of our studies people bring to mind similar kinds of reasons for liking the attitude object, and thus shift in a common direction. For example, in a study by Wilson, Lisle, and Schooler (1990), people analyzed why they felt the way they did about different kinds of posters. Two of them were reproductions of paintings by Impressionist artists. As it happened, people found it easiest to bring to mind negative attributes of these paintings when analyzing reasons, and thus changed their attitude toward them in a negative direction. People found it easiest to bring to mind positive attributes of the other type of poster (humorous pictures of animals with captions), and thus changed their attitude toward these in a positive direction.

Other times, however, analyzing reasons will not cause attitude change in a common direction. Instead, some people become more positive toward the attitude object, whereas others become more negative. One reason for this bi-directional attitude change is that different kinds of reasons are salient for different individuals. For example, when asked why they feel the way they do about a political candidate, people draw on different knowledge bases. The fact that is most salient to one person (e.g., that the candidate is anti-abortion) may be completely unknown to another. In addition, even if the same fact is available to everyone, such as the candidate's stance on abortion, it may be evaluated quite differently by different people, leading to attitude change in different directions. Consistent with these arguments, we found that people who analyzed reasons in the Wilson, Kraft, and Dunn study on political attitudes did change their attitudes, but not in a uniform direction. Some became more positive toward the candidates, others more negative. To assess this type of change we computed the absolute value of the difference between people's attitudes at Time 2 (after they had analyzed reasons) and at Time 1 (before they had analyzed reasons). As expected, the amount of absolute change was significantly higher for people who analyzed reasons than it was for people who did not.[1]

---

[1]Earlier we mentioned that the effects of merely thinking about an attitude object are different from the effects of analyzing the reasons for one's attitudes. It is possible, however, that these two kinds of thoughts have produced different effects only because different kinds of dependent measures have been used. We have found that analyzing reasons increases the absolute amount of change between a premeasure and a measure of attitudes taken right after the reasons analysis manipulation. This change is largest among people who are unknowledgeable about the attitude object (as discussed later in this chapter). Tesser found that merely thinking about the attitude object increases the percentage of people whose post-thought attitudes are more extreme on the same end of the scale as their pre-thought attitude. This type of change is largest among people who are knowledgeable about the attitude object.

It is possible that the key is not the different kinds of thought in which people engage, but the way in which attitude change is measured. For example, if Tesser's measure of polarization were included in some of our reasons analysis studies, perhaps we would replicate his results. To test this possibility, we assessed polarization in several of our studies (e.g., Wilson, Kraft, & Dunn, 1989, Study 2). It turns out that analyzing reasons does not lead to attitude polarization in either knowledgeable or unknowledgeable people. We also examined whether Tesser's mere thought manipulation causes changes on our absolute measure of attitude change that mirror the effects

HOW UNSTABLE ARE UNSTABLE ATTITUDES?
AND ARE ALL ATTITUDES UNSTABLE?

We have seen a considerable amount of evidence challenging the traditional assumption that attitudes are stable. Instead of reporting the contents of an attitude file, people often construct attitudes from the data that are most plausible
and accessible. These data can be people's behavior, their moods, or particular
beliefs about the attitude object that happen to be salient. The data people use
are influenced by the social context and the kind of thought they engage in.

Despite the evidence in support of these conclusions, they seem to belie common sense. Is it really the case that people are like chameleons, changing their
attitudinal colors from one extreme to the other at the spur of the moment?
It doesn't seem that way to us. Many of *our* attitudes have stayed the same
for years. Both of us have had the same political party affiliation throughout our
lives. One of us has always had a soft spot for old Dionne Warwick songs and
a long-standing aversion to anything Barbra Streisand sings. The other has always loved going to the ballet. And neither of us has ever liked anchovies on
our pizzas. It is possible, of course, that we are exceptions to the rule, rare
people whose attitudes are especially fossilized. Although one of us admits that
he has been accused of being an old curmudgeon, we trust that the reader shares
our view that many attitudes seem very stable, contrary to the evidence that
we have reviewed to this point. We believe there are several possible solutions
to this paradox, to which we now turn.

Attitudes Are Constructions, But Vary Only
Within a Latitude of Acceptance

Perhaps attitudes are constructed from the available data, but take on only a
limited range of positions from one time to the next. For example, according
to social judgment theory (M. Sherif & Hovland, 1961), people have a range
of positions that they find acceptable, and the attitudes people construct might
vary only within this range. Someone might be willing to endorse a variety of
positions about George Bush, from the view that he has done a very poor job
to the view that, on balance, he has succeeded in some areas and failed in others.
The position endorsed at any given point in time will, as we have argued, be
influenced by the data that are currently accessible. The latitude of acceptance,
however, might provide boundaries on how far this construction process will

---

of analyzing reasons. It did not in two studies by Tesser and Leone (1977). (We thank Abraham
Tesser for providing us with the data from these studies.) Finally, some studies have included both
types of thought manipulations and found that they have different effects (e.g., Tesser, Leone,
& Clary, 1978). Thus, analyzing reasons and thinking about the attitude object appear to be distinct
kinds of thought with distinct kinds of effects on people's attitudes.

go. If the data that are accessible are negative, people will endorse a position at the negative end of their latitude of acceptance. According to this view they will never endorse a position in their latitude of rejection, which consists of positions they find unacceptable.

This possibility has a certain intuitive appeal, because it explains the obvious fact that most people do not sway from one end of the attitude pole to the other according to the direction the contextual winds are blowing. If attitudes do vary only within a narrow range, however, the importance of the attitude-as-constructions model would be called into question. The bottom line would be that attitudes are relatively stable after all. Yes, you can make people endorse a slightly less liberal position than they endorsed before, but you cannot change a Democrat into a Republican simply by changing the context or altering how people think about political issues.

We are not aware of any evidence that directly assesses the possibility that attitudes vary only within a narrow, prescribed latitude of acceptance. There is evidence, however, that contextual changes in attitudes are sometimes far from trivial. Schwarz et al. (1987) found that people's moods had very large effects on their current life satisfaction, accounting for 24% of the variance. Tourangeau et al. (1989a) found that a minor change in the context of a survey changed people's support for increased spending for welfare from 62% to 44%, a difference of 18 percentage points. Further, as we see later, the attitude change caused by the kind of thought people engage in can be large, and can cause people to make decisions that are nonoptimal.

Attitudes Vary in Their Strength, and Weak Attitudes Are More Likely to Change with the Context

Another possible solution is that some attitudes are stable, much like the file drawer analogy suggests. Others are labile, varying according to the context and what people are thinking about. To borrow an analogy used by Abelson (1986), some attitudes are like family heirlooms that we treasure and hold on to throughout our lives. Others are like a piece of clothing that we don according to the weather, our mood, and current fashion. This view is consistent with the idea we have just reviewed concerning people's latitude of acceptance, as long as we assume—as social judgment theory does—that the width of the latitude of acceptance is wider for some attitudes than others (e.g., C. Sherif, 1980). When people are very involved in an issue they have a narrow latitude of acceptance (and a correspondingly large latitude of rejection). Their attitude is clearly defined, in that there are relatively few positions they are willing to endorse. Perhaps these attitudes are the ones that remain stable over time, and are immune to the effects of the context or what people are thinking about. When people are uninvolved in an issue they have a wide latitude of acceptance. These attitudes may be more susceptible to change by the social context and the different kinds of thought people engage in.

One difficulty with this hypothesis is that the concept of attitude strength is a thorny one, with several different meanings that appear unrelated to each other (Abelson, 1988; Krosnick & Abelson, in press; Raden, 1985; Wilson, Hodges, & Pollack, 1991). Nonetheless, there is evidence for the hypothesis that a strong attitude is a stable one (e.g., Converse, 1964; Fazio & Williams, 1986; Kendall, 1954; Krosnick, 1988; Petty & Cacioppo, 1986; Schuman & Presser, 1981; Taylor, 1983). Fazio and Williams, for example, found greater consistency between people's reports about whom they voted for in the 1984 presidential election and whom they said they supported 4 months earlier in people with accessible attitudes (as assessed with a reaction time procedure). Krosnick (1988) found that attitudes toward social issues that were important to people were less likely to change over the course of several months than were unimportant attitudes.

Interestingly, very few studies have tested the corollary hypothesis that people with weak attitudes are more influenced by the context or the kind of thought they engage in.[2] We have recently addressed this hypothesis in our research program on the effects of analyzing reasons on attitudes, at least indirectly. In the Wilson, Kraft, and Dunn (1989) study that looked at people's attitudes toward presidential candidates, we divided people into those who were knowledgeable about the candidates and those who were not, which was probably correlated with the strength of people's attitudes. Earlier we reported that the people who analyzed reasons were significantly more likely to change their attitudes. Actually, this was true only of people who were unknowledgeable about the candidates. As predicted, knowledgeable subjects were immune to the effects of analyzing reasons. The interaction between the reasons manipulation and people's amount of knowledge was significant.

One reason that knowledgeable people were immune to the effects of analyzing reasons might be that they were more likely to recall their previous attitude, and were thus less likely to generate reasons that conflicted with it. Consistent with this view, the correlation between the attitudes subjects expressed in their reasons and their initial attitudes was higher for knowledgeable than unknowledgeable people (see Table 2.1). There are other possible interpretations of

---

[2]An exception is a series of studies by Krosnick and Schuman (1988). They found in 27 surveys that people with intense, important, or certain attitudes were not less susceptible to such context effects as differences in question wording and response options. They suggested that the particular kinds of wording and response effects they examined did not cause genuine attitude change, but instead influenced how people interpreted the questions and how they chose to respond (i.e., self-presentational concerns). There is no reason to assume that weak attitudes are any more or less susceptible to such factors as self-presentational concerns or response biases. G. F. Bishop (1990) recently found evidence in support of the hypothesis we are considering here, namely that weak attitudes are more susceptible to actual attitude change in response to context effects.

TABLE 2.1
Correlations Between the Attitudes Expressed
in Reasons and Attitudes at Times 1 and 2

Correlation Between:	Low Knowledge	High Knowledge
Time 1 Attitude, Attitude Expressed in Reasons at Time 2	.71	.85
Time 2 Attitude, Attitude Expressed in Reasons at Time 2	.88	.89

Note: From Wilson, Kraft, and Dunn (1989, Study 2).

the moderating effects of knowledge. Lusk and Judd (1988), for example, found that unknowledgeable people are more likely to have cognitions about the attitude object that are evaluatively inconsistent; that is, they are more likely to have a mixture of positive and negative beliefs. When unknowledgeable people analyze reasons, then, they are more likely to focus on at least some beliefs that conflict with their initial attitude, resulting in attitude change. Consistent with this interpretation, unknowledgeable people in the Wilson, Kraft, and Dunn (1989) studies were significantly more likely to generate reasons that were evaluatively inconsistent than were knowledgeable people.

Attitudes Vary in Their Structure, and Some Kinds Are More Likely to Change with the Context

The key variable moderating attitude stability may be not attitude strength, but attitude structure. In recent years there has been a renewed interest in the structure of attitudes (Pratkanis et al., 1989; Tesser & Shaffer, 1990). The questions of interest for our purposes are whether structural variables moderate how stable an attitude is, and how easily the attitude can be changed by changing the context or the kind of thought people engage in. As to the first question, there is evidence that more complex attitudes are more stable (at least when multidimensional measures of attitudes are used; see Schlegel & DiTecco, 1982). Similarly, Rosenberg (1960) found that attitudes with consistent affective and cognitive components are more stable than ones with inconsistent components.

If consistent attitudes are the most stable, then we might expect that inconsistent ones would be most susceptible to the effects of the context and thought. There is a fair amount of evidence consistent with this proposition. For example, Chaiken and Baldwin (1981) found that people with inconsistent affective and cognitive components were most likely to change their attitudes toward the environment in response to a manipulation that made either pro- or anti-ecology behaviors temporarily salient. People with consistent components did not change their attitudes in response to this salience manipulation. Similarly, several interesting studies by Millar and Tesser (1986a, 1989, this volume) found that people who have inconsistent affective and cognitive components are most susceptible to the effects of analyzing reasons. When people analyze reasons, they suggest, they focus on the cognitive component of their attitude; that is, rational thoughts about the attitude object (see also Wilson et al., 1984). This can cause attitude change by turning what was an affectively based attitude into a cognitively based one. This attitude change, however, is only likely to occur to the extent that people's affect and cognitions are inconsistent with each other. If they are consistent, then focusing on one component versus the other will make little difference in how people feel.

We have found some support for the hypothesis that analyzing reasons is most likely to change people's attitudes if their *cognitions* are evaluatively inconsistent (Wilson, Kraft, & Dunn, 1989). We argue that when people analyze reasons they focus on a subset of their beliefs. The more inconsistent these beliefs are, the greater the likelihood that the subset people focus on will conflict with their previous attitude, leading to attitude change. (See our earlier discussion of the Wilson, Kraft, & Dunn, 1989 study.) Finally, there is evidence that context effects in surveys are more likely to occur if people have inconsistent, multidimensional beliefs about the attitude object (Schuman & Presser, 1981). For example, if people have inconsistent beliefs about gun control—such as the idea that people have the right to bear arms, but also that lax gun control laws contribute to the high murder rate in this country—then their attitude toward gun control will be more influenced by questions on a survey that highlight one or the other of these beliefs.

It is not entirely clear, however, how distinct structural variables such as the consistency or complexity of people's beliefs are from attitude *strength* (Abelson, 1988; Raden, 1985; Wilson et al., 1991). We can make a rough distinction between attitudes that are strong, complex, and made up of consistent feelings and cognitions versus those that are weak, not complex, and made up of inconsistent feelings and cognitions, and say that, with some exceptions, the former type of attitude is most likely to be stable and least likely to vary with the context. Very few studies, however, have examined whether the key moderating variable is strength, complexity, or consistency. An intriguing exception is a recent study by Tourangeau, Rasinski, Bradburn, and D'Andrade (1989b). They asked people how important several issues were to them, and how much they had mixed feelings and beliefs about these issues. They then observed how much an accessibility manipulation (i.e., questions in the survey that primed either positive or negative beliefs about the issues) influenced people's attitudes. Interestingly, the people who were most affected by this manipulation were those who had said that they had mixed feelings *and* that the issue was important. Thus, it may be that neither attitude strength nor structure by themselves moderate susceptibility to context effects. These two variables may interact in a more complex fashion.

Stable Attitudes Are Those with Stable Contexts

Another possible solution to our paradox is that some attitudes are stable because the context in which we express them, or the way in which we think about them, typically does not change. Some attitudes, such as our feelings about the annual church picnic or a colleague we see only at work, are expressed primarily in one, unvarying context, thus we use the same, unvarying data to construct them. Further, people do not exert much time thinking about many attitude objects or trying to analyze why they feel the way they do. If so, these attitudes will remain constant not because they are strong or structurally consistent, but because the context in which they are expressed does not vary.

Even if the context does vary, people might have a chronic way of constructing some attitudes, adding to their stability. That is, even if these attitudes vary according to the context people are in or what thoughts are accessible, people might "snap back" to a chronic way of construing the attitude object. This argument is similar to one made by Bargh et al. (1986; Bargh, Lombardi, & Higgins, 1988) about impression formation. These authors found that when people form impressions of others they have certain categories (e.g., shyness) that are chronically accessible, and that they view others in terms of these categories. The same may be true of some of people's attitudes more generally. If, over the years, we have found the annual church picnic to be dull and tedious, we are likely to construe it that way again this year (see Wilson, Lisle, Kraft, & Wetzel, 1989). We should stress that such attitudes are not immune to context effects. Our attitude toward the picnic is likely to be temporarily more positive if we are served a particularly delicious piece of fried chicken. The point is that, due to our chronic construction of such events, over time our negative attitude is likely to return. This possibility has some intriguing implications, which we discuss shortly.

People Overestimate the Stability of Their Attitudes

Finally, we should note that our examples about the constancy of our own attitudes about such things as Dionne Warwick and anchovies may be misleading, because there is a tendency for people to overestimate the extent to which their attitudes have remained constant (Bem & McConnell, 1970; Goethals & Reckman, 1973; G. Markus, 1986; Ross, 1989). Ross demonstrated that when people try to recall their past attitudes they assess how they currently feel and then consult their implicit theories about the stability of these feelings. Most people have the theory that attitudes do not change much over time (just as many social psychologists do), and therefore assume that how they feel now is how they have always felt. Because this theory is often incorrect, however, people overestimate how stable their attitudes have been. Thus, the fact that many of us can bring to mind examples of our own attitudes that have remained the same over the years does not necessarily mean that these attitudes really have remained constant.

Summary

We began this section with a paradox. There is a considerable amount of evidence that attitudes are constructed from the available data, and thus vary from time to time depending on the data that are accessible. On the other hand, it simply doesn't seem like this is true, at least for many of our own attitudes. We offered several possible solutions to this conundrum, namely that attitudes may vary only within a latitude of acceptance, that only some types of attitudes are unstable (e.g., weak attitudes or those consisting of inconsistent beliefs), that people have a chronic way of constructing some attitudes, and that attitudes are less stable than people believe, due to memory biases. Although there is much more evidence supporting some of these solutions than others, we believe there is at least a grain of truth in all of them.

DOES IT MATTER THAT ATTITUDES ARE SOMETIMES UNSTABLE?

Some of the solutions we offered might appear to minimize the importance of the idea that attitudes are often unstable. For example, if attitudes vary only within a narrow range of acceptance, then the attitude change that results from a change in the context or in what people are thinking about will probably not be very consequential. We have seen, however, that such attitude change is often not trivial. We turn now to evidence that it can also cause changes in people's attitudes that are nonoptimal.

We have already seen that when people think about why they feel the way they do, they often change their attitudes. We have recently posed the question of whether this change is beneficial, neutral, or harmful to people. Although it is unlikely to always be just one of these possibilities, we suggest that, at least at times, it can be harmful. There are two reasons for this. First, we assume that when people are left to their own devices, they often form satisfactory preferences and make good personal choices. People are certainly not perfect information processors, but they often manage to assign weights to the different attributes of the alternatives that produce a satisfactory choice (satisfactory to them). We assume that people often are not fully aware of how they are weighting the information, but often use schemes that work for them. The old adage that "I may not know why but I know what I like" probably has more than a grain of truth to it.

If so, what happens when people introspect about why they feel the way they do? This kind of introspection, we suggest, can change an optimal weighting scheme into a nonoptimal one. When people analyze reasons, we have argued that they focus on those attributes of the attitude object that are accessible in memory and seem like plausible causes of their evaluations. Those criteria that are accessible and plausible, however, might not have been weighted heavily before. Similarly, criteria that are not accessible or plausible—but were weighted heavily—will be overlooked. For example, when people evaluate a particular kind of food, they might be influenced by attributes of which they are unaware (e.g., an unknown ingredient) or that are difficult to verbalize (e.g., its texture or aroma). When asked to explain their reactions, they may assign less weight to these factors because they are difficult to put into words, and as a consequence change their preferences. Assuming that their original preference was fairly optimal, this change in weights might lead to a less optimal preference.

The second reason that explaining one's attitudes might lead to nonoptimal choices concerns the extent to which the attitude change caused by analyzing reasons persists over time. We have argued that attitudes are often constructed from the available data, and thus vary according to which data are accessible. As argued earlier, however, people often have a chronic way of constructing their attitudes. These attitudes can be altered when people encounter new contexts or think about the attitudes in new ways, but otherwise remain fairly constant. If this argument is true, what happens when people analyze reasons? The new attitude that results might be particularly unstable because it is contrary to the way people chronically construct the data in that domain.

For example, suppose someone is looking for something to hang over her mantle, and goes to a store that sells art posters. Suppose further that she is in a particularly introspective mood, and decides to analyze why she feels the way she does about each poster she examines. After doing so she decides which one she likes the best, purchases it, and takes it home. There is a good possibility, we suggest, that the act of analyzing reasons will change this person's mind about which poster to purchase. Trying to verbalize her reasons probably highlighted features of the posters that were not central to her initial evaluations, leading to a change in her preferences. Put differently, this person is probably not fully aware of how she usually (i.e., chronically) forms evaluations of works of art, leaving her open to the kinds of attitude change we have found so often in our studies. But what will happen over the next few weeks, as she looks at the poster over her mantle? Our suspicion is that the features she focused on when she analyzed reasons would probably no longer be salient. Instead, she would revert back to her chronic means of evaluating works of art, possibly causing her to regret her choice. We recently tested whether this sequence of events can occur.

Post-Choice Satisfaction with Consumer Choices

We asked subjects to evaluate five posters of the type college students hang in their rooms, and then choose one to take home (Wilson, Lisle, & Schooler, 1990). Two of the posters were reproductions of paintings by Impressionist artists, and were very popular with our student population. The remaining three were humorous posters, such as a photograph of a cat perched on a rope with the caption, "Gimme a Break." They were considerably less popular. In fact, in our control condition, where people were not asked to analyze reasons, 95% of the subjects chose one of the Impressionist paintings to take home.

Half of the subjects analyzed why they felt the way they did before evaluating the posters. As expected, this introspection changed the preferences of many of these subjects. People who analyzed reasons tended to focus on positive attributes of the humorous posters and negative attributes of the Impressionist paintings. As a result, they were significantly more likely to choose one of the humorous posters (see Table 2.2). So far, these results are the same as those we have obtained in many other studies: Analyzing reasons changes people's attitudes. The interesting finding is what happened after people took their posters home. We telephoned subjects 3 weeks later and asked them several questions assessing how satisfied they were with the poster they had chosen. As predicted, and as seen in the bottom row of Table 2.2, subjects in the reasons condition reported a lower satisfaction with their choice of poster, possibly because their initial attitude—that the Impressionist paintings were preferable—had by then returned.

According to our model, it should only have been people who convinced themselves they liked the unpopular humorous posters who later regretted their choice. As seen in Table 2.2, there was a tendency in this direction in that the difference in post-choice satisfaction between reasons and control subjects was greater among those who chose a humorous poster than those who chose an Impressionist poster. The interaction between condition and poster choice, however, was not significant. One reason for this might be that the control condition/humorous poster cell was represented by one person, making this value highly unreliable. We replicated the poster study with a new stimulus, felt-tip pens, and found results that were more consistent with our hypothesis. The people who were least satisfied with their choice of a pen were those in the reasons condition who convinced themselves that they liked one that was an unpopular color, and chose to take it home. When asked later how much they liked it, their original attitude seemed to have returned, making them relatively unhappy with their choice.

The Wilson, Lisle, and Schooler (1990) studies have some intriguing implications about the effects of other kinds of context effects on post-choice satisfaction. When people have a chronic way of constructing a preference or attitude, then any factor that alters this construction might cause people to make decisions they later regret. That is, suppose people changed their attitudes due to any of the context effects we have reviewed, be they question order effects on surveys or the kinds of priming effects studied in the impression formation literature. If they made an important decision based on this new way of constructing their attitude, they might regret this decision later, when their chronic way of viewing the attitude object returns.

TABLE 2.2
Results of the Wilson, Lisle, and Schooler (1990) Poster Study

	Control		Reasons	
Variable	Impressionist	Humorous	Impressionist	Humorous
Choice (%)	95	5	64	36
Post-Choice Satisfaction[a]	2.68	3.00	2.21	2.17

[a]Subjects were asked whether they still had the poster, whether they had hung it up, and whether they planned to take it home with them at the end of the semester. They received a zero if they said no to these questions and a one if they said yes. The satisfaction index is the sum of their three responses.

Comparing People's Attitudes to Expert Opinion

People's reported satisfaction with a choice is open to a number of biases, such as a tendency to feel that whatever the choice, it was the best one to make (Brehm, 1956). To add weight to our claim that analyzing reasons can lead to nonoptimal decisions, we used a different criterion in two other studies: expert opinion about which alternatives are the best (Wilson & Schooler, 1991). In the first study we compared the preferences of subjects toward a food item—strawberry jams—with the opinions of sensory panelists from *Consumer Reports* magazine. Subjects tasted five different brands. Half of the subjects analyzed why they liked or disliked each alternative, whereas half did not. All subjects then rated how much they liked each brand. We suggested earlier that, left to their own devices, people often make reasonably good decisions. Consistent with this hypothesis, the ratings made by control subjects corresponded fairly well with the experts' rating, resulting in a mean, within-subject correlation of .55. We have also suggested that trying to explain one's attitudes can influence the salience of certain attributes of the attitude object, causing people to change their evaluations. This prediction was also borne out, in that subjects who analyzed reasons ended up with significantly different preferences for the jams than did control subjects. Finally, consistent with our hypothesis that these preferences would be in some sense "worse," the ratings made by subjects who analyzed reasons did not correspond with the experts very well, mean correlation = .11. The difference between the mean correlations in the control and reasons conditions was significant.

The jam study examined people's preferences, without asking them to make an actual consumer decision. In a second study, Wilson and Schooler (1991) examined a real-life choice of some importance to college students: the decision of which courses to take. A sample of introductory psychology students, who had expressed an interest in taking more psychology classes, were seen at the beginning of the week when they registered for classes for the next semester. They were given a packet of information about each of the nine sophomore-level psychology classes being offered the next term. This packet contained such information as a description of the course content, the course evaluations of students who had previously taken the course, and whether a term paper was required. After reading through this information, subjects in the reasons condition were asked to describe why they might or might not take each course. Subjects in the control condition did not receive any special instructions about how to approach the course information.[3]

After examining the information about the courses, subjects were given a surprise recall test in which they were asked to write down everything they could remember about the courses. We used their recall as a rough indication of how they had weighted the different attributes when forming their preferences, comparing it to the opinions of faculty members as to which criteria *ought* to be used when choosing a course. Control subjects were significantly more likely to recall information that faculty members rated as important (e.g., who was teaching the course) than information faculty members rated as unimportant (e.g., when the class met), suggesting that these subjects were weighting the information fairly optimally (at least to the extent that we can consider the faculty members to be experts in this domain). In contrast, subjects who analyzed reasons were no more likely to recall the important information than they were the unimportant information.

We also examined (with subjects' permission) which courses they actually preregistered for. We assessed how good these choices were by comparing them to another kind of expert opinion: the course evaluations of students who had previously taken the courses. We assumed that it is advantageous for people to base their decisions of what courses to take on course evaluations, because these evaluations should predict how well they will enjoy the course. As discussed earlier, we assumed that, left to their own devices, people often make reasonably good choices. Control subjects were thus expected to base their choices, at least in part, on the course evaluations. We predicted that the reasons manipulation would change the criteria subjects used to make their choices, making them less likely to sign up for the highly rated courses. This prediction was confirmed, as seen in Table 2.3. Subjects in the control condition were significantly more likely to register for highly rated than for poorly rated courses. Subjects who analyzed reasons, however, showed only a slight preference for the highly rated courses. The Reasons Manipulation by Course Evaluation interaction was highly significant, $p < .001$.

We also included a long-term measure of subjects' behavior: the courses they

---

[3]We included a third condition as well, where subjects were asked to introspect about how each and every piece of information about every course influenced their preferences. For reasons of space we will omit a discussion of this condition here, except to note that we expected this kind of introspection to alter people's preferences in nonoptimal ways, albeit for different reasons. This prediction was confirmed (see Wilson & Schooler, 1991).

TABLE 2.3
Courses Preregistered for and Actually Taken, by Condition

Variable	Control	Reasons
Preregistration		
Highly Rated Courses	.41	.15
Poorly Rated Courses	.04	.10
Actual Enrollment		
Highly Rated Courses	.37	.21
Poorly Rated Courses	.03	.08

Note: Subjects were assigned a one if they registered for or actually took a course, and a zero if they did not register or take a course.

Table adapted from Wilson and Schooler (1991), copyright 1991 by the American Psychological Association.

were enrolled in at the end of the following semester. Subjects had the opportunity to add and drop courses at the beginning of the semester; thus, even though the reasons manipulation influenced their initial decision of which courses to take, they could revise these decisions later. We did not make firm predictions about the outcome of this measure. On the one hand, we have argued that the attitude change caused by analyzing reasons is relatively temporary, and will not influence long-term behavior. Consistent with this view, Wilson et al. (1984, Study 3) found that analyzing reasons did not influence dating couples' decisions about whether to break up several months after the study was completed. On the other hand, if analyzing reasons changes subjects' decisions about the courses for which they register, they might experience some inertia, such that they remain in these courses, even if they change their minds at a later point. Further, Millar and Tesser (1986a, 1989) found that analyzing reasons highlights the cognitive component of attitudes, and that these cognitively based attitudes will determine behaviors that are more cognitively based than affectively based. Given that the decision of whether to take a college course has a large cognitive component (e.g., whether it will advance one's career goals), the attitude change that results from analyzing reasons might cause long-term changes in behavior.

Consistent with this latter possibility, by the end of the following semester subjects who had analyzed reasons were still less likely than control subjects to be enrolled in courses that were highly rated and more likely to be enrolled in courses that were poorly rated (see Table 2.3). This effect had weakened over time, but the Reasons Manipulation by Course Evaluation interaction was still significant, $p < .05$. This is perhaps our strongest demonstration that analyzing reasons can be costly, leading to nonoptimal choices.

We should address some possible ethical objections to the course selection study, given that it involved a consequential, real-life decision on the part of the participants. It might be argued that we should not have asked subjects to think about why they felt the way they did about each course, given our hypothesis that this kind of introspection would change the courses for which they preregistered, and possibly even change the courses they actually took the following semester. We thought about this issue at some length before conducting the study, and discussed it with several colleagues. In the end we decided that the potential knowledge gained—discovering some detrimental effects of introspection—outweighed the possible harmful effects on the participants. We should emphasize that we did not give the participants any misinformation about the courses—all of the information we gave them, including the course evaluations, was accurate. What we did was to ask some of them to reflect more than they might ordinarily do when forming their preferences. According to the predominant theories of decision making (e.g., Janis & Mann, 1977), asking people to be more reflective about their choices should have beneficial effects. There are probably many decision analysts, counselors, and academic advisors who urge people to make decisions more reflectively. Given that the effects of our manipulations were predicted to be relatively benign—altering the psychology courses for which subjects preregistered, and possibly altering the courses they took the following semester—we felt it was worth testing the wisdom of such advice. We did not, of course, make this decision alone. The study was approved by a Human Subjects Committee.

SUMMARY AND CONCLUSIONS

We began this chapter by posing the question of whether attitudes are stable entities or temporary constructions, fashioned from whatever data are accessible when people evaluate an attitude object. We reviewed a considerable amount of evidence supporting the attitudes-as-constructions hypothesis, namely research showing that people's attitudes vary according to the context and what they are thinking about. We then considered several moderator variables specifying when attitudes are likely to be stable, like files that we retrieve from our memories, and when they are likely to be recomputed from the accessible data. Although the evidence is mixed, there is some support for the hypothesis that strong attitudes with consistent components are likely to be stable, whereas weak attitudes with inconsistent components are most likely to vary with the context and the kind of thought people engage in. The bottom line seems to be that when we ask what people's attitudes are, we first need to consider the context in which they were asked, and what they were thinking about at the time. Not all attitudes will be affected by such variables—but enough will that it is worthwhile to ask these questions. Considering the context and what people are thinking about is especially important because these variables can cause substantial changes in people's attitudes, and cause them to make nonoptimal decisions.

ACKNOWLEDGMENTS

The writing of this chapter was supported by a grant from the National Institute of Mental Health (MH41841) to the first author and a National Science Foundation Graduate Fellowship to the second author.

REFERENCES

Abelson, R. P. (1986). Beliefs are like possessions. *Journal for the Theory of Social Behaviour, 16*, 223–250.

Abelson, R. P. (1988). Conviction. *American Psychologist, 43*, 267–275.

Allport, G. W. (1935). Attitudes. In C. Murchison (Ed.), *A handbook of social psychology* (pp. 798–844). Worcester, MA: Clark University Press.

Allport, G. W. (1937). *Pattern and growth in personality.* New York: Holt, Rinehart & Winston.

Bargh, J. A., Bond, R. N., Lombardi, W. J., & Tota, M. E. (1986). The additive nature of chronic and temporary sources of construct accessibility. *Journal of Personality and Social Psychology, 50*, 869–878.

Bargh, J. A., Lombardi, W. J., & Higgins, E. T. (1988). Automaticity of chronically accessible constructs in person × situation effects on person perception: It's just a matter of time. *Journal of Personality and Social Psychology, 55*, 599–605.

Bem, D. J. (1972). Self-perception theory. In L. Berkowitz (Ed.), *Advances in experimental social psychology* (Vol. 6, pp. 1–62). New York: Academic Press.

Bem, D. J., & McConnell, H. K. (1970). Testing the self-perception explanation of dissonance phenomena: On the salience of premanipulation attitudes. *Journal of Personality and Social Psychology, 14*, 23–31.

Bennett, W. L. (1975). *The political mind and the political environment.* Lexington, MA: D. C. Heath.

Bishop, G. D., Hamilton, D. L., & McConahay, J. B. (1980). Attitudes and nonattitudes in the belief systems of mass publics. *The Journal of Social Psychology, 110*, 53–64.

Bishop, G. F. (1987). Experiments with the middle response alternative in survey questions. *Public Opinion Quarterly, 51*, 220–232.

Bishop, G. F. (1990). Issue involvement and response effects in public opinion surveys. *Public Opinion Quarterly, 54*, 209–218.

Brehm, J. W. (1956). Post-decision changes in desirability of alternatives. *Journal of Abnormal and Social Psychology, 52*, 384–389.

Brown, S. R. (1970). Consistency and the persistence of ideology. *Public Opinion Quarterly, 34*, 60–68.

Carlston, D. E., & Skowronski, J. J. (1986). Trait memory and behavior memory: The effects of alternative pathways on impression judgment response times. *Journal of Personality and Social Psychology, 50*, 5–13.

Chaiken, S., & Baldwin, M. W. (1981). Affective-cognitive consistency and the effect of salient behavioral information on the self-perception of attitudes. *Journal of Personality and Social Psychology, 41*, 1–12.

Chaiken, S., & Yates, S. M. (1985). Attitude schematicity and thought-induced attitude polarization. *Journal of Personality and Social Psychology, 49*, 1470–1481.

Cohen, A. R. (1962). An experiment on small rewards for discrepant compliance and attitude change. In J. W. Brehm & A. R. Cohen (Eds.), *Explorations in cognitive dissonance* (pp. 73–78). New York: Wiley.

Converse, P. E. (1964). The nature of belief systems in mass publics. In D. E. Apter (Ed.), *Ideology and discontent* (pp. 206–261). London: The Free Press of Glencoe.

Cook, T. D., & Flay, B. R. (1978). The persistence of experimentally induced attitude change. In L. Berkowitz (Ed.), *Advances in experimental social psychology* (Vol. 11, pp. 1–57). New York: Academic Press.

Eagly, A. H., & Chaiken, S. (1984). Cognitive theories of persuasion. In L. Berkowitz (Ed.), *Advances in experimental social psychology* (Vol. 17, pp. 267–359). Orlando, FL: Academic Press.

Ericsson, K. A., & Simon, H. A. (1980). Verbal reports as data. *Psychological Review, 87*, 215–251.

Fazio, R. H., & Williams, C. J. (1986). Attitude accessibility as a moderator of the attitude-behavior relation: An investigation of the 1984 presidential election. *Journal of Personality and Social Psychology, 51*, 505–514.

Feldman, J. M., & Lynch, J. G., Jr. (1988). Self-generated validity and other effects of measurement on belief, attitude, intention, and behavior. *Journal of Applied Psychology, 73*, 421–435.

Festinger, L. (1957). *A theory of cognitive dissonance.* Stanford, CA: Stanford University Press.

Fischhoff, B., Slovic, P., & Lichtenstein, S. (1980). Knowing what you want: Measuring labile values. In T. S. Wallsten (Ed.), *Cognitive processes in choice and decision behavior* (pp. 117–141). Hillsdale, NJ: Lawrence Erlbaum Associates.

Goethals, G. R., & Reckman, R. F. (1973). The perception of consistency in attitudes. *Journal of Experimental Social Psychology, 9*, 491–501.

Greenwald, A. G. (1980). The totalitarian ego: Fabrication and revision of personal history. *American Psychologist, 35*, 603–618.

Higgins, E. T. (1989). Knowledge accessibility and activation: Subjectivity and suffering from unconscious sources. In J. S. Uleman & J. A. Bargh (Eds.), *Unintended thought* (pp. 75–123). New York: Guilford Press.

Higgins, E. T., & King, G. (1981). Accessibility of social constructs: Information-processing consequences of individual and contextual variability. In N. Cantor & J. F. Kihlstrom (Eds.), *Personality, cognition, and social interaction* (pp. 69–121). Hillsdale, NJ: Lawrence Erlbaum Associates.

Higgins, E. T., Rholes, W. S., & Jones, C. R. (1977). Category accessibility and impression formation. *Journal of Experimental Social Psychology, 13*, 141–154.

Hippler, H. J., Schwarz, N., & Sudman, S. (Eds.). (1987). *Social information processing and survey methodology.* New York: Springer-Verlag.

Hogarth, R. M. (1982). *Question framing and response contingency.* San Francisco: Jossey-Bass.

James, W. (1910). *Psychology: The briefer course.* New York: Holt.

Janis, I. L., & Mann, L. (1977). *Decision making: A psychological analysis of conflict, choice, and commitment.* New York: The Free Press.

Judd, C. M., Drake, R. A., Downing, J. W., & Krosnick, J. A. (1991). Some dynamic properties of attitude structures: Context induced response facilitation and polarization. *Journal of Personality and Social Psychology, 60*, 193–202.

Judd, C. M., & Lusk, C. M. (1984). Knowledge structures and evaluative judgments: Effects of structural variables on judgment extremity. *Journal of Personality and Social Psychology, 46*, 1193–1207.

Kendall, P. (1954). *Conflict and mood: Factors affecting stability of response.* Glencoe, IL: The Free Press.

Krosnick, J. A. (1988). Attitude importance and attitude change. *Journal of Experimental Social Psychology, 24*, 240–255.

Krosnick, J. A., & Abelson, R. P. (in press). The case for measuring attitude strength in surveys. In J. Tanur (Ed.), *Questions about survey questions.* New York: Russell Sage.

Krosnick, J. A., & Schuman, H. (1988). Attitude intensity, importance, and certainty and susceptibility to response effects. *Journal of Personality and Social Psychology, 54*, 940–952.

Lingle, J. H., & Ostrom, T. M. (1981). Principles of memory and cognition in attitude formation. In R. E. Petty, T. M. Ostrom, & T. C. Brock (Eds.), *Cognitive responses in persuasion* (pp. 399–459). Hillsdale, NJ: Lawrence Erlbaum Associates.

Linville, P. W. (1982). The complexity-extremity effect and age-based stereotyping. *Journal of Personality and Social Psychology, 42,* 193–211.

Lusk, C. M., & Judd, C. M. (1988). Political expertise and the structural mediators of candidate evaluations. *Journal of Experimental Social Psychology, 24,* 105–126.

Markus, G. (1986). Stability and change in political attitudes: Observed, recalled, and "explained." *Political Behavior, 8,* 21–44.

Markus, H., & Kunda, Z. (1986). Stability and malleability of the self-concept. *Journal of Personality and Social Psychology, 51,* 858–866.

Martindale, C. (1980). Subselves: The internal representation of situational and personal dispositions. In L. Wheeler (Ed.), *Review of personality and social psychology* (Vol. 1, pp. 193–218). Beverly Hills, CA: Sage.

Marwell, G., Aiken, M., & Demerath, N. J. (1987). The persistence of political attitudes among 1960s civil rights activists. *Public Opinion Quarterly, 51,* 359–375.

McGuire, W. J., & Padawer-Singer, A. (1976). Trait salience in the spontaneous self-concept. *Journal of Personality and Social Psychology, 33,* 743–754.

Mead, G. H. (1934). *Mind, self, and society.* Chicago: University of Chicago Press.

Millar, M. G., & Tesser, A. (1986a). Effects of affective and cognitive focus on the attitude-behavior relationship. *Journal of Personality and Social Psychology, 51,* 270–276.

Millar, M. G., & Tesser, A. (1986b). Thought-induced attitude change: The effects of schema structure and commitment. *Journal of Personality and Social Psychology, 51,* 259–269.

Millar, M. G., & Tesser, A. (1989). The effects of affective-cognitive consistency and thought on the attitude-behavior relation. *Journal of Experimental Social Psychology, 25,* 189–202.

Nisbett, R. E., & Wilson, T. D. (1977). Telling more than we can know: Verbal reports on mental processes. *Psychological Review, 84,* 231–259.

Ottati, V. C., Riggle, E. J., Wyer, R. S., Schwarz, N., & Kuklinski, J. (1989). Cognitive and affective bases of opinion survey responses. *Journal of Personality and Social Psychology, 57,* 404–415.

Petty, R. E., & Cacioppo, J. T. (1981). *Attitudes and persuasion: Classic and contemporary approaches.* Dubuque, IA: Brown.

Petty, R. E., & Cacioppo, J. T. (1986). *Communication and persuasion: Central and peripheral routes to attitude change.* New York: Springer-Verlag.

Pratkanis, A. R., Breckler, S. J., & Greenwald, A. G. (Eds.). (1989). *Attitude structure and function.* Hillsdale, NJ: Lawrence Erlbaum Associates.

Raden, D. (1985). Strength-related attitude dimensions. *Social Psychology Quarterly, 48,* 312–330.

Rogers, C. R. (1951). *Client centered therapy.* New York: Houghton-Mifflin.

Rosenberg, M. J. (1960). A structural theory of attitude dynamics. *Public Opinion Quarterly, 24,* 319–341.

Ross, M. (1989). Relation of implicit theories to the construction of personal histories. *Psychological Review, 96,* 341–357.

Schlegel, R. P., & DiTecco, D. (1982). Attitudinal structures and the attitude-behavior relation. In M. P. Zanna, E. T. Higgins, & C. P. Herman (Eds.), *Consistency in social behavior: The Ontario Symposium* (Vol. 2, pp. 17–49). Hillsdale, NJ: Lawrence Erlbaum Associates.

Schuman, H., & Kalton, G. (1985). Survey methods. In G. Lindzey & E. Aronson (Eds.), *Handbook of social psychology* (3rd ed., Vol. 1, pp. 635–697). New York: Random House.

Schuman, H., & Presser, S. (1981). *Questions and answers in attitude surveys.* New York: Academic Press.

Schwartz, S. H. (1978). Temporal instability as a moderator of the attitude-behavior relationship. *Journal of Personality and Social Psychology, 36,* 715–724.

Schwarz, N., & Clore, G. L. (1983). Mood, misattribution, and judgment of well-being: Informative and directive functions of affective states. *Journal of Personality and Social Psychology, 45,* 513–523.

Schwarz, N., & Strack, F. (1985). Cognitive and affective processes in judgments of well-being: A preliminary model. In H. Brandstatter & E. Kirchler (Eds.), *Economic psychology* (pp. 439–447). Linz, Austria: Taubler.

Schwarz, N., Strack, F., Kommer, D., & Wagner, D. (1987). Soccer, rooms, and the quality of your life: Mood effects on judgments of satisfaction with life in general and with specific domains. *European Journal of Social Psychology, 17,* 69–79.

Shapiro, W. (1989, November 20). Breakthrough in Virginia. *Time,* pp. 54–57.

Sherif, C. W. (1980). Social values, attitudes, and involvement of the self. *Nebraska Symposium on Motivation, 27,* 1–64.

Sherif, M., & Cantril, H. (1947). *The psychology of ego-involvements: Social attitudes and identifications.* New York: Wiley.

Sherif, M., & Hovland, C. I. (1961). *Social judgment: Assimilation and contrast effects in communication and attitude change.* New Haven, CT: Yale University Press.

Sidis, B., & Goodhart, S. P. (1904). *Multiple personality: An experimental investigation into the nature of human individuality.* Englewood Cliffs, NJ: Prentice-Hall.

Smith, E. R., & Miller, F. D. (1978). Limits on perception of cognitive processes: A reply to Nisbett and Wilson. *Psychological Review, 85,* 355–362.

Smith, T. W. (1987). That which we call welfare by any other name would smell sweeter: An analysis of the impact of question wording on response patterns. *Public Opinion Quarterly, 51,* 75–83.

Srull, T. K., & Wyer, R. S. (1979). The role of category accessibility in the interpretation of information about persons: Some determinants and implications. *Journal of Personality and Social Psychology, 37,* 1660–1672.

Strack, F., & Martin, L. L. (1987). Thinking, judging, and communicating: A process account of context effects in attitude surveys. In H. J. Hippler, N. Schwarz, & S. Sudman (Eds.), *Social information processing and survey methodology* (pp. 123–148). New York: Springer-Verlag.

Swann, W. B., Jr. (1990). To be adored or to be known? The interplay of self-enhancement and self-verification. In E. T. Higgins & R. M. Sorrentino (Eds.), *Handbook of motivation and cognition: Foundations of social behavior* (Vol. 2, pp. 408–448). New York: Guilford Press.

Taylor, M. C. (1983). The black-and-white model of attitude stability: A latent class examination of opinion and nonopinion in the American public. *American Journal of Sociology, 89,* 373–401.

Tesser, A. (1978). Self-generated attitude change. In L. Berkowitz (Ed.), *Advances in experimental social psychology* (Vol. 11, pp. 289–338). New York: Academic Press.

Tesser, A., & Leone, C. (1977). Cognitive schemas and thought as determinants of attitude change. *Journal of Experimental Social Psychology, 13,* 340–356.

Tesser, A., Leone, C., & Clary, G. (1978). Affect control: Process constraints versus catharsis. *Cognitive Therapy and Research, 2,* 265–274.

Tesser, A., & Shaffer, D. (1990). Attitudes and attitude change. *Annual Review of Psychology, 41,* 479–523.

Tourangeau, R., & Rasinski, K. A. (1988). Cognitive processes underlying context effects in attitude measurement. *Psychological Bulletin, 103,* 299–314.

Tourangeau, R., Rasinski, K. A., Bradburn, N., & D'Andrade, R. (1989a). Belief accessibility and context effects in attitude measurement. *Journal of Experimental Social Psychology, 25,* 401–421.

Tourangeau, R., Rasinski, K. A., Bradburn, N., & D'Andrade, R. (1989b). Carryover effects in attitude surveys. *Public Opinion Quarterly, 53,* 495–524.

Turner, C. F., & Martin, E. (Eds.). (1984). *Surveying subjective phenomena* (Vol. 1). New York: Russell Sage Foundation.

Wilson, T. D. (1990). Self-persuasion via self-reflection. In J. Olson & M. P. Zanna (Eds.), *Self-inference processes: The Ontario Symposium* (Vol. 6, pp. 43–67). Hillsdale, NJ: Lawrence Erlbaum Associates.

Wilson, T. D., & Dunn, D. S. (1986). Effects of introspection on attitude-behavior consistency: Analyzing reasons versus focusing on feelings. *Journal of Experimental Social Psychology, 22,* 249–263.

Wilson, T. D., Dunn, D. S., Bybee, J. A., Hyman, D. B., & Rotondo, J. A. (1984). Effects of analyzing reasons on attitude-behavior consistency. *Journal of Personality and Social Psychology, 47,* 5–16.

Wilson, T. D., Dunn, D. S., Kraft, D., & Lisle, D. J. (1989). Introspection, attitude change, and attitude-behavior consistency: The disruptive effects of explaining why we feel the way we do. In L. Berkowitz (Ed.), *Advances in experimental social psychology* (Vol. 19, pp. 123–205). Orlando, FL: Academic Press.

Wilson, T. D., Hodges, S. D., & Pollack, S. E. (1991). *Effects of explaining attitudes on survey responses: The moderating effects of attitude accessibility.* Unpublished manuscript, University of Virginia, Charlottesville.

Wilson, T. D., Kraft, D., & Dunn, D. S. (1989). The disruptive effects of explaining attitudes: The moderating effect of knowledge about the attitude object. *Journal of Experimental Social Psychology, 25,* 379–400.

Wilson, T. D., Lisle, D. J., & Kraft, D. (1990). Effects of self-reflection on attitudes and consumer decisions. *Advances in Consumer Research, 17,* 79–85.

Wilson, T. D., Lisle, D. J., Kraft, D., & Wetzel, C. G. (1989). Preferences as expectation-driven inferences: Effects of affective expectations on affective experience. *Journal of Personality and Social Psychology, 56,* 519–530.

Wilson, T. D., Lisle, D. J., & Schooler, J. (1990). *Some undesirable effects of self-reflection.* Unpublished manuscript, University of Virginia, Charlottesville.

Wilson, T. D., & Schooler, J. (1991). Thinking too much: Introspection can reduce the quality of preferences and decision. *Journal of Personality and Social Psychology, 60,* 181–192.

Wilson, T. D., & Stone, J. I. (1985). More on telling more than we can know. In P. Shaver (Ed.), *Review of personality and social psychology* (Vol. 6, pp. 167–183). Beverly Hills, CA: Sage.

Wyer, R. S., & Hartwick, J. (1980). The role of information retrieval and conditional inference processes in belief formation and change. In L. Berkowitz (Ed.), *Advances in experimental social psychology* (Vol. 13, pp. 241–284). Orlando, FL: Academic Press.

Wyer, R. S., & Srull, T. K. (1980). The processing of social stimulus information: A conceptual integration. In R. Hastie, T. Ostrom, E. Ebbesen, R. Wyer, D. Hamilton, & D. Carlston (Eds.), *Person memory: The cognitive basis of social perception* (pp. 227–300). Hillsdale, NJ: Lawrence Erlbaum Associates.

Wyer, R. S., & Srull, T. K. (1989). *Memory and cognition in its social context.* Hillsdale, NJ: Lawrence Erlbaum Associates.

Zajonc, R. B. (1968). Attitudinal effects of mere exposure. *Journal of Personality and Social Psychology Monograph Supplement, 9,* 1–28.

Zanna, M. P. (1990). Attitude functions: Is it related to attitude structure? *Advances in Consumer Research, 17,* 98–100.

Zanna, M. P., & Rempel, J. K. (1988). Attitudes: A new look at an old concept. In D. Bar-Tal & A. W. Kruglanski (Eds.), *The social psychology of knowledge* (pp. 315–334). Cambridge, England: Cambridge University Press.

Unconscious Sources of Subjectivity and Suffering: Is Consciousness the Solution?

E. Tory Higgins
Columbia University

John A. Bargh
New York University

> *It would seem that we act all the more securely for our unawareness of the patterns that control us. It may well be that, owing to the limitations of the conscious life, any attempt to subject even the higher forms of social behavior to purely conscious control must result in disaster. . . . Is it not possible that the contemporary mind, in its restless attempt to drag all the forms of behavior into consciousness and to apply the results of its fragmentary or experimental analysis to the guidance of conduct, is really throwing away a greater wealth for the sake of a lesser and more dazzling one?*
>
> —Edward Sapir (1928, pp. 123–124)

In a recent volume one of us described varieties of automaticity that can occur outside conscious control and produce hidden biases in judgment (Bargh, 1989; see also Bargh, 1984), and the other discussed variables underlying knowledge activation that can function unconsciously to produce suffering as well as judgments and memories that are subjective in the sense of being involuntary, nonobjective, and even illusory (Higgins, 1989b; see also Higgins & King, 1981). What both of us were proposing (among other things) is that unconscious or preconscious processing can create problems.[1] This proposal is neither novel nor controversial. Indeed, by now psychologists take it for granted that the unconscious is a source of problems. Along with this notion is another, complementary notion that is also typically treated as a given—that consciousness is the

---

[1]It should be noted from the outset that by the term *unconscious* we are not referring to psychoanalytic variables such as repression and perceptual defenses. Rather, we are basically referring to processing that occurs automatically and without awareness.

solution to the problems associated with unconsciousness. The idea that unconsciousness is bad and consciousness is good has a long history in psychology. In the 17th and 18th centuries, the unconscious was considered to be both obscure and inhibited whereas the conscious was clear and uninhibited (see Heidbreder, 1933). A very similar viewpoint was expressed in psychoanalytic theories as well. Freud (1920/1952), for example, stated that symptoms are produced when a mental process has not been carried through to an end in a normal manner so that it could become conscious. When the mental process is unconscious, it has the power to construct a symptom. Indeed repression, which opposes the attempt to bring the unconscious into consciousness "is the essential preliminary condition for the development of symptoms" (p. 304). The unconscious, associated with the "pleasure-principle," is contrasted with the conscious, associated with the "reality-principle." The former is overwhelmed by instincts, whereas the latter is controlled by reason and facts.

The classic "hot" psychoanalytic distinction between the out-of-control consciousness and the reasonable, in-control conscious is mirrored in the "cold" information-processing distinction between *automatic,* unconscious processing and *controlled,* conscious processing (see, e.g., Posner, 1978; Shiffrin & Schneider, 1977). The information-processing perspective includes both the notion that unconscious processes can influence perception despite the current goals of the perceiver and the notion that conscious processes can inhibit the influence of unconscious processes. Thus, a conscious factual set can prevent unconscious processes, such as priming effects, from producing judgmental distortions. Other distinctions in the current literature, such as *mindful* versus *mindless* (see Langer, 1989) and *systematic* versus *heuristic* (see Chaiken, 1987), also involve the notion, at least to some extent, that conscious systematic processing is more controlled and realistic (i.e., data-oriented and reasoned) than unconscious automatic processing. It has also been common for cognitive perspectives on stereotyping to suggest that stereotyping is an especially difficult problem because it is uncontrolled, occurring without awareness or intent (for a recent review, see Fiske, 1989).

Psychological models designed to intervene and reduce mental suffering and bias have also traditionally assumed that making thoughts conscious will improve matters. The classic Freudian psychoanalytic approach attempts to initiate a process in which unconscious forms of thought press for realization and discharge. Clients are directed to "say whatever comes to mind." Psychoanalysis lures forbidden thoughts out of hiding so that the patient can wrestle with them. Only by consciously engaging the unconscious world can psychoanalytic treatment benefit the patient (see Freud, 1923/1961). Jungian treatment differs greatly from Freudian treatment but neurotic behavior is still handled on a conscious level and the main healing principle is to bring a person into greater contact with the deep (collective) unconscious (see Jung, 1954).

It is not only the hot psychotherapy treatments which assume that making the unconscious conscious is beneficial. The cold cognitive approaches do so as well. In cognitive-behavioral therapy, for example, a critical goal of the treatment is to help clients detect their dysfunctional *automatic thoughts* so that they can begin the unconscious healing process of reality testing (see Beck, Rush, Shaw, & Emery, 1979). Rational-emotive therapy (see Ellis, 1962) forbids anything hidden or unconscious and encourages clients to analyze their conscious assumptions and beliefs in order to make them more sensible. Mindfulness therapy (see Langer, 1989) is premised on the principle that taking conscious control over routinized thought and behavior patterns will foster adjustment and adaptation to one's life circumstances.

Making unconscious thoughts conscious is also considered to be beneficial in reducing judgmental biases. In the area of stereotyping, for example, it has been suggested that false beliefs will be difficult to alter as long as they remain unconscious. Positive change is deemed more likely to occur if people are made aware of their beliefs and then relate them to (disconfirming) evidence (see, e.g., Rothbart, 1981). Early on it was suggested that self-insight could help to reduce stereotyping and prejudice by making people aware of and concerned about their intolerance (see, e.g., Allport & Kramer, 1946; see also Fiske, 1989).

In summary, there is considerable agreement among psychologists that unconsciousness creates problems whereas consciousness solves problems; that is, unconsciousness is bad and consciousness is good. Our position in this chapter is that this basic proposition contains some truth but not the whole truth. Indeed, perhaps unconscious control is more functional than conscious control, as Edward Sapir suggested in the beginning quotation. Certainly the basic proposition needs to be reexamined more critically. In doing so, we describe some trade-offs involved in both conscious and unconscious processing. The chapter begins by illustrating in our own research the sort of phenomena that supports the key premise underlying the basic proposition that unconscious processing is bad and conscious processing is good—when unconscious processing produces subjectivity and suffering. Evidence for the second premise underlying this basic proposition is then briefly described—when conscious processing is relatively adaptive. We then review evidence that calls into question each of the premises underlying the basic proposition—when unconsciousness is good, and when consciousness is bad. Some implications of the trade-offs between consciousness and unconsciousness are then considered.

WHEN UNCONSCIOUSNESS IS BAD

Both hot and cold psychological theories agree that the unconscious can be a problem when it is associated with a lack of awareness and a loss of voluntary control. The general concept of automaticity captures both the out-of-awareness and out-of-control features of the purported role of the unconscious, although there are a variety of distinct features of automaticity that often do not co-occur (see Bargh, 1989). Knowledge accessibility and activation can produce subjectivity and suffering, but only some of its sources involve automatic processes. Indeed, the variables of momentary expectancies and motivational states included in Bruner's (1957) notion of category accessibility do not involve automatic processes. But other sources do, including variables that increase the prior likelihood that a particular construct rather than an alternative will be applied to an input.

Subjective Judgments from Knowledge Accessibility

A series of social psychological studies beginning in the late 1970s demonstrated that simply activating a construct in one task could increase the accessibility of the construct sufficiently to give it precedence when subjects later categorized a target person's behavior (for reviews, see Higgins, 1989b; Higgins & Bargh, 1987; Higgins & King, 1981; Wyer & Srull, 1981, 1986). Higgins, Rholes, and Jones (1977), for example, initially exposed subjects to one or another set of trait constructs as an incidental aspect of a study on perception. Next, the subjects participated in an "unrelated" study on reading comprehension where they read an essay describing the ambiguous behaviors of a target person. When the subjects later categorized the target person they were significantly more likely to use the constructs activated or primed in the "perception study" than alternative, equally applicable constructs—the now well-established *judgmental-assimilation bias*. Moreover, the priming effects on categorization unconsciously changed the subjective meaning of the target's behaviors over time, as indicated by changes in the subjects' own attitudes toward the target person 2 weeks later.

Many subsequent studies also found that recent priming can produce a judgmental-assimilation bias (e.g., Bargh, Bond, Lombardi, & Tota, 1986; Erdley & D'Agostino, 1988; Fazio, Powell, & Herr, 1983; Herr, 1986; Herr, Sherman, & Fazio, 1983; Higgins, Bargh, & Lombardi, 1985; Higgins & Chaires, 1980; Martin, 1986; Rholes & Pryor, 1982; Sinclair, Mark, & Shotland, 1987; Srull & Wyer, 1979, 1980). There is also evidence that frequent priming of a construct increases how long the construct will remain predominant (e.g., Higgins, Bargh, & Lombardi, 1985; Lombardi, Higgins, & Bargh, 1987; Srull & Wyer, 1979, 1980).

As an example of how both recent and frequent activation can produce the judgmental-assimilation bias, let us briefly consider the Higgins, Bargh, and Lombardi (1985) study. In a supposed "scrambled sentence task," undergraduate subjects were exposed across a number of trials to two different trait constructs that could be used to categorize the same behavior, with one trait being primed frequently and the other being primed only once but most recently. After delays of either 15 seconds or 120 seconds, the subjects began another task in which they were asked to categorize the same behavioral description of a target person. When categorizing the target person's behavior, the subjects tended to use the more recently activated construct after the brief delay but to use the more frequently activated construct after the long delay. This crossover pattern illustrates how variables extraneous to an input, such as prior activation and delay length, can unconsciously bias how an input is judged.

Other results of these studies suggest that the judgmental-assimilation bias is more likely to occur if perceivers are not conscious of the prior priming events when they later process the input than if they are conscious (see Lombardi et al., 1987). Indeed, the judgmental-assimilation bias disappears under experimental conditions that increase the likelihood of awareness, such as by using highly memorable priming stimuli or by actually reminding subjects of the priming events (see Herr, 1986; Herr et al., 1983; Lombardi et al., 1987; Martin, 1986; Newman & Uleman, 1990; Strack, Schwarz, Bless, Kubler, & Wanke, 1988). In a recent study by Newman and Uleman (1990, Experiment 2), for example, the priming manipulation consisted of asking a question about the trait prior to judging the behavior (e.g., "Is Molly *stubborn?*"). This type of priming did not produce a judgmental-assimilation bias. Other findings suggest that the assimilation-categorization bias is more likely to appear when subjects are motivated to suppress awareness of a priming event, such as when it would be unpleasant to remember (see, e.g., Martin, 1986).

Perhaps the most convincing evidence that knowledge accessibility can unconsciously produce a judgmental-assimilation bias as well as other kinds of subjective responding is provided by studies of chronic knowledge accessibility. Kelly (1955) stated that "construct systems can be considered as a kind of scanning pattern which a person continually projects upon his world. As he sweeps back and forth across his perceptual field he picks up blips of meaning" (p. 145). Higgins, King, and Mavin (1982) pointed out that there are two kinds of individual differences in construct systems. First, there are individual differences in the particular kinds of constructs that are present in memory for potential use in processing social input (differences in the kind of stored knowledge that is *available* for use). This is basically what Kelly (1955) meant by personal constructs. Second, there are individual differences in the readiness with which available constructs are actually used (differences in the *accessibility* or likelihood of using available constructs). Various studies have now shown that individuals' chronically accessible constructs can produce the judgmental-assimilation bias and other forms of subjectivity (e.g., Bargh & Pratto, 1986; Bargh & Thein, 1985; Higgins et al., 1982; King & Sorrentino, 1988; Lau, 1989; Strauman & Higgins, 1987).

In a couple of initial studies on chronic knowledge accessibility, Higgins et al. (1982) measured subjects' chronically accessible constructs by asking them to list the traits of a type of person that they liked, that they disliked, that they sought out, that they avoided, and that they frequently encountered. Chronic accessibility was defined either in terms of output primacy (i.e., those traits a subject listed first in response to the questions) or in terms of output frequency (i.e., those traits listed frequently in response to the questions). About 1 week later, subjects participated in an "unrelated" study conducted by a different experimenter. Each subject read an individually-tailored essay containing some behavioral descriptions of a target person that moderately exemplified the subject's accessible trait constructs, and other behavioral descriptions that moderately exemplified trait constructs that were not chronically accessible for the subject but were so for some other subject. (This was a *quasi-yoking* design that controlled across subjects for the content of the accessibility-related and -unrelated descriptions.) On a measure of subjects' recall of the behavioral descriptions, the study found that subjects were significantly more likely to exclude information unrelated to their chronically accessible constructs than information related to them.

Higgins et al. (1982) hypothesized that chronic individual differences in knowledge accessibility would function like temporary individual differences in knowledge accessibility (as produced by priming). Thus, combining in the same study both chronic and temporary individual differences in knowledge accessibility should enhance the judgmental-assimilation bias. The results of a study by Bargh et al. (1986) supported this hypothesis. They found that these chronic and temporary sources of knowledge accessibility combined additively to increase the likelihood that the construct would be used to interpret behavioral descriptions of a target person. An even more stringent test of this hypothesis was conducted by Bargh, Lombardi, and Higgins (1988). According to Higgins and King (1981), individual differences in chronic accessibility should function like temporary differences produced by frequent activation. Thus, Bargh et al. reasoned that the crossover pattern of results found in Higgins et al. (1985), where the input was categorized in terms of the most recently primed construct after a brief delay but in terms of the most frequently primed construct after a long delay, should be replicated if chronic individual differences in knowledge accessibility were substituted for the frequent priming manipulation. All subjects were primed by recent exposure to a trait construct (e.g., *persistent*) that could be used to categorize the ambiguous behavior of a target person that they read about in a subsequent task. Subjects were preselected so that the alternative trait construct that could be used to categorize the target person's behavior (e.g., *stubborn*) either was a chronically accessible construct for them *(Chronics)* or was not *(Nonchronics)*. As in our earlier study, the delay between the priming task and the categorization task was either brief (15 seconds) or long (120 seconds and 180 seconds).

The results confirmed the prediction. For Chronics, a crossover pattern was found. These subjects tended to use the recently primed construct after the short delay but the chronically accessible alternative construct after the longest delay. No such crossover pattern was found for Nonchronics. Thus, once again there was strong evidence that different sources of knowledge accessibility can produce an unconscious judgmental-assimilation bias. Another interesting result of this study was that as post-priming delay increased from 15 seconds to 180 seconds, the percentage of Chronic subjects who (correctly) used an ambiguous construct to categorize the ambiguous input decreased from 20% to only 6%. This decrease over time was evident only for the Chronics. (For the Nonchronics, approximately 25% used an ambiguous construct after both the 15-second delay and the 180-second delay.) Once again, this exemplifies how accessibility can bias judgments away from the input toward the most accessible construct.

Subjective Memory from Contextually Influenced Judgments

In the previous section we described how contextual priming can produce a judgmental-assimilation bias. In the case of priming, the influence of context on judgment can itself be unconscious. But even when the influence of context on judgment is not itself unconscious, the context-influenced judgment can have an unconscious effect on subsequent responses and memory.

It is well known that social judgments of a target person's behaviors can influence subsequent target-related judgments and behaviors (see, e.g., Carlston, 1980; Lingle & Ostrom, 1979; Manis, Cornell, & Moore, 1974; Sherman, Ahlm, Berman, & Lynn, 1978; for reviews, see Higgins & Stangor, 1988a; Wyer & Srull, 1986). Under certain conditions, these judgments can also produce errors in reconstructing the original target information (e.g., Higgins & Rholes, 1978). Such errors in reconstructive memory can be understood in terms of the following four commonly accepted premises (see, e.g., Anderson & Hubert, 1963; Carlston, 1980; Higgins & Rholes, 1978; Higgins & Stangor, 1988a; Lingle & Ostrom, 1979; Posner, 1978; Sherman et al., 1978; Wyer & Srull, 1986; Wyer, Srull, & Gordon, 1984): First, people's judgment of a target is influenced not only by the details or properties of the target but also by factors extraneous to the target's properties (such as mood, goals, standards, sets, knowledge accessibility). Second, when people encode a target they not only store the details of the target information but also their judgment of the target. Third, when people subsequently reconstruct the original target person information they use not only the represented target details but also their prior judgment of the target. Fourth, in using their prior judgment of the target as a basis for reconstruction, people do not take into account sufficiently the extent to which the judgment was based on factors extraneous to the properties of the input.

One interpretation of these errors in reconstructive memory is that people use their prior judgment as if its original source was solely the target's properties without (consciously) considering other sources of the judgment, such as contextual influences (see Higgins & Stangor, 1988a). One type of judgment-related reconstructive error that has been interpreted in these terms is the *change-of-standard* effect (see Higgins & Lurie, 1983; Higgins & Stangor, 1988b).

The change-of-standard effect refers to cases where people make an initial judgment of a target in relation to one standard and then later, when using the judgment in their current responding, reinterpret the meaning of that judgment in relation to a different standard without taking the change-of-standard into account sufficiently. Studies by Higgins and Lurie (1983) and Higgins and Stangor (1988b) showed that this change-of-standard effect can produce substantial errors in reconstructive memory.

Higgins and Lurie (1983) had subjects read about the sentencing decisions of a target trial judge in the context of reading about the decisions of other trial judges for the same kinds of criminal offenses. These other judges consistently gave either higher years of sentencing (the *harsh* context condition) or lower years of sentencing (the *lenient* context condition) than the target judge. A substantial context effect on subjects' judgments of the target's harshness or leniency as a judge was found. Subjects judged the same sentencing decisions of the target judge as more lenient in the harsh context condition than in the lenient context condition. This contrast effect of the standard provided by the immediate context on subjects' judgments of the target was consistent with many previous studies (see, e.g., Campbell, Hunt, & Lewis, 1958; Glucksberg, Krauss, & Higgins, 1975; Manis, 1967; Manis & Armstrong, 1971; Ostrom & Upshaw, 1968; Rosenberg & Cohen, 1966) and has since been directly replicated several times (see Higgins & Stangor, 1988b).

In addition to manipulating the standard provided by the immediate context in which subjects' initial target judgments were made, Higgins and Lurie (1983) also manipulated the overall category norm for trial judges' years of sentencing. This was accomplished by varying the sentencing decisions of the non-target trial judges that subjects read about both in the first session and in a second session held a few days later. In this way, it was possible to create conditions where the standard available at recall (the category norm) was basically the same as or different from the standard used to make the initial judgment (the context standard).

Higgins and Lurie (1983) found that when there was a change of standard there were substantial judgment-related errors in reconstructive memory. In those conditions in which subjects went from a harsh or a lenient context standard to a moderate category norm standard, the subjects' recall of the same target information differed substantially. It is interesting to note that the moderate category norm was designed to have the same average years of sentencing as the target's actual sentencing decisions. Nevertheless, subjects in the lenient context condition (who had categorized the target as harsh) recalled the target's sentencing decisions as being over 75% higher than subjects in the harsh context condition (who had categorized the target as lenient).

Higgins and Stangor (1988b) replicated and extended these basic findings.

Most important, their studies controlled for both subjects' initial judgments and the most recent exemplars of sentencing decisions and still found reconstructive memory errors when there was a change of standard. Higgins and Stangor's Study 3 accomplished this by varying the timing of subjects' judgments. In the first session, subjects read about only the sentencing decisions of three nontarget trial judges who were either generally harsh or generally lenient. It was not until 3 days later that the subjects read about the sentencing decisions of the target judge, Judge Jones. Half of the subjects made their judgments of the sentencing decisions of Judge Jones at the beginning of the second session. The comparison standard for these subjects, then, was the first session standard. The other half of the subjects read about the sentencing decisions of three additional trial judges at the beginning of the second session and then made their judgments of Judge Jones. The comparison standard for these subjects was the second session standard.

Table 3.1 shows the recall results for this study. (The actual total of Judge Jones' sentencing decisions was 15.) Subjects in Condition A and Condition G both had a harsh standard for their judgment, which produced the same lenient judgment, and both had the same most accessible (i.e., recent) exemplars (i.e., harsh exemplars). And, of course, Judge Jones' sentencing decisions were the same in both conditions. Still, subjects' recall of Judge Jones' sentencing decisions differed significantly between these conditions. This was because these two conditions happened to differ in their category norm standards and subjects in both conditions made the mistake of using the category norm standard to interpret the referential meaning of their judgment rather than the first or second session standards that actually determined these judgments. For the same reason, the recall of subjects in Conditions D and F was significantly different even though the initial judgments, most recent accessible exemplars, and target person information were all the same. The greater recall in Condition F than in Condition B and the greater recall in Condition C than in Condition G also demonstrate that simply the happenstance of when the judgment was made produced different recall of the same target person information. One would not expect

TABLE 3.1
Recall of Sentencing Decisions of Judge Jones as a Function of First and Second Session Contexts and Timing of Second Session Judgment

Context Condition	Timing of Judgment	
Session$_1$/Session$_2$	Judgment Before	Judgment After
Harsh$_1$/Harsh$_2$	21.5 (A)	19.0 (E)
Harsh$_1$/Lenient$_2$	11.3 (B)	14.5 (F)
Lenient$_1$/Harsh$_2$	17.8 (C)	14.7 (G)
Lenient$_1$/Lenient$_2$	10.5 (D)	12.9 (H)

Note: The letters in parentheses indicate condition labels as cited in the text.

people to be conscious of a factor like timing of judgment when they use their prior judgments in reconstructive memory.

Emotional Suffering from Self-Knowledge Activation

In an earlier section we described how the combination of chronic and temporary sources of accessibility can function unconsciously to produce subjective judgments, such as the judgmental-assimilation bias. In this section we discuss how this combination can also function unconsciously to produce emotional distress. As an illustration, let us consider the emotional consequences of people possessing self-discrepancies. People's self-knowledge includes both representations of the kind of person that they believe they actually are, their current self or self-concept, and representations of the kind of person that someone prefers or demands that they be, their valued end-states or self-guides. Two basic kinds of self-guides are the *ideal* self, which is a representation of someone's hopes or wishes for you, and the *ought* self, which is a representation of someone's beliefs about your duties and responsibilities (see Higgins, 1987).

People are motivated to make the attributes in their actual self congruent with the attributes in their self-guides. Self-discrepancy theory proposes that, first, discrepant relations between actual self and self-guide attributes represent, as a whole, a negative psychological situation, and, second, discrepant relations function as an available cognitive structure. A study by Higgins, Van Hook, and Dorfman (1988) provided some evidence that discrepant relations (i.e., mismatches between the actual self and a self-guide) do form a unified cognitive structure. Given that this available self-system has motivational significance, it should also be chronically accessible (see Higgins & King, 1981). Moreover, priming any part of it should increase the accessibility of the whole sufficiently to activate the self-discrepancy and produce distress.

Self-discrepancy theory (see Higgins, 1987, 1989a,c) predicts that activating an actual self:ideal self-guide discrepancy, which wholistically represents the "absence of positive outcomes," will produce dejection-related distress (e.g., feelings of sadness, disappointment, dissatisfaction). In contrast, activating an actual self:ought self-guide discrepancy, which wholistically represents the "expected presence of negative outcomes," is predicted to produce agitation-related distress (e.g., feelings of worry, nervousness, edginess).

Strauman and Higgins (1987) tested whether the combination of chronic and temporary sources of accessibility would unconsciously activate self-discrepancies and thereby produce distress. A covert, idiographic priming technique was used in a couple of studies to activate self-guide attributes in a supposedly nonself-relevant task investigating the "psychological effects of thinking about other people." Undergraduate subjects were given phrases of the form, "An X person is _____" (where X would be a trait adjective such as *friendly* or *intelligent*), and were asked to complete each sentence as quickly as possible. Because the trait adjectives that were used as primes were selected from subjects' self-guides, they were always positive. Thus, the primes were positive and the task directed attention to others. Nevertheless, the unconscious activation of self-discrepancies was expected to produce distress, with the nature of the distress varying depending on whether it was subjects' actual:ideal or actual:ought discrepancies that were activated. The subjects were preselected on the basis of their responses to the Selves Questionnaire to be either high in actual:ideal discrepancy or high in actual:ought discrepancy. For each sentence, each subject's total verbalization time and skin conductance response amplitude were recorded. Subjects' dejection-related and agitation-related emotions were also measured at the beginning and end of the session.

Both studies found that priming subjects' positive self-guide attributes produced a dejection syndrome in subjects who were high in actual:ideal discrepancy—a greater increase in dejection-related emotions than in agitation-related emotions, a decrease in standardized skin conductance response amplitudes, and a decrease in total verbalization time. In contrast, the priming produced an agitation syndrome in subjects who were high in actual:ought discrepancy—a greater increase in agitation-related emotions than in dejection-related emotions, an increase in standardized skin conductance response amplitudes, and an increase in total verbalization time. As shown in Figs. 3.1 and 3.2, the discriminant pattern across the different trials from priming ideal mismatches versus ought mismatches was quite striking for both the total verbalization times and skin conductance responses. In these figures, (S) denotes primes involving a self-related mismatch and (U) denotes primes involving a self-unrelated attribute.

Strauman (1989) tested whether these effects of unconsciously combining chronic and temporary sources of accessibility would be found in clinical samples as well. The subject samples included clinically diagnosed depressed patients and social phobic patients. As expected, the former sample possessed the highest level of actual:ideal discrepancy and the latter sample possessed the highest level of actual:ought discrepancy. Each subject was primed with both positive ideal self-guide attributes and ought self-guide attributes that were

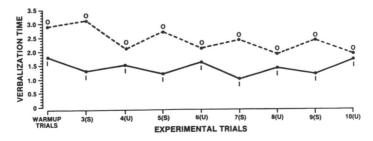

FIG. 3.1.

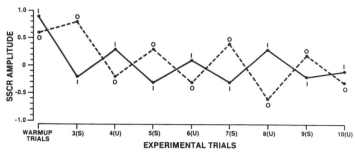

FIG. 3.2.

discrepant from the subject's actual self. The results replicated Strauman and Higgins (1987). Activating an actual:ideal discrepancy produced a dejection syndrome, which was most pronounced in the depressed subjects. Activating an actual:ought discrepancy produced an agitation syndrome, which was most pronounced in the social phobic subjects.

In summary, this section has illustrated how unconscious processing or a lack of consciousness can produce subjective judgments, subjective memory, and emotional suffering. Such findings are consistent with the notion that unconsciousness is the source of problems.

WHEN CONSCIOUSNESS IS GOOD

Compared to unconscious thought, conscious mentation is slow, inefficient, and limited because of its high consumption rate of scarce attentional resources. But it is also more flexible and adaptive, the source of novel responses to the environment. Consciousness is also the seat of control and inhibition, with the ability to suppress or override unconscious impulses (see, e.g., Logan, 1980; Posner & Snyder, 1975; Shallice, 1972).

Because of the complementary nature of the qualities of unconscious and conscious thought, when consciousness is good is precisely when unconsciousness is bad. In most situations, because we have been in them before, habitual, chronic, or instinctive responses are generated by the unconscious (i.e., unintentionally and immediately). If this routine response is in conflict with the current, conscious goal, however, consciousness is able to inhibit and control it, and to generate a more goal-appropriate response (Logan, 1980; Logan & Cowan, 1984; Posner & Snyder, 1975).

The classic experimental paradigm for studying this battle between conscious and unconscious influence has been the Stroop task and its variants (Logan, 1980; Stroop, 1935). In this task, subjects are presented with a word printed in one of a variety of ink colors. The subject's task is to name the color of the ink as quickly as possible—the word meaning itself is irrelevant to this purpose. Subjects cannot help but notice the meaning of the word, however, and it does influence their response latency. For example, people take longer to say "green" to the word *red* printed in green ink, than to the word *throw*, for example, printed in green ink. The reason for this is that the word *red* unconsciously suggests a response to the color-naming task (i.e., the response *red*) as does the color of the ink (i.e., the response *green*). Because only one response may be made, the inhibitory and response control quality of consciousness comes into play, inhibiting the incorrect, unconsciously generated response *red,* and permitting the correct response *green*—but at a cost of attentional resources and, therefore, time (see Logan, 1980).

The important point is that even though such responses take a bit longer to be made, still the response made is the correct one. Dramatic demonstrations of this ability of a flexible conscious response strategy to override habitual unconscious responses have been made by Neely (1977) and Logan and Zbrodoff (1979). In the Logan and Zbrodoff study, for instance, subjects were to indicate by a button press as quickly as they could whether a presented word was above or below a fixed point on the screen in front of them. Sometimes, the actual word *above* or *below* was presented. Analogously to the Stroop effect, on such trials subjects were faster when the word meaning agreed with the position of the word (e.g., *above* presented above the fixation point) than when it differed. However, Logan and Zbrodoff designed the study such that over the course of the experimental session, the word *above (below),* when presented, was usually placed below (above) the fixation point. The outcome was that subjects became faster to respond to *above (below)* when it was below (above) the point than when it appeared above (below)! Apparently, subjects developed a conscious response strategy to take advantage of the novel circumstances, which overrode the (inappropriate under the circumstances) unconscious influence.

These experimental demonstrations confirm what is a common, daily experience for most of us—that of controlling our impulses. Normal, polite social intercourse depends on our ability to closely monitor and control our true reactions and feelings (often disagreeable or intimate) regarding the people we are interacting with. An episode of the 1960s television series "Bewitched" illustrated this point nicely: Endora, the mother-in-law, mischievously gave Darrin and Samantha a present of a small statuette, which unbeknownst to them would cause anyone within 10 feet of it to speak the truth. Needless to say, there was social chaos later that evening at a dinner party in their home. We must constantly interact with people we don't like, who do things and hold beliefs we do not agree with, but we constantly control and censor what we really believe and what we would really like to say. If, as claimed by James (1890), habit is the flywheel of society, then control and inhibition must be its lubricant.

Speaking of habits, when they are undesirable or no longer appropriate (as when circumstances change), again it is conscious control and flexibility that can change them. Through constant, repeated suppression of the habitual impulse, and the substitution of a different, more acceptable or appropriate response, an undesirable unconscious response may be supplanted with a new, desired one—but only through deliberate, conscious effort. This formula has been applied by James (1890) to the "bad habit" of the after-dinner cigar, as well as by Beck, Rush, Shaw, and Emery (1979) to the bad habit of negative self-referential thoughts. Were it not for the control/flexibility qualities of consciousness, such changing of habitual, unconscious responses would be impossible.

Motivated conscious control has also been found recently to override unconscious biases in social judgment. One such bias is the pervasive tendency of people to attribute causes for a person's behavior to internal characteristics of the person, often ignoring strong situational influences (e.g., Heider, 1958; Jones & Davis, 1965; Ross, 1977). In part, this bias seems to be due to an unconscious tendency to categorize behavior in terms of personality constructs (see Higgins & Bargh, 1987; Newman & Uleman, 1990). Gilbert (1989) found in a variety of studies that when conscious control over the impression formation process is prevented, such as by distracting the subject or giving him or her something else to do while witnessing the relevant behavior, dispositional attributions are much more likely. Subjects only took situational causes into account when the ability to engage in effortful (and attention-demanding) conscious appraisal of the behavior was not prevented.

Just as the initial categorization of behavior in terms of trait constructs was found to be an unconscious, automatic process, so too has the categorization of people in terms of the age-, race-, occupation-, and gender-related stereotypes relevant to them (e.g., Brewer, 1988; Fiske & Neuberg, 1990; Pratto & Bargh, 1991). These stereotypes appear to be applied unconsciously to people as long as the person's obvious features (e.g., gender, skin color, clothing) match those of the stereotype representation in memory. The activated stereotype therefore would be likely to exert an unconscious influence on impressions and other judgments of the person.

Recent studies, however, have found that given sufficient motivation—such as when one expects to have to justify one's judgments, or when one is motivated to be nonprejudiced—a social perceiver will exert conscious control over the judgment process, and override stereotypical influences with effortfully gained individuating information (Devine, 1989; Devine, Sedikides, & Fuhrman, 1989; Fiske, 1989; Fiske & Neuberg, 1990; Tetlock, 1985). In other words, unconscious influences serve as the default in the judgment process unless they are countermanded by motivated conscious judgment strategies (Bargh, 1988, 1989). The motivation for the necessary conscious effort expenditure can come from a variety of sources, from one's chronic values to one's temporary situational goals, but without *some* motivational support the conscious effort does not occur, and the unconscious bias prevails by forfeit.

In summary, consciousness is good to have around when unconsciously generated influences on decisions and responses are undesirable or inappropriate to current goals, or lacking altogether (as in completely novel circumstances). The control and flexibility qualities of conscious thought enable us to overcome the vicissitudes of early, unquestioned learning, such as prejudices passed down by one's parents, to change a habitual pattern of behavior that formerly served one well but has become inappropriate (e.g., a man holding doors for women in a small, traditional town vs. a sophisticated modern city), and to figure out what to do when faced with a situation one has never been in before. But if consciousness is good when unconsciousness is bad, it may be less helpful when unconsciousness itself is good. In the next section evidence is presented which suggests that unconsciousness can, indeed, be good. And following that section, findings are described that suggest that, rather than being the solution, consciousness can itself be a source of problems.

WHEN UNCONSCIOUSNESS IS GOOD

It would not be an exaggeration to say that human life would not be possible in any of its current forms without unconscious mental processes. It is very easy to unwittingly minimize their importance, for by their very nature, one is unaware of them. Yet if relatively slow, serial, limited conscious thought had to take over everything typically handled by unconscious processes, then, as Miller, Galanter, and Pribram (1960) put it, we would not be able even to get out of bed in the morning. The amount of conscious attention it would require to monitor, direct, and coordinate all of the muscle movements needed to stand up would overwhelm the limits of conscious thinking capacity.

Given the limits on conscious attentional capacity (e.g., Miller, 1956), and its relatively slow, serial nature, it would make little sense for all of cognition to be conscious. Whatever *can* be handled unconsciously *should* be, therefore, reserving consciousness for just those functions that cannot be (see preceding section). And this is just what happens—through frequent and consistent experience, skills of attention, perception, judgment, and motor control become more efficient, eventually requiring little if any conscious attention or direction (see Newell & Rosenbloom, 1981; Schneider & Shiffrin, 1977; Smith & Lerner, 1986).

As Bateson (1972) argued, the purpose of conscious awareness is to deal with what is going on in the world, not with the details of how one knows it. It would be of little functional value for one to be aware of each step along the way from sensation to feature detection to pattern recognition; better to save limited conscious awareness and attention for the final output of those preliminary, preconscious processes (see Ericsson & Simon 1980; Nisbett & Wilson, 1977). Accordingly, the perception of any object, scene, or behavior involves an extensive preconscious analysis, with the results furnished as the givens or starting blocks of conscious processing (Neisser, 1967; Werner, 1956). In other words, we perceive the schoolteacher, the snowbank, and the hamburger immediately, as givens, without awareness of the considerable interpretative work necessary to produce those direct perceptions. Such meanings are not self-evident in the sensory information alone. Rather, extensive unconscious inferential activity, involving the activation of stored knowledge as well as feature synthesis and integration, are necessary to arrive at what only seem to be self-evident perceptual conclusions. We see the snowbank because it is January in Wisconsin, not July in Florida; we are drawing on stored knowledge and occupational stereotypes to "know" that the adult woman leading thirty-five 9-year-olds in a museum is a schoolteacher.

A study by Friedman (1979) demonstrated just how immediately such stored knowledge is brought to bear in perception. She showed subjects photographs of common scenes, such as a kitchen and a farmyard, and measured the location and duration of first eye fixations—where the eyes went to first in scanning the photograph, and where they lingered longest. Subjects spent very little time looking at the expected, usual features of each scene, but took considerably more time on objects that did not belong or were out of place in the scene (e.g., a toaster in the sink; a hippopotamus in the farm pond). This relative attention allocation—little to the expected, much more to the unexpected—is notable because it occurred immediately, the first time the subject's eyes encountered the object. Thus, relevant stored knowledge was immediately and unconsciously (unintentionally and nonstrategically) activated by the scene. It then facilitated the processing of the expected, usual features of the scene, such that minimal conscious attention was needed for them. Consequently, conscious attention was automatically drawn to those features for which it was most needed—the unusual and novel, those which unconscious processing alone could not handle (see previous section).

The extent of preconscious analysis has long been a topic of debate (see, e.g., Deutsch & Deutsch, 1963; Neisser, 1967; Norman, 1968). Recent evidence, however, indicates that it extends to the detection and categorization of frequently experienced types of social behavior, such as honesty, kindness, and stupidity (Bargh & Pratto, 1986; Bargh & Thein, 1985; Higgins, King, & Mavin, 1982). Just as Friedman (1979) found for common visual scenes, the regularities of one's social environment are also detected immediately and unconsciously, without the need of conscious, attentional processing. For example, Bargh and Thein (1985) found that when conscious processing ability was severely constrained, behaviors that corresponded to a subject's chronically accessible constructs (i.e., those that had presumably been used frequently and consistently in the past; see Bargh, 1984; Higgins & King, 1981) were nonetheless detected and influential in impressions of the target person. Behaviors relevant to the subject's inaccessible social constructs were not. Using the Stroop paradigm, Bargh and Pratto (1986) found that information relevant to one's chronic constructs could not be ignored, relative to other trait information. Thus, subjects pick up and are influenced by such behavioral information unconsciously, such as when conscious processing of it is prevented.

Why is this preconscious processing of social information good? Because the unconscious activation and use of stored knowledge relevant to the current situation, and the detection and registration of its regular features, keeps a working model of the world preactivated and ready at all times. Moreover, as in Friedman's (1979) research, any occurrence that does not match this implicit model immediately "kicks out" to conscious attentional processing. Examples of such chronic salience effects include the greater attention given to red-headed people, paraplegics, or pregnant women (see McArthur, 1981), to extremely pro- or anti-social behavior (Fiske, 1980), and to angry faces in a crowd (Hansen & Hansen, 1988). Such features do not fit our chronic, normative, unconsciously generated expectations for social situations, and so automatically attract conscious processing. The operation of this unconscious *social reality monitor* (Bargh, 1989) is sensitive, vigilant, and reliable, as it does not depend on the vagaries of the current focus or the availability of conscious attention, or the current processing goal—all of which are conditions needed for the *conscious* detection of events.

Another form of preconscious analysis has only recently come to light, that of the immediate unconscious classification of people, events, and objects as good or bad based on previously stored evaluative responses to them. It appears from recent evidence that all perceived stimuli activate their associated evaluative responses immediately, unintentionally, and outside of awareness. This *auto-evaluation process* (Bargh, Litt, Pratto, & Spielman, 1989) involves a simple dichotomous response to the person, object, or event as positive or negative; it does not report on the extent or degree of the goodness or badness.

The evidence of this phenomenon comes from several independent studies (Bargh, Chaiken, Govender, & Pratto, in press; Fazio, Sanbonmatsu, Powell, & Kardes, 1986; Greenwald, Klinger, & Liu, 1989). Greenwald et al. used a priming paradigm in which a prime word was presented for a brief moment (500 milliseconds) preceding presentation of a target word. Subjects were to evaluate the target as quickly as they could, using buttons labeled *good* and *bad*. The prime words were presented in such a way (through backward dichoptic masking) that subjects were never aware of their presence. Nonetheless, the primes facilitated responses to targets of the same valence, and interfered with responses (i.e., slowed them down) to targets of the opposite valence. Fazio et al. reported similar findings, but in their experiments the effect appeared to be limited to the subject's strongest and most accessible attitudes in memory.

In both of these studies, the priming stimuli apparently activated their associated evaluative responses unconsciously, because in one case (Fazio et al., 1986) subjects were not intending to evaluate the prime (just the target), and in the other (Greenwald et al., 1989) they weren't even aware of the prime's presence. Moreover, the duration of the prime prior to the target presentation was too brief in both studies for it to have been evaluated consciously and intentionally (see Neely, 1977).

The generality of this effect was demonstrated in a further series of studies (Bargh et al., in press; Bargh, Chaiken, Raymond, & Hymes, 1991). The point of these experiments was to eliminate successively as many of the conscious, strategic aspects of the subject's task from the procedure, in order to gauge the extent to which the effect was truly preconscious—that is, independent of conscious, strategic processes. For example, instructing the subject to evaluate the target word as good or bad would, of course, induce the conscious goal of evaluation, and as a result the prime might also be consciously evaluated due to this strategic mind-set (see also Bargh, 1990; Gollwitzer, 1990). Bargh et al. (1991) had subjects pronounce the target words as quickly as possible instead of evaluate them. Still, the same pattern of results was produced as with the evaluation task. Importantly, as the conscious and strategic aspects of the subject's task were removed in the successive experiments by Bargh et al. (in press), the preconscious evaluation effect became, if anything, stronger. Thus, the effect seems only to be interfered with when consciousness is involved, much as well-practiced skills (e.g., tennis, typing) deteriorate when performed consciously and deliberately.

Although the exact mechanism and the consequences (e.g., for emotional experience or further cognition) of the preconscious evaluation effect remain to be mapped out, the adaptive nature of the effect seems obvious. Assuming, as is the case with other preconscious processes (see Bargh, 1988, 1989), that the evaluative classification of a stimulus serves as input for subsequent decisions and behavioral responses, the immediate knowledge that a person, object, or situation is liked or disliked would be a boon to quick, on-line decisions as to how to respond. And given the frequent need to make such quick, snap decisions in the course of interacting with others (see Rothbart, 1981), immediate and direct evaluation would enable such decisions to be based on long-term preferences instead of the current, temporary contents of consciousness alone.

One other quality of unconscious thought should be highlighted for its beneficial nature. Unconsciousness is also good when the problem-solving strategies of conscious processing are unsuccessful. As discussed in the preceding section, the serial nature of conscious thought is made possible by its ability to inhibit other, competing lines of thought (e.g., Milner, 1957; Posner & Snyder, 1975; Shallice, 1972). Whereas this inhibitory function preserves the phenomenal "stream of consciousness," it also deters thinking from entering the less well-trodden paths that might be necessary to produce a solution. Unconscious thought, on the other hand, operates in parallel and without the inhibition of any one line of thought by another.

The creative aspect of unconscious thought is well-known. There is considerable anecdotal evidence from famous artists and scientists that solutions to problems they had been unable to crack after days or even months of intense conscious thought would suddenly occur to them in dreams, or when thinking about something else entirely, such as while shaving (causing Einstein, for one, to cut himself; see the compilation of Ghiselin, 1952). Apparently, extensive unsuccessful conscious effort at reaching a processing goal eventually results in the unconscious operation of that goal, and solutions that appear "out of nowhere" (see Bargh, 1990; Kuhl, 1986). A common example is the "tip of the tongue" phenomenon, in which one knows that one knows something, but cannot retrieve that knowledge from memory—only to have it pop into consciousness later on, unannounced (e.g., Brown & McNeil, 1966; Norman & Bobrow, 1976). The solution or answer that could not be attained consciously, due to the inhibitory feature of consciousness, was achieved unconsciously, when the inhibition was no longer operating.

In summary, it really is not a question of *when* unconsciousness is good, because it is constantly operating to keep an accurate model of the world and one's place in it ready and waiting for conscious use. This model includes one's frequent interpretations and evaluations of people, objects, and places one has encountered in the past. It is clearly operating even as one sleeps, for it is right there waiting for us when we awaken, providing continuity of phenomenal experience. Its representation of the chronic, usual features of one's life is illustrated by the common experience of travelers feeling disoriented for a moment or two upon awakening in strange surroundings, until conscious thought can figure out where one is. The notable point here is that the necessity of such conscious reasoning on waking is the exception, not the rule.

WHEN CONSCIOUSNESS IS BAD

It is not possible in this paper to provide an exhaustive review of all the possible ways in which consciousness can create rather than solve problems. Instead, we discuss three basic ways in which consciousness can be problematic and draw a set of conclusions that question the premise that consciousness is the solution.

Consciousness as a Source of Problematic Content

Earlier we described how self-discrepancies could be unconsciously activated and produce suffering even when positive attributes were primed and individuals were focusing on other people. Given the chronic accessibility of self-discrepancies, it takes very little additional excitation to activate them. It is not necessary that people consciously attend to their self-discrepancies or think about their self-guides in order for them to be activated and produce distress. Indeed, the traditional perspective in which consciousness is considered the solution to the problem implies that if people did think about their self-discrepancies they would be less likely to suffer from them. Presumably, consciousness would facilitate dealing with negative beliefs, such as by changing perspective (from child to adult) or finding counterevidence. Let us now consider what happens when people are asked explicitly to think about their self-guides or about self-discrepancies.

In an early study by Higgins, Bond, Klein, and Strauman (1986, Study 2), undergraduates' self-discrepancies were measured several weeks before the experimental session. On the basis of their responses, two groups of subjects were recruited for the experiment: (a) subjects who were relatively high on both actual:ideal discrepancy and actual:ought discrepancy; and (b) subjects who were relatively low on both types of discrepancies. Ostensibly as part of a life-span developmental study, subjects were asked to describe either the kind of person that they and their parents (now and in the past) would ideally like them to be and the attributes that they hoped they would have (Ideal-self focus), or the kind of person that they and their parents (now and in the past) believed they ought to be and the attributes that they believed it was their duty or obligation to have (Ought-self focus). Both before and after this manipulation of self-guide focus, subjects rated the extent to which they were currently feeling dejection-related emotions and agitation-related emotions. The study found that focusing on a self-guide produced an increase in discomfort only for those subjects who had self-discrepancies available to be activated (i.e., subjects high in both types of self-discrepancies). Moreover, the kind of discomfort that these subjects experienced depended on the type of self-guide they focused upon—an increase in dejection-related emotions when the Ideal self-guide was the focus and an increase in agitation-related emotions when the Ought self-guide was the focus.

This study involved priming a part of subjects' self-discrepancies, and this in turn produced emotional distress. To this extent, the results of this study are similar to those described earlier. But the priming manipulation was very different. In the studies of Strauman (1989) and Strauman and Higgins (1987), subjects were not aware that the priming events had anything to do with their self-guides. Indeed, they did not even know that the events were self-relevant. In contrast, subjects in the present study were explicitly asked to remember and think about their self-guides (i.e., their personal goals and standards). The results of the study demonstrate that such conscious activation of the self-system produces the same kind of distress as unconscious activation.

In another study by Higgins et al. (1986, Study 1), undergraduates were asked to imagine either a positive event in which performance matched a common standard (e.g., receiving a grade of A in a course) or a negative event in which performance failed to match a common standard (e.g., receiving a grade of D in a course that was necessary for obtaining an important job). Subjects' moods were measured both before and after they engaged in imagining the positive or negative event. To measure change in mood, the contribution to subjects' post-manipulation moods from their pre-manipulation moods was statistically removed. The partial correlational analyses on the mood change measures are

TABLE 3.2
Partial Correlations Between Types of Self-Discrepancies and Types
of Postmanipulation Mood in the Positive Event and Negative Event Conditions[1]

| | Guided-Imagery Manipulation Task | | | |
| | Positive Event Imagined | | Negative Event Imagined | |
Type of Self-Discrepancy	Dejection Emotions	Agitation Emotions	Dejection Emotions	Agitation Emotions
Actual:ideal	.17	.13	.39**	−.33*
Actual:ought	.05	.26#	−.04	.46**

Note: Partial correlations shown have premanipulation mood and the alternative type of self-discrepancy partialled out of each.
# $p < .10$; * $p < .05$; ** $p < .01$.

shown in Table 3.2, where the contribution to the relation between each type of discrepancy and each type of mood from their common association to the alternative type of discrepancy was also statistically removed. As Table 3.2 shows, the magnitude and type of subjects' actual:self-guide discrepancies predicted the amount and kind of mood change that they experienced weeks later when they imagined the events. Moreover, these relations were clearly evident only when subjects imagined an event to which the self-discrepancies, as negative psychological situations, were applicable (i.e., the negative event condition).

Again, the results of this study are consistent with the results of the studies by Strauman (1989) and Strauman and Higgins (1986). But in this study subjects were asked to *imagine* a discrepancy. Thus, not only was the discrepancy consciously focused on, but the discrepancy was imaginary! If consciousness reduces suffering by instigating objective, here-and-now cognitive responses, then one might expect that such responses should be especially effective for a discrepancy that is only imagined. After all, given that the subjects were first-year undergraduates, they could have reasoned that the imagined negative event (e.g., receiving a D in a course necessary to obtain an important job) had not happened to them (nor was it ever likely to). Nevertheless, subjects who chronically possessed greater self-discrepancies experienced more distress when they focused on an imaginary negative event.

One additional aspect of the results of both of the studies by Higgins et al. (1986) should be highlighted. In general, when the subjects with high self-discrepancies began the experimental session they were not experiencing much distress. Thus, the unconscious self-discrepancies per se were not producing discomfort. But after the subjects *consciously* focused on their self-guides or imagined a discrepancy they did begin to experience distress. In these studies, therefore, consciousness caused an increase in discomfort. (A positive mood manipulation was used at the end of each study to ensure that subjects felt good when they left.)

The increase in discomfort found in these studies is not surprising from the perspective of self-discrepancy theory because the conscious processing in these studies would be expected to activate available self-discrepancies that represent negative psychological situations. It is the activation of the self-discrepancy that matters and not the source of activation. Indeed, people do not generally know or consider the sources of their activated knowledge (see Bargh, 1989; Higgins, 1989b). Thus, consciousness is just another source of knowledge activation. And knowledge activation can produce distress when the knowledge is problematic, as in the case of self-discrepancies. Moreover, without consciousness the knowledge may remain unactivated, at least for the moment. Certainly, the subjects in these studies were feeling better *before* they focused on self-guides and discrepancies.

In summary, the results of these studies suggest the following conclusion: "When stored knowledge is problematic, unconscious nonactivation can be preferable to conscious activation." Sometimes it is better not to think about issues that could be problematic, as suggested in the old adage, "Let sleeping dogs lie." This is true even when the knowledge that is activated to deal with an issue is itself realistic or objective. But the activated knowledge can also be unrealistic or even illusionary. Self-guides, for example, often make unrealistic demands on individuals, and people's negative beliefs about their actual selves are often mistaken. When a person fails on a task, for example, it is rarely the case that a lack of ability attribution can be made with certainty given the wide range of alternative attributions that could be made, such as task difficulty and, especially, lack of effort or practice (see, e.g., Heider, 1958; Weiner & Kukla, 1970). The subjectivity in self-attributions and how it produces suffering is well documented (see, e.g., Abramson & Martin, 1981; Anderson & Arnoult, 1985; Dweck & Goetz, 1978). It should also be noted that it is dysfunctional to make a person conscious of a problem if there is no solution to the problem. Telling a male friend, "Women don't find you attractive because you're so short," may increase his consciousness of the problem, but it is unlikely to improve matters.

Focusing on subjective knowledge not only can activate the problem represented in that knowledge. It can also *increase* the problem. There are a variety of ways that this can occur. For example, people will consciously suppress painful thoughts. Although suppression can be momentarily successful in avoiding unwanted thoughts, it can produce a rebound of preoccupation with the problem. In severe cases, people can become obsessed with the thoughts. Indeed, there is evidence that conscious suppression of thoughts can hamper coping, lead to relapse, and produce distress (for a review, see Wegner & Schneider, 1989). In addition, active avoidance of thinking about certain traumatic events is associated with people avoiding thinking about *any* significant topic in any depth, which produces new problems (see Pennebaker, 1989).

Rumination, or "conscious thinking directed toward a given object for an extended period of time" (Martin & Tesser, 1989, p. 306), can result from conscious suppression of unwanted thoughts. But it can occur for other reasons, too, as when a daughter can't stop thinking about her father after he dies. Rather than solving the problem, this prolonged conscious attention to the problem often makes matters worse. Indeed, certain features of disorders, such as the "spiraling down" phenomenon in depression, are not only maintained by ruminations but are even instigated by them (for reviews, see Martin & Tesser, 1989; Tait & Silver, 1989). It should also be noted that the classic psychodynamic literature describes defense mechanisms involving conscious processing (for preconscious goals) that increase problems, such as intellectualization and rationalization. These particular defenses, moreover, are recognized as major obstacles to therapeutic progress (see Cameron, 1963).

Conscious attention to attitudes can also be dysfunctional. James (1890/1948), Bartlett (1932), and others early on recognized that stored knowledge is not simply retrieved in its original trace form but is reconstructed. And paying attention to a sensation makes it stronger. Thus, thinking about some topic changes the available information on the topic. It tends to make the information more evaluatively consistent, for example. This phenomenon formed the underpinning for Tesser's now-classic work on self-generated attitude change (see Tesser, 1978). Tesser found that when people thought about some person, object, or idea their feelings about it often intensified or polarized. For instance, when subjects evaluated a target person, the more they thought about the target the more negatively they evaluated a dislikable target and the more positively they evaluated a likable target. Moreover, such polarization effects were found even when the target was present while they thought about it; that is, reality constraints did not remove the effect (although they may have reduced it).

Attitude polarization in itself is not necessarily bad. But our point here is that it is not necessarily good, either. What is clear is that changes occur in the available information. Such changes could make the knowledge less veridical. In addition, the evaluation or feelings become intensified and polarized. As Tesser (1978) pointed out, this can produce problems in certain cases, such as in a catharsis therapy in which clients are encouraged to focus on emotional issues. He reported the results of a study in which an emotional focus treatment *increased* subjects' anxiety.

A fascinating case of consciousness being dysfunctional was discovered by Wilson (for a review, see Wilson, 1990, and this volume). In his studies, subjects were simply asked to explain why they felt the way they did about something they knew little about. This self-reflection can cause people to generate a biased sample of reasons for their feelings. When these reasons imply an attitude that is different from their original attitude, people will change their attitude to be consistent with the reasons, and then, shortly after, will behave in a manner consistent with the new attitude. But the reasons are not necessarily representative of their true feelings. Thus, consciously focusing on their reasons can cause people to behave in a way that is dysfunctional for them. Wilson found, for example, that self-reflection influenced subjects' decisions about which type of poster to take home, and that later they regretted the decision. More recently, Wilson and Schooler (1991) found that self-reflection led undergraduates to make choices among different brands of strawberry jam and even among different college courses that corresponded less with expert opinion than the choices of undergraduates who did not engage in self-reflection.

As we discussed earlier, one of the reasons that consciousness has been considered good is precisely because it leads to self-reflection. Wilson's research suggests that too much self-reflection can be a mistake. He also points out that even the kind of self-reflection involved in Fishbein and Ajzen's (1975) theory of reasoned action can be a problem because requiring people to think about the different components can produce new thoughts that are unrelated to the original behavioral intentions (see also Budd, 1987). In summary, these studies lead to a second conclusion: "Conscious attention to knowledge (e.g., an opinion, belief, or attitude) can make the knowledge biased and dysfunctional."

Consciousness as a Source of Problematic Process

We discussed earlier how increasing knowledge accessibility through priming can produce a judgmental-assimilation bias. We also noted that this effect occurred when the priming events were likely to be unconscious at the time that the judgment was made. Otherwise, the judgmental-assimilation bias disappeared. These results are apparently consistent with the notion that consciousness is the solution to the problem, in this case the judgmental-assimilation bias. Before accepting this conclusion, however, we need to consider some additional findings in these studies. To begin with, let us consider the Higgins et al. (1985) and Lombardi et al. (1987) studies in more detail.

In order to test the possibility that the priming effects on judgment were simply due to episodic memory, Higgins et al. (1985) separated subjects who could remember the priming events from those who could not. If memory was the source of the judgmental-assimilation bias, then the bias should be stronger for subjects who could remember the priming events and should be weaker for subjects who could not remember. As reported earlier, however, the opposite was true. The judgmental-assimilation bias was stronger for subjects who could *not* remember the primes. Unfortunately, there were not enough subjects who could remember the primes to determine exactly what was happening in this condition. Thus, a study was conducted by Lombardi et al. (1987, Experiment 1) to compare the priming effects of subjects who could remember the primes and subjects who could not.

The study was an exact replication of Higgins et al. (1985) except that an intermediate delay period of 60 seconds between the last prime and the target information was included. To assess memory for the priming events, subjects were asked to write down all of the sentences they could remember forming in the scrambled sentences task (the priming task). They were given as much time as they needed and were encouraged to write down anything they remembered even if they were unsure of its source. A lenient criterion was used to score recall. It was sufficient for a subject to recall a prime regardless of whether the original sentence in which it occurred was recalled.

Table 3.3 shows the priming effects on judgment for those subjects who recalled any of the primes (Recall subjects) and those subjects who recalled none of the primes (No-Recall subjects). The top half of Table 3.3 shows the results for the No-Recall subjects. These results clearly replicate the findings of Higgins et al. (1985). No-Recall subjects' judgments were assimilated to the most recent prime at the short delay but were assimilated to the most frequent prime at the long delay.

The bottom half of Table 3.3 shows the results for the Recall subjects. Again consistent with the findings of Higgins et al. (1985), no judgmental-assimilation bias was found in this condition. But this does not mean that consciousness eliminated biased judgments. Instead, a new bias appeared. As shown in Table 3.3, Recall subjects' judgments were contrasted to the most recent prime at the short delay but were contrasted to the most frequent prime at the long delay. That is, a *judgmental-contrast bias* was found.

One explanation for these results is that consciousness of the priming events leads people to treat the events as exemplars or instances of people possessing a trait to a greater extent than the average person and these exemplars are then used as reference points for judging the target information. Given that the target information represents the trait ambiguously or vaguely, it is judged as

TABLE 3.3

Categorization of the Target Person as a Function of Type of Priming, Post-Priming Delay (in Seconds), and Recall of Priming Events

	Post-Priming Delay		
	Brief	*Medium*	*Long*
	15s	60s	120s
Type of Priming *Frequent/Recent*			
	No-Recall Subjects		
Persistent/Stubborn	5.3 (S)	3.5 (S/P)	2.9 (P)
Stubborn/Persistent	2.9 (P)	4.3 (S)	4.8 (S)
	Recall Subjects		
Persistent/Stubborn	2.8 (P)	3.2 (P)	4.3 (S)
Stubborn/Persistent	5.4 (S)	4.1 (S)	2.9 (P)

Note: Scores > 3.5 = Stubborn categorization (S); Scores < 3.5 = Persistent categorization (P)

a poor instance of the trait in comparison to the prime as trait exemplar (i.e., a contrast effect). The recency and frequency manipulation simply influences which prime is likely to be used as the exemplar (see Higgins, 1989c). It should also be noted that the measure of consciousness of the priming events (i.e., recall) was independent of which exemplar was relatively more accessible at the moment of judgment (see Lombardi et al., 1987). Thus, it is unlikely that the judgmental-contrast bias found in this study was due simply to demand effects.

As evident in Table 3.3, the judgmental-contrast bias found for the Recall subjects was just as strong as the judgmental-assimilation bias found for the No-Recall subjects. Thus, consciousness did not eliminate bias. Rather, consciousness changed the judgmental process such that a new bias emerged. Other studies have also found that when subjects are likely to remember category instances or exemplars provided by the priming events (i.e., when subjects are likely to be conscious of the primes at the moment of judgment), a judgmental-contrast bias appears (e.g., Herr, 1986; Herr et al., 1983; Martin, 1986; Newman & Uleman, 1990; Strack et al., 1988). There is also evidence suggesting that under certain conditions consciousness of primes can produce the judgmental-assimilation bias as well (see Lombardi et al., 1987, Experiment 2; Martin, 1986). These studies, then, suggest another conclusion: "Consciousness can produce new biases by introducing new problematic processes."

Consciousness of priming events is not the only case of consciousness introducing problematic processes. Indeed, we discussed earlier Tesser's (1978) account of attitude polarization which suggested that thinking about an object can introduce biased processing that produces evaluatively consistent cognitions. More generally, consciousness is controlled processing and controlled processing has characteristics that can introduce problems and limitations. It is well known, for example, that smooth, well-practiced routines, such as driving a car or playing the piano, can be disrupted by conscious attention. The attention responses involved in controlled processing can themselves introduce problems. First, they can restrict the amount of information or number of alternatives considered. Second, they can increase the influence of momentary, and often irrelevant, contextual factors, such as temporal or spatial order effects (see, for example, Nisbett & Wilson, 1977). Third, they can inhibit the use of stored knowledge acquired through long experience. Such effects of attention responses introduced by controlled processing can impair performance in various ways, such as decreasing the amount of relevant information used in problem-solving.

Such cases suggest the following conclusion: "The controlled nature of conscious processing can introduce limitations."

Consciousness without Understanding

As discussed earlier, the change-of-standard effect exemplifies how context effects can unconsciously produce errors in reconstructive memory. In a recent study, Higgins and Liberman (1991) investigated whether increasing people's awareness of the context of judgment would eliminate the change-of-standard effect. The question they addressed was, Why do people fail to take into account sufficiently the standard in relation to which their initial judgment was made when they later use that judgment? Two basic types of answers were considered—one having to do with consciousness or awareness and one having to do with understanding. By *awareness* is meant "noticing with a degree of controlled thought or observation" (*Webster's Ninth New Collegiate Dictionary*, 1989, p. 279). By *understanding* is meant "to be thoroughly familiar with the character and propensities of [something]; to achieve a grasp of the nature, significance, or explanation of something" (*Webster's Ninth New Collegiate Dictionary*, 1989, p. 1287).

With regard to awareness, it is possible that people are unaware that their initial judgment of the target person is made not only in relation to the target person's behaviors but also in relation to the standard defined by the immediate context of non-target persons' behaviors (Awareness 1). It is also possible that people are aware when they make their initial judgment that it is made in relation to the context standard but that when they later use the judgment they are no longer aware of the context in which the judgment was made (Awareness 2). In either case, a lack of awareness of the context standard in relation to which their initial judgment was made could lead people to use this judgment without taking this standard into account sufficiently, thus producing reconstructive memory errors.

An alternative answer to why a change-of-standard produces judgment-related reconstructive memory errors is that people do not understand that when they use a prior judgment of a target in subsequent target-related responses they must take into account the fact that this judgment was initially made in relation to a particular standard. They may be perfectly aware that they made their initial judgment in relation to the context standard, both when they made their judgment and when they later used that judgment, but they do not understand the implications of this fact for *how* they should reconstruct the referential meaning of the judgment.

In order to take the judgmental context standard into account sufficiently, a person must understand two rules. First, it is appropriate (indeed, normative) to make judgments of a target stimulus in relation to the immediate context of alternative stimuli. Second, the fact that one did make a judgment in relation to a context standard must be taken into account when later using that judgment. Although most people understand the first rule (see, e.g., Glucksberg et al., 1975; Higgins, 1981; Rosenberg & Cohen, 1966), many may not understand the second rule. If this is the case, a change-of-standard would produce judgment-related reconstructive memory errors.

To test these two alternative accounts of how and when a change-of-standard produces judgment-related reconstructive memory errors, Higgins and Liberman (1991) replicated the basic design of previous change-of-standard studies but added independent manipulations of Awareness 1 and Awareness 2. Awareness 1 was manipulated by instructing half of the subjects, "Please be sure to use the other judges' sentences for comparison to help decide how harsh or lenient Judge Jones is." (Judge Jones was the target judge.) In this *salient judgmental context* condition, subjects consciously attended to the fact that their judgment of Judge Jones' behaviors was made in relation to a standard defined by the immediate context of non-target persons' behaviors. The remaining half of the subjects were in the standard condition of previous change-of-standard studies in which subjects' attention is not drawn to the immediate context of non-target judges as an explicit standard. Subjects in both conditions, however, were expected to use the context standard when judging Judge Jones.

Awareness 2 was manipulated when subjects returned for the second session. Half of the subjects in each condition were asked to recall the sentencing decisions of the non-target judges that they had read about in the previous session. This *reinstatement of judgmental context* condition was designed to make subjects, prior to recalling Judge Jones' behaviors, consciously attend to the non-target behaviors that formed the immediate context standard of their original judgment of Judge Jones. The remaining half of the subjects were in the standard condition in which there was no reinstatement of the judgmental context standard.

This study, then, examined whether it was a lack of one particular kind of awareness, or both kinds together, that underlay the change-of-standard effect. If a lack of understanding contributed to the change-of-standard effect, however, then even the combination of a salient judgmental context and reinstatement of the judgmental context would be insufficient to eliminate the change-of-standard effect.

As expected, subjects made their judgments of Judge Jones' sentencing decisions in relation to the immediate context standard. In all conditions, Judge Jones was categorized as harsh in the lenient first session context and as lenient in the harsh first session context. Most important, and contrary to both the Awareness 1 *and* Awareness 2 notions, there was still a change-of-standard effect on recall in the Salient/Reinstatement condition. In this condition the subjects' contextually tailored judgments of Judge Jones significantly influenced their recall of his sentencing decisions. If increasing awareness was the answer to eliminating the change-of-standard effect, then one would expect that the combination of salience and reinstatement would be effective in eliminating the effect. This combination did not eliminate the effect, however.

Although it is rare in the literature for studies to examine directly whether or not increasing people's awareness increases their understanding, there are findings suggesting that it often does not. Nisbett and Wilson (1977), for example, described studies in which people consciously considered the possible causes for their actions but did not provide accurate answers. Increasing awareness did not produce understanding. Indeed, when people are given the correct answer to a problem they often reject it because of a lack of understanding of the principles underlying the correct answer (see Nisbett & Ross, 1980). Moreover, focusing on the wrong answer could inhibit unconscious processes that would otherwise provide alternatives, including the correct alternative. The disadvantages of focusing on the incorrect dominant response rather than allowing one's mind to roam freely has been well documented in the literature on creativity, such as the work on *functional fixedness* (see, e.g., Duncker, 1945).

In a classic study, Bruner and Postman (1949) presented subjects tachistoscopically with playing cards, and asked subjects to identify what they saw. The cards were first presented for only a very brief duration that increased until the cards were successfully identified. On some trials, an incongruous playing card, such as a red six of spades, was presented. On those trials subjects tended to persist with incorrect hypotheses about what they were seeing, taking much longer than for congruous cards to identify them correctly. What was notable was the persistence of the incorrect conscious expectation in the face of clearly visible disconfirming information.

Research by Ross, and his colleagues (Ross, Lepper, & Hubbard, 1975) on the *perseverence effect* demonstrated how even conscious awareness of the faulty basis of a belief does not result in a change of the belief. Subjects who were given false feedback concerning their ability to correctly detect true suicide notes from fakes persisted in believing that feedback (i.e., that they did or did not possess the sensitivity needed to detect true notes) following debriefing in which the bogus nature of the feedback was disclosed. Moreover, Lord, Ross, and Lepper (1979), Crocker, Hannah, and Weber (1983) and others (see review by Higgins & Bargh, 1987) repeatedly found that when one becomes aware of information disconfirming one's belief, one does not change the belief. Instead, one mentally reworks the disconfirming evidence (e.g., by discrediting its validity, or through a situational attribution) in order to preserve the prior belief. Clearly, awareness of new, relevant information alone is insufficient to increase one's understanding.

The results of these studies suggest the following conclusion: "Conscious awareness without understanding can fail to solve the problem. Indeed, it can even increase the problem."

CONCLUDING COMMENTS

The Webster's Dictionary (*Webster's Ninth New Collegiate*, 1989) defines *conscious* as "perceiving, apprehending, or noticing with a degree of controlled thought or observation" (p. 279) and defines *consciousness* as "the upper level of mental life of which the person is aware as contrasted with unconscious processes" (p. 279). Consciousness is also defined as "acting with critical awareness," as marked by "will," "design," and "volition" (p. 279). What is noteworthy about these definitions is that they reflect not only the idea that consciousness involves controlled thought but also the notion that such thought reflects a higher level of mental processing than unconsciousness. This chapter has presented evidence consistent with this common notion that, compared to unconscious processing, conscious processing, by involving controlled thought, can solve problems. But this chapter has also presented evidence consistent with an opposite conclusion—conscious processing, compared to unconscious processing, can create problems!

There are three major reasons why conscious processing is not always an advantage and can even be a disadvantage relative to unconscious processing. The first reason has to do with the controlled nature of conscious processing. Being "in control" clearly has its benefits. But it necessarily uses up resources and restrains processing. Under some conditions the resource expenditure may be worthwhile and the restraint necessary. But it is not always so. The second reason has to do with the directed attention aspect of conscious processing. Conscious processing has the advantage of orienting to the here and now, not being a prisoner of the past. But the here and now can be less informative than prior experience and can even be misleading. The third reason is that consciousness implies awareness but not understanding. If understanding is lacking, conscious processing per se is not going to solve the problem. Indeed, it can make matters worse.

When considering the advantages and disadvantages of consciousness, it might be useful to distinguish *consciousness of the problem* and *conscious problem solving*. When people are functioning maladaptively, it may be necessary for them to become conscious that there is a problem before the problem can be addressed. In this sense, consciousness may be critical to problem solving. This does not imply, however, that conscious processing is the best way to solve the identified problem. Creative solutions that maximally benefit from the wealth of a person's past experiences may require unconscious processing. Once one has identified the problem, perhaps the best next step is to "sleep on it." To attempt control at this stage may restrain rather than facilitate discovering a solution.

It may also be useful to distinguish the *generation of solutions* and the *assessment of solutions*. Unconscious processing may be most effective and efficient when attempting to generate the broadest range of possible solutions. Conscious processing, on the other hand, may be best when assessing the comparative utility of alternative solutions. The point is that the relative advantages and disadvantages of conscious versus unconscious may vary for different stages and aspects of problem-solving. One direction for future research would be to examine the consequences of varying conscious attention to different stages and aspects of problem-solving. Just as priming effects on judgment can vary dramatically as a function of consciousness, so too could different facets of problem solving. Could solutions to the problems of dissonance, imbalance, inequity, and so on vary depending on whether and when consciousness was involved? And would consciousness produce better or worse solutions?

One final comment: Neither conscious nor unconscious processing is inherently good or bad. Here is a case where content and not just process must be carefully considered. If conscious processing directs attention to relevant information, then it is good. But if it inhibits the use of relevant stored knowledge, then it is bad. Both relevant or appropriate information and irrelevant or inappropriate information can be activated by either conscious or unconscious processing. Similarly, problem solving with or without understanding can be performed either consciously or unconsciously. Thus, whether and when conscious processing is advantageous compared to unconscious processing depends on the contents likely to be activated by conscious versus unconscious processing. As there is no necessary relation between the contents and the processes of consciousness and unconsciousness, it is not reasonable to promote consciousness as a solution to problems. In therapy, for example, it would be more reasonable to promote either conscious or unconscious processing depending on which type of processing (at different stages) increased the likelihood of activating adaptive knowledge. To do so effectively, it is useful to appreciate the trade-offs of conscious and unconscious processing that we have described.

ACKNOWLEDGMENTS

Support for the preparation of this chapter and for the studies herein described was provided by Grant MH39429 from the National Institute of Mental Health to the first author, and by Grant MH43265 from the National Institute of Mental Health to the second author. We thank Walter Mischel and the editors for helpful comments on an earlier draft.

REFERENCES

Abramson, L. Y., & Martin, D. J. (1981). Depression and the causal inference process. In J. H. Harvey, W. Ickes, & R. F. Kidd (Eds.), *New directions in attribution research* (Vol. 3, pp. 117–168). Hillsdale, NJ: Lawrence Erlbaum Associates.

Allport, G. W., & Kramer, B. M. (1946). Some roots of prejudice. *Journal of Psychology, 22*, 9–39.

Anderson, C. A., & Arnoult, L. H. (1985). Attributional style and everyday problems in living: Depression, loneliness, and shyness. *Social Cognition, 3*, 16–35.

Anderson, N. H., & Hubert, S. (1963). Effects of concomitant verbal recall on order effects in personality impression formation. *Journal of Verbal Learning and Verbal Behavior, 2*, 379–391.

Bargh, J. A. (1984). Automatic and conscious processing of social information. In R. S. Wyer, Jr., and T. K. Srull (Eds.), *Handbook of social cognition* (Vol. 3, pp. 1–43). Hillsdale, NJ: Lawrence Erlbaum Associates.

Bargh, J. A. (1988). Automatic information processing: Implications for communication and affect. In L. Donohew, H. Sypher, & E. T. Higgins (Eds.), *Communication, affect, and social cognition* (pp. 9–32). Hillsdale, NJ: Lawrence Erlbaum Associates.

Bargh, J. A. (1989). Conditional automaticity: Varieties of automatic influence in social perception and cognition. In J. S. Uleman & J. A. Bargh (Eds.), *Unintended thought* (pp. 3–51). New York: Guilford Press.

Bargh, J. A. (1990). Auto-motives: Preconscious determinants of thought and behavior. In E. T. Higgins, & R. M. Sorrentino (Eds.), *Handbook of motivation and cognition* (Vol. 2, pp. 93–130). New York: Guilford Press.

Bargh, J. A., Bond, R. N., Lombardi, W. J., & Tota, M. E. (1986). The additive nature of chronic and temporary sources of construct accessibility. *Journal of Personality and Social Psychology, 50,* 869–878.

Bargh, J. A., Chaiken, S., Govender, R., & Pratto, F. (in press). The generality of the automatic attitude activation effect. *Journal of Personality and Social Psychology.*

Bargh, J. A., Chaiken, S., Raymond, P., & Hymes, C. (1991). *Automatic evaluation effects with a pronunciation task: Eliminating potential strategic influences.* Unpublished manuscript, New York University, New York.

Bargh, J. A., Litt, J., Pratto, F., & Spielman, L. A. (1989). On the preconscious evaluation of social stimuli. In A. F. Bennett & K. M. McConkey (Eds.), *Cognition in individual and social contexts* (pp. 357–370). Amsterdam: Elsevier/North-Holland.

Bargh, J. A., Lombardi, W. J., & Higgins, E. T. (1988). Automaticity of chronically accessible constructs in Person X Situation effects on person perception: It's just a matter of time. *Journal of Personality and Social Psychology, 55,* 599–605.

Bargh, J. A., & Pratto, F. (1986). Individual construct accessibility and perceptual selection. *Journal of Experimental Social Psychology, 22,* 293–311.

Bargh, J. A., & Thein, R. D. (1985). Individual construct accessibility, person memory, and the recall-judgment link: The case of information overload. *Journal of Personality and Social Psychology, 49,* 1129–1146.

Bartlett, F. C. (1932). *Remembering.* Cambridge, England: Cambridge University Press.

Bateson, G. (1972). *Steps to an ecology of mind.* New York: Ballantine.

Beck, A. T., Rush, A. J., Shaw, B. F., & Emery, G. (1979). *Cognitive therapy of depression.* New York: Guilford Press.

Brewer, M. B. (1988). A dual process model of impression formation. In T. K. Srull & R. S. Wyer, Jr. (Eds.), *Advances in social cognition* (Vol. 1, pp. 1–36). Hillsdale, NJ: Lawrence Erlbaum Associates.

Brown, R., & McNeil, D. (1966). The "tip of the tongue" phenomenon. *Journal of Verbal Learning and Verbal Behavior, 5,* 325–337.

Bruner, J. S. (1957). Going beyond the information given. In H. E. Gruber, K. R. Hammond, & R. Jessor (Eds.), *Contemporary approaches to cognition* (pp. 41–69). Cambridge, MA: Harvard University Press.

Bruner, J. S., & Postman, L. (1949). On the perception of incongruity: A paradigm. *Journal of Personality, 18,* 206–223.

Budd, R. J. (1987). Response bias and the theory of reasoned action. *Social Cognition, 5,* 95–107.

Cameron, N. (1963). *Personality development and psychopathology.* Boston: Houghton Mifflin.

Campbell, D. T., Hunt, W. A., & Lewis, N. A. (1958). The relative susceptibility of two rating scales to disturbance resulting from shifts in stimulus context. *Journal of Applied Psychology, 42,* 213–217.

Carlston, D. E. (1980). Events, inferences, and impression formation. In R. Hastie, T. M. Ostrom, E. B. Ebbesen, R. S. Wyer, Jr., D. L. Hamilton, & D. E. Carlston (Eds.), *Person memory: The cognitive basis of social perception* (pp. 89–119). Hillsdale, NJ: Lawrence Erlbaum Associates.

Chaiken, S. (1987). The heuristic model of persuasion. In M. P. Zanna, J. M. Olson, & C. P. Herman (Eds.), *Social influence: The Ontario symposium* (Vol. 5, pp. 3–39). Hillsdale, NJ: Lawrence Erlbaum Associates.

Crocker, J., Hannah, D. B., & Weber, R. (1983). Person memory and causal attributions. *Journal of Personality and Social Psychology, 44,* 55–66.

Deutsch, J. A., & Deutsch, D. (1963). Attention: Some theoretical considerations. *Psychological Review, 70,* 80–90.

Devine, P. G. (1989). Stereotypes and prejudice: Their automatic and controlled components. *Journal of Personality and Social Psychology, 56,* 5–18.

Devine, P. G., Sedikides, C., & Fuhrman, R. W. (1989). Goals in social information processing: The case of anticipated interaction. *Journal of Personality and Social Psychology, 56,* 680–690.

Duncker, K. (1945). On problem solving. *Psychological Monographs, 58,* (5, Whole No. 270).

Dweck, C. S., & Goetz, T. E. (1978). Attributions and learned helplessness. In J. H. Harvey, W. Ickes, & R. F. Kidd (Eds.), *New directions in attribution research* (Vol. 2, pp. 157–179). Hillsdale, NJ: Lawrence Erlbaum Associates.

Ellis, A. (1962). *Reason and emotion in psychotherapy.* New York: Lyle Stuart.

Erdley, C. A., & D'Agostino, P. R. (1988). Cognitive and affective components of automatic priming affects. *Journal of Personality and Social Psychology, 54,* 741–747.

Ericsson, K. A., & Simon, H. A. (1980). Verbal reports as data. *Psychological Review, 87,* 215–251.

Fazio, R. H., Powell, M. C., & Herr, P. M. (1983). Toward a process model of the attitude-behavior relation: Accessing one's attitude upon mere observation of the attitude object. *Journal of Personality and Social Psychology, 44,* 723–735.

Fazio, R. H., Sanbonmatsu, D. M., Powell, M. C., & Kardes, F. R. (1986). On the automatic activation of attitudes. *Journal of Personality and Social Psychology, 50,* 229–238.

Fishbein, M., & Ajzen, I. (1975). *Belief, attitude, intention, and behavior: An introduction to theory and research.* Reading, MA: Addison-Wesley.

Fiske, S. T. (1980). Attention and weight in person perception: The impact of negative and extreme behavior. *Journal of Personality and Social Psychology, 38,* 889–906.

Fiske, S. T. (1989). Examining the role of intent: Toward understanding its role in stereotyping and prejudice. In J. S. Uleman & J. A. Bargh (Eds.), *Unintended thought* (pp. 253–283). New York: Guilford Press.

Fiske, S. T., & Neuberg, S. L. (1990). A continuum of impression formation, from category-based to individuating processes: Influences of information and motivation on attention and interpretation. *Advances in Experimental Social Psychology, 23,* 1–74.

Freud, S. (1952). *A general introduction to psychoanalysis.* New York: Washington Square Press. (Original work published 1920)

Freud, S. (1961). The ego and the id. In J. Strachey (Ed. and Trans.), *Standard edition of the complete psychological works of Sigmund Freud* (Vol. 19, pp. 3–66). London: Hogarth Press. (Original work published 1923)

Friedman, A. (1979). Framing pictures: The role of knowledge in automatized encoding and memory for gist. *Journal of Experimental Psychology: General, 110,* 341–362.

Ghiselin, B. (Ed.). (1952). *The creative process.* New York: New American Library.

Gilbert, D. T. (1989). Thinking lightly about others: Automatic components of the social inference process. In J. S. Uleman & J. A. Bargh (Eds.), *Unintended thought* (pp. 189–211). New York: Guilford Press.

Glucksberg, S., Krauss, R. M., & Higgins, E. T. (1975). The development of referential communication skills. In F. Horowitz, E. Hetherington, S. Scarr-Salapatek, & G. Siegel (Eds.), *Review of child development research* (Vol. 4, pp. 305–345). Chicago: University of Chicago Press.

Gollwitzer, P. M. (1990). Action phases and mind-sets. In E. T. Higgins & R. M. Sorrentino (Eds.), *Handbook of motivation and cognition* (Vol. 2, pp. 53–92). New York: Guilford Press.

Greenwald, A. G., Klinger, M. R., & Liu, T. J. (1989). Unconscious processing of dichoptically masked words. *Memory and Cognition, 17,* 35–47.

Hansen, C. H., & Hansen, R. D. (1988). Finding the face in the crowd: An anger superiority effect. *Journal of Personality and Social Psychology, 54,* 917–924.

Heidbreder, E. (1933). *Seven psychologies.* New York: Appleton-Century-Crofts.

Heider, F. (1958). *The psychology of interpersonal relations.* New York: Wiley.

Herr, P. M. (1986). Consequences of priming: Judgment and behavior. *Journal of Personality and Social Psychology, 51,* 1106–1115.

Herr, P. M., Sherman, S. J., & Fazio, R. H. (1983). On the consequences of priming: Assimilation and contrast effects. *Journal of Experimental Social Psychology, 19,* 323–340.

Higgins, E. T. (1981). The "communication game": Implications for social cognition and persuasion. In E. T. Higgins, C. P. Herman, & M. P. Zanna (Eds.), *Social cognition: The Ontario symposium* (Vol. 1, pp. 343–392). Hillsdale, NJ: Lawrence Erlbaum Associates.

Higgins, E. T. (1987). Self-discrepancy: A theory relating self and affect. *Psychological Review, 94,* 319–340.

Higgins, E. T. (1989a). Continuities and discontinuities in self-regulatory and self-evaluative processes: A developmental theory relating self and affect. *Journal of Personality, 57,* 407–444.

Higgins, E. T. (1989b). Knowledge accessibility and activation: Subjectivity and suffering from unconscious sources. In J. S. Uleman & J. A. Bargh (Eds.), *Unintended thought* (pp. 75–123). New York: Guilford Press.

Higgins, E. T. (1989c). Self-discrepancy theory: What patterns of self-beliefs cause people to suffer? In L. Berkowitz (Ed.), *Advances in experimental social psychology* (Vol. 22, pp. 93–136). New York: Academic Press.

Higgins, E. T., & Bargh, J. A. (1987). Social perception and social cognition. *Annual Review of Psychology, 38,* 369–425.

Higgins, E. T., Bargh, J. A., & Lombardi, W. (1985). The nature of priming effects on categorization. *Journal of Experimental Psychology: Learning, Memory, and Cognition, 11,* 59–69.

Higgins, E. T., Bond, R. N., Klein, R., & Strauman, T. (1986). Self-discrepancies and emotional vulnerability: How magnitude, accessibility, and type of discrepancy influence affect. *Journal of Personality and Social Psychology, 51,* 5–15.

Higgins, E. T., & Chaires, W. M. (1980). Accessibility of interrelational constructs: Implications for stimulus encoding and creativity. *Journal of Experimental Social Psychology, 16,* 348–361.

Higgins, E. T., & King, G. A. (1981). Accessibility of social constructs: Information processing consequences of individual and contextual variability. In N. Cantor & J. Kihlstrom (Eds.), *Personality, cognition, and social interaction* (pp. 69–121). Hillsdale, NJ: Lawrence Erlbaum Associates.

Higgins, E. T., King, G. A., & Mavin, G. H. (1982). Individual construct accessibility and subjective impressions and recall. *Journal of Personality and Social Psychology, 43,* 35–47.

Higgins, E. T., & Liberman, A. (1991). *How context-driven judgments produce reconstructive memory errors: A problem of awareness or understanding?* Unpublished manuscript, Columbia University.

Higgins, E. T., & Lurie, L. (1983). Context, categorization, and memory: The "change-of-standard" effect. *Cognitive Psychology, 15,* 525–547.

Higgins, E. T., & Rholes, W. S. (1978). "Saying is believing": Effects of message modification on memory and liking for the person described. *Journal of Experimental Social Psychology, 14,* 363–378.

Higgins, E. T., Rholes, W. S., & Jones, C. R. (1977). Category accessibility and impression formation. *Journal of Experimental Social Psychology, 13,* 141–154.

Higgins, E. T., & Stangor, C. (1988a). A "change-of-standard" perspective on the relations among context, judgment, and memory. *Journal of Personality and Social Psychology, 54,* 181–192.

Higgins, E. T., & Stangor, C. (1988b). Context-driven social judgment and memory: When "behavior engulfs the field" in reconstructive memory. In D. Bar-Tal & A. W. Kruglanski (Eds.), *The social psychology of knowledge* (pp. 262–298). New York: Cambridge University Press.

Higgins, E. T., Van Hook, E., & Dorfman, D. (1988). Do self attributes form a cognitive structure? *Social Cognition, 6,* 177–207.

James, W. (1890). *Principles of psychology* (2 vols.). New York: Holt.

James, W. (1948). *Psychology.* New York: World. (Original work published 1890)

Jones, E. E., & Davis, K. E. (1965). From acts to dispositions: The attribution process in social perception. *Advances in Experimental Social Psychology, 2,* 219–266.

Jung, C. G. (1954). *The practice of psychotherapy: Vol. 16. The collected works of C. G. Jung.* New York: Bollingen Series.

Kelly, G. A. (1955). *The psychology of personal constructs.* New York: Norton.

King, G. A., & Sorrentino, R. M. (1988). Uncertainty orientation and the relation between accessible constructs and person memory. *Social Cognition, 6,* 128–149.

Kuhl, J. (1986). Motivation and information processing: A new look at decision making, dynamic change, and action control. In R. M. Sorrentino & E. T. Higgins (Eds.), *Handbook of motivation and cognition* (Vol. 1, pp. 404–434). New York: Guilford Press.

Langer, E. J. (1989). Minding matters: The consequences of mindlessness-mindfulness. In L. Berkowitz (Ed.), *Advances in experimental social psychology* (Vol. 22, pp. 137–173). New York: Academic Press.

Lau, R. R. (1989). Construct accessibility and electoral choice. *Political Behavior, 11,* 5–32.

Lingle, J. H., & Ostrom, T. M. (1979). Retrieval selectivity in memory-based judgments. *Journal of Personality and Social Psychology, 37,* 180–194.

Logan, G. D. (1980). Attention and automaticity in Stroop and priming tasks: Theory and data. *Cognitive Psychology, 12,* 523–553.

Logan, G. D., & Cowan, W. B. (1984). On the ability to inhibit thought and action: A theory of an act of control. *Psychological Review, 91,* 295–327.

Logan, G. D., & Zbrodoff, N. J. (1979). When it helps to be misled: Facilitative effects of increasing the frequency of conflicting stimuli in a Stroop-like task. *Memory and Cognition, 7,* 166–174.

Lombardi, W. J., Higgins, E. T., & Bargh, J. A. (1987). The role of consciousness in priming effects on categorization. *Personality and Social Psychology Bulletin, 13,* 411–429.

Lord, C. G., Ross, L., & Lepper, M. R. (1979). Biased assimilation and attitude polarization: The effects of prior theories on subsequently considered evidence. *Journal of Personality and Social Psychology, 37,* 2098–2109.

Manis, M. (1967). Context effects in communication. *Journal of Personality and Social Psychology, 5,* 326–334.

Manis, M., & Armstrong, G. W. (1971). Contrast effects in verbal output. *Journal of Experimental Social Psychology, 7,* 381–388.

Manis, M., Cornell, S. D., & Moore, J. C. (1974). Transmission of attitude-relevant information through a communication chain. *Journal of Personality and Social Psychology, 30,* 81–94.

Martin, L. L. (1986). Set/reset: Use and disuse of concepts in impression formation. *Journal of Personality and Social Psychology, 51,* 493–504.

Martin, L. L., & Tesser, A. (1989). Toward a motivational and structural theory of ruminative thought. In J. S. Uleman & J. A. Bargh (Eds.), *Unintended thought* (pp. 306–362). New York: Guilford Press.

McArthur, L. Z. (1981). What grabs you? The role of attention in impression formation and causal attribution. In E. T. Higgins, C. P. Herman, & M. P. Zanna (Eds.), *Social cognition: The Ontario symposium* (Vol. 1, pp. 201–246). Hillsdale, NJ: Lawrence Erlbaum Associates.

Miller, G. A. (1956). The magical number seven, plus or minus two: Some limits on our capacity for processing information. *Psychological Review, 63,* 81–97.

Miller, G. A., Galanter, E., & Pribram, K. H. (1960). *Plans and the structure of behavior.* New York: Holt.

Milner, P. M. (1957). The cell assembly: Mark II. *Psychological Review, 64,* 242–252.

Neely, J. H. (1977). Semantic priming and retrieval from lexical memory: Roles of inhibitionless spreading activation and limited-capacity attention. *Journal of Experimental Psychology: General, 106,* 225–254.

Neisser, U. (1967). *Cognitive psychology.* New York: Appleton-Century-Crofts.

Newell, A., & Rosenbloom, P. S. (1981). Mechanisms of skill in acquisition and the law of practice. In J. R. Anderson (Ed.), *Cognitive skills and their acquisition* (pp. 1–55). Hillsdale, NJ: Lawrence Erlbaum Associates.

Newman, L. S., & Uleman, J. S. (1990). Assimilation and contrast effects in spontaneous trait inference. *Personality and Social Psychology Bulletin, 16,* 224–240.

Nisbett, R. E., & Ross, L. D. (1980). *Human inference: Strategies and shortcomings of informal judgment.* Century Series in Psychology. Englewood Cliffs, NJ: Prentice-Hall.

Nisbett, R. E., & Wilson, T. D. (1977). Telling more than we can know: Verbal reports on mental processes. *Psychological Review, 84,* 231–259.

Norman, D. A. (1968). Toward a theory of memory and attention. *Psychological Review, 75,* 522–536.

Norman, D. A., & Bobrow, D. G. (1976). On the role of active memory processes in perception and cognition. In C. N. Cofer (Ed.), *The structure of human memory* (pp. 114–132). San Francisco: Freeman.

Ostrom, T. M., & Upshaw, H. S. (1968). Psychological perspective and attitude change. In A. G. Greenwald, T. C. Brock, & T. M. Ostrom (Eds.), *Psychological foundations of attitudes* (pp. 217–242). New York: Academic Press.

Pennebaker, J. W. (1989). Stream of consciousness and stress: Levels of thinking. In J. S. Uleman & J. A. Bargh (Eds.), *Unintended thought* (pp. 327–350). New York: Guilford Press.

Posner, M. I. (1978). *Chronometric explorations of the mind.* Hillsdale, NJ: Lawrence Erlbaum Associates.

Posner, M. I., & Snyder, C. R. R. (1975). Attention and cognitive control. In R. L. Solso (Ed.), *Information processing and cognition: The Loyola symposium* (pp. 55–85). Hillsdale, NJ: Lawrence Erlbaum Associates.

Pratto, F., & Bargh, J. A. (1991). Stereotyping based on apparently individuating information: Trait and global components of sex stereotypes under attention overload. *Journal of Experimental Social Psychology, 27,* 26–47.

Rholes, W. S., & Pryor, J. B. (1982). Cognitive accessibility and causal attributions. *Personality and Social Psychology Bulletin, 8,* 719–727.

Rosenberg, S., & Cohen, B. D. (1966). Referential processes of speakers and listeners. *Psychological Review, 73,* 208–231.

Ross, L. (1977). The intuitive psychologist and his shortcomings: Distortions in the attribution process. *Advances in Experimental Psychology, 10,* 170–224.

Ross, L., Lepper, M. R., & Hubbard, M. (1975). Perseverance in self-perception and social perception: Biased attribution processes in the debriefing paradigm. *Journal of Personality and Social Psychology, 32,* 880–892.

Rothbart, M. (1981). Memory processes and social beliefs. In D. L. Hamilton (Ed.), *Cognitive processes in stereotyping and intergroup behavior* (pp. 145–181). Hillsdale, NJ: Lawrence Erlbaum Associates.

Sapir, E. (1928). The unconscious patterning of behavior in society. In *The unconscious: A symposium* (pp. 114–142). New York: Alfred A. Knopf.

Schneider, W., & Shiffrin, R. M. (1977). Controlled and automatic human information processing: I. Detection, search, and attention. *Psychological Review, 84,* 1–66.

Shallice, T. (1972). Dual functions of consciousness. *Psychological Review, 79,* 383–393.

Sherman, S. J., Ahlm, K., Berman, L., & Lynn, S. (1978). Contrast effects and their relationship to subsequent behavior. *Journal of Experimental Social Psychology, 14,* 340–350.

Shiffrin, R. M., & Schneider, W. (1977). Controlled and automatic human information processing: II. Perceptual learning, automatic attending, and a general theory. *Psychological Review, 84,* 127–190.

Sinclair, R. C., Mark, M. M., & Shotland, R. L. (1987). Construct accessibility and generalizability across response categories. *Personality and Social Psychology Bulletin, 13,* 239–252.

Smith, E. R., & Lerner, M. (1986). Development of automatism of social judgments. *Journal of Personality and Social Psychology, 50,* 246–259.

Srull, T. K., & Wyer, R. S. (1979). The role of category accessibility in the interpretation of information about persons: Some determinants and implications. *Journal of Personality and Social Psychology, 37,* 1660–1672.

Srull, T. K., & Wyer, R. S., Jr. (1980). Category accessibility and social perception: Some implications for the study of person memory and interpersonal judgments. *Journal of Personality and Social Psychology, 38,* 841–856.

Strack, F., Schwarz, N., Bless, H., Kubler, A., & Wanke, M. (1988). *Remember the priming events! Episodic cues may determine assimilation vs. contrast effects.* Unpublished manuscript, University of Mannheim, West Germany.

Strauman, T. J. (1989). Self-discrepancies in clinical depression and social phobia: Cognitive structures that underlie emotional disorders? *Journal of Abnormal Psychology, 98,* 14–22.

Strauman, T. J., & Higgins, E. T. (1987). Automatic activation of self-discrepancies and emotional syndromes: When cognitive structures influence affect. *Journal of Personality and Social Psychology, 53,* 1004–1014.

Stroop, J. R. (1935). Studies of interference in serial verbal reactions. *Journal of Experimental Psychology, 18,* 643–662.

Tait, R., & Silver, R. C. (1989). Coming to terms with major negative life events. In J. S. Uleman & J. A. Bargh (Eds.), *Unintended thought* (pp. 351–382). New York: Guilford Press.

Tesser, A. (1978). Self-generated attitude change. In L. Berkowitz (Ed.), *Advances in experimental social psychology* (Vol. 11, pp. 289–338). New York: Academic Press.

Tetlock, P. E. (1985). Accountability: A social check on the fundamental attribution error. *Social Psychology Quarterly, 48,* 227–236.

Webster's Ninth New Collegiate Dictionary. (1989). Springfield, MA: Merriam.

Wegner, D. M., & Schneider, D. J. (1989). Mental control: The war of the ghosts in the machine. In J. S. Uleman & J. A. Bargh (Eds.), *Unintended thought* (pp. 287–305). New York: Guilford Press.

Weiner, B., & Kukla, A. (1970). An attributional analysis of achievement motivation. *Journal of Personality and Social Psychology, 15,* 1–20.

Werner, H. (1956). Microgenesis and aphasia. *Journal of Abnormal and Social Psychology, 52,* 347–353.

Wilson, T. D. (1990). Self-persuasion via self-reflection. In J. M. Olson and M. P. Zanna (Eds.), *Self-inference processes: The Ontario symposium* (Vol. 6, pp. 43–67). Hillsdale, NJ: Lawrence Erlbaum Associates.

Wilson, T. D., & Schooler, J. W. (1991). Thinking too much: Introspection can reduce the quality of preferences and decisions. *Journal of Personality and Social Psychology, 60,* 181–192.

Wyer, R. S., & Srull, T. K. (1981). Category accessibility: Some theoretical and empirical issues concerning the processing of social stimulus information. In E. T. Higgins, C. P. Herman, & M. P. Zanna (Eds.), *Social cognition: The Ontario symposium* (Vol. 1, pp. 161–197). Hillsdale, NJ: Lawrence Erlbaum Associates.

Wyer, R. S., & Srull, T. K. (1986). Human cognition in its social context. *Psychological Review, 93,* 322–359.

Wyer, R. S, Srull, T. K., & Gordon, S. E. (1984). The effects of predicting a person's behavior on subsequent trait judgments. *Journal of Personality and Social Psychology, 43,* 674–688.

II

Research Supporting
New Assumptions

4

The Role of Exemplars
in Social Judgment

Eliot R. Smith
Purdue University

The used-car salesman promises you that this car is a real creampuff—the former owner serviced it every 3,000 miles and nothing can possibly go wrong with it. Do you believe him and buy the car? Any theory of social judgment, applied to situations like this, must contain answers to two basic questions. First; What information does the perceiver use? Are your readings of the salesman's non-verbal cues, the words he speaks, or your belief that used-car salesmen are typically dishonest brought to bear in making this decision? Second; How is the information processed? Are the available items of information simply weighted and combined, or used in some more complex, configural way to categorize or characterize the judgment target? In this chapter, I briefly review the major current theories of social judgment within this framework. I then describe a new theory that gives very different answers to these two basic questions. In the rest of the chapter I cite some preliminary evidence that, I hope, gives my advocacy of the theory more credibility than the used-car salesman's claims.

EXISTING THEORIES OF SOCIAL JUDGMENT

Two basic classes of model have been developed to describe social judgment. Attribute-based linear models of judgment, exemplified by Information Integration Theory (Anderson, 1981), assumed that perceivers identify attributes of the stimulus person that have implications for the dimension of judgment, then weight and combine those implications algebraically into an overall judgment.

Thus, the perceiver is assumed to draw on knowledge concerning many person attributes (smiles, has shifty gaze, is a used-car salesman) and their positive or negative implications for many possible judgmental dimensions (honesty, likability). In processing this information, the implications of the available attributes are weighted and averaged to yield an overall judgment.

Schematic models assume that perceivers categorize persons or other stimulus objects, then use knowledge about the category's typical characteristics to flesh out available information about the particular stimulus. The knowledge on which perceivers draw is assumed to be abstract, generic knowledge structures or schemas (see Higgins & Bargh, 1987). In the domain of person perception, the most obvious form of such schematic knowledge is *stereotypes:* knowledge about the traits or other attributes (dishonest, ingratiating) that the perceiver believes are typically associated with a social category or group (used-car salesmen). The assumed judgmental process is somewhat more complex than that postulated by information integration theory. First, the target is categorized, based on observable attributes that are cues to category membership. Once a category is chosen, judgments about the target are based on schematic knowledge rather than on the direct implications of the stimulus information itself.

Some theorists (Brewer, 1988; Fazio, 1986; Fiske & Neuberg, 1988; Lambert & Wyer, 1990) developed *dual-process models* in which both schematic and attribute-based judgment processes come into play under different circumstances. For example, a stimulus person who is seen as highly typical of a category may be judged on the basis of the perceiver's knowledge about the category, while category-atypical targets may be judged with a more individuated, attribute-by-attribute process (Fiske & Neuberg, 1988). Or (at least for categories that are seen as low in variability) the extent of the target's fit to its category may itself be taken as an evaluatively important attribute (Lambert & Wyer, 1990). Someone who is seen as an atypical member of a negative category (like used-car salesmen) might be liked for that reason. These dual-process models, too, assume that general, abstract cognitive representations (schematic knowledge and knowledge about attribute–judgment relationships) underlie social judgments.

Algebraic and schematic models of social judgment have been popular and have some important strengths. However, they cannot account for several phenomena that have been the focus of intensive recent investigation. Most fundamentally, human memory is strikingly specific. For example, low-level details like the typeface in which a word was read or its location on the page are preserved in memory over long delays, though a purely schematic account of memory would predict that only the semantic content of an item should be represented (Alba & Hasher, 1983). If we move toward recognizing the existence and widespread effects of very specific cognitive representations—as researchers studying memory and cognitive processes are increasingly doing (e.g., Brooks, 1987; Logan, 1988)—then the potential role of specific representations in judgment should also be explored. For example, might specific representations of individual persons (as well as general stereotypes about social groups) affect judgments about other individuals?

EXEMPLAR-BASED SOCIAL JUDGMENT

I have recently been exploring the relevance of exemplars and cognitive procedures for several issues within social cognition including stereotyping, category accessibility effects, illusory correlation, and person perception (Smith, 1990, 1991; Smith & Branscombe, 1988; Smith & Zarate, 1990). Many of these specific effects can be encompassed in an integrative model of exemplar-based social judgment (Smith & Zarate, 1992). The postulates of this new model—and its basic differences from existing models—can be illustrated by considering the way it answers the two questions of what information people use in judgments and how they process it.

What Information Is Used?

In making social judgments, perceivers access exemplar representations stored in memory. A definition is obviously required here. For present purposes (dealing in this chapter mostly with judgments about individuals and groups as targets), an *exemplar* is a cognitive representation of a person. Several implications of this definition need expansion:

1. An exemplar (by this definition) differs from a prototype or schema, which is generally taken to involve abstract knowledge about the typical or expected properties of a social group. Exemplars (cognitive representations of individuals) can range from very detailed, complete representations of specific people (my mother or my colleague) to minimal representations involving only two or three attributes. Reading a newspaper story that identifies a White male, aged 20, as a suspect in a burglary might lead to the formation of such a minimal representation (White, male, 20, criminal). Stock figures drawn from our fiction and general culture (Don Corleone, Walter Cronkite, Robin Hood) are also exemplars, represented in more or less detail. In fact, an individual who is subjectively typical of a social category ("Joe Sixpack" or a "typical fraternity member") can also be constructed and represented cognitively. Such a representation might (confusingly) be called a "prototype" of the category, but by definition it is also an exemplar. In the model presented here, it would be accessed and used just like any other individual exemplar, rather than having any special status because it is subjectively representative of a whole group. Thus, a person need not be encountered face-to-face to be represented in memory, but may

be imagined or experienced via the media or a secondhand account (see Linville, Fisher, & Salovey, 1989).

2. Exemplars that influence perception and categorization may not be accessible to conscious recollection. That is, exemplars that affect the identification, categorization, or evaluation of a stimulus may not be the same ones that are retrieved in an explicit memory task like recall or recognition (Brooks, 1987; Jacoby, 1983; Jacoby & Kelley, 1987; Lewicki, 1986). This point is elaborated on later in the chapter.

3. An exemplar is a representation of the stimulus person as interpreted by the perceiver, rather than a veridical or "pictoliteral" (Brewer, 1988) copy of the available stimulus information. For instance, if a prejudiced individual encounters a member of an ethnic minority and infers that the target is hostile, the attribute of hostility will probably be stored as part of the exemplar representation of the target person—even in the absence of any actual hostile behaviors by the target. This process can generate seeming support for the initial stereotype, in a circular and self-fulfilling manner.

How Is the Information Processed?

The fundamental processing assumption of this model is that exemplar representations are stored in memory and can be retrieved later to influence judgments. Specifically, suppose you encounter Person A who is tall and humorless; you store a representation of Person A's attributes in memory. Later you encounter Person B, whom you can see is tall. In common with others (Kahneman & Miller, 1986), I assume that this encounter triggers the retrieval of other exemplars that are similar to Person B from memory. This retrieval attempt makes sense as an effort to determine whether you have any stored knowledge about this specific person (B). Even if you do not, stored information about others who are similar to Person B is likely to prove helpful in dealing with Person B in the current situation. Person B's similarity to Person A on the dimension of height may lead you to retrieve Person A (among other representations).

Once exemplars that are similar to the target are retrieved from memory, their known attributes constitute expectations or inferences about the target as well: You may assume that Person B is also humorless. So if the used-car salesman's smile or overall appearance reminds me of my cousin Bob, who always tells the truth, I might assume that the salesman is honest. But if I only retrieve exemplars of used-car salesmen that are known to be dishonest, I am likely to infer that this individual too is dishonest.

But definition and elaboration is needed regarding the concept of *similarity*. Similarity cannot be assumed to be a simple, fixed, context-independent property of a set of stimuli. Rather, similarity depends on the way the perceiver processes and interprets the stimuli. One way to express this dependence is to say that perceived similarity depends on the perceiver's theory concerning the identity and relations among the stimuli (Medin, 1989). A theory may indicate what attributes are of central importance (perhaps those that have causal implications for other correlated attributes). Certainly social perceivers have no shortage of theories about people and social groups, such as the notion that females are naturally suited for a nurturing role so that gender causes differences in psychological characteristics like empathy. Such a theory influences the amount of attention that perceivers allocate to stimulus dimensions—gender may receive more attention than other, less basic attributes.

The effect of attention on stimulus identification and categorization processes has been formalized in the context model (Medin & Schaffer, 1978; Nosofsky, 1987). In this chapter I avoid mathematical detail, but simply illustrate the effects of the model's assumptions (see Smith & Zarate, 1992). Paying more attention to a given stimulus dimension exaggerates differences along that dimension. For example, consider stimuli YM, YF, and OM (a young male, young female, and old male, respectively). Figure 4.1 displays the effect of the perceiver's attention to dimensions on the similarities among these stimuli. Figure 4.1a shows a high weight (much attention) given to gender, which magnifies differences in gender relative to age differences. Stimulus YM is seen as more similar to OM than to YF. Figure 4.1b shows a high weight on age, with YM now seen as more similar to YF than to OM. Research with nonsocial stimuli (e.g., Nosofsky, 1986) shows that attentional shifts like this can be produced by training subjects on category structures in which one or another stimulus attribute is a better cue to category membership. So we would expect that if subjects were predicting each target's membership in the National Organization for Women versus membership in the American Association of Retired Persons, different patterns of attention to dimensions (and hence different perceptions of similarity among the targets) would result. As I discuss later, other factors, including a range of social, motivational, and contextual variables, may also affect the way perceivers process stimulus dimensions.

Evidence for Exemplar-Based Social Judgment

Effects of exemplars on social judgments have several characteristics that are difficult to accommodate in a purely schematic or algebraic model (see Smith, 1990). For instance, characteristics of a previously encountered person (A) may influence judgments about a target (B) who is similar to A. Alternatively, any characteristic of B or the context that makes the retrieval of A more likely may increase its influence on judgment, even if that characteristic is intrinsically irrelevant to the judgment. Many people appear to judge that Saddam Hussein is aggressive in part because he reminds them of Hitler. How much is the retrievability of the Hitler exemplar, and the judgment of Saddam's aggressiveness, increased by the fact that Hussein wears a mustache?

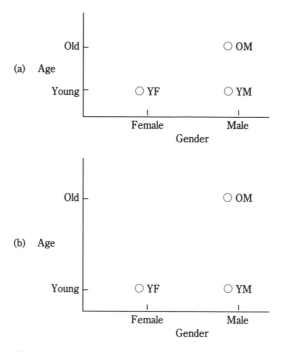

FIG. 4.1.   Effects of perceiver's attention on similarity relations among stimuli (a: effect of giving more attention to gender than to age; b: effect of giving more attention to age than to gender).

Though research attention to this area remains sparse to date, scattered evidence shows exemplar- or analogy-based effects on social judgments. In one study (Lewicki, 1986, p. 200), people encountered an experimenter who insulted them as they were filling out a questionnaire. Later the subjects were instructed to take their completed experimental materials to the assistant who was not busy when the subjects entered the room. When the subjects got there, both assistants were free, requiring an arbitrary choice. Subjects who had been insulted by the experimenter tended to avoid one assistant whose hair style resembled that of the experimenter. Control subjects who were not insulted by the experimenter showed no such tendency. The effects identified by Lewicki in this and other studies are not dependent on the subject's drawing a conscious analogy between the target person and the earlier experience, for the subjects uniformly denied that the earlier encounter had any effect on their later behavior.

Gilovich (1981) demonstrated similar exemplar-based inferences by giving subjects (who were sportswriters and college football coaches) brief descriptions of fictitious college football players. Some descriptions were constructed to create a linkage between the described player and a highly successful professional player. The linkage was logically irrelevant to the college player's ability or future success. (For example, the college player had won the "Joe Montana Award" at his school, or the college player came from the same hometown as the pro.) Nevertheless, these players were rated as having significantly higher potential for future success than were comparable control descriptions where no such linkage existed. White and Shapiro (1987, Experiment 2) had subjects hold a several-minute phone conversation with a target who either did or did not resemble the perceiver's close friend. After the conversation, perceivers rated the familiar-appearing targets as more similar to the friend on important personality dimensions.

Can a known exemplar influence judgments about a target person even more strongly than an abstract stereotypic knowledge structure? Andersen and Cole (1990, Study 3) had subjects generate a list of attributes of a specific individual they knew well, and also attributes of a well-known social stereotype (e.g., *redneck*) and an abstract trait category (e.g., *honest person*). In a supposedly unrelated memory experiment, subjects then read descriptions of fictitious stimuli persons and were tested on them with a recognition procedure. When the description of a stimulus person included some attributes drawn from the subject's description of a specific friend, subjects were likely to falsely report that the description had also included the friend's other attributes. For instance, suppose the subject had described a friend as *tall, intelligent, ambitious, humorless*. If a fictitious character description included the first three of these traits intermixed with some fillers, the subject would be likely to falsely recognize *humorless* as also having been part of the description. When Andersen and Cole used subjects' descriptions of a social stereotype and a trait category instead of a friend to construct the stimulus materials, the tendency to falsely recognize the related but unpresented traits was significantly weaker. Thus, representations of well-known individuals can serve as more powerful bases of inferences than such general knowledge representations as stereotypes and traits.

Common to all these examples is the theme that a judgment or evaluation of a target person is influenced by the perceiver's previous experiences with other individuals (exemplars). The most reasonable interpretation of these effects appears to be that the target serves as a cue for the retrieval of exemplar representations from memory, allowing stored information or the perceiver's attitude toward the stored exemplars to be accessed and applied to the current target. Other theories of social judgment have difficulty with observations of this sort. One could argue that a single encounter with a hostile long-haired individual could alter one's schematic knowledge (stereotype) about long-haired people, but that hardly seems plausible. And if it is argued that a single experience can have a major impact on schematic knowledge, even for a short time, then any clear conceptual distinction between general, abstract schematic knowledge and memory traces of specific experiences or episodes is lost—the very meaning of the term *schema* is destroyed (Jacoby, Baker, & Brooks, 1989). Similarly, in an information integration perspective, one would be hard pressed to argue that the valuation or the weight of specific person attributions should be changed in a lasting way by a single experience with an individual.

SOME QUESTIONS ABOUT THE EXEMPLAR-BASED MODEL

Despite (what I hope is now) the general plausibility of the exemplar view and its consistency with evidence such as that summarized, several key issues and questions probably remain for the reader. I try next to anticipate those questions and provide tentative answers to them.

Can Exemplars Influence Judgment Without the Perceiver's Awareness?

Many people interpret the idea of exemplar-based judgment as involving the conscious retrieval and evaluation of exemplars, and reject the whole idea on the basis of introspection. They may say "My evaluation of Ronald Reagan doesn't depend on the fact that he reminds me of old Uncle Edmund, who sometimes lost touch with reality a little bit!" But theorists who suggest that exemplars can influence judgments have been consistent in postulating that this process does not require conscious awareness (e.g., Kahneman & Miller, 1986, p. 136).

The empirical evidence supporting this postulate is clear. In fact, the evidence suffices to establish a somewhat broader point: Memory traces of specific past experiences can influence all sorts of task performances and subjective reactions to stimuli (not just social judgments about stimuli), independent of the perceiver's ability to consciously recollect the past experience. This phenomenon is generally termed *implicit memory* (Schacter, 1987; Smith & Branscombe, 1988). The reader can refer to Schacter's (1987) review for a broader view of the evidence, but a few examples will be illustrative.

In the nonsocial domain, a previous exposure to a particular stimulus item has been found to facilitate later processing of the same item, even in the absence of conscious recollection of the initial exposure. Any account of such an effect clearly requires the assumption that a memory trace of the item was stored initially, and is (nonconsciously) retrieved later to influence the judgment or task performance. These effects can be remarkably long-lasting. For example, Kolers (1976) had subjects practice reading text in various inverted or reversed orientations. When he retested them a year later, he found that specific pages of inverted text that subjects had read a year earlier could still be read faster than new pages, even if subjects did not recognize them as old. Mitchell and Brown (1988) had subjects name objects depicted in simple drawings, and found that previously named pictures could be named faster than new pictures—even 6 weeks after the initial presentation, and even if the picture was not recognized as having been previously seen. And Sloman, Hayman, Ohta, Law, and Tulving (1988) observed that completion of fragmented words was facilitated by earlier practice reading the word, for as long as 16 months after the initial study (at which time subjects spent an average of less than 7 seconds studying each word in a long list). Such facilitation has also been found to be independent of subjects' ability to consciously recognize the studied words.

Similar effects hold for judgments. Some researchers have had subjects read plausible general-knowledge statements, and then later given them a list of mixed old and new statements and asked for judgments of their validity. Statements that are familiar because of prior presentations are subjectively rated as more valid than comparable novel sentences (Begg, Armour, & Kerr, 1985; Hasher, Goldstein, & Toppino, 1977). Presumably subjects misattribute the familiarity, taking it as evidence of the sentence's truth. This process could not depend on the subjects' conscious recollection of the previous encounters with the statements, or they would not make this incorrect attribution.

My own research has investigated trait judgments concerning behaviors (Smith, 1989; Smith, Branscombe, & Bormann, 1988). Subjects read behaviors on a computer screen one at a time and judge whether each behavior was *friendly* or *intelligent,* responding yes or no by pressing a key. Some behaviors among a subject's hundreds of trials (spread over two sessions one day apart) are repeated, at various lags. Some behaviors are repeated within a block of 50 trials; others are repeated from one block to the next (with an average of 50 other behaviors intervening); and still others between sessions with 24 hours in between. The interest is in whether repeated behaviors can be judged more quickly than new ones. In fact, they can be, even after a 24-hour delay. A long-lasting trace of the behavior must be established by just a single presentation, which enables people to respond more quickly when the behavior is repeated. Further, the facilitation of response to a repeated behavior was just as large when the subject did not even recognize that the word had been presented earlier as it was when the word was recognized (Smith, 1989). Thus, like other types of implicit memory performance (Schacter, 1987) the facilitation of social judgments from repetition does not depend on subjects' conscious awareness of the earlier experience.

Thus, the answer to this question is that exemplar influences on social judgment do not require the perceiver's awareness. In fact, a stronger statement is warranted: Memory representations of specific previous experiences can have all sorts of effects on judgment and performance (e.g., processing speed) independent of the perceiver's ability to consciously recollect those experiences.

Do People Retrieve Exemplars
When General Knowledge Would Suffice?

In many of the aforementioned examples, a memory trace of a previous experience clearly is not necessary for the subject to perform his task. The perceiver could in principle perform some tasks on the basis of his or her general knowledge, as in naming the object in a drawing (Mitchell & Brown, 1988) or judging the validity of a statement (Begg et al., 1985). But in fact, effects of specific prior experiences on semantic tasks like reading a word (Jacoby, 1983) or making a trait judgment about a behavior (Smith, 1989) are ubiquitous—even though Jacoby's subjects could all read and Smith's subjects could all make trait judgments about behaviors that they had not encountered before in the experiment. Why, one might ask, should subjects bother to retrieve traces of previous experiences when they can refer to their general (schematic) knowledge, or to simple cognitive procedures, which will allow them to perform the task perfectly adequately?

But this question answers itself once it is framed this way: Subjects retrieve exemplars because they allow them to perform the task more quickly than they could by using only their general knowledge. One might postulate a "race" model, in which processes of exemplar-based judgment (or response, more generally) and processes deriving a judgment or response from generic knowledge operate in parallel. The first process that runs to completion "wins" and its response is output. The evidence of response-time facilitation by a memory trace of a previous experience in a very diverse collection of tasks is consistent with such a model. The evidence also shows that in many cases (not necessarily all) the exemplar-based response process wins the race. In fact, Logan (1988) postulated exactly this sort of race model involving exemplar-based responding as a general explanation for the automatization of task performance with practice. As subjects repeatedly respond to stimuli within a particular domain, they accumulate more and more memory traces of specific stimuli and the associated response. The retrieval of any one of these traces and therefore the ability to give a memory-based response becomes faster (on average) as more are accumulated in memory.

What about nonspeeded tasks, in which response time is not the main concern? Without time pressure, might subjects reject a quick exemplar-based response and go on to process stimuli based on their general schematic knowledge? Jacoby, Kelley, Brown, and Jasechko (1989) believed that subjects can choose between alternative "analytic" and "nonanalytic" strategies of task performance. In their study, subjects judged whether each name in a list (e.g., Sebastian Weisdorf) was that of a famous person. The list consisted of mixed famous and nonfamous names. Previously, subjects had studied another list of names, which they were (correctly) told were all nonfamous. Now consider: Subjects could make a fame judgment either in analytic fashion, calling a name

famous only if the subject could actually recall what the person did, or in nonanalytic fashion, simply responding to the subjective familiarity of each name. Subjects who use the latter strategy can be misled: Previously studied nonfamous
names may be familiar enough that they will be misperceived as famous, and
in fact subjects tended to false-alarm on these old nonfamous names. (The design of this experiment cleverly establishes that the feeling of familiarity for those
names must be an implicit memory phenomenon, for if the subjects consciously
recognized the names as having been studied, they would have been able to
confidently respond that they were nonfamous.) Jacoby suggests that by turning to the alternate, analytic strategy for responding, subjects would be able
to avoid having their judgments influenced by memory traces of previous experiences. But presumably such a strategy is more effortful than the default
nonanalytic strategy that relies on the subjective feeling of familiarity, explaining why most subjects chose the latter approach.

Thus, the answer to this question is that exemplars are retrieved and used
in judgment because often that process is quicker or less effortful than alternative procedures for making the judgment—if the latter are even available at all.

Does the Way the Exemplar Was Processed
Make a Difference?

I emphasized that an exemplar is a representation of a stimulus as processed.
What evidence is there that the way an exemplar was interpreted or processed
makes a difference in the effects it has later, above and beyond the exemplar's
objective attributes? Several studies using nonsocial stimuli make this point clearly
(e.g., Jacoby, Baker, & Brooks, 1989; Whittlesea, 1987). But it can also be
illustrated with my work on social judgments (behavior-trait inferences).

In my previously described study, specific behaviors that were repeated could
be judged significantly faster than comparable behaviors that were encountered
for the first time (Smith, 1989). However, this result was obtained only when
the behaviors were repeated while subjects were making the same trait judgment (e.g., friendliness). Some behaviors were repeated from one block to the
next across a change in the trait subjects were judging (e.g., they changed from
making judgments about the friendliness of the behaviors to judging their intelligence). Even though processing was strongly facilitated (by 141 ms) for a behavior repeated between blocks of trials when the trait was unchanged, there
was no facilitation whatever for repeated behaviors across a change in the trait
(−5 ms facilitation, not significantly different from zero). Note that this pattern
of results rules out a simple speedup of reading or accessing the behavior's
memory representation as a cause of the facilitation. If a repeated behavior could
simply be read or comprehended faster, equal facilitation for a repeated behavior
would be observed even if the type of trait judgment had changed. Instead, the

results demonstrate that the memory trace that is stored on the original encounter with the behavior, and is retrieved to facilitate responding upon its repetition, involves not only the specific behavior but also the way it was processed
or interpreted. It must be that subjects store, for example, not just "punch"
(a behavior) but rather "punch—unfriendly" (a behavior and its interpretation;
cf. Logan, 1988). This trace facilitates a later (repeated) judgment of the same
behavior's friendliness, but does not speed the response at all if subjects later
have to judge whether "punch" is an intelligent behavior.

The way a behavior was processed on a previous encounter can affect the
content of judgments as well as response speed. Smith, Stewart, and Buttram
(in press) had subjects make trait judgments about behaviors in two sessions
24 hours or 7 days apart, answering yes/no questions about whether a few
hundred behaviors were *friendly* or *intelligent*. In this study, the behaviors were
not just single verbs as in Smith (1989), but brief phrases like "billed a client
for services rendered." At the conclusion of the study, subjects completed an
ostensibly unrelated questionnaire, evaluating a number of behaviors on a general
positivity or social desirability dimension. Some behaviors embedded in this questionnaire were constructed to be intelligent but unfriendly, others were unintel-
ligent but friendly. Consistent with previous results (Smith, 1989), questionnaire
behaviors that the subject had not previously encountered in the experiment
were evaluated more in line with the trait implication that subjects were more
practiced and efficient in drawing. For example, a subject who had made intelligence judgments would evaluate the intelligent/unfriendly behaviors more favorably than the unintelligent/friendly ones. More important, this effect was
significantly greater for specific behaviors that the subject had previously encountered among his or her hundreds of judgment trials—even those that were
seen 1 or 7 days earlier. A memory trace of the specific behavior, along with
the way it was processed at the initial encounter (that is, what trait implication
was assessed), must be assumed to affect subjects' judgments on the questionnaire.

My assumption that interpretations or judgments are stored in memory as
part of an exemplar representation is similar to Fazio's (1986) claim that an object-
evaluation association constitutes the structural representation for an attitude.
Fazio holds that when the same object is encountered again, the evaluation is
quickly retrieved from memory and can direct the individual's perceptions and
action toward the object. In this exemplar-based model, a memory representation
and whatever response(s) are associated with it can be retrieved when *similar*
exemplars are encountered (not just the identical one). (Though he has not been
explicit on the point, Fazio might well share this assumption.) But I also assume that what is stored with an exemplar representation depends on the type
of processing the perceiver performed when the exemplar was encoded. Surely evaluation is a fundamental judgment that is often involved when social objects are encountered. But it is not the only important type of judgment. One's

living-room furnishings might be assessed for weightiness by a mover, for portability and value by a burglar, and for fashionability by an interior decorator.

Thus, different processing goals at the time an exemplar is originally encoded will result in the storage of different inferences (responses, judgments) as part of the exemplar representation. Differences in what is stored will in turn affect the type of influence the exemplar will have on judgments when it is later retrieved.

What Factors Influence Which Exemplars Are Retrieved?

A target stimulus is assumed to be judged on the basis of knowledge about the most similar stored exemplars. Similarity depends in turn on the perceiver's attention to stimulus dimensions or attributes. For example, giving most attention to occupation when evaluating the target used-car salesman will result in the perception that all members of that occupation are highly similar, and the retrieval of other used-car salesmen as exemplars. We might say that the target has been categorized by occupation and stereotyped accordingly. However, in this exemplar model there is no cognitive representation directly corresponding to a category or a stereotype (i.e., general knowledge about the category); only stored knowledge about exemplars is used. Attention to height, eye color, or some other dimension instead of occupation would yield a quite different map of perceived similarity (as in Fig. 4.1), and the retrieval of a different set of exemplars.

But answering questions about why perceivers attend to some stimulus dimensions (such as race, occupation, and gender) and not to others (such as eye color) requires going beyond the types of cognitive processes outlined above, to enter the realm of social, motivational, and contextual factors. Effects of such factors on judgment have long been investigated in social psychology (McGuire, McGuire, Child, & Fujioka, 1978; Tajfel, 1978; Turner, 1987; Wilder, 1981) and to some extent in cognitive psychology (Barsalou, 1987; Roth & Shoben, 1983). For example, the relative numbers of members of two groups in the immediate social context, the perceiver's degree of prejudice, and cooperation or competition between groups all influence categorization and stereotyping along group lines. I propose that all such factors modulate stimulus similarity by affecting perceivers' allocation of attention to specific stimulus attributes. These factors will therefore influence which exemplars are retrieved when any given target serves as the cue, and hence how the target is categorized and judged. Here is an incomplete list of such factors:

1. Perceiver's Goal. Research with nonsocial stimuli shows that perceivers' attention to dimensions (and the similarity relations among exemplars) depends on the categorization task at hand (Nosofsky, 1986). Thus, the perceiver's goal (to categorize stimuli in one way or another) influences attention and perceived similarity. For example, evaluating stimulus persons with the goal of choosing a study partner versus a date would be predicted to result in allocation of more attention (respectively) to intellectual versus social attributes of the targets.

2. Perceiver's Past Experiences.

Perceivers may learn over a lifetime that certain dimensions are often important in categorizing people, and hence chronically pay attention to such dimensions even if they are irrelevant for the specific task at hand. This constitutes a theory about social attributes and categories, of the sort that is cited by Medin (1989) as a key influence on perceivers' categorization and judgments. Attributes like age, gender, and race are powerful determinants of many important social roles, and hence may be processed automatically by most adults in our society (Brewer, 1988). For example, men and women are unequally distributed into the roles of employee and homemaker, which are assumed to demand quite different psychological characteristics (Eagly & Steffen, 1984). People assume that employees are characterized by agentic qualities like task orientation and rationality, and homemakers by communal qualities like interpersonal orientation and empathy. How would a female employee be perceived? General experience might well lead perceivers to pay attention to gender even if it is locally irrelevant for categorization (e.g., among a group of male and female employees in an organization). Attention to gender, by exaggerating perceived differences along that dimension relative to other dimensions (as in Fig. 4.1a) would make female employees be seen as more similar to female homemakers than to male employees, and so be attributed homemakers' typical traits (communal rather than agentic qualities). In short, it would cause perceivers to apply the traditional female stereotype. Conversely, attention to the role dimension would result in female employees being seen as more similar to male employees than to female homemakers, so they would be seen as more agentic.

3. Trait Chronicity and Perceiver's Self-Relevant Attributes.

Higgins (e.g., Higgins, King, & Mavin, 1982) developed a model of *chronicity*, a perceiver's stable tendency to use a particular trait dimension in describing and evaluating other persons. One who is "chronic" for intelligence, for example, will tend to describe others in terms of their standing on that dimension, form impressions of other people's intelligence relatively quickly, and better remember intelligence-related behaviors than other behaviors (Bargh & Thein, 1985; Higgins et al., 1982). Therefore, perceivers who are chronically attuned to a dimension should give it more weight in perceived similarity. For Higgins, chronicity is developed by frequent use of the trait construct over time (see also Smith, 1989).

Self-relevant or self-schematic attributes also receive more processing by perceivers, even in other people (Fong & Markus, 1982; Lewicki, 1984). Self-relevant attributes should function like chronically accessible attributes in person perception. That is, one who characteristically views himself or herself in terms of a trait like *independence* will pay attention to that dimension, exaggerating differences among stimulus exemplars along that dimension in comparison to differences on other dimensions. Tajfel and Wilkes (1964) found that subjects made more extreme judgments of others on those personality dimensions the subjects considered important. This is consistent with the prediction that attention to a particular dimension will increase perceived differences along that dimension.

4. Frequency of Exposure. Differential frequency of exposure to specific exemplars may be important in real life, for perceivers will rarely be equally familiar with every individual member of a group. Here I do not refer to increasing familiarity such as might result from extensive interaction over time with an exemplar of a specific category (e.g., gays), which would have multiple and complex effects, such as exposing the perceiver to the individual's personal or counter-stereotypic attributes. Instead, I am referring simply to repeated exposure to the same information about the exemplar—as when a particular TV advertisement is seen several times per day over a period of weeks or months. Nosofsky (1988) showed that frequently-presented stimuli, and other stimuli that are similar to them, become more accessible and more likely to be retrieved and influence judgments. With social stimuli, it may be that for most Americans, Dan Quayle is now subjectively experienced as a relatively typical member of the category "Hoosier Politician" and is the exemplar most readily retrieved if an evaluation of that group is to be given. This is the case even though, objectively, Quayle is not particularly typical of that group. Similarly, greater frequency of exposure to Willie Horton than to Bill Cosby may alter the types of exemplars that people retrieve when they evaluate Blacks as a category or individual Black persons.

5. Ingroup–Outgroup Dynamics. Perceiver characteristics may also play a role in person perception by defining ingroups and outgroups (Tajfel & Turner, 1985). Zarate and Smith (1990) found ingroup–outgroup effects in a social categorization task, in which subjects categorized stimulus photographs by gender or race. Subjects classified same-sex photos by sex faster than opposite-sex photos. This effect held across White and Black subjects in Zarate and Smith's Experiment 1, and was replicated in two different experiments using different stimulus sets. These results are related to those of Brigham and Barkowitz (1978), who found that Black and White subjects are more accurate in recognizing same-race targets than other-race targets. Using still another dependent measure, Park and Rothbart (1982; Experiment 4) presented subjects with short stories about numerous individuals, and later asked subjects to recall all they could remember about the target's characteristics. They found that subjects' memory for subordinate details (e.g., occupation) was better for same-sex targets than for opposite-sex targets. Finally, people tend to view outgroup members as more similar to each other than ingroup members (Judd & Park, 1988; Linville et al., 1989; Park & Rothbart, 1982).

All these factors suggest a clear prediction for application of this exemplar-based model to social judgment in an ingroup–outgroup context. More attention is devoted to the individuating (non-category-defining) attributes of the self and fellow ingroup members, and more to the category-defining attribute(s) of outgroup members. For example, a male processing a female target would pay particular attention to gender, thereby perceiving her as relatively similar to other females (outgroup homogeneity) and in particular as similar to housewives (thus viewing her in stereotypic, communal terms; Eagly & Steffen, 1984). Conversely, a male perceiving a male target would devote more attention to his other attributes (occupation, traits), perhaps because less time is required to process the ingroup gender attribute (Zarate & Smith, 1990). This attention allocation would result both in perceptions that males are quite diverse, and in better memory for their individuating attributes (Park & Rothbart, 1982). Though the basic exemplar-similarity model of Nosofsky (1987) assumes that attention to a given dimension (e.g., gender) is constant across stimuli, Medin and Edelson (1988) proposed a version in which attention to a dimension can vary depending on the other attributes of the stimulus, the same assumption that appears to be called for here.

Messick and Mackie (1989, p. 56), Mullen (in press), and Turner (1987) have adopted different versions of the assumption that ingroup and outgroup members are processed differently. I do not assume that the representation is dichotomous (e.g., the outgroup represented by a prototype and ingroup members as exemplars). Instead, there is a single representational format (all groups are represented by exemplars), with the qualification that differential attention and encoding processes alter the representation of those exemplars so that outgroup members appear more similar to each other because their individuating attributes receive less attention.

6. Cultural Defaults. A culture may define particular person attributes as expected or default values. For example, in our culture it has been claimed that male gender, White racial identity, nonhandicapped physical status, heterosexual orientation, and young age are treated as cultural defaults or expectations (Eagly & Kite, 1987; Goffman, 1963). In cases where a cultural default exists, a departure from such an expected attribute value becomes a stigma that will be likely to attract attention and be the basis for categorizing the target.

Zarate and Smith (1990) reported three studies that measured the speed with which subjects can categorize photographs of people along various dimensions (*White, Black, male, female*). This measure can be used to reveal the specific categorization that people use when more than one is applicable to a target individual (as is always the case with real people). Results show that targets who differ from a cultural default of White and male are categorized according to that deviation. Thus, Black males are categorized as *Black* rather than as *male;* White females are categorized as *female,* not *White.*

Another study (reported in Zarate, 1990) applied a novel frequency-estimation measure. Subjects in a baseline condition saw 24 slides of faces, six of each type (race × gender) randomly ordered, for 1 sec each. They were instructed in essence just to look at the photos and anticipate later questions about them. They were then asked to rank order the four categories *Black, White, male,* and *female* by the number of photos of each type. In another condition, 4 additional Black male photos were added. Subjects were predicted to encode Black males as *Black* rather than as *male,* because only their race differs from a cultural default. As predicted, in this condition estimates of the number of Blacks significantly exceeded the number of males (while in reality, equal numbers of Blacks and males were seen). Likewise, White females were predicted to be encoded as *female* rather than *White.* When extra White female photos were included, subjects did estimate that they saw more females than Whites. Thus, these results suggest that subjects encoded a culturally nondefault attribute of a photo, but not both the sex and race attributes.

7. Numbers in the Social Context. Numerical relationships can influence intergroup perceptions and behavior (Taylor & Fiske, 1978; Mullen, in press). When one category is larger than another (e.g., more males than females) and particularly when a minority is so small as to constitute a token one or two individuals, the dimension (e.g., gender) becomes highly salient relative to the case of a more equal split (Taylor & Fiske, 1978). A prediction for the current model is that as the sizes of two groups become more unequal more attention will be paid to dimensions that differentiate them, so that the two groups will be seen as more different while perceived within-group similarity should increase.

A second prediction is parallel to that for ingroups and outgroups. Members of a minority group are generally seen as more similar to each other than members of a majority (e.g., Mullen, in press; Simon & Brown, 1987). Thus, observers give more attention to individuating or non-category-defining attributes of the majority (like ingroup members) and more attention to the category-defining attribute of the minority (like outgroup members). This has implications for social inference processes. For example, an attribute should be generalized from one minority member to another more readily than from one majority-group member to another.

I have described three separate but related effects: Members of an outgroup, of a category culturally defined as nondefault, and of a minority in the local context are all processed in terms of their category-defining attribute rather than their individuating characteristics. Often these three effects will overlap and reinforce each other, as when a White (member of a majority, culturally default group) views a Black in a situation where Blacks constitute a small minority. But the effects can also be put into conflict. There are hints that cultural defaults outweigh effects of the perceiver's own group membership. For example, female subjects as well as males give frequency estimates that suggest they attend to female rather than male gender as a nondefault value (Zarate, 1990). Nor did Black subjects' racial categorizations differ from Whites in the one study that involved Black subjects (Zarate & Smith, 1990, Experiment 1), though this conclusion must be tentative due to relatively low power. But whether cultural defaults or local numerical context is a stronger effect remains to be determined.

Three other factors are mentioned briefly and speculatively:

8. Intergroup Conflict or Competition. Competition can sharpen the salience of group boundaries (Brewer, 1979; Judd & Park, 1988), exaggerating within-group similarities and between-group differences.

9. Outcome Dependency. Outcome dependency or other motivational factors can cause perceivers to pay attention to individuating attributes of specific others on whom they are dependent (Messick & Mackie, 1989, p. 57; Neuberg & Fiske, 1987).

10. Mere Existence of a Stereotype. Simply being aware of a stereotype or having a theory concerning a particular attribute, like Medin's (1989) theory concerning an attribute's importance, may cause perceivers to pay attention to the attribute (Krueger, Rothbart, & Sriram, 1989; cf. Turner's "normative fit," 1987). So if you learn that there are day people and night people, or Aquarians and Sagittarians, you might begin noting the category membership of people you know. Paying attention to the attribute (however arbitrary it may be) would make you see more within-category homogeneity and more between-category differences, confirming the idea that the dimension is important.

Summary. The answer to this final question is that an open-ended list of social, motivational, and contextual factors may influence the way perceivers allocate attention to a target exemplar, and therefore the set of other exemplars that they will retrieve from memory and use in judgment. This process represents a crucial interface between the social world in which perceivers are embedded and the internal cognitive processing and representation of social stimuli.

IMPLICATIONS OF EXEMPLAR-BASED JUDGMENT FOR STEREOTYPING

What changes in our thinking about stereotyping might flow from adopting an exemplar-based judgment model? Consider the possibility that some racially prejudiced people may not have negative attitudes toward, or stereotypic beliefs about, Blacks per se. Perhaps such individuals (a) pay attention to race when they encounter a Black target because Blacks constitute an outgroup, are culturally defined as nondefault, and are a minority; (b) therefore perceive Blacks as homogeneous; and (c) have available exemplars of a few disliked, widely publicized Blacks like Willie Horton. Then a Black stimulus person—encountered on the street, perhaps—would trigger the retrieval of those exemplars, leading to a negative attitude and to expectations of criminal conduct. In another context (e.g., watching Bill Cosby on TV) a different set of exemplars (other comedians) might be retrieved, because the context makes role more salient than race. This type of analysis, then, suggests that racial attitudes and stereotypes should be markedly context sensitive. If some instances of stereotypic beliefs and prejudiced attitudes stem from this source, it would theoretically be possible to remedy them by increasing the importance of other dimensions in the perceiver's view. Consistent with this suggestion, increasing the salience of cross-cutting dimensions is known to reduce intergroup bias in minimal intergroup situations (Deschamps & Doise, 1978).

Another example is one cited by Rothbart (1981) from Jean-Paul Sartre. A woman says she hates Jews because of her "most horrible experience with all (Jewish) furriers." Sartre asks: "But why did she choose to hate Jews rather than furriers? Why Jews or furriers rather than such and such a Jew or such and such a furrier?" (Rothbart, 1981, p. 156). The model presented here suggests, first, that representations of the negative experiences with Jewish furriers were stored in memory. Second, these exemplars were retrieved in future encounters with Jews rather than furriers, males, or other social targets, because the perceiver paid more attention to ethnicity than to occupation, gender, or other dimensions. This attention allocation results in all Jews being seen as quite similar to each other and as quite different from non-Jews. Third, the social and motivational reasons that caused the woman to attend to ethnicity particularly might include ingroup–outgroup dynamics (the woman is probably not herself a Jew), numerical context (Jews probably constitute a minority), and social learning (her culture may emphasize ethnicity over other dimensions).

Stereotyping Versus Individuation

The literature on stereotyping has raised two prominent general issues to which the exemplar-based model is relevant. First, many researchers have considered the relative weight of categorical and individuating information in social judgment (Fiske & Neuberg, 1988; Locksley, Hepburn, & Ortiz, 1982). In making judgments about an individual, perceivers often rely on stereotypic information about the target's social category. However, some conditions (e.g., the provision of individuating information about the target) lead perceivers to lessen their reliance on stereotypes (Krueger & Rothbart, 1988). Brewer (1988) proposed a fixed distinction between categorical and individuated modes of person perception, and others (e.g., Fiske, 1988; Turner, 1987) a more realistic view of a continuum between these two. In the current framework, the balance between attention to group-defining attributes (e.g., gender) and individuating attributes (e.g., traits) will determine the relative weight of individuating and categorical information in judgments. That is, more attention to group-defining attributes will emphasize within-group similarities and between-group differences and hence increase stereotypic perceptions (Krueger et al., 1989; Turner, 1987, chapter 3). Attention to occupation means that all used-car salesmen appear quite similar to each other—and in particular any such individual may cue the retrieval of a socially learned, crooked, used-car-salesman exemplar—while more attention to individuating attributes will make individuals appear as unique and distinct.

Which Stereotype Will be Used?

A second issue whose importance is gradually being recognized in the stereotyping literature is what category will be applied to a stimulus person who can be categorized in different ways (Messick & Mackie, 1989; Oakes & Turner, in press; Zarate & Smith, 1990), both horizontally overlapping (e.g., race, gender, age, or occupation) and vertically structured (e.g., woman or career woman). Many researchers have studied informational and motivational determinants of perceivers' use of hierarchically organized types and subtypes (e.g., Brewer, Dull, & Lui, 1981; Fiske & Neuberg, 1988). In the framework advanced here, attention to one dimension (e.g., gender) rather than crosscutting (e.g., race) or subordinate dimensions (e.g., those defining gender subtypes) will determine the perceived similarity of the target stimulus to others (cf. Fig. 4.1). This similarity in turn will determine whether the target is categorized (and stereotyped) by gender, by race, or by a gender subtype. Thus, the major issues that have been considered in this literature—including the balance between individual- and category-level information in person perception, and the question of which category is accessed—promise to be encompassed within a single framework.

Inconsistent Group-Level and Individual-Level Knowledge

With social categories, social learning is no doubt an important source of knowledge at the group rather than individual level. Someone might be told that all politicians are corrupt, that all Palestinians are terrorists, or that "big boys don't cry," for instance, in the absence of supportive experience with specific exemplars (Messick & Mackie, 1989, p. 48). In fact, socially learned group-level (stereotypic) information may even be contradicted by the majority of the individual's experiences with specific group members, a possibility that presumably could not arise if group-level knowledge was acquired only by induction from specific exemplars. Certainly the "bigot with the heart of gold," who dislikes an outgroup as a generality but is personally accepting of individually encountered outgroup members, is a stock figure in popular culture (as is the opposite, professedly nonracist but personally intolerant type). Of course, if a perceiver possesses mixed and inconsistent group-level and exemplar-level representations, the issue of which representation is accessed and used to make any particular judgment comes to the fore.

Because a stimulus acts as a cue for the perceiver to retrieve similar past instances, the nature of the cue—the stimulus the perceiver is reacting to—is one potential determinant. In particular, a verbal label for a group, like *a Black person,* may be more likely to retrieve group-level representations, and a specific individual more likely to retrieve other persons (exemplars). This is because a group label is semantically linked to group-level attributes, whereas a specific individual will always have non–group-specific, individuating attributes as well (height, eye color, specific behaviors, occupation, clothing style). On the assumption that representations of groups often contain stereotypic negative information while encounters with individual group members are mostly benign, this hypothesis is consistent with the "person positivity effect" found by Sears (1983). For example, Sears pointed out that most Americans express quite a negative view concerning Congress, while routinely re-electing their own individual Congressional representatives at a rate approaching 100%.

Of course, there will rarely be complete independence between knowledge about groups and about individual group members. Perceivers may sometimes access their group-level knowledge when thinking about or evaluating an individual (e.g., "I think well of my representative, but the Congress as a whole has not been doing very well on the nation's problems—maybe it's time for a change."). And group-level information may be used to interpret ambiguous exemplar information, as when a group member's ambiguous behavior comes to be seen in stereotype-consistent terms (e.g., Darley & Gross, 1983). This may be particularly likely when the perceiver has few or no specific exemplars stored in memory, but has strong and easily accessible group-level knowledge. This might be the situation of a young child in his or her first encounters with members of a racial outgroup in public school. Unfortunately, access of negative group-level knowledge in this situation can lead to a self-perpetuating stereotype, as specific individuals may be inferred to have group-typical negative characteristics and be stored as negative specific exemplars of the group.

Measurement of Stereotypes

Our perspective, together with the logic just outlined, has significant implications for the assessment of stereotypes. Since the classic study of Katz and Braly (1933) and continuing to the present day (e.g., Deaux & Lewis, 1984; Devine, 1989) most researchers have provided subjects with verbal group labels as stimuli to assess group stereotypes. It is possible that such measurement techniques will assess knowledge structures that are real, but are *not* those accessed by the perceivers in everyday encounters with individual group members. There is a real need for the development of assessment techniques that can reveal which exemplars or other knowledge structures are accessed when a real person is the cue—perhaps along the lines pioneered by Malt (1989). Unfortunately, there are bound to be many complexities in that effort: Exemplar retrieval will depend on perceived similarity, which in turn varies with the current focus of attention, contextual salience, perceivers' individual differences, and the like.

CONCLUSIONS

Existing models of social judgment, whether algebraic or schematic, have emphasized the role of the perceiver's abstract, schematic knowledge (Alba & Hasher, 1983). It may be time to recognize the role of specific experiences and exemplar representations as well. In contrast to the often-noted stability and self-perpetuating tendencies of general schemas, social knowledge embodied in exemplars can be specific, concrete, and malleable by recent experiences. It can also affect our judgments and reactions to people without our conscious awareness (Lewicki, 1986). The model outlined here may serve as a starting point for the investigation of exemplar effects in social judgment, and for the incorporation of a range of social, motivational, and contextual effects (such as ingroup–outgroup dynamics, numerical context, the perceiver's self-schema, and the like) on judgments. Even if this model proves to be applicable and fruitful, many significant issues yet remain to be addressed. Perhaps chief among them is the integration of exemplar-based judgment with more analytic judgmental processes that draw largely on general knowledge. To date we have the suggestion that subjects can choose between alternative nonanalytical (exemplar-based) and analytical judgment strategies (Jacoby, Kelley, Brown, & Jasechko, 1989), but more subtle forms of interaction between these two types of processing no doubt need to be explored. But at least a first step toward resolving these ultimate issues is to broaden our theoretical thinking about social judgment, recognizing the importance of specific exemplar representations as well as abstract, schematic knowledge (Smith, 1990).

ACKNOWLEDGMENT

Preparation of this chapter was facilitated by the National Science Foundation under grant BNS-8613584, and by a sabbatical award from the James McKeen Cattell Fund.

REFERENCES

Alba, J., & Hasher, L. (1983). Is memory schematic? *Psychological Bulletin, 93,* 203-231.

Andersen, S. M., & Cole, S. W. (1990). "Do I know you?" The role of significant others in general social perception. *Journal of Personality and Social Psychology, 59,* 384-399.

Anderson, N. H. (1981). *Foundations of information integration theory.* New York: Academic Press.

Bargh, J. A., & Thein, R. D. (1985). Individual construct accessibility, person memory, and the recall-judgment link: The case of information overload. *Journal of Personality and Social Psychology, 49,* 1129-1146.

Barsalou, L. W. (1987). The instability of graded structure: Implications for the nature of concepts. In U. Neisser (Ed.), *Concepts and conceptual development* (pp. 101-140). Cambridge, England: Cambridge University Press.

Begg, I., Armour, V., & Kerr, T. (1985). On believing what we remember. *Canadian Journal of Behavioral Science, 17,* 199-214.

Brewer, M. B. (1979). In-group bias in the minimal intergroup situation: A cognitive-motivational analysis. *Psychological Bulletin, 86,* 307-323.

Brewer, M. B. (1988). A dual process model of impression formation. In R. S. Wyer & T. K. Srull (Eds.), *Advances in social cognition* (Vol. 1, pp. 1-36). Hillsdale, NJ: Lawrence Erlbaum Associates.

Brewer, M. B., Dull, V. T., & Lui, L. (1981). Perceptions of the elderly: Stereotypes as prototypes. *Journal of Personality and Social Psychology, 41,* 656-670.

Brigham, J. C., & Barkowitz, P. (1978). Do "they all look alike?" The effect of race, sex, experience, and attitudes on the ability to recognize faces. *Journal of Applied Social Psychology, 8,* 306-318.

Brooks, L. R. (1987). Decentralized control of cognition: The role of prior processing episodes. In U. Neisser (Ed.), *Concepts and conceptual development* (pp. 141-174). Cambridge, England: Cambridge University Press.

Darley, J. M., & Gross, P. H. (1983). A hypothesis-confirming bias in labeling effects. *Journal of Personality and Social Psychology, 44,* 20-33.

Deaux, K. K., & Lewis, L. L. (1984). Structure of gender stereotypes: Interrelationships among components and gender label. *Journal of Personality and Social Psychology, 46,* 991-1004.

Deschamps, J. C., & Doise, W. (1978). Crossed category memberships in intergroup relations. In H. Tajfel (Ed.), *Differentiation between social groups* (pp. 141-158). London: Academic Press.

Devine, P. G. (1989). Stereotypes and prejudice: Their automatic and controlled components. *Journal of Personality and Social Psychology, 56,* 5-18.

Eagly, A. H., & Kite, M. E. (1987). Are stereotypes of nationalities applied to both women and men? *Journal of Personality and Social Psychology, 53,* 451-462.

Eagly, A. H., & Steffen, V. J. (1984). Gender stereotypes stem from the distribution of women and men into social roles. *Journal of Personality and Social Psychology, 46,* 735-754.

Fazio, R. H. (1986). How do attitudes guide behavior? In R. M. Sorrentino & E. T. Higgins (Eds.), *Handbook of motivation and cognition* (pp. 204-243). New York: Guilford Press.

Fiske, S. T. (1988). Compare and contrast: Brewer's dual process model and Fiske et al.'s continuum model. In T. K. Srull & R. S. Wyer (Eds.), *Advances in social cognition* (Vol. 1, pp. 65-76). Hillsdale, NJ: Lawrence Erlbaum Associates.

Fiske, S. T., & Neuberg, S. L. (1988). A continuum model of impression formation: From category-based to individuating processes as a function of information, motivation, and attention. *Advances in Experimental Social Psychology, 23,* 1-108.

Fong, G. T., & Markus, H. (1982). Self-schemas and judgments about others. *Social Cognition, 1,* 191-204.

Gilovich, T. (1981). Seeing the past in the present: The effect of associations to familiar events on judgments about decisions. *Journal of Personality and Social Psychology, 40,* 797-808.

Goffman, E. (1963). *Stigma.* Englewood Cliffs, NJ: Prentice-Hall.

Hasher, L., Goldstein, D., & Toppino, T. (1977). Frequency and the conference of referential validity. *Journal of Verbal Learning and Verbal Behavior, 16,* 107–112.

Higgins, E. T., & Bargh, J. A. (1987). Social cognition and social perception. *Annual Review of Psychology, 38,* 369–427.

Higgins, E. T., King, G. A., & Mavin, G. H. (1982). Individual construct accessibility and subjective impressions and recall. *Journal of Personality and Social Psychology, 43,* 35–47.

Jacoby, L. L. (1983). Perceptual enhancement: Persistent effects of an experience. *Journal of Experimental Psychology: Learning, Memory, and Cognition, 9,* 21–38.

Jacoby, L. L., Baker, J. G., & Brooks, L. R. (1989). Episodic effects on picture identification: Implications for theories of concept learning and theories of memory. *Journal of Experimental Psychology: Learning, Memory, and Cognition, 15,* 275–281.

Jacoby, L. L., & Kelley, C. M. (1987). Unconscious influences of memory for a prior event. *Personality and Social Psychology Bulletin, 13,* 314–336.

Jacoby, L. L., Kelley, C. M., Brown, J., & Jasechko, J. (1989). Becoming famous overnight: Limits on the ability to avoid unconscious influences of the past. *Journal of Personality and Social Psychology, 56,* 326–338.

Judd, C. M., & Park, B. (1988). Outgroup homogeneity: Judgments of variability at the individual and group levels. *Journal of Personality and Social Psychology, 54,* 778–788.

Kahneman, D., & Miller, D. T. (1986). Norm theory: Comparing reality to its alternatives. *Psychological Review, 93,* 136–153.

Katz, D., & Braly, K. (1933). Racial stereotypes in one hundred college students. *Journal of Abnormal and Social Psychology, 28,* 280–290.

Kolers, P. A. (1976). Reading a year later. *Journal of Experimental Psychology: Human Learning and Memory, 2,* 554–565.

Krueger, J., & Rothbart, M. (1988). The use of categorical and individuating information in making inferences about personality. *Journal of Personality and Social Psychology, 55,* 187–195.

Krueger, J., Rothbart, M., & Sriram, N. (1989). Category learning and change: Differences in sensitivity to information that enhances or reduces intercategory distinctions. *Journal of Personality and Social Psychology, 56,* 866–875.

Lambert, A., & Wyer, R. S. (1990). Stereotypes and social judgment: The effects of typicality and group heterogeneity. *Journal of Personality and Social Psychology, 59,* 676–691.

Lewicki, P. (1984). Self-schema and social information processing. *Journal of Personality and Social Psychology, 47,* 1177–1190.

Lewicki, P. (1986). *Nonconscious social information processing.* Orlando, FL: Academic Press.

Linville, P. W., Fisher, G. W., & Salovey, P. (1989). Perceived distributions of the characteristics of ingroup and outgroup members. *Journal of Personality and Social Psychology, 57,* 165–188.

Locksley, A., Hepburn, C., & Ortiz, V. (1982). Social stereotypes and judgments of individuals: An instance of the base-rate fallacy. *Journal of Experimental Social Psychology, 18,* 23–42.

Logan, G. D. (1988). Toward an instance theory of automatization. *Psychological Review, 95,* 492–527.

Malt, B. C. (1989). An on-line investigation of prototype and exemplar strategies in classification. *Journal of Experimental Psychology: Learning, Memory, and Cognition, 15,* 539–555.

McGuire, W. J., McGuire, C. V., Child, P., & Fujioka, T. (1978). Salience of ethnicity in the spontaneous self-concept as a function on one's ethnic distinctiveness in the social environment. *Journal of Personality and Social Psychology, 15,* 511–520.

Medin, D. L. (1989). Concepts and conceptual structure. *American Psychologist, 44,* 1469–1481.

Medin, D. L., & Edelson, S. M. (1988). Problem structure and the use of base-rate information from experience. *Journal of Experimental Psychology: General, 117,* 68–85.

Medin, D. L., & Schaffer, M. M. (1978). Context theory of classification learning. *Psychological Review, 85,* 207–238.

Messick, D. M., & Mackie, D. M. (1989). Intergroup relations. *Annual Review of Psychology, 40,* 45–81.

Mitchell, D. B., & Brown, A. S. (1988). Persistent repetition priming in picture naming and its dissociation from recognition memory. *Journal of Experimental Psychology: Learning, Memory, and Cognition, 14*, 213–222.

Mullen, B. (in press). The phenomenology of being in a group: Integrations of social cognition and group processes. *Personality and Social Psychology Bulletin.*

Neuberg, S. L., & Fiske, S. T. (1987). Motivational influences on impression formation: Outcome dependency, accuracy driven attention, and individuating processes. *Journal of Personality and Social Psychology, 53*, 431–444.

Nosofsky, R. M. (1986). Attention, similarity, and the identification-categorization relationship. *Journal of Experimental Psychology: General, 115*, 39–57.

Nosofsky, R. M. (1987). Attention and learning processes in the identification and categorization of integral stimuli. *Journal of Experimental Psychology: Learning, Memory, and Cognition, 13*, 87–108.

Nosofsky, R. M. (1988). Similarity, frequency, and category representations. *Journal of Experimental Psychology: Learning, Memory, and Cognition, 14*, 54–65.

Oakes, P. J., & Turner, J. C. (in press). Is limited information processing capacity the cause of social stereotyping? In M. Hewstone & W. Stroebe (Eds.), *European review of social psychology* (Vol. 1). Chichester, England: Wiley.

Park, B., & Rothbart, M. (1982). Perception of out-group homogeneity and levels of social categorization: Memory for the subordinate attributes of in-group and out-group members. *Journal of Personality and Social Psychology, 42*, 1051–1068.

Roth, E. M., & Shoben, E. J. (1983). The effect of context on the structure of categories. *Cognitive Psychology, 15*, 346–378.

Rothbart, M. (1981). Memory processes and social beliefs. In D. L. Hamilton (Ed.), *Cognitive processes in stereotyping and intergroup behavior* (pp. 145–181). Hillsdale, NJ: Lawrence Erlbaum Associates.

Schacter, D. (1987). Implicit memory: History and current status. *Journal of Experimental Psychology: Learning, Memory, and Cognition, 13*, 501–518.

Sears, D. O. (1983). The person-positivity bias. *Journal of Personality and Social Psychology, 44*, 233–250.

Simon, B., & Brown, R. (1987). Perceived homogeneity in minority-majority contexts. *Journal of Personality and Social Psychology, 53*, 703–711.

Sloman, S. A., Hayman, C. A. G., Ohta, N., Law, J., & Tulving, E. (1988). Forgetting in primed fragment completion. *Journal of Experimental Psychology: Learning, Memory, and Cognition, 14*, 223–239.

Smith, E. R. (1989). Procedural efficiency: General and specific components and effects on social judgment. *Journal of Experimental Social Psychology, 25*, 500–523.

Smith, E. R. (1990). Content and process specificity in the effects of prior experiences. Target article in T. K. Srull & R. S. Wyer (Eds.), *Advances in social cognition* (Vol. 3, pp. 1–59). Hillsdale, NJ: Lawrence Erlbaum Associates.

Smith, E. R. (1991). Illusory correlation in a simulated exemplar-based memory. *Journal of Experimental Social Psychology, 27*, 107–123.

Smith, E. R., & Branscombe, N. R. (1988). Category accessibility as implicit memory. *Journal of Experimental Social Psychology, 24*, 490–504.

Smith, E. R., Branscombe, N. R., & Bormann, C. (1988). Generality of the effects of practice on social judgment tasks. *Journal of Personality and Social Psychology, 54*, 385–395.

Smith, E. R., Stewart, T. L., & Buttram, R. (in press). Inferring a trait from a behavior has long-term, highly specific effects. *Journal of Personality and Social Psychology.*

Smith, E. R., & Zarate, M. A. (1990). Exemplar and prototype use in social categorization. *Social Cognition, 8*, 243–262.

Smith, E. R., & Zarate, M. A. (1992). Exemplar-based model of social judgment. *Psychological Review, 99*, 3–21.

Tajfel, H. (1978). *Differentiation between social groups*. London: Academic Press.

Tajfel, H., & Turner, J. (1985). The social identity theory of intergroup behavior. In S. Worchel & W. G. Austin (Eds.), *Psychology of intergroup relations* (pp. 7–24). Chicago: Nelson-Hall.

Tajfel, H., & Wilkes, A. L. (1964). Salience of attributes and commitment to extreme judgments in the perception of people. *British Journal of Social and Clinical Psychology, 2,* 40–49.

Taylor, S. E., & Fiske, S. T. (1978). Salience, attention, and attribution: Top of the head phenomena. In L. Berkowitz (Ed.), *Advances in experimental social psychology* (Vol. 11, pp. 249–288). New York: Academic Press.

Turner, J. C. (1987). *Rediscovering the social group: A self-categorization theory*. Oxford: Blackwell.

White, G. L., & Shapiro, D. (1987). Don't I know you? Antecedents and social consequences of perceived familiarity. *Journal of Experimental Social Psychology, 23,* 75–92.

Whittlesea, B. W. A. (1987). Preservation of specific experiences in the representation of general knowledge. *Journal of Experimental Psychology: Learning, Memory, and Cognition, 13,* 3–17.

Wilder, D. A. (1981). Perceiving persons as a group: Categorization and intergroup relations. In D. L. Hamilton (Ed.), *Cognitive processes in stereotyping and intergroup behavior* (pp. 213–257). Hillsdale, NJ: Lawrence Erlbaum Associates.

Zarate, M. A. (1990). *Cultural normality and social perception*. Unpublished doctoral dissertation, Purdue University, Lafayette, IN.

Zarate, M. A., & Smith, E. R. (1990). Person categorization and stereotyping. *Social Cognition, 8,* 161–185.

5

Cognitive Phenomenology: Feelings and the Construction of Judgment

Gerald L. Clore
*University of Illinois
at Urbana-Champaign*

It is a truism in the history of science that the last thing to be studied is that which is closest to the scientist. If the stars were the first object of study, perhaps it was inevitable that research on the experience of thought and emotion would be long delayed. Even contemporary psychologists generally avoid dealing with consciousness—especially feelings and other experiential aspects of consciousness. We are better prepared to study the content of thought than the experience of thinking, preferring to relegate observations about experience itself to phenomenologists, poets, and drug addicts. Even investigators concerned with the role of emotion in social cognition have avoided focusing on experience, despite the fact that one of the most distinctive aspects of emotions is that they are felt. If there is a necessary ingredient in emotion, it is surely experience. One can have an emotion without doing anything or saying anything, but not without feeling anything. It is odd, therefore, that current accounts of emotion and social cognition have left out the experiential aspect altogether. But, while psychologists avoid focusing on conscious experience, the same may not be true of our subjects. Recent research suggests that affective and cognitive feelings are central to a surprising variety of judgments and decisions. Rather than being idle by-products of information processing, affective and cognitive feelings I argue are gainfully employed in the construction of everyday social judgments.

Perhaps the amazing fidelity of our senses is responsible for our failure to accord experience its rightful place. Rarely does one have occasion to focus on sensations apart from what they signify. Normally, we focus on the outside world and can safely ignore the fact that sensations of the world and the world itself are not the same. One is more likely, for example, to say, "Feel the velvet fabric," than to say "Feel your skin against the velvet fabric," even though, strictly speaking, our skin is all that we can ever feel. Mostly we separate experience and reality only when confronted with sensory anomalies, as when, at a baseball game, we hear the crack of the bat only after we see the ball sailing into left field. Magic shows, perceptual illusions, and distorting mirrors are all fascinating, presumably because the connection between experience and reality is usually so seamless. We instinctively believe our senses and our feelings above all else, and it is surprising to discover that they can be in error. Indeed, the very phraseology of this discussion shows how delicate the problem is. Error cannot actually be a property of feelings and senses, but only of the inferences we draw from the information they provide. The conditions of such errors are the focus of much of this chapter.

I focus on two kinds of feelings, emotional and nonemotional feelings, and discuss their respective roles in affective and nonaffective judgment. In the first part of this chapter, a model developed to understand how mood and emotion affect judgment is discussed, along with relevant research. In the second part, I argue that the same processes that govern the role of mood in judgment also govern the role of nonemotional feelings in nonaffective judgments.

EMOTIONAL FEELINGS AND JUDGMENT

The most reliable phenomenon in the cognition-emotion domain is the effect of mood on evaluative judgment. The rose-colored glasses effect and its reverse can be readily observed in everyday life and easily produced in the laboratory. Forgas and Moylan (1987), for example, interviewed nearly 1,000 people as they left movie theaters after they had seen one of several movies. The movies had been previously classified as happy, sad, or aggressive in affective tone. The interviews covered views on political figures, future events, crime, and life satisfaction. In response to these questions, viewers made judgments that clearly reflected the affective tone of the films they had seen. There were no such differences among patrons entering the theaters, suggesting that the bias was indeed due to their momentary mood states. The list of demonstrations that moods affect judgment in this way is long (see Forgas & Bower, 1988). Rather than review them here, however, let us turn directly to possible explanations of the effect.

In the service of parsimony, most investigators have assumed that the concepts and processes needed to explain emotional phenomena would be found within traditional cognitive psychology. For example, emotions have been treated as equivalent to semantic concepts (e.g., Bower, 1981; Isen, Shalker, Clark, & Karp, 1978). In general, spreading activation theory characterizes both abstract concepts and concrete memories as nodes in an associative network (Anderson & Bower, 1973). In this approach to cognitive processes, activation is believed to spread from one memory or concept to another along associative pathways. By observing the precise time required to go from one concept to another it has been possible to map aspects of a person's implicit cognitive structure (Posner, 1978). Spreading activation theory offers an explanation for many of the effects of emotion on recall and judgment. To make the theory applicable to affective phenomena, emotions and moods are considered to be additional nodes in a network and are assumed to share many of the properties of the concepts and memories to which they are connected. This view, which I refer to as the *priming model*, remains a powerful approach, and one that offers a compelling account of many affective phenomena.

A different explanation is offered by the feelings-as-information view (Schwarz & Clore, 1983, 1988). According to this approach, whether or not mood influences a particular judgment is governed by the degree to which the feelings occasioned by being in a mood state are seen as a reaction to the object of judgment. When one makes an affective appraisal, some affective feedback in the form of feelings and thoughts is produced that serves as input to subsequent processes. The quality of the affective experience provides information about the nature of the personal relevance of a situation. The quantity or intensity of the experience provides information about the relative importance of the situation for one's concerns. On the basis of this feedback, one makes implicit decisions regarding action, the distribution of attention (Frijda, 1986) and processing priorities (Simon, 1967). The affective feedback from this appraisal process involves cues that are not different in kind from the affective feedback characteristic of moods and emotions. In the case of moods, which are often ongoing and of low intensity, one may fail to attend to such cues until the occasion arises to make a decision or judgment. During the judgment process, as one attends to the output of the appraisal process, it is generally not possible to discriminate appraisal-produced cues from pre-existing, mood-produced cues. This, we have suggested, is one process whereby moods affect judgments and decisions.

Mood as Information

For readers not familiar with the basic data of the mood-as-information approach, I now review the studies reported by Schwarz and Clore (1983) which can be thought of as a prototype for the other studies considered: Two experiments were conducted using a misattribution paradigm. The basic procedure in each case involved inducing a happy or a sad mood and making an external plausible cause for subjects' feelings salient for some subjects but not others. The results showed that moods influenced evaluative judgments in a mood-congruent manner, but when an external plausible cause was made salient, this effect disappeared.

In the first of these experiments, moods were induced by having subjects spend 15 minutes writing a detailed description of a happy or a sad event in their recent past. A check at the end of the experiment showed that subjects who had written about a happy event were indeed in a better mood than those who had written about a sad event. After the writing task, subjects answered two questions about life satisfaction which served as the primary dependent variable. Those who were in the happy mood condition rated themselves as more satisfied with their life as a whole than did those in the sad mood condition.

In addition, the salience of a possible external cause for subjects' momentary feelings of happiness or sadness was varied. The experiment was conducted in a small and unusual sound-proof room with its own ventilation and lighting system. Before they began, half of the subjects were given reason to think that the room might make them feel tense. They were told that other subjects had reported that being in the sound-proof room made them feel tense after a period of time, a technique used previously by Fazio, Zanna, and Cooper (1977). To lend credibility to this story, subjects were asked to fill out a questionnaire about the room, the lighting, the ventilation. The results showed that making salient a plausible external cause for subjects' feelings eliminated the effect of mood on judgments, as shown in Fig. 5.1. These subjects misattributed their negative feelings to the room, and were therefore less likely to read them as an indication of how they felt about their life as a whole. The moods reported by subjects in the external attribution group did not differ from the moods reported by other subjects, but their implicit understanding of these momentary affective experiences did differ.

The results were consistent with the idea that the proximal cue for many kinds of affective judgments is the information provided by one's feelings as one considers the object of judgment. Schwarz and Clore (1983) interpreted them as support for an informational hypothesis rather than a cognitive priming hypothesis, because priming is supposed to be an automatic cognitive process. Spreading activation theory offers no reason to assume that such automatic and unconscious priming processes should depend on subjects' conscious attributions about their momentary affective experience.

The second experiment was a field replication of the first. Following research by Cunningham (1979), the weather was used as a naturalistic mood manipulation. The research was conducted on the first warm and sunny days of spring and a few days later when, as is inevitably the case in the Midwest, the weather turns cold and damp again. The life satisfaction data were collected in telephone interviews in which the same two questions were asked as in the laboratory experiment. Results showed that people were indeed in a better mood on sunny than on rainy days, and that mood affected their life satisfaction ratings just as before. In order to manipulate attributions, the caller pretended to be telephoning from a Chicago survey organization. This allowed the caller to ask at the beginning of some but not all of the calls, "By the way, how's the weather down

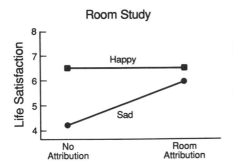

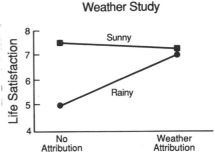

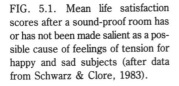

FIG. 5.1. Mean life satisfaction scores after a sound-proof room has or has not been made salient as a possible cause of feelings of tension for happy and sad subjects (after data from Schwarz & Clore, 1983).

FIG. 5.2. Mean life satisfaction scores for respondents interviewed on rainy or sunny days when weather was or was not made salient as a source of their mood states (after data from Schwarz & Clore, 1983).

there?'' It was expected that answering this question would make the weather salient as a plausible (and in this case true) cause of subjects' momentary affective feelings. As before, the results showed that the effect of mood on life satisfaction ratings was disrupted by having an external plausible cause made salient (see Fig. 5.2).

Two additional things are worthy of note in these experiments. First, in both experiments the misattribution effect occurred for negative moods only. A possible reason for this result is that the mood manipulation had been successful only in the negative and not also in the positive condition. Indeed, in the first experiment, subjects in the happy conditions did not differ in mood from subjects in a no-mood control condition. Because college students generally rate themselves as in a somewhat positive mood anyway, it may be easier to decrease than to increase their moods. In addition, mood affects processing style (Schwarz, 1990). People in happy moods are more likely to rely on heuristic strategies and less likely to be analytical. Negative moods, on the other hand, signal problems and tend to elicit analytical problem solving that may make subjects more alert to possible causes of their affect. Such a mental set should also make them more susceptible to attributional manipulations.

A second, and especially important, fact about the results is that the attribution manipulations affected subjects' life satisfaction ratings but not their moods. Responses to a mood item collected afterward showed that positive and negative mood groups still differed, and that their attributions had not affected their moods. Attributing their experience to the soundproof room or to the weather did not influence the intensity of subjects' moods, but only interpretations of their mood-based feelings. This fact is important because some alternative explanations for the results of misattribution studies (e.g., Calvert-Boyanowsky

& Leventhal, 1975) assume that attribution manipulations decrease or eliminate moods.

The results of this experiment are consistent with our emphasis on the fact that emotions involve experiential states, and these experiential states convey information. By and large, this is not the position that has been taken in the literature. The more common priming view outlined earlier is that the effects of emotion on judgment operate automatically and unconsciously, and that the person is passive in the process. Our view was inspired by Wyer and Carlston's (1979) book, in which they suggested that one way that affect might influence cognition is by serving as information to judges about their own reactions. Like the role of touch in allowing one to locate an object in a drawer without looking, affective experience allows one to navigate the interpersonal world (Ortony, 1991). Affective feelings are a readout of the computations involved in appraising events. They serve as feedback from such processes around which evaluations of associated stimuli are formed. But because we have only one window on our affective experience, the merging of appraisal-based cues and mood-based cues tends to result in bias.

Direct Versus Indirect Effects of Mood

Underlying the issue of whether mood effects are due to the priming of concepts or to the conscious experience of feelings is a more basic question. This question concerns whether mood acts directly on judgment, by being interpreted as evidence of one's reaction to the object of judgment, or only indirectly on the stored representation of the object that is then retrieved and judged.

Indirect Effects. It has long been assumed that most influences on judgment are mediated by changes in beliefs (or in the weights attached to beliefs) about the object of judgment (e.g., Anderson, 1981; Fishbein & Ajzen, 1975), or in a more cognitive account, by changes in one's interpretation of presented information (e.g., Higgins, Rholes, & Jones, 1977). During the last decade or so, social cognition research has been preoccupied with problems of how information about people is represented, stored, and retrieved (Wyer & Srull, 1984). As attention has turned toward the effects of mood and emotion on social judgment, a natural tendency has been to devise accounts that use this same framework. Thus, according to the priming model, as indicated earlier, emotions activate emotion-congruent facts or beliefs in memory (Bower, 1981; Isen, 1984). From this view, mood is believed to have its effects on the interpretation or encoding of new material (Bower, 1981) or on the retrieval of material about known objects. In either case the effects of mood are mediated by changes in either one's temporary or one's permanent representation of the object of judgment.

However, a variety of findings have cast doubt on some of these proposals. In many cases, for example, little or no relationship is evident between memory and judgment, leading to the inference that many judgments may not be based on memory (Schwarz & Clore, 1988). Also, unlike most priming effects, which generally occur when encoding new material (Srull & Wyer, 1979), mood effects are frequently found to occur at the judgment stage (Clore, Parrott, Schwarz, & Wilkin, 1990; Fiedler & Stroehm, 1986).

Direct Effects. By contrast, the feelings-as-information approach (e.g., Clore & Parrott, 1991; Schwarz & Clore, 1983, 1988), maintains that emotions affect judgment and decisions directly rather than indirectly. By *directly* I mean that emotion enters the equation at the judgment stage rather than solely at the encoding or the retrieval stages. It contributes to impressions by combining with stimulus information additively; that is, mood affects subjects' evaluations independently of their representation of the object of judgment (Schwarz, Robbins, & Clore, 1985).

As an analogy, consider how we would answer related questions about food. To answer the question, "How much do you like your lunch?" we would attend to our momentary gustatory sensations and reply accordingly. Most models of evaluative judgment imply that we would answer such questions by listing the ingredients in our lunch, accessing stored evaluations of them, and adding up the values. Or we might categorize the dish as a whole (as say, lasagna) and then look up the stored value for that. In other words, "I must like my lunch because it is lasagna, and I know I like lasagna." Such an account is quite odd, and this oddity suggests that the traditional approach is wrong or at least that its domain of application is limited. (In addition, it suggests that one might want to avoid judgment theorists as dining companions.) As an alternative view, I assume that the liking judgment includes information directly from the enjoyment of the taste of the food. A similar process presumably underlies other on-line affective appraisals. For example, if asked how much we like a person we have only recently met, we are likely to formulate an answer by bringing the person to mind and noting any overall affective reactions. Often we may not be able to say why we like them, because we may not have accessed reasons when we made our appraisal—rather, we simply read off our momentary experience.

This basic issue is in fact an old one in social psychology. In the 1970s, for example, the affective model of interpersonal attraction also assumed direct effects (Byrne & Clore, 1970; Clore, 1966; Clore & Byrne, 1974). It focused on how the affective reactions occasioned by rewards and punishments from others influenced liking and disliking. The theory, and the research surrounding it, sparked some debate on this same issue. At the time, standard judgment theory maintained that liking and other evaluative social judgments derived solely from pre-existing evaluative beliefs about the person or inferences from those beliefs (e.g., Ajzen, 1974; Fishbein & Ajzen, 1975; Kaplan & Anderson, 1973a, 1973b). These theories assumed that affect and emotion influence judgment only indirectly, by first influencing a person's beliefs about the object of judgment.

The *reinforcement-affect model of attraction*, as it was referred to, proposed instead that emotion had direct effects on judgment (e.g., Byrne, Clore, Griffitt, Lambreth, & Mitchell, 1973a, 1973b; Clore & Byrne, 1974). Indeed, to avoid an infinite regress, it was felt that some source for judges' evaluations other than prior evaluative beliefs was logically required. The local question in the similarity-attraction experiments around which the model was designed was whether being agreed with by someone affected liking for that person directly (through associated affect) or only indirectly (through belief change). The idea that the influence of affective states was not always mediated by belief change was supported by evidence that liking was affected even when affective states were due to completely irrelevant causes. These included happy and sad films (Gouaux, 1971), hot and crowded rooms (Griffitt & Veitch, 1971), and good or bad news on the radio (Veitch & Griffitt, 1976). In each case, being in a good or bad mood influenced social judgments in a mood-congruent way. Thus, the issue in this subliterature was similar to the issue in the recent mood literature—to what degree do changes of judgment necessarily reflect changes in beliefs about the object of judgment? Because the intervening years have seen increased attention to questions about how social information is represented, this issue has even greater relevance to contemporary social cognition research than it did to the impression formation and interpersonal attraction research of that period.

A question that arises concerns the relation between information from one's momentary affective reactions and information from the retrieval of previously stored values. Are these two kinds of information comparable; are they integrated into the same mental equation? Schwarz and Clore (1988) have characterized mood effects as the result of a heuristic process, suggesting that one either bases one's judgment on beliefs about the object or uses the *how-do-I-feel-about-it* heuristic. However, many judgments may involve a two-stage process in which both are involved. One may first retrieve or compute an evaluation by integrating the values of one's beliefs about the object (as in traditional judgment theory), and then appraise how one feels about that tentatively evaluated object (the feelings-as-information heuristic). Even if one has a clear opinion, one must often make a further evaluation to answer the question posed—"I know I like the person, but on a 10-point scale, how much do I like him?"

NON-EMOTIONAL FEELINGS AND JUDGMENT

Some of the clearest examples of the role of feelings in judgment involve the influence of affective feelings on evaluative judgments. I argue, however, that the same kinds of feedback processes govern the role of nonaffective feelings in nonevaluative judgments. I take *affect* to refer to something *valenced*, that is, something that is positive or negative, and I take *affective appraisal*, to be an appraisal of some event, action, or object with respect to one's own goals, standards, or attitudes (Ortony, Clore, & Collins, 1988). The term *feelings* is often assumed to refer to affective feelings, but this need not be the case. Many of the most common feelings are not affective. For example, when we say we feel hungry, tired, or dizzy, we are not referring to emotions but to bodily feelings. Such feelings also provide information that affects judgment and decision making, but the information concerns the state of one's body rather than the state of one's goals, standards, and attitudes. Similarly, when we say we feel certain, confused, or surprised, these are not assertions primarily about the state of our goals, or the state of our body, but about our state of knowledge. Saying that these are not affective does not mean that they cannot be the cause of affective or emotional reactions. We may find it distressing that we are tired, happy that we are certain about something, or frustrated that we are confused, but being tired or certain or confused are not themselves emotional feelings (Clore, Ortony, & Foss, 1987).

I now attempt to show that these nonaffective cognitive experiences or feelings also affect judgment and decision making, and that when they do, they obey the same principles that guide decisions based on affective feelings. In the studies to be discussed, some momentary cognitive experience is induced, some attributional variable is generally manipulated, and some judgment is made. Depending on the attributional manipulation, all produce some form of assimilation or contrast effects in a predictable way. The content of each of these factors varies widely, and with them the nature of the implications for different judgment domains. Few of the authors would, a priori, have grouped their study with the others. Their similarity lies in the fact that some aspect of a person's phenomenal experience of thinking is used as data for making a judgment in each study, and, I argue, each involves a common set of processes. To make clearer the similarity, the following summary information is given for each of the major studies: (a) the momentary experience studied, (b) the method of inducing the experience, (c) the kind of judgment, (d) the method of manipulating attributions, if any, and (e) the results.

Uncertainty and Understanding

If "cognitive feelings" refer to feelings about knowing, one of the most prototypical cognitive feelings is the experience of understanding something. Exactly how such feelings are produced is unclear, but the feeling or sense that one does or does not understand something is presumably familiar to everyone. Moreover, using this self-produced information for decision-making is common. Such cues are often the basis for deciding to ask a question, deciding to read something a second time, and so on. To study such experiences, Clore and

Parrott (1990) attempted to induce feelings of uncertainty in order to determine whether these feelings play a role in judgments of knowing analogous to the role played by affective feelings in judgments of liking.

Clore and Parrott (1990) administered a standard group test of hypnotic susceptibility to a large audience as part of a hypnosis demonstration. During the hypnosis, subjects were given a guided fantasy designed to induce feelings of uncertainty and confusion. The feelings were induced by having subjects imagine being in a confusing lecture on computer programming. Most people in an unselected group are not particularly hypnotizable, and these nonhypnotizable subjects were therefore available as a control group. As expected, the highly hypnotizable subjects reported feeling more uncertain and confused than the low hypnotizable, control subjects. For half of the subjects in both groups, hypnosis was made salient as the cause of their feelings after they awoke. For the other half no explanation for the feelings was made salient. High versus low hypnotizability was crossed in a 2 × 2 design with instructions making the cause of feelings of uncertainty either salient or not. Subjects were then given a short poem by Rudyard Kipling. They were asked to read it and rate how well they felt they understood it and how well they could explain what the author had in mind. The results in Fig. 5.3 show that the low hypnotizable subjects, who did not feel particularly uncertain, thought that they understood the poem reasonably well. Highly hypnotizable subjects did report experiencing feelings of uncertainty. Among these, the subjects for whom hypnosis was made salient as a cause for their feelings also thought they understood the poem reasonably well. But as predicted, highly hypnotizable subjects whose feelings of uncertainty remained unexplained were significantly less sure that they had understood the poem.

Clore and Parrott (1990)
Experience: Feeling of uncertainty
Induction: Guided fantasy in hypnotized subjects
Judgment: Degree to which they felt they understood a poem
Attribution manipulation: Reminding subjects of hypnotic suggestion or not
Results: Subjects attributing their feelings of uncertainty to an external cause (hypnotic suggestion) felt they understood the poem, but subjects experiencing the same feelings without such an explanation did not.

In a second experiment the effect was replicated with a different fantasy and in a different setting. The fantasy used in the replication was about feelings of uncertainty experienced when trying to decide between two equally attractive apartments to rent. The results were the same, showing that feelings of uncertainty that do not involve confusion have the same effect.

As in the emotional mood experiments, these cognitive feelings appear to

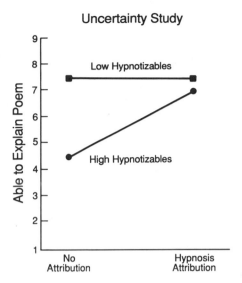

FIG. 5.3. Mean self-ratings of their understanding of a peom made by high and low hypnotizable subjects after a fantasy inducing them to feel uncertain (after data from Clore & Parrott, 1990).

inform the experiencer about his own state. In this case the feelings were metacognitive feelings, and the state was the subject's state of knowledge. The results suggest that one of the proximal cues for deciding how well one understands something is the presence of feelings of uncertainty or confusion.

The Availability Heuristic

Psychologists have generally approached the study of decision making as a search for the algorithm that people use to weight and combine the available information. An exception to this trend was Kahneman and Tversky's (1973) work on heuristics. What was innovative and exciting about the idea of heuristics was that Kahneman and Tversky looked for an explanation of various judgmental effects in a place that no theorist focusing on normative variables would ever have looked: They focused on the phenomenology rather than the content of cognition. They suggested that people attend to the experience of thinking itself—for example, to the ease with which an idea comes to mind. In the case of the availability heuristic people's likelihood estimates for certain events were inflated by manipulating the readiness with which relevant examples occurred to them. When one finds it easy to imagine a given scenario or to retrieve from memory a given example, one is likely to judge it as more probable or more frequent than events that are less easy to imagine.

Despite the volume of research stimulated by the heuristic notion, psychologists have by and large failed to pick up on the most revolutionary aspect of the conceptualization—the notion that an important input to judgment and decision making is the information provided by the momentary experience of aspects of one's own cognitive processes. Such a heuristic is subject to error, however, because one is generally unable to say whether the experience of ease resulted from the frequency of the event or from an irrelevant property of the event that made it salient. Like the other examples I cite, the subjective experience involved is subject to misattribution, as can be seen by considering an experiment reported by Schwarz, Bless, Strack, Klumpp, Rittenauer-Schatka, and Simons (1991).

Subjects participated in an experiment on autobiographical memory. They were asked either to recall situations in which they had behaved assertively and felt at ease or to recall situations in which they behaved unassertively and felt insecure. In each of these conditions, half were instructed to recall 6 examples and half to recall 12 examples. Afterward, subjects made a series of ratings purportedly to explore their interest in an assertion-training program. They were also asked to evaluate their assertiveness, feelings of security, and feelings of anxiety. Together these served as a measure of assertiveness.

The results showed a significant interaction between the number of examples requested (6 vs. 12) and the content of recall (assertive vs. unassertive). Subjects who had described 6 examples of assertive behavior rated themselves as more assertive than those describing 12 examples (and vice versa for recalling examples of unassertiveness). This was the case even though subjects in the 12-example condition came up with more examples. One explanation is that subjects were attending, not to the number of examples they thought of, but to the ease with which examples of a certain kind came to mind. The authors considered the possibility that the results might simply reflect a tendency for subjects required to think of more examples to come up with poorer ones, but ratings of the last few examples given in each case showed no difference in the quality of examples in the 12-example as opposed to the 6-example condition.

Schwarz, Bless, Strack, Klumpp, Rittenauer-Schatka, and Simons (1991)

Experience: Ease of retrieval
Induction: Asked to recall either 6 or 12 examples of assertive (or unassertive) behavior
Judgment: Own assertiveness
Attribution manipulation: Music was played that was said to facilitate memories of being insecure or memories of being assertive.
Results: Assertiveness judgments depended on the ease of retrieval (6-example condition) rather than the number of examples recalled (12-example condition). The effect was eliminated when subjects misattributed the experience of ease to an external source (music).

In an additional experiment, the same basic procedure was used but the apparent diagnosticity of the ease or difficulty was varied. This was done by having subjects listen to "meditation music" over headphones as they completed the recall task. In half of the cases, subjects were told that the music was known to facilitate the recall of autobiographical memories either concerned with assertiveness or concerned with insecurity. In conditions where the music was believed to facilitate the kind of recall requested, the experienced ease of retrieval would have been seen as nondiagnostic of one's true assertiveness, whereas in conditions where the music was believed to facilitate the opposite kind of recall, experienced ease would have been diagnostic.

The results of this manipulation showed that the effect of experienced feelings on judgment depend on their apparent informativeness. A significant three-way interaction showed the action of the availability heuristic in the high diagnostic condition, but not in the low diagnostic condition. Indeed, in the low diagnostic condition, the reverse was found. That is, when diagnostic, subjects used the experience of the ease of bringing relevant examples to mind as information about their own assertiveness. But when their feelings were assumed to be nondiagnostic, subjects attended to the number of examples retrieved rather than to the experience of ease.

Familiarity and Fame

A prime example of the processes I have in mind can be seen in the experiments on perceived famousness by Jacoby and his collaborators. In one particular study (Jacoby, Kelley, Brown, & Jasechko, 1989), a list of nonfamous names was presented for subjects to read. They were informed that all of the names were nonfamous, and that the study concerned the factors that influence the pronunciation of names. In a second part, the names were presented again along with some new nonfamous names and some famous names. The task was to indicate which were in fact famous. The famous names were only moderately well known, ones that undergraduates would be likely to recognize as famous without necessarily being able to recall why—Helmut Schmidt, Marsha Mason, Anne Hathaway, Arthur Rubinstein, Thomas Hobbes, and so forth. The list of comparable nonfamous names included such names as Sandra Brophy, Adrian Marr, Sebastian Weisdorf, Joseph Parcenti, and Larry Jacoby.

The results showed that when nonfamous names were familiar, they were sometimes assumed to be famous. A comparison was made between judgments of old and new nonfamous names made immediately or delayed to the next day. Compared to the immediate condition, judgments after a delay showed a small but significant familiarity effect: Nonfamous names that had appeared in the initial list were more likely to be judged famous than nonfamous names that had not been presented.

It is noteworthy that the effect occurred only in the delayed condition. Subjects had been told at the time that the names on the first list were nonfamous. If they recognized a name as having been presented earlier, therefore, they knew it was not famous. Because this true source of familiarity was relatively more salient in the immediate condition, the same effect was not seen there. A test of reaction times showed parallel effects. Subjects were slower to decide about the famousness of old nonfamous names than new nonfamous names on the delayed test. With time, the source of the feelings of familiarity apparently became harder to identify.

Jacoby, Kelley, Brown, and Jasechko (1989)

Experience: Feelings of familiarity
Induction: Having subjects read names as part of a separate study of name pronunciation
Judgment: Whether or not names were famous
Attribution manipulation: Judgments made either immediately after or a day after initial name presentation
Results: When the prior presentation of nonfamous names was not salient (delay condition), familiar names were more often judged famous than when the prior presentation was salient (immediate condition).

Consistent with the approach taken here, Jacoby et al. interpreted the results as indicating that participants made famousness judgments on the basis of feelings of familiarity in response to the names they had previously seen. They also had a similar view of the key role of attribution. The effect requires that subjects assumed their experience of familiarity to have been caused by the famousness of the names rather than by their prior presentation in the experiment. Knowing why the names seemed familiar would not have made them seem any less familiar, of course, but it would have changed the diagnostic value of the experience for judging fame.

This kind of experiment works because the experience of familiarity is the proximal cue for identifying both previously presented names and famous names. If, instead of identifying which were famous, subjects had been asked which names they had seen the day before, some of the famous names would presumably have been falsely identified as nonfamous names that had been previously seen. The effect depends only on the presence of cues that are relevant to the judgment goal and that are not attributed to an irrelevant source.

There are other examples of this same set of processes that I do not discuss in detail. One particularly nice example cited by Jacoby (1988) showed that prior presentation of a statement of trivia resulted in increased judgments of its truth (Begg, Armour, & Kerr, 1985). These results suggest that one of the cues we use to judge whether something is true is whether or not it is familiar. It is often observed that if one tells a lie often enough, people begin to believe it.

Distraction and Boredom

A somewhat different example of this process can be seen in a recent study by Damrad-Frye and Laird (1989). Subjects made a series of self-ratings after listening to a tape-recorded presentation of a *Psychology Today* article. As they listened, distracting sounds came from the next room from which a television soap opera could be overheard. Of primary interest were subjects' ratings of how bored they were. The noise from the next room was loud in one condition, only moderately loud in another, and absent in a third. When present, the noise tended to distract subjects' attention from the tape. When subjects in the loud condition were asked why their minds wandered, they correctly identified the external stimulus as the source of their distraction. In the moderately loud condition, subjects were equally distracted, but the source of their distraction was less salient. As a result, they perceived the tape to be boring. Damrad-Frye and Laird's interpretation is quite compatible with the present view. They concluded that:

> When subjects were distracted by an outside noise but did not recognize the role of that noise, they reported feeling bored and did not enjoy the task. Apparently then, their feeling of boredom came from the recognition that they were not attending to what they should have been. Lacking any other explanation for their inattention, they had no alternative except to believe that they were bored with the material. (p. 319)

Damrad-Frye and Laird, 1989
  Experience: Distraction, inability to pay attention
  Induction: Soap opera playing on TV in next room
  Judgment: How bored while listening to taped lecture
  Attribution manipulation: Varying silence of true cause of distraction, barely
                                audible TV versus loud TV
  Results: Experience of being unable to attend led to self-perception of boredom, but making the external cause of the distraction more salient (loud TV) eliminated the effect.

The authors placed their study in the context of self-perception theory (Bem, 1972), and they discussed the implications of the theory for understanding emotion (and other nonemotional experiences such as boredom). According to self-perception theory, "Emotional feelings are presumed to arise from emotional actions rather than the reverse" (Damrad-Frye & Laird, 1989, p. 315). Although this view has generated interesting research, it mistakenly assumes that because the emotion cycle can be activated by expression, that expression is therefore the seat of emotion. In fact, emotion can be triggered by entering the system at any of a number of places. This fact indicates only that the components of the emotion system are richly intertwined and influence each other, not that behavior or expression is more basic than, say, thought or feeling.

Self-perception theory may be too committed to a behavioral view to yield a successful general account of emotion. A cardinal principle of the theory is that the subjective experience of emotion depends on the same cues that outside observers might use. Such a starting point requires us to assume that facial and behavioral expressions are essential to emotional experience. In contrast, the mood-as-information hypothesis (Schwarz & Clore, 1983, 1988) simply stresses the informative properties or the feedback functions of momentary subjective experience, regardless of whether the experience is of one's behavior, thoughts, or feelings.

Expectations

Another set of phenomena susceptible to the same analysis are expectation effects. A strong expectation that a particular event may occur shares many of the properties with an actual occurrence of the event. Indeed, to be in a state of expectation regarding a particular experience (as opposed to simply holding the belief that a particular experience is possible) may sometimes involve simulating some level of the experience itself. A related point was made by Neisser (1976) with regard to the relationship between perceptual and imaginal experience: "I believe the experience of having an image is just the inner aspect of a readiness to perceive the imagined object" (p. 130). As Neisser pointed out, imagining is not normally confused with perceiving in the moment, because the latter involves the continual pick-up of new information. When retrieved at a later time, however, the imaginal and perceptual experience of a situation might be more difficult to separate. Indeed the neuropsychological evidence indicates that an imagined image of a particular scene involves the same circuitry as a perceived image of the same scene (Farah, 1989).

An analogous state of affairs may exist for expectation. It may sometimes be difficult to disentangle the cognitive content left from prior experience and the cognitive content left from prior expectation unless the two are well marked in memory. Indeed, whether prior expectation leads to contrast or assimilation effects in judgment might be controlled by whether or not subjects verbalize their expectations before they have the experience itself. Labeling the expectations, rating their strength, or otherwise isolating expectations mentally should create contrast effects when experience does not match expectations. But if such mental segmentation is not encouraged by the procedures, one might expect assimilation effects in which judgments tend to conform to expectations. This was the case in a series of studies undertaken by Wilson and his colleagues.

Wilson, Lisle, Kraft, and Wetzel (1989) had subjects judge cartoons that they either expected to be funny or about which they had no expectation. From the perspective of the analysis outlined here, it seems likely that expectation-based cues would mingle with perception-based cues in subjects' experience, and such intermingling of cues would produce expectation effects. The results showed that funniness ratings were indeed affected by expectations for some cartoons. Specifically, expectations influenced ratings of cartoons that were not very funny, but did not do so for truly funny cartoons. Reactions were not affected for truly funny cartoons presumably because the expectation-based cues were redundant with perception-based cues. And reactions were affected for less funny cartoons presumably because the combination of expectation-based cues of funniness and perception-based cues were funnier than perception-based cues of unfunniness alone.

Wilson, Lisle, Kraft, and Wetzel (1989)

Experience: Expectation that cartoons would (or would not) be funny
Induction: False information about reactions of previous subjects
Judgment: Funniness ratings of cartoons
Attribution manipulation: None
Results: Judgments were expectation-congruent, and expectation-congruent judgments were faster and accompanied by more (or less) facial mirth.

In this study, however, expectation appeared to induce an experiential change rather than merely a rating bias. Evidence for this comes from the fact that for the three cartoons that were not very funny, subjects not only rated them as funnier but showed more facial mirth when they expected them to be funny than when they had no expectations. This is of some interest given Neisser's argument, cited previously, that imagination is unlikely to be confused with perception because of the continual pick-up of information in perception. In this situation, however, it appears that expectation can be confused with on-line experience. This is presumably due to the peculiar nature of humor. The action in humor occurs all at once when the elements of a joke come together in the punch line (or analogously in the moment of comprehension of a cartoon). Unlike Neisser's example of visual perception, humor does not involve a continual pick-up of information, but only a single moment at which expectation and experience come together to create a single experience.

Well-known comedians presumably enjoy similar expectation-driven effects. In many cases, the audience may begin to smile and even to laugh before the comedian actually says anything. There is no way to correct for our expectations because we generally do not focus on having an expectation as a separable event. Under conditions in which one is led to isolate one's expectations or specify them with precision, a contrast effect may occur when expectations and experience do not match. However, no contrast effects were found in the studies by Wilson et al. (1989).

Feelings of Knowing

What have been referred to as *cognitive feelings* (Clore & Parrott, 1991) have not been a common topic of psychological inquiry, perhaps because they so rarely occur apart from the mental content that elicits them. There are also times, however, when such feelings do occur without relevant mental content, as in the tip-of-the-tongue phenomenon or in feelings of knowing. Some relevant work has been done by developmental psychologists interested in metamemory and in reading. In these areas one can encounter studies of such topics as *the illusion of knowing* (Glenberg, Wilkinson, & Epstein, 1982), *subjective certainty* (DeLoache & Brown, 1984), *realizing that you don't know* (Markman, 1977), and *feeling of knowing experiences* (Wellman, 1977). For example, Harris, Kruithof, Meerum Terwogt, and Visser (1981) studied the reactions of 8- and 11-year-old readers to anomalous sentences in a brief story. Only the older group was able to pick out the anomalous line as not fitting the story, but both groups read the anomalous sentences more slowly. The authors interpreted their results as an indication that at both ages children generate internal signals of comprehension failure, but that the older children tend to have learned better how to use such signals as information to locate the source of their comprehension difficulty.

Where Harris, and others, have tended to use the more neutral term *internal signals*, I have used the term *feelings*. In part, this is because my goal is to study the similarity between such signals and affective feelings. I propose that the important function of cognitive and bodily feelings, as well as affective feelings, is precisely their signal or information value. We cannot claim, however, that the nature and source of cognitive feelings is at all clear. Most of us have had the experience of holding steadfastly to a position in an argument because we felt certain, and also perhaps, with the emergence of new information or a different perspective, of having the feeling of certainty fade along with our persistence. Perhaps finding a match between the content of one's working hypothesis and the momentary content of memory produces a distinctive feeling, a sort of low level "Ah-ha" experience. In any case, we usually experience cognitive feelings in conjunction with focal cognitions about things that are familiar, surprising, confusing, or obvious.

The feeling-of-knowing experience is a good example of cognitive feelings. Cognitive feelings refer to the feedback from one's own cognitive processes, feedback that informs experiencers about their own state of knowledge. A paradigm for studying this experience, first developed by Hart (1965), can be seen in a study by Nelson, Leonesio, Landwehr, and Narens (1986). They asked subjects to try to answer a variety of general knowledge questions, such as, "What is the capital of Chile?" and "What was the name of Tarzan's girlfriend?" When subjects failed to answer correctly a preset number of times, say 12, these items were then re-presented in pairs on a computer screen. Subjects indicated for which question of each pair they experienced greater feelings of knowing.

Subsequently, the items reappeared in a recognition test to assess the accuracy of the feeling of knowing.

The basic validity of feeling of knowing experiences has been demonstrated in many studies. In this one, the authors compared the relative validity of each individual's feelings with two other criteria—the base rate item difficulty (normative probabilities of correct recall) and normative feelings of knowing. An individual's feeling of knowing was shown to accurately predict which items subjects would in fact be able to recognize later. These predictions were not as good as those provided by a knowledge of item difficulty (the base rates of correct recalls), but they were more accurate than simply averaging the feeling of knowing of the group. That is, subjects do have access to idiosyncratic experiential knowledge about what they know.

Nelson, Leonesio, Landwehr, and Narens (1986)

Experience: Feeling of knowing
Induction: Posing general knowledge questions that subjects could not answer but for which they could recognize answers
Judgment: Ability to recognize correct answer
Attribution manipulation: None
Results: Individual feelings of knowing did predict later recognition performance.

From a system design point of view, it would seem like a useful feature for the individual to have access to whether or not something is in memory without actually having to retrieve it. Without such access, memory searches might be quite inefficient. Of course, we can know with high likelihood that we do not know certain kinds of information simply because it is not the sort of thing we would know. But for questions in domains of possible knowledge, the feeling and its absence serves as a signal for whether to keep searching or whether to abort the search. By such a process valuable processing time can be saved and endless, unproductive searches avoided. The basis of such experiences may include partial retrieval of the information sought. Yaniv and Meyer (1987) suggested that such experiences may function to keep a problem in one's mental cue until the missing parts are retrieved.

The Nelson et al. (1986) study differed from those discussed above in that there was no attempt to influence subjects' interpretations of their feelings through misattribution manipulations, but it seems likely that such procedures would be successful.

PRIMED THOUGHTS AND JUDGMENT

I have discussed the role of feelings in judgment and have focused on the curious process whereby we are often in the position of being informed about our appraisal of a situation by our feelings. Evidence was presented in the first section to show this process with respect to affective appraisals (appraisals of value). The process was seen to generalize in the second section to cognitive appraisals (appraisals of knowledge). In this section, three experiments are presented to suggest that similar processes are at work when the output of the appraisal process is in the form of thoughts rather than feelings. In such situations also, we have little access to our appraisal processes except through our awareness of the output in the form of the concepts that come to mind. The emergent nature of the output is more obvious in the case of feelings, but the processes involved turn out to be very similar.

Ortony, Clore, and Collins (1988) recently sketched one view of the process of affective appraisal, outlining the kinds of computations that may be involved when goals, standards, and attitudes eventuate in affective reactions. The products of these unconscious mental computations are sometimes thoughts and sometimes feelings, and sometimes it is difficult to distinguish the two (Parrott, 1988). I argue that the relevance of emergent thoughts and feelings to one's ongoing judgments is often established on strictly circumstantial evidence. Like intuitions, our thoughts and feelings often appear as from nowhere. The circumstantial evidence that links them to objects in the world is usually simply the fact that they occur in the right place and at the right time to be implicated in a judgment. So when asked, "Do you like Mary?" one may base an answer on how one feels when considering Mary or on what concepts come to mind, or both. Prior moods or primed concepts can both contaminate judgment because, in the main, one has access only to the results of appraisals rather than to the process itself. If they occur at the same time, one may have no way of separating the feelings and thoughts of appraisals from the feelings of mood and the thoughts stimulated by priming manipulations.

The heuristics involved in studies of feeling and in studies of primed thoughts are similar. In studies of mood, for example, the heuristic is, essentially, *If I experience positive feelings when I consider Mary, then my attitude to Mary must be positive.* In studies of primed concepts, the heuristic is, *If I experience positive thoughts when I consider Mary, then my attitude to Mary must be positive.* When subjects are searching for a concept and a primed concept comes to mind at just the right moment, the experience that it represents one's reaction to the object of judgment is compelling. The apparent causal connection is no less compelling than the connection between the motion of one billiard ball and the motion of another that it hits. Indeed, in priming studies, the experimenter has to make the irrelevant source of the primed concept especially salient to prevent subjects from experiencing the appearance of the concept as a reaction to the object of judgment.

The studies to be described next are ones in which concepts are primed and are shown to have the potential to influence judgment. The primed thoughts are not feelings. The link between the studies of feelings and these studies of primed concepts is the emergent nature of the experiences of having a particular feeling or thought, the information value of these experiences, and the pivotal role played by subjects' attributions about them.

Subtle Priming and Reminding

The priming process has been the cornerstone of research in social cognition for the past decade or more. The procedure appears to offer a tool whereby investigators can map unconscious cognitive structure. Innumerable studies have been done in which primed concepts have been shown to influence recall and judgment. And in the domain of affect, priming is the primary alternative to the informational view as an explanation of mood effects. But the results of some recent studies suggest that priming, too, is mediated by the same experiential and attributional processes. Merely activating a concept is not sufficient for insuring that judgment and recall will be influenced in the direction of a primed concept. Priming requires subtlety. The priming words are sometimes presented subliminally (Bargh & Pietromonaco, 1982), sometimes as background stimuli in a Stroop task (Higgins, Rholes, & Jones, 1977), and are sometimes embedded in irrelevant tasks (Srull & Wyer, 1979). When activated in a blatant way, judgments are either unaffected by the prime or show the opposite (i.e., contrast) effects. Such results force one to the conclusion that priming effects depend on subjects' tacit assumptions about why particular thoughts have so readily come to mind (Clore, 1988; Clore & Parrott, 1991). It turns out, therefore, that priming research provides eloquent testimony to the importance of experiential processes. Explicit tests of the hypothesis that the use of particular mental content depends on how one punctuates one's experience comes from three interesting priming studies.

In a study by Strack, Schwarz, Bless, Kubler, and Wanke (1990), tones were preceded or followed by a word, and subjects were to indicate whether the tone was high or low and to write down the word that preceded the tone. Four of the 10 words were synonyms either of *friendly/helpful* (positive prime) or of *dishonorable* (negative prime). This was followed by a distractor task in which subjects had to circle two-digit numbers that were divisible by 7. Half of the subjects then answered questions that reminded them of the first task. The dependent variables were evaluative judgments about an ambiguous target person who was described as having helped a friend by supplying him with answers for an exam. The behavior of the character was evaluatively ambiguous, because it could be seen both as helpful and as dishonest. The usual priming effect was found when the source of their primed mental content was not obvious. But when subjects were reminded of the priming episode, the opposite was found. Consistent with our logic, whether assimilation or contrast effects occurred depended on how salient it was to subjects that the concepts that had come to mind were from the priming task rather than from their reaction to the person they had just read about.

> **Strack, Schwarz, Bless, Kubler, and Wanke (1990)**
>
> **Experience:** Salience of certain words
> **Induction:** Incidental priming
> **Judgment:** Liking for person described ambiguously
> **Attribution manipulation:** Reminded of priming by rating aspects of the
>   priming task
> **Results:** Contrast when reminded, congruence when not reminded.

Strack et al. suggested that a two-stage model of priming is needed. They argued that theorists need to go beyond the determinants of activation; they also need to consider the factors that govern the use of activated information. Relevant data also come from studies by Martin (1986) and Lombardi, Higgins, and Bargh (1987), and from a study by Martin, Seta, and Crelia (1990), which is examined next.

Blatant Priming and Distraction

Martin, Seta, and Crelia (1990) conducted an experiment in which positive or negative concepts were blatantly primed, after which subjects were asked to rate an ambiguous paragraph (the Donald paragraph from Higgins, Rholes, & Jones, 1977). Because of the obviousness of the priming manipulation, subjects generally showed contrast effects in their judgments. That is, the ambiguous character was rated more positively after negative concepts were primed and more negatively after positive concepts were primed. But some subjects were distracted as they formed their impression by a secondary task in which they had to keep track mentally of the number of digits presented in a tape recording. This distraction kept the true source of their primed thoughts from being salient. Hence, the presence of positive thoughts in consciousness as they considered the character led subjects to like him, and the presence of negative thoughts led them to dislike him. But for conditions without the distracting secondary task, the external source of the passing thoughts was more salient. Under these conditions, the positive or negative thoughts were attributed to the priming task and therefore were not used as data for subjects' judgment about the character.

> **Martin, Seta, and Crelia (1990)**
>
> **Experience:** Salience of positive or negative concepts
> **Induction:** Blatant priming; having subjects paraphrase positive and negative
>   self-referent (Velton) statements
> **Judgment:** Liking for person described ambiguously
> **Attribution manipulation:** Presence or absence of secondary task
> **Results:** With a secondary task, mood congruence was found; without a sec-
>   ondary task, contrast effects were found (because subjects could focus
>   on the blatantness of the prime).

There are now a number of studies by Martin and others in which varying the obviousness versus the nonobviousness of priming manipulations yielded similar results. The consistency of results shows that there is nothing automatic about the effects on judgment of priming manipulations. One interpretation of these effects is that the key to the use of the momentary contents of consciousness in judgment lies in perceptions of the causal belongingness of the information to the task at hand. When one experiences relevant mental content as one is posing the judgment question, one is likely to use the information. Whether one uses it or discounts it depends on one's perception of its source. If no disqualifying information is encountered, it is likely to be taken by default as the answer. If, for example, one is asked the capital of Virginia and finds the word *Madison* in consciousness, one might assume Madison to be the capital. But if it were salient that one had just been introduced to someone named *Madison,* then one would be likely to discount that information and search further.

Anchoring and Salience

An elegantly simple demonstration of this same process was reported by Kubovy (1977), in a study in which he asked subjects to generate a random number. By varying the exact wording of the instruction, he was able to both implant a suggested number and vary the degree to which his suggestion of a particular number was obvious. For example, when asked to "name the first digit that comes to mind," about 2% of the subjects came up with the number 1, but when asked to "name the first *one* digit that comes to mind," 18% chose the number 1. When made subtly salient in consciousness in this way, the number 1 was quite frequently chosen by subjects. But when the number was made still more salient by telling subjects to "name the first one digit that comes to mind, like one," this process was reversed. With this more blatant suggestion, only about 5% gave 1 as a response.

Kubovy (1977)

> **Experience:** Encountering a certain number in consciousness
> **Induction:** Mentioning a number in the instructions to the task
> **Task:** Choosing a random number
> **Attribution manipulation:** Varying the obviousness with which the number is suggested
> **Results:** Suggested number was chosen more frequently when it was salient in consciousness, but less frequently when the external source of its salience was obvious.

Kubovy proposed a two-step model that is quite compatible with the logic of feelings-and-cognitive-experience-as-information model. He suggested that one first retrieves an answer to the question posed and then checks on the appropriateness or representativeness of the answer. When it is relatively clear that the source of the number was the suggestion of the experimenter, then the number is rejected by most subjects because it is not, therefore, a good example of a random number. Here again, the use of cognitive content that one finds in working memory depends on one's attributions about its source.

Switzer and Sniezek (1991) applied this same technique in a study of anchoring and adjustment effects. They showed that a completely irrelevant number that is made salient can influence how subjects set performance goals. They had subjects work on a computer to unscramble and make sense of scrambled sentences that had been mixed together from two completely different passages. In addition to performing this task, subjects were to indicate how many they expected to be able to solve. They found that subjects' expectations were influenced by whatever numbers were floating around in their heads, regardless of the numbers' relevance. Sometimes the number referred to the previous subjects' performance, but other times it was simply the number of the experiment that had been mentioned. When making such a judgment, subjects pose the question to themselves and attempt to generate a number with which to answer it. If a number is already present in working memory, it is likely to be used unless it is either explicitly tagged as referring to something irrelevant or is in some more subtle way perceptually grouped with distinctively different events.

PUNCTUATING MENTAL EXPERIENCE

This chapter has focused on judgment bias, but that emphasis merely reflects the fact that studying bias is a convenient research strategy. The overall goal is to understand how human social judgment ordinarily works so well. The research discussed suggests that experiential factors play a larger and more direct role in these judgments than has previously been realized, and, importantly, that this is an adaptive arrangement. Although the practice of basing judgments on momentary feelings and passing thoughts sometimes leads to suboptimal outcomes, the main lesson from the evidence is not so much that such feelings and intuitions lead us astray, but that they are utterly basic to whatever it is that we mean by human judgment.

The guiding criterion for whether or not particular thoughts or feelings will be integrated into a judgment concerns their apparent appropriateness. The authors of the chapters in this book agree on this point, referring variously to the critical variable as *appropriateness* (Martin et al., 1990), *relevance* (Schwarz, this volume), or *representativeness* (Strack, this volume). But at a more fundamental level, what underlies appropriateness, relevance, and representativeness is how people parse the moment to moment flow of their experience. In a study by Martin (1986), for example, simply varying whether subjects perceived that they had finished the priming task or not determined the results. The key to the results was whether subjects mentally punctuated the experience or let it run on into the next experience. Keeping in mind the gestalt principles of Heider (1958) on which attribution theory is based, what one needs to know to predict judgment is the perceptual grouping of relevant experiences. Indeed, appropriateness, relevance, and representativeness in this context simply refer to the degree to which a perceiver tacitly sees one cognitive feedback experience as grouped with or as belonging to another experience—the experience of the object to be judged. That grouping can be based on an explicit causal attribution or on any of a variety of more passive processes that also result in the separation or lumping of two experiences.

Some years ago, we conducted a series of studies concerned with order effects in impression judgments (e.g., Clore, Wiggins, & Itkin, 1975; Stapert & Clore, 1969). Of interest in these studies was whether impressions formed on the basis of positive information would be more positive (assimilation) or less positive (contrast) when preceded by negative information. The key to finding assimilation or contrast effects in such studies turned out to depend on whether subjects segmented the information string into one or two parts. Contrast effects occur when the two parts are separated by preliminary judgments made in the middle of the sequence, and assimilation effects occur when no intervening judgments are made. Interestingly, it is not necessary for subjects actually to make intervening judgments; merely thinking about making them is enough (Byrne, Lambreth, Palmer, & London, 1969). What is important is the segmentation of the judge's own experience. The same principle appears to govern the occurrence of assimilation and contrast effects in mood research and priming research. Making attributions about the source of our affective experience, as in the Schwarz and Clore studies, is simply one way of governing how subjects organize their experience.

In the above research, segmentation was influenced by the salience of certain factors and the timing of questions. It can also be based on qualitative differences among feelings. Gallagher and Clore (1985), for example, showed that pre-existing feelings of anger sometimes bias blame judgments, but not risk estimates. Similarly, fear can bias risk estimates but not blame judgments. In these cases, experiential data and judgmental requirements were grouped qualitatively. Just as one would not look in the refrigerator for one's car keys, one would not focus on hunger cues to assess blame. Having said that, however, one can immediately think of cases where tired and hungry children (or adults) do show a greater propensity for reacting with anger and blame. It seems likely, however, that in such cases they are not actually focusing on these bodily hunger cues but on affective ones. Presumably, when one runs out of energy to cope with the demands of civilized social interaction, even the smallest obstacle can cause a sizeable frustration reaction. When the tired and hungry father screams at his child for spilling her milk, his appraisal of blame is not based on feelings of tiredness or hunger directly, but on feelings of frustration caused by a momentary lack of coping resources. Unlike feelings of hunger, feelings of frustration, of course, are often a completely appropriate element in judgments of blame. Although the father might reasonably be expected to be able to differentiate his experience of hunger and tiredness from his frustration of the child's accident, he would have much more difficulty distinguishing his experience of frustration at things in general from his frustration with this incident, hence such unseemly punitiveness is very common.

I have emphasized the role of attribution and the punctuation of one's momentary experience as the gate that controls the effect of emotion on judgment. A different view was taken by Allen, Kenrick, Linder, and McCall (1989). They studied the effect of irrelevant arousal on men's reaction to an attractive woman. The arousal was induced in some cases by exercise and in some cases by threat of electric shock. They found that aroused men were more sexually attracted to the woman regardless of whether the true source of the arousal was made salient, a finding that argues against the misattribution explanation. However, what is required for attributional discounting is for subjects to see the explanation offered as adequate to account for their experience. It seems likely that subjects had a different implicit theory about their experience of sexual attraction than the investigators. Explanations of fear- or exercise-induced arousal probably seemed relevant to subjects' experience of sexual attraction. What might have been required is an alternative explanation of their experience of sexual attraction rather than of their experience of arousal.

CONSTRUCTIVISM

What unites research on momentary feelings and thoughts and research on the variety of other influences on judgment covered in this volume is that they argue for a constructivist view of judgment (Martin, this volume). The underlying theme of this book is the observation that the normative or received view of human judgment may be wrong-headed in some fundamental respects. It has been widely assumed that when a judgment is made, stored beliefs are accessed and combined on the basis of some implicit calculation about their weighted relevance to a particular domain of judgment. An expressed judgment is thus seen as a more or less direct reflection of this calculated value. In test theory terms, the assumption is that there is an internal true score for a judgment and that expressed judgments tap that true score plus some error.

One of the points of disagreement between a constructivist view and the standard view concerns the extent to which there is such an internal true score. A constructivist view (or an ecological view) implies that judges may not know themselves as well as the standard model assumes, and that the computations one engages in are highly context specific or situated. In the spirit of self-observation theory (Bem, 1972), people do not have full access to what they think, so that even if such a true score model were appropriate, the inner view that gives one privileged access to one's own beliefs is murky at best. As a result, one is in the odd position of having to observe one's own mental life to divine what one thinks (just as others might have to observe one's behavior).

A second subtheme in this constructivist view is the idea expressed by those espousing a *garbage can model* of decision making (Cohen, March, & Olsen, 1972). According to their model, judgment and decision making is like the art of found objects: One tends to make the best composition one can with whatever is at hand. The resulting judgment is therefore heavily dependent on what is cognitively salient at the time. Laboratory studies of judgment tend not to observe this process because they control the information presented. This found-object aspect of judgment would not necessarily be problematic if one could weight each found object appropriately. Many irrelevant considerations could simply be weighted zero, as is done in the computational algorithms for multidimensional scaling solutions. But a corollary of the garbage can approach seems to be that whatever factors show up in consciousness, however tangentially related, get a more or less equal vote in the decision. This is perhaps a consequence of the self-observation aspect of the process. One tends to assume that a factor is relevant simply by virtue of the fact that it has crossed one's mind while considering the object of judgment. It is within this context that it seems likely that mood and emotion have direct effects on judgment rather than, or in addition to, indirect effects.

SUMMARY

The theme of this chapter is that social cognition theorists have overlooked the role of immediate experience. The study of emotion tends to highlight the importance of immediate experience, because one of the most distinctive aspects of emotions is that they are experienced. The cognitive activity that leads to emotions results in a distinctive experiential state involving feelings, thoughts, and urges. I have argued that this experiential state is not an epiphenomenon, but rather that it plays a causal role in other cognitive processes; that it is a form of self-produced feedback that serves as input to subsequent cognitive processes. Schwarz and Clore's (1983) study of mood, misattribution, and judgment was reviewed and the mood-as-information model was contrasted with explanations based on priming. In addition, I argued that emotion and mood exercise their influence on judgment directly rather than solely indirectly, as traditional judgment theory has insisted.

I also proposed that the use of feelings as information is not unique to emotion but probably characterizes all feeling-based judgments. In support of this claim, evidence from several different areas of research was reviewed, including uncertainty and understanding, the availability heuristic, the overnight-fame effect, the role of distraction in boredom, expectation effects, and feelings of knowing. I also noted the similarity between the processes governing the role of feelings in judgment to those governing the role of primed concepts in judgment. Several experiments were reviewed including studies of subtle priming and reminding, blatant priming and distraction, and anchoring and salience. The critical feature determining whether or not feedback from one mental process affected the next in these studies lay in the manipulations of procedural variables and how they influenced subjects' punctuation of their own momentary mental experience. A theme that was hinted at, but not fully explored in this chapter, is that all judgments necessarily involve some such feeling-based or appraisal stage, and that this is really what we mean when we refer to *human judgment*. Finally, I argued that the effects observed when such experientially based judgments are studied encourage a constructivist view of judgment.

ACKNOWLEDGMENTS

Preparation of this chapter was supported in part by National Science Foundation Grant BNS 83-18077. The author benefited from stimulating conversation on this topic with a number of people, including Joyce Pfennig, Lenny Martin, Jerry Parrott, Andrew Ortony, Bill Brewer, Doug Medin, and Norbert Schwarz.

REFERENCES

Ajzen, I. (1974). Effects of information on interpersonal attraction: Similarity versus affective value. *Journal of Personality and Social Psychology, 29,* 374–380.

Allen, J. B., Kenrick, P. T., Linder, D. E., & McCall, M. A. (1989). Arousal and attraction: A response-facilitation alternative to misattribution and negative reinforcement models. *Journal of Personality and Social Psychology, 57,* 261–270.

Anderson, J. R., & Bower, G. H. (1973). *Human associative memory.* Washington, DC: Winston & Sons.

Anderson, N. H. (1981). *Foundations of information integration.* New York: Academic Press.

Bargh, J. A., & Pietromonaco, P. (1982). Automatic information processing and social perception: The influence of trait information presented outside of conscious awareness on impression formation. *Journal of Personality and Social Psychology, 43,* 437–449.

Begg, I., Armour, V., & Kerr, T. (1985). On believing what we remember. *Canadian Journal of Behavioral Science, 17,* 199–214.

Bem, D. J. (1972). Self-perception theory. In L. Berkowitz (Ed.), *Advances in experimental social psychology* (Vol. 6, pp. 1–62). New York: Academic Press.

Bower, G. H. (1981). Mood and memory. *American Psychologist, 36,* 129–148.

Byrne, D., & Clore, G. L. (1970). A reinforcement model of evaluative responses. *Personality: An International Journal, 1,* 103–128.

Byrne, D., Clore, G. L., Griffitt, W., Lambreth, J., & Mitchell, H. E. (1973a). One more time. *Journal of Personality and Social Psychology, 23,* 323–324.

Byrne, D., Clore, G. L., Griffitt, W., Lambreth, J., & Mitchell, H. E. (1973b). When research paradigms converge: Confrontation or integration? *Journal of Personality and Social Psychology, 23,* 105–111.

Byrne, D., Lambreth, J., Palmer, J., & London, O. (1969). Sequential effects as a function of explicit and implicit interpolated attraction responses. *Journal of Personality and Social Psychology, 13,* 70–78.

Calvert-Boyanowsky, J., & Leventhal, H. (1975). The role of information in attenuating behavioral responses to stress: A reinterpretation of the misattribution phenomenon. *Journal of Personality and Social Psychology, 32,* 214–221.

Clore, G. L. (1966). *Discrimination learning as a function of awareness and magnitude of attitudinal reinforcement.* Unpublished doctoral dissertation, University of Texas, Austin.

Clore, G. L. (1988, August). *Moods and their vicissitudes: Thoughts and feelings as information.* Paper presented at the symposium of the International Congress of Psychology, Sydney, Australia.

Clore, G. L., & Byrne, D. (1974). A reinforcement-affect model of attraction. In T. L. Huston (Ed.), *Foundations of interpersonal attraction* (pp. 143–170). New York: Academic Press.

Clore, G. L., Ortony, A., & Foss, M. A. (1987). The psychological foundations of the affective lexicon. *Journal of Personality and Social Psychology, 53,* 751–766.

Clore, G. L., & Parrott, W. G. (1990). *Cognitive feelings and metacognitive judgments.* Unpublished manuscript, University of Illinois, Urbana-Champaign.

Clore, G. L., & Parrott, W. G. (1991). Moods and their vicissitudes: Thoughts and feelings as information. In J. Forgas (Ed.), *Emotion and social judgment* (pp. 107–123). Oxford: Pergamon.

Clore, G. L., Parrott, W. G., Schwarz, N., & Wilkin, N. (1990). *Does emotional bias occur during encoding or judgment?* Unpublished manuscript.

Clore, G. L., Wiggins, N., & Itkin, S. (1975). Gain and loss in attraction: Attributions from nonverbal behavior. *Journal of Personality and Social Psychology, 31,* 706–712.

Cohen, D., March, J. G., & Olsen, J. P. (1972). A garbage can model of organizational choice. *Administrative Science Quarterly, 17,* 1–25.

Cunningham, M. R. (1979). Weather, mood, and helping behavior: Quasi-experiments with the sunshine samaritan. *Journal of Personality and Social Psychology, 37,* 1947–1956.

Damrad-Frye, R., & Laird, J. D. (1989). The experience of boredom: The role of the self-perception of attention. *Journal of Personality and Social Psychology, 57,* 315–320.

DeLoache, J. S., & Brown, A. L. (1984). Where do I go next? Intelligent searching by very young children. *Developmental Psychology, 20,* 37–44.

Farah, M. J. (1989). Is visual imagery really visual? Overlooked evidence from neuropsychology. *Psychological Review, 95,* 307–317.

Fazio, R. H., Zanna, M. P., & Cooper, J. (1977). Dissonance and self-perception: An integrative view of each theory's proper domain of application. *Journal of Experimental Social Psychology, 13,* 464–479.

Fiedler, K., & Stroehm, W. (1986). What kind of mood influences what kind of memory: The role of arousal and information structure. *Memory & Cognition, 14,* 181–188.

Fishbein, M., & Ajzen, I. (1975). *Belief, attitude, intention, and behavior.* Reading, MA: Addison-Wesley.

Forgas, J. P., & Bower, G. H. (1988). Affect in social and personal judgments. In K. Fiedler & J. P. Forgas (Eds.), *Affect, cognition, and social behavior* (pp. 183–208). Toronto: Hogrefe.

Forgas, J. P., & Moylan, S. (1987). After the movies: The effects of mood on social judgments. *Personality and Social Psychology Bulletin, 13,* 465–477.

Frijda, N. H. (1986). *The emotions.* New York: Cambridge University Press.

Gallagher, D. J., & Clore, G. L. (1985, May). *Emotion and judgment: Effects of fear and anger on relevant and irrelevant cognitive tasks.* Paper presented at the meeting of the Midwestern Psychological Association, Chicago.

Glenberg, A. M., Wilkinson, A. C., & Epstein, W. (1982). The illusion of knowing: Failure in the self-assessment of comprehension. *Memory & Cognition, 10,* 597–602.

Gouaux, C. (1971). Induced affective states and interpersonal attraction. *Journal of Personality and Social Psychology, 20,* 37–43.

Griffitt, W., & Veitch, R. (1971). Hot and crowded: Influences of population density and temperature on interpersonal behavior. *Journal of Personality and Social Psychology, 17,* 92–98.

Harris, P. L., Kruithof, A., Meerum Terwogt, M., & Visser, T. (1981). Children's detection and awareness of textual anomaly. *Journal of Experimental Child Psychology, 31,* 212–230.

Hart, J. T. (1965). Memory and the feeling-of-knowing experience. *Journal of Educational Psychology, 56,* 208–216.

Heider, F. (1958). *The psychology of interpersonal relations.* Hillsdale, NJ: Lawrence Erlbaum Associates.

Higgins, E. T., Rholes, W. S., & Jones, C. R. (1977). Category accessibility and impression formation. *Journal of Experimental Social Psychology, 13,* 141–154.

Isen, A. M. (1984). Toward understanding the role of affect in cognition. In R. S. Wyer & T. K. Srull (Eds.), *Handbook of social cognition* (pp. 179–236). Hillsdale, NJ: Lawrence Erlbaum Associates.

Isen, A. M., Shalker, T. E., Clark, M., & Karp, L. (1978). Affect, accessibility of material in memory, and behavior: A cognitive loop? *Journal of Personality and Social Psychology, 36,* 1–11.

Jacoby, L. L. (1988). Memory observed and memory unobserved. In U. Neisser & E. Winograd (Eds.), *Remembering reconsidered: Ecological and traditional approaches to the study of memory* (pp. 145–177). Cambridge, England: Cambridge University Press.

Jacoby, L. L., Kelley, C. M., Brown, J., Jasechko, J. (1989). Becoming famous overnight: Limits on the ability to avoid unconscious influences of the past. *Journal of Personality and Social Psychology, 56,* 326–338.

Kahneman, D., & Tversky, A. (1973). On the psychology of prediction. *Psychological Review, 80,* 237–251.

Kaplan, M. F., & Anderson, N. H. (1973a). Information integration theory and reinforcement theory as approaches to interpersonal attraction. *Journal of Personality and Social Psychology, 28,* 301–312.

Kaplan, M. F., & Anderson, N. H. (1973b). Comment on "When research paradigms converge: Confrontation or integration?" *Journal of Personality and Social Psychology, 28,* 321–322.

Kubovy, M. (1977). Response availability and the apparent spontaneity of numerical choices. *Journal of Experimental Psychology: Human Perception and Performance, 3,* 359–364.

Lombardi, W. J., Higgins, E. T., & Bargh, J. A. (1987). The role of consciousness in priming effects on categorization: Assimilation versus contrast as a function of awareness of the priming task. *Personality and Social Psychology Bulletin, 13,* 411–429.

Markman, E. M. (1977). Realizing that you don't understand: A preliminary investigation. *Child Development, 48,* 986–992.

Martin, L. L. (1986). Set/reset: Use and disuse of concepts in impression formation. *Journal of Personality and Social Psychology, 51,* 493–504.

Martin, L. L., Seta, J. J., & Crelia, R. A. (1990). Assimilation and contrast as a function of people's willingness and ability to expend effort in forming an impression. *Journal of Personality and Social Psychology, 59,* 27–37.

Neisser, U. (1976). *Cognition and reality.* San Francisco: Freeman.

Nelson, T. O., Leonesio, R. J., Landwehr, R. S., & Narens, L. (1986). A comparison of three predictors of an individual's memory performance: The individual's feeling of knowing versus the normative feeling of knowing versus base rate item difficulty. *Journal of Experimental Psychology, 12,* 279–287.

Ortony, A. (1991). Value and emotion. In G. Kessen, A. Ortony, & F. Craik (Eds.), *Memories, thoughts and emotions: Essays in memory of George Mandler* (pp. 337–353). Hillsdale, NJ: Lawrence Erlbaum Associates.

Ortony, A., Clore, G. L., & Collins, A. (1988). *The cognitive structure of emotions*. New York: Cambridge University Press.

Parrott, W. G. (1988). The role of cognition in emotional experience. In W. J. Baker, L. P. Mos, H. V. Rappard, & H. J. Stam (Eds.), *Recent trends in theoretical psychology* (pp. 327–337). New York: Springer-Verlag.

Posner, M. I. (1978). *Chronometric explorations of mind*. Hillsdale, NJ: Lawrence Erlbaum Associates.

Schwarz, N. (1990). Happy but mindless? Mood effects on problem-solving and persuasion. In R. M. Sorrentino & E. T. Higgins (Eds.), *Handbook of motivation and cognition* (Vol. 2, pp. 527–561). New York: Guilford Press.

Schwarz, N., Bless, H., Strack, F., Klumpp, G., Rittenauer-Schatka, H., & Simons, A. (1991). Ease of retrieval as information: Another look at the availability heuristic. *Journal of Personality and Social Psychology, 61*, 195–202.

Schwarz, N., & Clore, G. L. (1983). Mood, misattribution, and judgments of well-being: Informative and directive functions of affective states. *Journal of Personality and Social Psychology, 45*, 513–523.

Schwarz, N., & Clore, G. L. (1988). How do I feel about it? The informative function of affective states. In K. Fiedler & J. Forgas (Eds.), *Affect, cognition, and social behavior* (pp. 44–62). Toronto: Hogrefe.

Schwarz, N., Robbins, M., & Clore, G. L. (1985, May). *Explaining the effects of mood on social judgment*. Paper presented at the meeting of the Midwestern Psychological Association, Chicago.

Simon, H. A. (1967). Motivational and emotional controls of cognition. *Psychological Review, 74*, 29–39.

Srull, T. K., & Wyer, R. S., Jr. (1979). The role of category accessibility in the interpretation of information about persons: Some determinants and implications. *Journal of Personality and Social Psychology, 37*, 1660–1672.

Stapert, J. C., & Clore, G. L. (1969). Attraction and disagreement-produced arousal. *Journal of Personality and Social Psychology, 13*, 64–69.

Strack, F., Schwarz, N., Bless, H., Kubler, A., & Wanke, M. (1990). *Remember the priming episode. Episodic cues may determine assimilation vs. contrast effects*. Manuscript submitted for review.

Switzer, F. S., III, & Sniezek, J. (1991). Judgment processes and motivation: Anchoring and adjustment effects on judgment and behavior. *Organizational Behavior and Human Decision Processes, 49*, 208–229.

Veitch, R., & Griffitt, W. (1976). Good news-bad news: Affective and interpersonal effects. *Journal of Applied Social Psychology, 6*, 69–75.

Wellman, H. M. (1977). Tip of the tongue and feeling of knowing experiences: A developmental study of memory monitoring. *Child Development, 48*, 13–21.

Wilson, T. D., Lisle, D. J., Kraft, D., & Wetzel, C. G. (1989). Preferences as expectation-driven inferences: Effects of affective expectations on affective experience. *Journal of Personality and Social Psychology, 56*, 519–530.

Wyer, R. S., Jr., & Carlston, D. E. (1979). *Social cognition, inference, and attribution*. Hillsdale, NJ: Lawrence Erlbaum Associates.

Wyer, R. S., Jr., & Srull, T. K. (Eds.). (1984). *Handbook of social cognition* (Vol. 1). Hillsdale, NJ: Lawrence Erlbaum Associates.

Yaniv, I., & Meyer, D. E. (1987). Activation and metacognition of inaccessible stored information: Potential bases for incubation effects in problem solving. *Journal of Experimental Psychology: Learning, Memory, and Cognition, 13*, 187–205.

The Influence of Mood State on Judgment and Action: Effects on Persuasion, Categorization, Social Justice, Person Perception, and Judgmental Accuracy

Robert C. Sinclair
University of Alberta

Melvin M. Mark
The Pennsylvania State University

There is considerable current interest in the influence of affective state on various spheres of human judgment and behavior (e.g., Baron, 1990; Bodenhausen, in press; Forgas & Bower, 1987, 1988; Isen, 1984, 1987; Johnson & Tversky, 1983; Mackie & Worth, 1989, 1991; Petty, Cacioppo, Sedikides, & Strathman, 1988; Petty, Gleicher, & Baker, 1991; Schwarz, 1988, 1990; Schwarz, Bless, & Bohner, 1991; Schwarz & Clore, 1983, 1988; Sinclair, 1988; Sinclair & Mark, 1991). In this chapter, we address the impact of mood states on decision making and performance in several areas. Our focus is primarily on the role of processing strategy as a possible mediator of the effects of mood.

MOOD AND PROCESSING STRATEGY: TOWARD A MODEL

A number of different explanations have been offered in an attempt to account for the effects of mood state on social judgments and behavior (see, e.g., Mackie & Worth, 1989; Schwarz, 1990). However, converging evidence, from research examining different outcome variables, is consistent with the proposition that mood state affects processing strategy, which in turn affects judgments and behavior. Specifically, subjects in a positive mood (e.g., happy subjects) appear to process information in a way that can be characterized as less systematic, more heuristic, more superficial, and less careful. For instance, happy subjects: attend more to heuristic cues than to argument strength (Bless, Bohner, Schwarz, & Strack, 1990; Mackie & Worth, 1989; Schwarz et al., 1991; Worth & Mackie, 1987); seem to act more impulsively when facing a potential helping situation (Schaller & Cialdini, 1990); respond more quickly (Isen & Means, 1983); and are more likely to rely on stereotypes in making social judgments (Bodenhausen, in press; Bodenhausen & Kramer, 1990, 1991). In contrast, subjects in a negative mood (e.g., sad subjects) appear to process information in a way that can be characterized as more systematic, less heuristic, less superficial, and more careful. For instance, sad subjects: attend more to argument strength in processing a persuasive message (Bless et al., 1990); seem to engage more in a cost/benefit analysis when facing a potential helping situation (Schaller & Cialdini, 1990); and show the least halo bias and most accuracy in a performance appraisal task (Sinclair, 1988). Schwarz (1990) similarly suggested that "individuals in a bad mood are more likely to spontaneously engage in effortful, detail-oriented analytic processing strategies than individuals in an elated mood" (p. 42).

We refer to the hypothesized effect, whereby those in a positive mood are more heuristic, less systematic, more superficial and less careful in their processing of social information, while those in a negative mood process in the opposite fashion, as a *processing strategy* explanation for the effects of mood. In this chapter, we review a wide range of evidence that is consistent with a processing strategy explanation, including much of the work cited previously, plus several recent, yet-unpublished studies. We also consider the conditions under which the proposed processing strategy effects may not occur, and discuss the role of possible mediators of mood effects other than processing strategy. Our primary focus, however, is on the converging evidence in support of a processing strategy explanation.

The Causes of Processing Strategy Differences

Figure 6.1 presents a model representing our current beliefs about the role of processing strategy as a mediator of mood effects. As shown in the figure, mood state is thought to elicit three processes, each of which may contribute to processing strategy effects.

Cognitive Capacity. Evidence exists that positive moods bring more, and more diverse, material to mind (e.g., Isen & Daubman, 1984; Isen, Johnson, Mertz, & Robinson, 1985). Such activation of material may limit the available amount of limited cognitive capacity, forcing subjects in positive moods to rely on heuristic strategies and simplification in problem solving (e.g., Isen & Means, 1983). Mackie and Worth (1989) provide evidence to support the restricted capacity view. They found that happy subjects failed to elaborate on persuasive

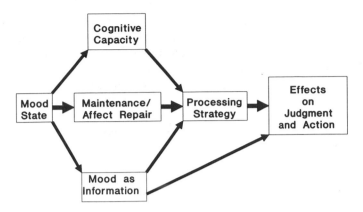

FIG. 6.1. A model of processing strategy as a mediator of mood effects.

messages only when the time to complete the task was restricted. When time was not restricted, happy subjects did not differ from controls. Such evidence suggests happy states elicit cognitive capacity limitations, which in turn result in happy subjects' propensity to engage in less systematic (or more heuristic) processing.

However, other results seem to us to indicate that capacity arguments alone cannot account for all mood effects or for mood-related processing strategy differences in general. For example, in research on the effects of mood on categorization (described more fully later), Murray, Sujan, Hirt, and Sujan (1990) did not restrict the time subjects had to complete their task; yet they found categorization effects consistent with a differential processing strategy explanation. Further, Murray et al. found that happy subjects took less time to complete their task. If restricted capacity alone accounted for the effects, as in Mackie and Worth (1989), (a) happy subjects should have taken longer to complete the task, and (b) Murray et al. should have found no effect. A similar argument can be made for other research (e.g., that of Bodenhausen, in press, on mood and stereotyping), including all of our research presented in this chapter. We did not restrict the time subjects had to complete their tasks, yet we found mood effects, even when subjects had the opportunity to take the time that should have afforded them the opportunity to overcome any capacity deficiencies. It could be counterargued that Mackie and Worth's happy subjects had restricted capacity and were motivated to process fully in the absence of time restrictions, whereas our subjects and those of Murray et al. (and others) were not motivated to work longer to overcome their capacity deficits. Although possible, we instead believe that more than a restricted capacity explanation is required to explain many, if not most, mood effects.

Mood Maintenance/Affect Repair.   Motivational processes, in the form of mood maintenance and affect repair, are likely to contribute to the effects of mood on processing strategy. When one is in a good mood, engaging in systematic problem solving could decrease the experience of positive affect (cf. Arkes, Herren, & Isen, 1988; Schaller & Cialdini, 1990); thus, happy people may be motivated to avoid engaging in systematic processing. Conversely, those in a bad mood may engage in systematic processing as an attempt to repair their affective state; that is, sad people may be motivated to engage in systematic processing to distract themselves from their mood (cf. Schaller & Cialdini). Such distraction (Morrow & Nolen-Hoeksema, 1990), especially if paired with successful problem solving, may result in affect repair.

Isen (1984) presented evidence to support the affect repair/mood maintenance position. For example, she suggested that, relative to controls, happy subjects were less willing to help others when the helping is incompatible with subjects' positive moods. Conversely, Cialdini, Darby, and Vincent (1973) and Isen, Horn, and Rosenhan (1973) showed that subjects in negative moods will help in situations in which helping can result in affect repair (see Schaller & Cialdini, 1990, for a review).

By considering the mood maintenance/affect repair explanation of the processing strategy effects of mood, we can generate hypotheses about when mood may not elicit the processing strategy differences previously described. Specifically, positive mood subjects may not avoid systematic, effortful processing if such processing would maintain the positive mood state. Such a reversal of the more common mood maintenance effect on strategy could occur (a) if the processing involved detailed review of positively valenced or personally relevant stimuli (Forgas, 1989; Wegener, Petty, & Richman, 1991) or (b) if, through directions to process carefully, the person develops an expectation that performance will be evaluated by the self or by another, such that the failure to process systematically would threaten the mood state. We believe that such expectations may have developed in research by Bless et al. (1990), who found that happy subjects can carefully scrutinize arguments when explicitly instructed to do so.

Mood as Information. Schwarz (1990) proposed two ways in which mood can serve as an informational cue in judgments and decision making. First, for some types of evaluative judgments, such as one's self-perceived life satisfaction, mood can serve directly as information relevant to the judgment. Schwarz and Clore (1983, 1988), Schwarz (1990), and Clore (1990) suggested that moods have such an impact on judgments of well-being and life satisfaction only when the mood is perceived as providing information about one's life. For example, Schwarz and Clore (1983) led some subjects to attribute their mood states to a strange room or to the weather. These subjects showed mood change but, when asked to report on their general well-being and life satisfaction, they were unaffected by mood. Subjects in negative moods who had no external attribution for their state reported lower life satisfaction, relative to subjects in good moods and to subjects in bad moods who externalized their moods; this pattern shows the informational use of mood in evaluative judgments when mood is perceived as relevant to the judgment. Clore (1990) replicated this effect with chronic depressives. A direct informational effect of mood on evaluative judgments, such as that shown in Schwarz and Clore (1983), is represented in Fig. 6.1 as the path from "mood as information" to "effects on judgment and action."

Of greater interest here, the mood as information phenomenon can also elicit processing strategy differences as a mediator. Schwarz (1990) suggested that mood may serve as an informational cue that influences motivation in decision-making tasks. He posited that good moods lead people to believe that they make good judgments (and that their lives are satisfactory); bad moods may provide information that their judgments have been inadequate (and that their lives are not satisfactory). Thus, in good moods, people might assume that there is no reason to reevaluate their decision-making processes because they tend to make good decisions; hence, they do not deliberate as much or as carefully in their decisions. However, in bad moods, people might realize that there is need to reevaluate their decision-making processes and to engage in systematic problem solving. Thus, the mood as information hypothesis suggests processing differences between good and bad moods.

With respect to boundary conditions on processing strategy effects of mood, one limitation can be inferred from previous work on the direct informational effects of mood on evaluative judgments. Specifically, it can be hypothesized that external attributions for moods would reduce processing strategy effects on other judgments, such as responses to persuasive appeals (cf. Schwarz & Clore, 1983). We are presently collecting data to test this hypothesis.

A Summary of the Model

A great deal of evidence has accumulated which, we believe, is consistent with the position that positive mood states lead to less systematic information processing than do neutral states (e.g., Isen & Daubman, 1984; Isen & Means, 1983; Isen, Means, Patrick, & Nowicki, 1982; Mackie & Worth, 1989; Worth & Mackie, 1987), while negative states lead to more systematic processing (e.g., Mark & Sinclair, 1990; Schwarz, 1988, 1990; Schwarz & Bless, 1991; Schwarz, Bless, & Bohner, 1991; Sinclair, 1988; Sinclair & Mark, 1990, 1991). As summarized in Fig. 6.1, we believe that at least three processes mediate mood's processing strategy effects: cognitive capacity, mood maintenance/affect repair, and mood as information. Consideration of these three processes leads to three important realizations. First, processing strategy effects seem to be multiply determined, rather than attributable to a single source. Second, for each of the processes posited to lead to processing strategy differences, there are boundary conditions under which they should not lead to processing strategy effects: Cognitive capacity limitations may not lead to processing strategy effects if adequate time is provided for processing (Mackie & Worth, 1989, 1991; Worth & Mackie, 1987) and the person is motivated to attempt to overcome the capacity limitations; mood maintenance, on the part of happy subjects, may not lead to less systematic processing if the task itself is seen as enhancing one's positive mood (cf. Forgas, 1989; Wegener et al., 1991) and, correspondingly, affect repair, in the case of sad subjects, may not lead to more systematic processing if the task is seen as intensifying or lengthening one's negative mood (Wyer & Srull, 1989); and mood as information may not lead to processing strategy differences if mood is attributed externally (cf. Schwarz & Clore, 1983). Concerning the mood as information pathway to processing strategy differences, we can also suggest that negative mood may not lead to more systematic processing if it is so intense that the person believes he or she is highly unlikely to engage in effective problem solving (cf. Marsh & Weary, 1989, on the difference between mildly and severely depressed individuals). Third, we do not know the relative magnitude of the alternative pathways from mood state to processing strategy shown in Fig. 6.1. However, as our earlier comments imply, we do not expect that the path from cognitive capacity to processing strategy is as strong as the others, particularly the path from mood maintenance/affect repair. Note that, because of our uncertainty about the magnitude of the three pathways from mood to processing strategy differences, we are uncertain about the relative importance of the boundary conditions associated with each pathway. Thus, we do not know, for example, if the mood maintenance pathway were reversed because a happy subject was faced with a pleasurable task, whether this would be sufficient to overwhelm the cognitive capacity and mood as information pathways. We also do not know about the extent to which individual difference or situational variables may modify the magnitude of the causal pathways shown in Fig. 6.1 though, like Bodenhausen (in press), we expect that these may be important. Indeed, situational characteristics may even eliminate some of the mediating processes shown in Fig. 6.1 or require the addition of situation-specific mediators; for example, some tasks may entail mood congruency effects, whereas others may not.

MOOD AND SYSTEMATICITY OF PROCESSING IN MULTIPLE DOMAINS

It is not possible to evaluate fully the model shown in Fig. 6.1. However, there is considerable evidence, from research on mood's effect on a variety of different outcomes, that allows us to evaluate the central tenet of the model. Specifically, we can evaluate the proposition that mood state influences processing strategy, which in turn leads to effects on judgment and action. For the most part, the effect of mood on processing strategy will be inferred from the pattern of effects on the various outcome measures employed. Thus, it is important to note that the supporting research employs quite dissimilar experimental tasks and paradigms.

We review research concerning the effects of mood on judgments in several domains. We begin by reviewing briefly research conducted by others on the effects of mood on persuasion. Here, and throughout, we have borrowed from the work of others who have conducted considerable influential research on the effects of mood. Following that, we review our own recent research on the effects of mood on several domains of judgment; specifically, categorization, judgments of social justice, person perception, and judgmental accuracy. We review only literature on temporarily induced mood state; suffice it to say that a growing body of research on individual differences in mood state can also be seen as supporting a processing strategy approach (e.g., Gleicher & Weary, 1991; Lewicka, Piegat, & Krzyzak, 1991; Marsh & Weary, 1989).

We believe that, across the variety of domains reviewed, the processing strategy explanation (of the form that views happy subjects as less systematic and less effortful in their judgmental processes, and unhappy subjects as more systematic and more effortful) is an important and useful explanatory model. Further, we suggest that, if taken as *the* explanation of processing strategy differences, the cognitive capacity explanation would be inadequate. While we advocate a processing strategy explanation, a cautionary note also may be warranted: It seems premature to identify the processing strategy explanation as *the* explanation of all mood effects or even of the sort we review. Thus, in some instances, we will note other processes that may operate simultaneously with the processing strategy mechanism.

Finally, note that, although we have discussed possible boundary conditions for each of the pathways linking mood and processing strategy, in the review that follows we do not focus on boundary conditions. Instead, we emphasize evidence on the linkages between mood, processing strategy, and various mood effects. We do so (a) because these linkages constitute the central tenet of our model, and (b) because research probing possible boundary conditions is rare.

Mood and Responses to Persuasion

The Elaboration Likelihood Model of persuasion identifies both central and peripheral routes for persuasion (Petty & Cacioppo, 1986) and explicates when elaboration is more or less likely to occur. Central persuasive appeals (e.g., message quality) have greatest impact on persuasion when elaboration is high; peripheral appeals (e.g., source attractiveness) have greatest impact when elaboration is low. Cacioppo, Petty, and Morris (1983) showed that subjects who are low on need for cognition, who scrutinize messages less and engage in less effortful processing, do not discriminate between strong and weak arguments in persuasive appeals, while subjects who are high on need for cognition, who scrutinize more and engage in more effortful processing, do discriminate between strong and weak arguments. Presumably, this is because subjects low on need for cognition fail to elaborate and thus fail to differentiate messages based on quality, while subjects high on need for cognition engage in elaboration and thus differentiate (see also Petty, 1990).

Good moods appear to result in processing strategies similar to those used by low need-for-cognition subjects, whereas bad moods appear to lead to strategies similar to those used by high need-for-cognition subjects. That is, subjects in good moods often fail to elaborate, do not discriminate between strong and weak messages, and are relatively more persuaded by weak messages and by peripheral appeals (Bless et al., 1990; Mackie & Worth, 1989; Worth & Mackie, 1987). In contrast, subjects in bad moods seem to engage in elaboration, discriminate between strong and weak arguments, are persuaded by strong but not weak arguments, and respond to central rather than peripheral appeals (Bless et al., 1990; also see Schwarz, 1990; Schwarz et al., 1991). Such findings, of course, can alternatively be framed in terms of Chaiken's (1980, 1987) position that when people respond to message content, it is through careful attention to the arguments presented and results from systematic processing; conversely, responses to cues such as attractiveness, perceived expertise or likeability, without careful attention to message, result from heuristic processing.

Schwarz et al. (1991) provided a review of the evidence regarding the effects of mood state on responses to persuasion. They concluded that mood-related processing strategy differences account for differential responses to persuasive communications (see also Bless et al., 1990; Mackie & Worth, 1989; Petty, Gleicher, & Baker, 1991; Worth & Mackie, 1987). For example, Bless et al. changed subjects' moods and had them hear either strong or weak arguments directed toward an increase in student fees. Consistent with the processing strategy position, subjects in bad moods discriminated between strong and weak arguments and were persuaded only by strong arguments; subjects in good moods failed to discriminate and were equally persuaded by strong and weak arguments. An analysis of subjects' cognitive responses showed that subjects in bad moods reported more favorable thoughts in the strong condition, indicating systematic elaboration on message content; subjects in good moods failed to show systematic elaboration. Worth and Mackie (1987) had earlier shown a similar effect with subjects in good moods, relative to controls. In a recent study that replicated this effect, Sinclair, Mark, and Clore (1991) telephoned subjects on days with either good or bad weather (see Schwarz & Clore, 1983). Half of the subjects were cued to the weather and half were not. Subjects were then read either strong or weak arguments advocating the institution of comprehensive final exams for graduating seniors (from Petty & Cacioppo, 1984). The results were consistent with the processing strategy position. Regardless of weather cue, happy subjects failed to discriminate between strong and weak arguments and were equally persuaded by both argument types; in contrast, sad subjects discriminated between strong and weak arguments and were persuaded only by strong arguments.

Mackie and Worth (1989) found that such mood-related differences between happy and control subjects were apparent only when time to make judgments was restricted. They argued that good moods limit processing capacity, resulting in the use of heuristics that prevent further strain on capacity. Removal of time constraints, they suggested, allows happy subjects the additional time to process information and thereby overrides restricted capacity, resulting in no mood-related differences in persuasion. However, as in other areas of research, mood effects on persuasion are sometimes apparent in the absence of time constraints (or other obvious unavoidable capacity limitations; see Bless et al., 1990; Sinclair et al., 1991), so that the differential processing strategy position does not seem to reduce to a cognitive capacity explanation.

Although the processing strategy position usefully accounts for findings in the mood and persuasion literature (Schwarz et al., 1991), it is not without competing explanations (Wyer & Srull, 1989). Further, even if one takes as true the processing strategy explanation, it can be argued that other mechanisms will sometimes mediate the effect of mood on persuasion, as Petty et al. (1991) suggested. For instance, in some cases mood may serve as relevant information, as in the direct mood as information phenomenon. In addition to serving as relevant information, affect could serve as a peripheral cue, or could bias processing (see Petty et al., 1991). Further, there may be situations in which happy subjects do engage in systematic processing; specifically, Wegener et al. (1991) provided evidence that happy subjects will discriminate between strong and weak arguments when elaboration is expected to be "uplifting" and thus leads to mood maintenance.

Mood and Categorization

Isen and Daubman (1984) found that elated subjects categorize more broadly than do controls. That is, relative to controls, happy subjects perceived relatively nonprototypic exemplars of a category as more prototypic (e.g., they were more likely to rate a camel as a vehicle). Further, happy subjects created fewer categories on a category creation task. Isen and Daubman posited at least three potential explanations for this effect: (a) "positive affect may prime an affective dimension of material that is not normally seen as affective and this in turn serves to change or broaden the relations perceived" (p. 1212); (b) positive affect promotes heuristic use (p. 1213); and (c) positive affect may result in "more material and more diverse material" coming to mind (p. 1213).

More recently, Murray et al. (1990) suggested that happy subjects are not simply broad categorizors, but rather, they are flexible in their categorization. In a television program categorization task, Murray et al. found that subjects in good moods categorized most broadly when they were asked to focus on similarities among stimuli, and categorized most narrowly when asked to focus on differences among stimuli. Consistent with the work of Isen, Daubman, and Nowicki (1987) and Isen et al. (1985), they also found that subjects in positive moods responded in a more creative manner. Murray et al. suggested heuristic use as one explanation of their findings (cf. Sinclair, 1988); however, they appeared to prefer an explanation consistent with Pretty and Seligman (1984), who suggested that positive moods increase intrinsic interest in the task. This increased interest then guides cognitive strategies in the categorization task. We believe that the Murray et al. (1990) findings are more consistent with an interpretation based on processing strategy differences. That is, happy subjects may avoid systematic processing because of limited cognitive capacity, in order to maintain their moods, or because their positive moods provide information that their decisions are generally good (Schwarz, 1990). In any case, because of their less systematic processing, they may overly respond to experimenter-provided cues.

Let us consider the categorization breadth/flexibility research further from the perspective that mood influences processing strategy. We believe it can be argued that, in the context of the Isen and Daubman paradigm, broad categorization is a simple strategy to implement. Thus, we would expect that subjects who are in good moods, and who therefore process nonsystematically, would adopt the simplest strategy—broad categorization. However, we would make different predictions if subjects were provided with cues specifying the modes in which they should categorize; note that the Murray et al. (1990) manipulation can be interpreted as providing such cues. Elated subjects, who avoid effortful processing, should be most responsive to experimenter-provided cues. Thus, if situational cues suggest broad categorization, positive-mood subjects should rely on these cues as a heuristic for categorization, and create very few categories; if the cues suggest narrow categorization, elated subjects should create very many categories. In responding this way, positive-mood subjects can attend to the task in a less thoughtful manner. Subjects in bad moods, however, should be much less affected by the experimenter-provided breadth cues and instead engage in systematic processing, potentially to distract themselves from their negative moods or because their mood serves as a cue that their decision-making is suspect and requires further attention.

We attempted to explore the issue of mood-based systematic versus nonsystematic processing on a categorization task (Sinclair, Mark, & Weisbrod, 1990). Using an unrelated second study paradigm (Higgins, Rholes, & Jones, 1977), in an initial study we induced elated, neutral, or depressed moods in subjects. In a subsequent study, conducted by a second experimenter, we provided subjects with a categorization breadth cue (whereas Murray et al., 1990, asked subjects to focus on similarities or differences among television programs and to sort programs into piles; i.e., categories); we simply asked subjects to think carefully and create very few large groups or many small groups. Thus, experimenter-provided cues explicitly suggested that subjects create few large groups or many small groups (or they received no grouping instructions) on a categorization task (e.g., categorize the number of skiers on a ski hill). Our predictions that happy subjects would be most, and sad subjects least, affected by the breadth cue were supported. That is, happy subjects who were cued to create very few large groups categorized most broadly, whereas happy subjects who were cued to create very many small groups categorized most narrowly. It appears that happy subjects are most responsive to experimenter-provided cues. The results seem to support the position that categorization effects may arise because happy subjects avoid effortful processing, whereas sad subjects engage in effortful processing. Thus, we can question whether Murray et al.'s (1990) findings indicate that people in a positive mood are flexible categorizors; rather, they may be avoiding effortful processing.

Alternative interpretations of these results remain. Our results, and those of Murray et al., could be due to positive-mood subjects being more solicitous or having a greater desire to please the experimenter. To test this hypothesis, we conceptually replicated the study just described. However, the experimenter conducting the first study told subjects that he was interested in how differences in people relate to the amount of mood change caused by the mood induction. Subjects' moods were changed; they completed a mood measure; and they completed the Crownc–Marlowe (Crowne & Marlowe, 1964) measure of social desirability (a measure of describing oneself in socially desirable terms to achieve approval). Breadth cue was manipulated by introducing experimenter bias in the "unrelated" second study. For example, subjects in the broad condition were told that we were attempting to replicate some well-documented effects indicating that subjects tend to create very few large groups. We measured the number of categories created, liking for the experimenter conducting the second study, and retrieval of the breadth cue manipulation. Again, happy subjects created the fewest categories when the breadth cue suggested broad categorization, but created the most categories when the breadth cue suggested narrow categorization. Sad subjects were less affected by the breadth cue manipulation. Further, happy subjects scored higher on the Crowne–Marlowe measure than did sad subjects. However, analyses of covariance indicated that neither social desirability scores nor liking for the experimenter mediated the effect of mood on responsiveness to the breadth cues. Thus, solicitousness and liking do not appear to be viable alternative explanations. Finally, no mood-related differences were seen in retrieval of the breadth cue manipulation; both happy and sad subjects attended to the information but, consistent with the processing strategy position, happy subjects made most use of the breadth cues.

When viewed from the processing strategy perspective, the evidence reviewed thus far suggests that when external cues signal that processing should be narrow (or broad), positive-mood subjects respond to these cues the most, and negative-mood subjects, the least. In the absence of external cues or heuristics to the contrary, happy subjects categorize most broadly, presumably based on their use of simple/effortless strategies that do not interfere with their moods. Subjects in bad moods, on the other hand, appear to process more systematically, leading to narrower categorization, if external cues are absent. Based on these differences in processing, we decided to explore the effects of mood in judgments of social justice, where subjects have to make judgments of how valued resources should be distributed in society and, in doing so, make discriminations between the inputs and outcomes of people (Mark & Sinclair, 1990). Our focus was on judgment in the absence of explicit external cues.

Mood and Judgments of Social Justice

Major theoretical approaches to perceived justice seek to describe how valued resources are allocated in groups and how people respond to resource allocations (Adams, 1965; Berger, Zelditch, Anderson, & Cohen, 1972; Homans, 1961; Walster, Berscheid, & Walster, 1973). Most theories include both cognitive and affective or motivational components, which are presumed to predominate at different stages of the process through which people judge and react to resource allocation. For instance, in the case of equity theory, perceptions of equity/inequity are thought to result from the comparison, across persons, of input and outcome ratios. The computation of equity is conceived as a cognitive task; in contrast, the causes of preferences for equity and many consequences of inequity are presumed to be motivational or affective. Most research has addressed the cognitive basis of justice judgments and has paid little attention to the interaction of affect and cognition in perceived justice.

What are the implications of mood-related differential processing strategies in the area of equity judgments? Recall that we have interpreted the effects of mood on categorization breadth in terms of processing strategy. We could conceptualize some justice judgments as a categorization task: Does a particular allocation of resources fall into the category *fair*? Conceived in this light, if mood, by affecting processing strategy, impacts on categorization breadth, it should also have an effect on perceived justice. In particular, if positive moods lead to nonsystematic processing, failure to discriminate among stimuli, and thus the use of broader categories, then people in good moods should perceive less variation in fairness as rewards become more or less equitable, relative to subjects in other moods. Although they do not interpret their data in this manner, O'Malley and Davies (1984) found effects consistent with this suggestion. O'Malley and Davies first induced happy, neutral, or sad moods, and then told subjects that they performed better or worse than another subject on a task. Subjects were then asked to allocate rewards to themselves and the other subject. Relative performance had no effect among happy subjects, while better and worse performers did allocate differently in the neutral and, especially, the negative mood conditions. We would interpret the failure of the happy group to react significantly to performance as being due to positive moods leading to nonsystematic processing, to failure to discriminate, and to the use of broad categories. In contrast, neutral and, especially, negative moods led to more systematic processing strategies, to finer discrimination and thus narrower categorization, and therefore to greater sensitivity to variations in performance.

We conducted research to address this explanation of equity judgments; three studies are reported here (Mark & Sinclair, 1990). In the first study, we borrowed conceptually and methodologically from the categorization literature (Isen & Daubman, 1984; Rosch, 1975). In categorization tasks, subjects are generally presented with a range of stimuli, some of which are prototypic category exemplars and others of which are weak exemplars; subjects are asked to rate the extent to which each stimulus is a category member. In the first study, subjects in induced elated, neutral, or depressed moods read about work situations in which two targets performed at different levels, and then subjects rated the fairness of six alternative pay allocations. The pay allocations varied from *equality*, where both targets received the same amount of payment (inequitable underpayment of the superior performing individual), to *equity*, where the ratio of pay was equal to the ratio of performance, to *inequitable overpayment* (IOP) of the more productive individual (see Brickman & Bryan, 1973; Brickman, Folger, Goode, & Schul, 1981). Of course, we would expect equity to be perceived as most fair, and deviations from equity in either direction perceived as more unfair (with larger deviations from equity being perceived as more unfair). Thus, treating the six payment allocations as a dimension ranging from equality to equity to IOP, and ignoring mood for the moment, we predicted a significant quadratic trend component in fairness ratings (i.e., an inverted-U function relating payment allocations and fairness). Given our assumption about how mood leads to differential processing strategies and categorization breadth, we expected that subjects in good moods would have a more restricted range in fairness judgments (a flatter inverted-U) and subjects in bad moods would show most range in fairness ratings (the steepest inverted-U). Moreover, subjects in bad moods were expected to perceive equity as most fair and deviations from equity as most unfair, relative to the other groups, given their more effortful and careful processing.

We did indeed find that the quadratic component of trend in fairness ratings differed across the mood groups. This effect is illustrated in Fig. 6.2. Consistent with our predictions, negative mood subjects' fairness ratings showed the greatest change across pay allocations and happy subjects' ratings showed least. This lends some support to our position that equity judgments can be conceptualized as a categorization task. The results are also consistent with the position that happy subjects use a processing strategy that results in less attention to detail, less discrimination across payment allocations, and less variability across fairness ratings, while subjects in bad moods adopt a strategy that results in the opposite. However, our results would have been more conclusive if we had directly measured subjects' fairness of payment categories. We conducted a second study to explore this issue.

We had subjects listen to music that was designed to make them feel good

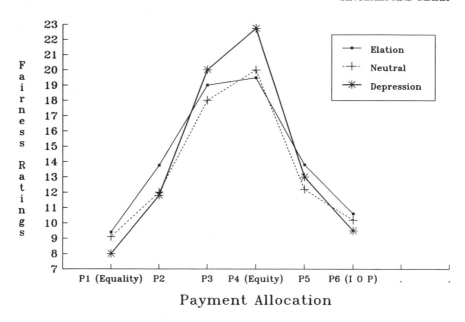

FIG. 6.2.   Fairness of payment ratings as a function of induced mood and payment allocation.

or bad, and then read a series of vignettes describing two workers. Half of the vignettes described low productivity ratios, where the two workers produced about the same; half described high productivity ratios, where one worker substantially outproduced the other. We asked subjects to divide a pot of money between the two workers and to tell us the least and the most that a person could get while still keeping the distribution of resources fair. The difference between the least and most ratings served as a measure of breadth of fair payment. We expected subjects in good moods, who process nonsystematically and thus differentiate less across stimuli, to show broadest fair payment categories; we expected subjects in bad moods, who differentiate more, to show narrowest fair payment categories. Further, we expected this difference to be most apparent for high productivity ratios where there is greater possibility for conflict between alternative rules of justice (i.e., equity and equality); at low productivity ratios, where people produce about the same, the division of resources is less ambiguous because an equality rule and equity rule lead to about the same division. The results were exactly as predicted: Subjects in a positive mood had the broadest categorization of fair payment, especially at high productivity ratios. We interpret this effect in terms of mood-related differences in processing strategy, with subjects in good moods differentiating less, leading to a broader categorization of what is a fair payment. Moreover, the results indicate the utility of conceptualizing equity judgments as a categorization task.

Nevertheless, we wanted to manipulate processing strategy in another manner than through a mood induction, in order to better test the linkage between processing strategy and breadth of fair payment. We used an unrelated second study paradigm. In an initial study purportedly assessing how subjects group stimuli, we primed subjects on an initial categorization task to either a high differentiation (i.e., create many small groups) or low differentiation (i.e., create few large groups) condition, or subjects were assigned to a no prime control group. In the second study, ostensibly assessing perceptions of work situations, subjects provided the least-most ratings described above. We perfectly replicated the results of the previous study. Subjects in the low differentiation condition had a larger range of payments classified as fair, especially at high productivity ratios. It appears that changes in processing strategy, whether induced by mood or by priming, affect justice judgments. Strategies that result in attention and finer differentiation lead to narrower fair payment categories; strategies that result in less differentiation lead to broad fair payment categories.

We conducted an additional study to address the effects of mood on another aspect of perceived justice, that is, relative endorsement of microjustice and macrojustice principles (Sinclair & Mark, 1991). *Microjustice principles* refer to "the fairness of rewards to individual recipients," whereas *macrojustice* has been described as "the aggregate fairness of reward in society" (Brickman et al., 1981, p. 183; see also, Mark, 1980). Thus, *equity* is an example of a microjustice principle in resource allocation, whereas a minimum income or cap on maximum salaries are examples of macrojustice principles. Although our focus has been on processing strategy, there are several mechanisms through which mood may affect the relative endorsement of these two types of principles. First, people in positive moods report greater liking for others and more positive conceptions of people; people in negative moods show the opposite (Forgas & Bower, 1987; Griffitt, 1970; Veitch & Griffitt, 1976). Liking of others is likely associated with more egalitarianism and less concern for equity (e.g., Deutsch, 1975; Lamm & Schwinger, 1980). Thus, good moods should increase endorsement of egalitarian, macrojustice principles by enhancing people's judgments of others, and negative moods should do the opposite. Further, consider the evidence that moods result in differential processing, and consider that microjustice principles require the use of individually differentiating information (e.g., inputs) whereas macrojustice principles do not (i.e., they may require less cognitive effort to institute). Accordingly, subjects in bad moods, who engage in more effortful, more systematic processing, may prefer equity-based microjustice principles, which require greater cognitive effort and individually differentiating information to institute. Subjects in positive moods, on the other hand, may prefer the less cognitively effortful macrojustice principles. Of course, we might expect this processing strategy effect to have greater impact on actual resource allocation; however, it might also affect the evaluation of justice principles because subjects may consider the processing required to implement a principle, and may prefer principles consistent with their current processing strategy. Finally, if, as we have argued, mood affects categorization breadth through processing strategy, happy subjects may prefer the use of macrojustice principles, which are instituted by viewing (at least some) people as alike; in contrast, subjects in bad moods may prefer microjustice principles, which involve differentiating individuals based on their personal characteristics, such as discriminating according to levels of merit.

To test the effects of mood on endorsement of justice principles, we had subjects in induced happy, neutral, or depressed moods indicate their relative endorsement of both macrojustice (e.g., "There should be a minimum income guaranteed for everyone") and microjustice (e.g., "Each person's income should be based on how hard he or she works relative to others") principles in resource allocation. Consistent with our predictions, we found that happy subjects showed more endorsement of egalitarian macrojustice principles than did depressed subjects. Further, elated subjects discriminated least between microjustice and macrojustice principles, whereas depressed subjects discriminated most.

Based on our results in the area of mood and justice, we developed a model of the mechanisms through which mood may have impact on perceived justice and resource allocation. This model, as presented in Fig. 6.3, emphasizes processing strategy, but also includes other mechanisms that could influence perceived justice through a confluence of processes. Borrowing from Schwarz (1990), Petty et al. (1988) and others, we suggest that affective states have three direct, major consequences. First, they affect processing strategies such that happy subjects use more heuristic, less systematic processing strategies, whereas sad subjects use more deliberate, more effortful strategies. (Note that earlier in this chapter we presented a model which specified three pathways linking mood state and processing strategy; see Fig. 6.1.) Second, mood serves as an informational cue; for example, in assessing a target's likability, people may assess their feelings toward the target and, in doing so, be influenced by

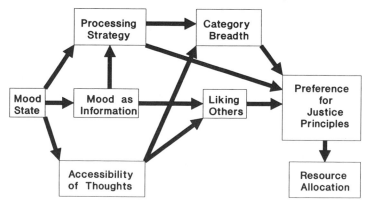

FIG. 6.3. A hypothesized model of the process by which mood influences justice principles and resource allocation.

mood state (Clore, 1990; Schwarz, 1990; Schwarz & Clore, 1983). Third, affective state may influence the accessibility of material in memory such that good moods lead to the retrieval of positive thoughts (e.g., Clark & Isen, 1982; Petty et al., 1988).

These three mechanisms can instigate other processes. The nonsystematic strategy of happy subjects will often lead to broad categorization (as discussed previously). Good moods may also make accessible thoughts about the basic similarity of all people, leading to broader categorization (cf. Isen & Daubman, 1984). Liking for others will be influenced by the use of mood as a cue, by retrieval of mood-congruent thoughts, and by processing strategy (in that a positive response to others may be an effortless, nonsystematic response; cf. Fiske, 1980; Sears, 1983). Through a variety of mechanisms, then, we would expect that good moods would lead to a relative preference for egalitarian macrojustice principles and bad moods to a preference for microjustice principles. Of course, preference for justice principles should affect resource allocation.

The model presented in Fig. 6.3 illustrates a fundamental point of this chapter. We believe that processing strategy has a prominent place in mediating the effects of mood. Further, the empirical evidence reviewed in this section, as in the preceding sections, is consistent with a processing strategy explanation. However, we do not see processing strategy as the only process mediating the effect of mood on outcome variables, as indicated by the other pathways linking mood and preferences for justice principles in Fig. 6.3. But we do believe that processing strategy is relatively pervasive across domains of judgment and action; the following two sections further illustrate the scope of processing strategy accounts.

Mood, Person Perception, and Accuracy of Impressions

There is ample evidence to suggest that mood impacts on information encoding and retrieval in a manner consistent with an accessibility hypothesis (Bower, 1981; Esses, 1989; Isen, 1984, 1987; Isen, Shalker, Clark, & Karp, 1978; Snyder & White, 1982; Teasdale & Fogarty, 1979; Teasdale & Russell, 1983). That is, subjects in positive moods generally encode and subsequently retrieve mood-congruent information that results in mood-consistent impressions. Such mood-related accessibility effects have been found in the area of person perception (Baron, 1987; Forgas & Bower, 1987; Sinclair, 1988).

The position that positive and negative moods have differential effects on processing strategies leads to another prediction. Given a valid measure of accuracy, we might expect that happy subjects, who engage in less systematic processing, would be least accurate in person perception judgments, whereas depressed subjects, who engage in systematic processing, would be most accurate. However, it is difficult to assess whether moods affect accuracy in the area of person perception, because there are few criteria for accuracy of impressions.

Sinclair (1988) attempted to test this hypothesis about mood and accuracy in person perception. Subjects read about a target person and were provided with both positive and negative behavioral information that mapped onto specific behavioral categories (e.g., *sensitivity, answering questions, delivering lectures*). Later, in induced elated, neutral, or depressed moods, subjects evaluated the likability of the target and made evaluations of the target on scales related to the specific behavioral categories (e.g., *sensitivity*). As expected, based on the accessibility hypothesis, happy subjects formed more positive impressions than depressed subjects. However, depressed subjects made evaluations of the target that better mapped onto the valence of the encoded information in each of the behavioral categories. For example, depressed subjects were more likely to evaluate the target as positive on a dimension for which the behavioral information was positive and as negative on a dimension for which the behavioral information was negative, relative to elated subjects. Thus, in the sense of correspondence to the target person's characteristics across categories, depressed subjects were more accurate. Further, happy subjects displayed most halo in their judgments; that is, consistent with the categorization breadth effects, they failed to discriminate across behavioral dimensions when making evaluations when, in fact, discrimination was called for. Finally, depressed subjects' specific behavioral ratings gave more information about (i.e., allowed greater predictability of) their global evaluation of the target than was the case for happy subjects. Sinclair concluded that elated subjects may be forming sweeping global impressions, whereas depressed subjects may be assessing more facts and making more discrete judgments. He argued that categorization breadth effects may be due to the use of loose heuristic strategies on the part of happy subjects and more algorithmic strategies on the part of depressed subjects.

Given these results, and given our beliefs about mood-based differences in processing strategy, we decided to further explore processing strategy differences in another person perception study (Sinclair & Mark, 1990). We varied subjects' moods and later, in a purportedly unrelated study, varied the degree to which the behavioral information that subjects encoded about a target was initially positive or negative (although all subjects encoded the same total information; cf. Asch, 1946; Farr, 1973; Farr & York, 1975; Luchins, 1957; Sinclair, 1988). Thus, we had a 2 (mood: elated, depressed) × 2 (primacy: initial positive information, initial negative information) design. Later, in neutral moods, subjects evaluated target likability and recalled all information that they could about the target.

If subjects in good versus bad moods had been merely presented with a random array of positive and negative information about a target, we would expect the typical mood-congruent accessibility at encoding effect (Bower, 1981; cf. Isen et al., 1978), with subjects in good moods encoding and retrieving positive information and distorting information in a positive manner, and subjects in bad moods encoding and retrieving negative information and distorting information in a negative manner. However, given our belief that elated subjects and depressed subjects use different processing strategies, a different set of predictions would be made when mood at encoding is paired with a primacy manipulation at encoding. Recall the processing strategy position that depressed subjects process more systematically or more actively and accurately, make more careful judgments, and weight more information in making decisions, relative to elated subjects who process less systematically and less accurately, weigh less information, and make quick and easy judgments. Based on such processing differences, we would expect elated subjects to be more affected by the primacy manipulation. That is, those elated subjects who encode initially positive information about a target should form a very positive impression. Conversely, those elated subjects who encode initially negative information should form a very negative impression. Our rationale was that elated subjects, being less deliberate and more apt to use heuristics in their processing, are likely to be greatly influenced by initial information and to discount or even fail to attend to subsequent information because the initial information should provide a heuristic for impression formation. In contrast, depressed subjects should more deliberately process and more equally weigh all information in forming impressions, and thus should be less affected by primacy.

Indeed, we found the predicted pattern. Elated subjects were most affected by the primacy manipulation. That is, elated subjects who encoded initial positive information formed the most positive impressions, whereas elated subjects who encoded initial negative information formed the most negative impressions; depressed subjects were less affected by the primacy manipulation. It appears that depressed subjects weigh more information in their impressions, and are thus less affected by primacy; elated subjects appear to form quick and easy judgments about targets based on initial information and discount or distort subsequent information.

We also examined the information that subjects retrieved about the target. Happy subjects tended to distort information (whether it was objectively positive or negative) in a manner consistent with the valence of their primacy condition; depressed subjects distorted to a lesser extent. Thus, *how* the information was encoded was affected interactively by mood and primacy. It appears that happy subjects are more influenced by primacy, and that for happy subjects initial information sets the tone for the encoding and interpretation of subsequent information more than for depressed subjects. It is as though the initial information (primacy) provides a heuristic for encoding, and thus reduces processing effort; elated subjects rely on this information in order to avoid effortful processing, while depressed subjects engage in more effortful processing and thereby make less use of the primacy heuristic. Finally, we should point out that, whereas we found differences in how information was encoded and subsequently retrieved as a function of mood (i.e., our distortion data), we did not find any mood-related differences in the amount of positive or negative information retrieved about the target.

We should note that the retrieval findings, in conjunction with the fact that our method did not restrict the time subjects had to make their judgments, suggest that differential cognitive capacity restriction is implausible in this research, both in terms of accounting for why processing strategy differences occurred and as a separate explanation. We believe that the restricted capacity view would have led to the prediction that: (a) no mood-related effects would be found because happy subjects were given unlimited time to encode information and to make their judgments (cf. Mackie & Worth, 1989); and (b) restricted capacity for subjects in good moods should have led to retrieval decrements for those subjects. We believe that the results of the two person-perception studies described in this section seem consistent with the position that induced mood elicits processing strategy differences, which result in differential accuracy and bias in impression formation. However, it is somewhat unclear what *accuracy* is in this context. Thus, we conducted additional research assessing the effects of mood states on judgmental accuracy in a nonsocial domain.

Affect, Arousal, and Accuracy

The issue of accuracy in perception as a function of affect is not a new one. Much research in the area of clinical depression, stemming from the reformulation of learned helplessness, has addressed this issue. For example, chronically depressed subjects tend to make more accurate attributions about performance and more accurately perceive control relative to nondepressed subjects (e.g., Abramson, Alloy, & Rosoff, 1981; Alloy & Abramson, 1979, 1982; Alloy, Abramson, & Viscusi, 1981). Further, chronic depression has been associated with heightened sensitivity to social cues, more extensive social inference activity, and greater interest in social information (e.g., Gleicher & Weary, 1991; Hildebrand-Saints & Weary, 1989; Marsh & Weary, 1989; Weary, Elbin, & Hill, 1987; Weary, Jordan, & Hill, 1985). Finally, Ruehlman, West, and Pasahow (1985) found that nondepressed subjects showed a positivity bias in attributions and perceptions, mildly depressed subjects showed no bias, and severely depressed subjects showed a negativity bias. The research just cited involved trait or chronic depression rather than induced depressed moods; further, the judgments examined in that research tended to be self-relevant (e.g., perceived control). It is unclear whether temporarily induced negative mood states would have a similar relationship to judgmental accuracy on tasks lower in self-relevance. However, given our other results, which suggest that happy subjects use heuristic strategies while subjects in depressed moods engage in more effortful/algorithmic processing, we would expect greater accuracy for subjects in negative moods.

We decided to assess the accuracy issue in the context of judgments for which there was an unambiguous accuracy criterion (Sinclair & Mark, 1990). We changed subjects' moods and then had them report the magnitude and direction of correlation coefficients from scatterplots. Subjects were research methods students, familiar with correlations, who believed that the mood induction was for their first lab. They thought that the correlation estimation task was part of their course work. We found that happy subjects were least accurate in their estimates. Further, happy subjects used fewer digits in their estimates than did depressed subjects (e.g., a happy subject would report that a correlation was .7, whereas a sad subject would report that the correlation was .72). It would appear that happy subjects process less systematically and make less precise snap judgments.

We replicated this effect in a study in which we factorially manipulated the affective and arousal content of our mood induction (Sinclair & Mark, 1990; cf. Russell, 1980; Sinclair & Thayer, 1991; Tanaka & Huba, 1984a, 1984b). Subjects were exposed to *active positive* (i.e., elation), *active negative* (i.e., anxiety; see Andrews & Borkovec, 1988), *passive positive* (i.e., serenity), or *passive negative* (i.e., depression) mood inductions and then made correlation estimates. We found that arousal had little influence on accuracy (cf. Kahneman, 1973; Yerkes & Dodson, 1908; Zajonc, 1965), but that subjects in positive moods were less accurate than subjects in negative moods. Again, subjects in positive moods used fewer digits in their estimates than did subjects in negative moods. We also had subjects describe their strategies for estimating the correlations, give examples of correlational relationships, and estimate the amount of concentration they expended while making their estimates. Consistent with the differential strategy position, happy subjects reported concentrating less while completing the task, they used less accurate strategies, gave less accurate examples, used less detail, wrote less comprehensible descriptions, addressed fewer aspects of correlations in their descriptions, and wrote fewer words than did subjects in bad moods. These effects suggested that, regardless of arousal level, subjects in bad moods were accessing and assessing more information, and more pertinent information when making their judgments. Interestingly, happy subjects appeared to use more creative descriptions of correlations and more creative examples. So, happy people were more creative, but they were wrong. Finally, consistent with Murray et al. (1990) (although nonsignificant in our case), subjects in positive states took less time to complete their correlation estimates.

These results suggest that happy subjects are less accurate when performing nonsocial tasks. They appear to use heuristic strategies (e.g., snap judgments) and haphazard processing strategies relative to subjects in bad moods. In recent research consistent with this position, Melton (1990) showed that happy subjects performed worse than controls on a syllogism task, and that they used heuristic strategies, and selected more universal rather than particular conclusions (i.e., they failed to discriminate among arguments). Finally,

Melton found that happy subjects took less time to complete the task than did a control group (cf. Mackie & Worth, 1989). Once again, it appears that a restricted-capacity argument alone cannot account for the effects of mood on processing strategy.

Mood and Stereotyping

If happy subjects process less systematically and rely more on heuristics, they should be more likely to rely on stereotypes in social judgments, given that stereotypes can be viewed as a type of heuristic (Bodenhausen, in press; Bodenhausen & Wyer, 1985). Bodenhausen (in press) and Bodenhausen and Kramer (1990, 1991) provided evidence consistent with this hypothesis. Happy subjects' judgments were more affected by stereotypes than were subjects in other moods. These findings on the effect of mood on stereotyping seem closely related to our findings on mood and susceptibility to primacy effects, discussed earlier.

Further, Bodenhausen and Kramer (1991) suggested that the effect of mood on stereotype use occurs even when the mood induction used does not involve rumination-based capacity restriction. In particular, Bodenhausen and Kramer found that positive mood subjects rely more on stereotypes even when the positive mood induction involves a ruse through which subjects were led to smile, under the pretext of a "cognitive-motor coordination" study (see e.g., Adelman & Zajonc, 1989 on the effectiveness of such techniques). Such a manipulation should not constrain cognitive capacity in the same way as would asking subjects to recall and re-experience previous life events. Thus, the research on mood and stereotyping is also consistent with the processing strategy explanation.

CONCLUSIONS

Our research, and the work of others from which we have drawn in this chapter, is consistent with the position that mood affects processing strategy, such that: (a) good moods lead to less systematic, less effortful processing, with a greater reliance on heuristics, while (b) bad moods lead to more systematic processing and more effortful processing strategies that rely less on heuristics. Such differences are observed in processing information and in making judgments ranging from estimates of correlations to responses to persuasive appeals, from justice judgments to stereotyping. Viewed from this perspective, subjects in bad moods are seen as often making better and more thoughtful judgments than subjects in good moods.

Individual findings that support a processing strategy interpretation of mood effects can sometimes be reinterpreted in terms of other, indeed, essentially opposite, explanations. For example, Wyer and Srull (1989) suggested that Bless et al.'s (1990) findings on mood and persuasion could be interpreted in terms of positive mood subjects' greater cognitive activity. However, we believe that the pattern of findings reviewed is more reasonably and parsimoniously explained by the processing strategy position as we have described it.

We would like to make two points about a processing strategy approach to mood. First, although processing strategy may be an important mechanism, it is probably not the only mechanism through which many mood effects are mediated. Indeed, some phenomena may both causally underlie processing strategy effects and also have independent, direct effects on at least some types of judgments, as we have suggested is the case for mood as information (see Fig. 6.1). That is, there may be no single mediator, but a multiply-determined causal system, as illustrated in our model of the effects of mood on justice principles (see Fig. 6.3). Further, a given mediator may be more important for some situations and for some people. For example, we expect that mood as information would have stronger direct effects on judgments of subjective well-being than on judgments about the magnitude of correlations.

Second, the processing strategy effect of mood is itself likely to be multiply determined, as illustrated in Fig. 6.1. Various of the mechanisms we cited may be important, with the magnitude of their contributions possibly varying as a function of situational or person characteristics. People may be generally motivated to maintain their positive moods (by avoiding effortful processing) and to repair their negative moods (by attending to a task carefully); however, these mood maintenance/affect repair processes may be weaker for some individuals and may even reverse for some types of tasks. Concerning mood as information, if the mood provides information that a person's judgments are good, the person may fail to engage in more systematic processing. If the information that the mood provides is negative, the person may engage in more systematic processing that distracts from the mood and can lead to better problem solving, which should help prevent any further mood decrement. We have suggested that mood-based capacity restriction cannot fully account for mood effects in several areas, but restricted capacity can only accentuate strategy differences and thus, the effects of mood on judgments.

In this chapter, we have focused on the role of processing strategy as a mediator of mood effects. This focus could seem to imply a robust advantage for those in a negative mood, whose processing strategy is characterized as more systematic, less heuristic, and more careful and effortful. However, more systematic processing does not inevitably lead to better decisions (see Isen & Means, 1983, regarding heuristic strategies). Further, while those in a positive mood can be characterized negatively with respect to processing strategy, a more positive characterization can also be offered: Positive moods may lead to creative thinking (Isen et al., 1987), broad (Isen & Daubman, 1984) or flexible (Murray et al., 1990) categorization, and other modes of expansive thinking that have potential benefits. In addition, people in positive moods can at least sometimes be characterized as being more motivated (Pretty & Seligman, 1984) and as having higher expectations about their ability to achieve positive outcomes (Kavenaugh & Bower, 1985). Because of the benefits of positive moods, happy people may be more willing to risk potentially negative decisions because their mood provides information that their decisions are good and that life is good. Further, although there may be negative consequences for making an improper decision, the person in a positive mood may be able to afford it (cf. Hollander, 1958). Additionally, we can speculate that those in good moods may be more willing and better able to juggle the demands of multiple tasks. Conversely, while negative moods may lead to more systematic processing, they may also lead to less risk taking, and to less creative and more pragmatic thinking. People in negative states may not be able to afford the risk of a more expansive or creative strategy. Further, negative mood may serve as a cue to focus more narrowly on the task at hand (Frijda, 1988). It may be that the differential processing strategy effects of mood that we have described are robust, but that the extent to which they impact positively or negatively on a given task vary as a function of the properties of the task.

ACKNOWLEDGMENTS

This chapter benefited from conversations with Jerry Clore, Mel Jaffa, Diane Mackie, Lenny Martin, Rich Petty, George Ronan, and Norbert Schwarz. Lenny Martin, Rich Petty, and Abe Tesser provided valuable feedback on a previous version of this chapter. Amy Alonso, Toni Babin, Jim Doherty, Bruce Friedman, Becky Gibson, Shannon Gilin, Jennifer Hoffman, Sandy Kanouse, Kim Lange, Becky Miles, Marty Murphy, Lynn Niemi, Tracie Pickering, Gary Reeder, Carol Ryan, Elaine Stypula, Eileen Tait, Joe Tedesco, Bruce Wallis, Mitch Weisbrod, and Stephanie Wrzensinski assisted in collecting and coding the data reported here.

REFERENCES

Abramson, L. Y., Alloy, L. B., & Rosoff, R. (1981). Depression, and the generation of complex hypotheses in the judgment of contingency. *Behaviour Research and Therapy, 19,* 35–45.
Adams, J. S. (1965). Inequity in social exchange. In L. Berkowitz (Ed.), *Advances in experimental social psychology* (Vol. 2, pp. 267–299). New York: Academic.
Adelman, P. K., & Zajonc, R. B. (1989). Facial efference and the experience of emotion. *Annual Review of Psychology, 40,* 249–280.
Alloy, L. B., & Abramson, L. Y. (1979). Judgment of contingency in depressed and non-depressed students: Sadder but wiser? *Journal of Experimental Psychology: General, 108,* 441–485.
Alloy, L. B., & Abramson, L. Y. (1982). Learned helplessness, depression, and the illusion of control. *Journal of Personality and Social Psychology, 42,* 1114–1126.
Alloy, L. B., Abramson, L. Y., & Viscusi, D. (1981). Induced mood and the illusion of control. *Journal of Personality and Social Psychology, 41,* 1129–1140.

Andrews, V. H., & Borkovec, T. D. (1988). The differential effects of inductions of worry, somatic anxiety, and depression on emotional experience. *Journal of Behaviour Therapy and Experimental Psychiatry, 19,* 21–26.

Arkes, H. R., Herren, L. T., & Isen, A. M. (1988). The role of potential loss in the influence of affect on risk-taking behavior. *Organizational Behavior and Human Decision Processes, 42,* 181–191.

Asch, S. E. (1946). Forming impressions of personality. *Journal of Abnormal and Social Psychology, 41,* 258–290.

Baron, R. A. (1987). Interviewer's mood and reactions to job applicants: The influence of affective states on applied social judgments. *Journal of Applied Social Psychology, 17,* 911–926.

Baron, R. A. (1990). Environmentally induced positive affect: Its impact on self-efficacy, task performance, negotiation, and conflict. *Journal of Applied Social Psychology, 20,* 368–384.

Berger, J., Zelditch, M., Jr., Anderson, B., & Cohen, B. P. (1972). Structural aspects of distributive justice: A status-value formulation. In J. Berger, M. Zelditch, Jr., & B. Anderson (Eds.), *Sociological theories in progress* (Vol. 2, pp. 119–146). Boston, MA: Houghton Mifflin.

Bless, H., Bohner, G., Schwarz, N., & Strack, F. (1990). Mood and persuasion: A cognitive response analysis. *Personality and Social Psychology Bulletin, 16,* 331–345.

Bodenhausen, G. V. (in press). Emotions, arousal, and stereotypic judgments: A heuristic model of affect and stereotyping. In D. M. Mackie & D. L. Hamilton (Eds.), *Affect, cognition, and stereotyping: Interactive processes in group perception.* San Diego, CA: Academic Press.

Bodenhausen, G. V., & Kramer, G. P. (1990, June). *Affective states trigger stereotypic judgments.* Paper presented at the annual convention of the American Psychological Society, Dallas, TX.

Bodenhausen, G. V., & Kramer, G. P. (1991, May). *Smiling and stereotyping: Does happiness trigger stereotypic judgments?* Paper presented at the annual meeting of the Midwestern Psychological Association, Chicago, IL.

Bodenhausen, G. V., & Wyer, R. S., Jr. (1985). Effects of stereotypes on decision making and information processing strategies. *Journal of Personality and Social Psychology, 48,* 262–282.

Bower, G. (1981). Mood and memory. *American Psychologist, 36,* 129–148.

Brickman, P., & Bryan, J. H. (1973). Moral judgment of theft, charity, and third-party transfers that increase or decrease equity. *Journal of Personality and Social Psychology, 31,* 156–161.

Brickman, P., Folger, R., Goode, E., & Schul, Y. (1981). Microjustice and macrojustice. In M. J. Lerner & S. C. Lerner (Eds.), *The justice motive in social behavior* (pp. 173–202). New York: Plenum.

Cacioppo, J. T., Petty, R. E., & Morris, K. J. (1983). Effects of need for cognition on message evaluation, recall, and persuasion. *Journal of Personality and Social Psychology, 45,* 805–818.

Chaiken, S. (1980). Heuristic versus systematic information processing and the use of source versus message cues in persuasion. *Journal of Personality and Social Psychology, 39,* 752–766.

Chaiken, S. (1987). The heuristic model of persuasion. In M. P. Zanna, J. M. Olson, & C. P. Herman (Eds.), *Social influence: The Ontario symposium* (Vol. 5, pp. 3–39). Hillsdale, NJ: Lawrence Erlbaum Associates.

Cialdini, R. B., Darby, B., & Vincent, J. (1973). Transgression and altruism: A case for hedonism. *Journal of Experimental Social Psychology, 9,* 502–516.

Clark, M. S., & Isen, A. M. (1982). Toward understanding the relationship between feeling states and social behavior. In A. H. Hastorf & A. M. Isen (Eds.), *Cognitive social psychology* (pp. 73–108). New York: Elsevier North Holland.

Clore, G. L. (1990, October). *The information function of affective states.* Paper presented at the annual meeting of the Society for Experimental Social Psychology, Buffalo, NY.

Crowne, D., & Marlowe, D. (1964). *The approval motive.* New York: Wiley.

Deutsch, M. (1975). Equity, equality, and need: What determines which value will be used as the basis of distributive justice? *Journal of Social Issues, 31,* 137–149.

Esses, V. M. (1989). Mood as a moderator of acceptance of interpersonal feedback. *Journal of Personality and Social Psychology, 57,* 769–781.

Farr, J. L. (1973). Response requirement and primacy-recency effects in a simulated selection interview. *Journal of Applied Psychology, 57,* 228–232.

Farr, J. L., & York, C. M. (1975). Amount of information and primacy-recency effects in recruitment decisions. *Personnel Psychology, 28,* 233–238.

Fiske, S. T. (1980). Attention and weight in person perception: The impact of negative and extreme behavior. *Journal of Personality and Social Psychology, 38,* 889–906.

Forgas, J. P. (1989). Mood effects on decision making strategies. *Australian Journal of Psychology, 41,* 197–214.

Forgas, J. P., & Bower, G. H. (1987). Mood effects on person-perception judgments. *Journal of Personality and Social Psychology, 53,* 53–60.

Forgas, J. P., & Bower, G. H. (1988). Affect in social and personal judgments. In K. Fiedler & J. Forgas (Eds.), *Affect, cognition, and social behavior* (pp. 183–208). Toronto: Hogrefe.

Frijda, N. H. (1988). The laws of emotion. *American Psychologist, 43,* 349–358.

Gleicher, F., & Weary, G. (1991). The effect of depression on the quantity and quality of social inferences. *Journal of Personality and Social Psychology, 61,* 105–114.

Griffitt, W. B. (1970). Environmental effects on interpersonal affective behavior: Ambient effective temperature and attraction. *Journal of Personality and Social Psychology, 15,* 240–249.

Hildebrand-Saints, L., & Weary, G. (1989). Depression and social information gathering. *Personality and Social Psychology Bulletin, 15,* 150–160.

Higgins, E. T., Rholes, W., & Jones, C. R. (1977). Category accessibility and impression formation. *Journal of Experimental Social Psychology, 13,* 141–154.

Hollander, E. P. (1958). Conformity, status, and idiosyncrasy credit. *Psychological Review, 65,* 117–127.

Homans, G. C. (1961). *Social behavior: Its elementary forms.* New York: Harcourt, Brace, & World.

Isen, A. M. (1984). Toward understanding the role of affect in cognition. In R. S. Wyer & T. K. Srull (Eds.), *Handbook of social cognition* (Vol. 3, pp. 179–236). Hillsdale, NJ: Lawrence Erlbaum Associates.

Isen, A. M. (1987). Positive affect, cognitive processes, and social behavior. In L. Berkowitz (Ed.), *Advances in experimental social psychology* (Vol. 20, pp. 203–353). New York: Academic Press.

Isen, A. M., & Daubman, K. A. (1984). The influence of affect on categorization. *Journal of Personality and Social Psychology, 47,* 1206–1217.

Isen, A. M., Daubman, K. A., & Nowicki, G. P. (1987). Positive affect facilitates creative problem solving. *Journal of Personality and Social Psychology, 52,* 1122–1131.

Isen, A. M., Horn, N., & Rosenhan, D. L. (1973). Effects of success and failure on children's generosity. *Journal of Personality and Social Psychology, 27,* 239–247.

Isen, A. M., Johnson, M. M. S., Mertz, E., & Robinson, G. F. (1985). The influence of positive affect on the unusualness of word associations. *Journal of Personality and Social Psychology, 48,* 1413–1426.

Isen, A. M., & Means, B. (1983). The influence of positive affect on decision making strategy. *Social Cognition, 2,* 18–31.

Isen, A. M., Means, B., Patrick, R., & Nowicki, G. (1982). Some factors influencing decision making and risk taking. In M. S. Clark & S. T. Fiske (Eds.), *Affect and cognition: The seventeenth annual Carnegie symposium on cognition* (pp. 241–261). Hillsdale, NJ: Lawrence Erlbaum Associates.

Isen, A. M., Shalker, T. E., Clark, M. S., & Karp, L. (1978). Positive affect, accessibility of material in memory, and behavior: A cognitive loop? *Journal of Personality and Social Psychology, 36,* 1–12.

Johnson, E., & Tversky, A. (1983). Affect, generalization, and the perception of risk. *Journal of Personality and Social Psychology, 45,* 20–31.

Kahneman, D. (1973). *Attention and effort.* Englewood Cliffs, NJ: Prentice-Hall.

Kavenaugh, D. J., & Bower, G. H. (1985). Mood and self-efficacy: Impact of joy and sadness on perceived capabilities. *Cognitive Therapy and Research, 9,* 507–525.

Lamm, H., & Schwinger, T. (1980). Norms concerning distributive justice: Are needs taken into consideration in allocation decisions? *Social Psychology Quarterly, 43*, 425–429.

Lewicka, M., Piegat, A., & Krzyzak, K. (1991). *Mood related differences in predecisional search strategies.* Unpublished manuscript, University of Warsaw.

Luchins, A. S. (1957). Primacy-recency in impression formation. In C. Hovland (Ed.), *The order of presentation in persuasion* (pp. 33–61). New Haven, CT: Yale University Press.

Mackie, D. M., & Worth, L. T. (1989). Processing deficits and the mediation of positive affect in persuasion. *Journal of Personality and Social Psychology, 57*, 27–40.

Mackie, D. M., & Worth, L. T. (1991). Feeling good, but not thinking straight: The impact of positive mood on persuasion. In J. Forgas (Ed.), *Emotion and social judgments* (pp. 201–219). London: Pergamon.

Mark, M. M. (1980). *Justice in the aggregate: The perceived fairness of the distribution of income.* Unpublished doctoral dissertation, Northwestern University, Evanston.

Mark, M. M., & Sinclair, R. C. (1990). *Mood, categorization breadth, and perceived justice: A processing strategy interpretation.* Unpublished manuscript, The Pennsylvania State University, University Park.

Marsh, K. L., & Weary, G. (1989). Depression and attributional complexity. *Personality and Social Psychology Bulletin, 15*, 325–336.

Melton, R. J. (1990). *Effects of induced moods on analytic task performance.* Unpublished manuscript, Indiana University, Bloomington, IN.

Morrow, J., & Nolen-Hoeksema, S. (1990). Effects of responses to depression on the remediation of depressive affect. *Journal of Personality and Social Psychology, 58*, 519–527.

Murray, N., Sujan, H., Hirt, E. R., & Sujan, M. (1990). The influence of mood on categorization: A cognitive flexibility interpretation. *Journal of Personality and Social Psychology, 59*, 411–425.

O'Malley, M. N., & Davies, D. K. (1984). Equity and affect: The effects of relative performance and moods on resource allocation. *Basic and Applied Social Psychology, 5*, 273–282.

Petty, R. E. (1990, October). *Attributions and persuasion: A new look.* Paper presented at the annual meeting of the Society for Experimental Social Psychology, Buffalo, NY.

Petty, R. E., & Cacioppo, J. T. (1984). The effects of involvement on responses to argument quantity and quality: Central and peripheral routes to persuasion. *Journal of Personality and Social Psychology, 46*, 69–81.

Petty, R. E., & Cacioppo, J. T. (1986). The elaboration likelihood model of persuasion. In L. Berkowitz (Ed.), *Advances in experimental social psychology* (Vol. 19, pp. 124–203). New York: Academic Press.

Petty, R. E., Cacioppo, J. T., Sedikides, C., & Strathman, A. (1988). Affect and persuasion: A contemporary perspective. *American Behavioral Scientist, 31*, 355–371.

Petty, R. E., Gleicher, F., & Baker, S. M. (1991). Multiple roles for affect in persuasion. In J. Forgas (Ed.), *Emotion and social judgments* (pp. 181–200). London: Pergamon.

Pretty, G. H., & Seligman, C. (1984). Affect and the overjustification effect. *Journal of Personality and Social Psychology, 46*, 1241–1253.

Rosch, E. (1975). Cognitive representation of semantic categories. *Journal of Experimental Psychology: General, 104*, 192–233.

Ruehlman, L. S., West, S. G., & Pasahow, R. J. (1985). Depression and evaluative schemata. *Journal of Personality, 53*, 46–92.

Russell, J. A. (1980). A circumplex model of affect. *Journal of Personality and Social Psychology, 39*, 1161–1178.

Schaller, M., & Cialdini, R. B. (1990). Happiness, sadness, and helping: A motivational integration. In E. T. Higgins & R. M. Sorrentino (Eds.), *Handbook of motivation and cognition: Foundations of social behavior* (Vol. 2, pp. 265–296). New York: Guilford Press.

Schwarz, N. (1988, August). *Happy but mindless? Mood effects on problem solving and persuasion.* Paper presented at the twenty-fourth International Congress of Psychology, Sydney, Australia.

Schwarz, N. (1990). Feelings as information: Informational and motivational functions of affective states. In E. T. Higgins & R. M. Sorrentino (Eds.), *Handbook of motivation and cognition: Foundations of social behavior* (Vol. 2, pp. 527–561). New York: Guilford Press.

Schwarz, N., & Bless, H. (1991). Happy and mindless, but sad and smart? The impact of affective states on analytic reasoning. In J. Forgas (Ed.), *Emotion and social judgments* (pp. 55–71). London: Pergamon.

Schwarz, N., Bless, H., & Bohner, G. (1991). Mood and persuasion: Affective states influence the processing of persuasive communications. In M. Zanna (Ed.), *Advances in experimental social psychology* (Vol. 24, pp. 161–199). New York: Academic Press.

Schwarz, N., & Clore, G. L. (1983). Mood, misattribution, and judgments of well-being: Informative and directive functions of affective states. *Journal of Personality and Social Psychology, 45*, 513–523.

Schwarz, N., & Clore, G. L. (1988). How do I feel about it? The information function of affective states. In K. Fiedler & J. Forgas (Eds.), *Affect, cognition and social behavior* (pp. 44–62). Lewiston, NY: Hogrefe.

Sears, D. O. (1983). The person-positivity bias. *Journal of Personality and Social Psychology, 44*, 233–250.

Sinclair, R. C. (1988). Mood categorization breadth, and performance appraisal: The effects of order of information acquisition and affective state on halo, accuracy, information retrieval, and evaluations. *Organizational Behavior and Human Decision Processes, 42*, 22–46.

Sinclair, R. C., & Mark, M. M. (1990). *The effects of mood state on processing strategy, accuracy, and impression formation: Strategy versus capacity.* Unpublished manuscript, Central Michigan University, Mt. Pleasant, MI.

Sinclair, R. C., & Mark, M. M. (1991). Mood and the endorsement of egalitarian macrojustice principles versus equity-based microjustice principles. *Personality and Social Psychology Bulletin, 17*, 369–375.

Sinclair, R. C., Mark, M. M., & Clore, G. L. (1991). *Mood, misattribution, and persuasion: The informational impact of mood on processing strategy.* Unpublished manuscript, University of Alberta, Edmonton, Canada.

Sinclair, R. C., Mark, M. M., & Weisbrod, M. S. (1990). *The effects of mood states on categorization breadth: Processing strategy or cognitive flexibility?* Unpublished manuscript, Central Michigan University, Mt. Pleasant, MI.

Sinclair, R. C., & Thayer, J. F. (1991). *The structure of affective states and the use of the Multiple Affect Adjective Check List: Evidence for orthogonal bipolar affect and activity dimensions.* Unpublished manuscript, Central Michigan University, Mt. Pleasant, MI.

Snyder, M., & White, P. (1982). Mood and memories: Elation, depression, and the remembering of one's life. *Journal of Personality, 50*, 149–167.

Tanaka, J. S., & Huba, G. J. (1984a). Confirmatory hierarchical factor analyses of psychological distress models. *Journal of Personality and Social Psychology, 46*, 621–635.

Tanaka, J. S., & Huba, G. J. (1984b). Structures of psychological distress: Testing confirmatory hierarchical models. *Journal of Consulting and Clinical Psychology, 52*, 719–721.

Teasdale, J. D., & Fogarty, S. J. (1979). Differential effects of induced moods on retrieval of pleasant and unpleasant events from episodic memory. *Journal of Abnormal Psychology, 88*, 248–257.

Teasdale, J. D., & Russell, M. L. (1983). Differential effects of induced mood on the recall of positive, negative, and neutral words. *British Journal of Clinical Psychology, 22*, 163–172.

Veitch, R., & Griffitt, W. (1976). Good news–bad news: Affective interpersonal effects. *Journal of Applied Social Psychology, 6*, 69–75.

Walster, E., Berscheid, E., & Walster, G. W. (1973). New directions in equity research. *Journal of Personality and Social Psychology, 25*, 151–176.

Weary, G., Elbin, S., & Hill, M. G. (1987). Attributional and social comparison processes in depression. *Journal of Personality and Social Psychology, 52*, 605–610.

Weary, G., Jordan, J. S., & Hill, M. G. (1985). The attributional norm of internality and depressive sensitivity to social information. *Journal of Personality and Social Psychology, 49,* 1283–1293.

Wegener, D. T., Petty, R. E., & Richman, S. A. (1991). Positive mood and processing of persuasive communications. *Proceedings and Abstracts of the Annual Meeting of the Midwestern Psychological Association, 63,* 151.

Worth, L. T., & Mackie, D. M. (1987). Cognitive mediation of positive affect in persuasion. *Social Cognition, 5,* 76–94.

Wyer, R. S., & Srull, T. K. (1989). *Memory and cognition in its social context.* Hillsdale, NJ: Lawrence Erlbaum Associates.

Yerkes, R. M., & Dodson, J. D. (1908). The relation of strength of stimulus to rapidity of habit-formation. *Journal of Comparative Neurology of Psychology, 18,* 459–482.

Zajonc, R. B. (1965). Social facilitation. *Science, 149,* 269–274.

Beyond Accessibility:
The Role of Processing
Objectives in Judgment

Leonard L. Martin
John W. Achee
University of Georgia

People are not stupid. At least, they are not stupid in the way that some of the initial work in social cognition seemed to suggest. Consider, for example, the work on concept priming. It was assumed (e.g., Higgins & King, 1981; Wyer & Srull, 1980, 1981) that in the course of forming impressions, people searched for concepts with which to interpret a target person's behaviors. As soon as they found such a concept, they stopped searching, even when a little further searching might have revealed a concept that provided a better or equally good fit. One implication of this assumption was that "judgments of people may often be affected by quite fortuitous events that lead one or another concept to be more accessible at the time the information about these people is first received" (Wyer & Srull, 1980, p. 282). More generally, social perceivers were characterized as "cognitive misers" who tended to devote no more effort to processing than they had to, and who preferred instead to use whatever information was on the "top of their heads" (Fiske & Taylor, 1984).

While we do not dispute the findings of this research, we do suggest that the findings may have presented an incomplete view of the social perceiver. There is reason to believe that perceivers are much more sophisticated in their use of information than the initial work seemed to suggest. In this chapter, we explore some ways in which people appear to seek specific kinds of information while forming an impression. We briefly review the initial work on concept priming and the models that grew out of that work. Then, we discuss more recent models of concept priming (i.e., Lombardi, Higgins, & Bargh, 1987; Martin, 1986; Martin, Seta, & Crelia, 1990), and the research bearing on these models. Finally, we discuss the implications of this research for a more complex view of the social perceiver.

THE FEATURE MATCH MODELS:
ASSIGNMENT TO A CATEGORY

The initial work on concept priming grew out of Bruner's (1957) work on *perceptual readiness* (see Higgins & King, 1981). The basic assumption was that when a person received information with the goal of forming an impression, the first cognitive operation the person had to perform was encoding the information in terms of a knowledge structure (e.g., a trait concept). Presumably, it was not until the behavioral information had been encoded in terms of such a structure that it became useful in forming an impression. As Bruner (1957) described it, "All perception is generic in the sense that whatever is perceived is placed in and receives its meaning from a class of percepts with which it is grouped" (p. 124). Thus, a behavior like *never changes his mind* is informative with regard to impression formation only after perceivers have encoded it as either persistent or stubborn.

Assignment of an action to a concept was assumed to depend, in part, on the degree of match between the features of the action and those of the concept. The more features an action and a concept had in common, the more likely it was that the action would be encoded in terms of that concept. The action *never changes his mind*, for example, would be more likely to be interpreted as stubborn or persistent than as sociable or neat. Stubborn and persistent denote a singleness of purpose that is consistent with never changing one's mind, but sociable and neat do not denote singleness of purpose. Hence, they are inapplicable for interpreting the behavior *never changes his mind*.

When an action is interpretable in terms of more than one concept, individuals are assumed to use the concept that is more accessible (i.e., most easily retrieved). A concept's accessibility is determined by, among other things, recent or frequent use (see Higgins & King, 1981). Thus, the behavior *never changes his mind* would be interpreted as stubborn by someone in whom the concept *stubborn* had recently been activated, but as persistent by someone in whom the concept *persistent* had recently been activated.

Two models of concept use in impression formation were initially proposed (Higgins & King, 1981; Wyer & Srull, 1980). Although these models differed from one another in a number of ways, they were similar in their basic predictions. These predictions were summarized succinctly by Higgins and Chaires (1980):

> Thus, both approaches suggest that recent and frequent activation of a construct increases the likelihood that the construct will be selected or retrieved first to

apply to the stimulus information. If the construct is applicable to the stimulus (i.e., there is a sufficient match between the features of the construct and the features of the stimulus), then it will be used to encode or characterize the stimulus. (p. 351)

Evidence for this general model has been obtained in a variety of experiments (for reviews, see Higgins & King, 1981; Wyer & Srull, 1980, 1981). Higgins, Rholes, and Jones (1977), for example, had subjects perform in what were ostensibly two experiments. In the first, subjects were asked to memorize words that were presumably distractors in a perceptual task. In reality, the words served to prime (i.e., increase the accessibility of) various trait concepts. In the second experiment, subjects were presented with a description of a person and asked to form an impression of that person. The description included actions that could be construed in either favorable or unfavorable terms. The act of skydiving, for example, could be construed as either adventurous or reckless.

For some subjects, the distractor words in the first experiment primed concepts that were favorable and applicable for interpreting the description in the second experiment (e.g., *adventurous*). For other subjects, the distractors primed concepts that were unfavorable and applicable (e.g., *reckless*). The remaining subjects received inapplicable concepts that were either favorable (e.g., *obedient*) or unfavorable (e.g., *listless*).

When the primed concepts were applicable for interpreting the actions of the target person, subjects' impressions of the target were assimilated toward the implications of those concepts. That is, subjects in whom concepts such as *adventurous* were primed construed the target's risk-taking behaviors as adventurous. Subjects in whom concepts such as *reckless* were primed construed these same behaviors as reckless. When the subjects had been primed with inapplicable concepts, however, their impressions were not significantly affected by the priming. These results suggest that subjects interpreted the information about the target person in terms of the concepts that had been most recently activated, but only when these concepts were applicable (i.e., denotatively similar) to the target information.

Subsequent work (e.g., Herr, 1986; Herr, Sherman, & Fazio, 1983) suggested that when the most accessible concept is related to but much more extreme than the target information along the dimension of judgment, subjects contrast their impressions with the implications of the concept. Thus, a target person who engages in moderately hostile behavior, for example, would be judged to be very hostile by perceivers who had just been thinking of Gandhi or Shirley Temple but as not very hostile by perceivers who had just been thinking of Hitler or Genghis Khan (Herr, 1986). According to Herr et al. (1983), when the most accessible concept is inconsistent with the implications of the target information, people do not use that concept to interpret the information. Rather, they use it as a standard of comparison, and this leads to a shift in judgment away from the implications of the concept (e.g., Sherif & Hovland, 1961).

To summarize, the models of concept use that grew out of the initial priming work placed the onus of concept use/disuse on two qualities of the primed information: applicability and accessibility. As long as a concept was accessible and applicable to information, it was used to interpret that information (Higgins & Chaires, 1980, p. 351). When the concept was inconsistent with the implications of the target behavior, it was used as a standard of comparison, producing shifts in judgment away from the implications of the primed concept (i.e., a contrast effect).

Problems With the Feature Match View

One weakness with the view that concept use is determined by a concept's similarity (i.e., applicability) to the target information is that similarity, by itself, is not an explanatory concept. Explanations in terms of similarity, noted Medin (1989):

> will prove useful only to the extent that one specifies which principles determine what is to count as a relevant property and which principles determine the importance of particular properties. It is important to realize that the explanatory work is being done by the principles which specify these constraints rather than the general notion of similarity. In that sense similarity is more like a dependent variable than an independent variable. (p. 1474)

Consider, for example, the range of features that a plum and a lawn mower have in common (Murphy & Medin, 1985). Both weigh less than 1,000 kg, both are found on earth, both are found in our solar system, both cannot hear well, both have an odor, both are not worn by elephants, both are used by people, both can be dropped, and so on. How do we decide which of these features to consider in our judgment of similarity? The features themselves do not say. Factors outside of the features must tell us what is relevant and what is not and how much to weigh each of the relevant features (Medin, 1989; Tversky, 1977).

Defining applicability in terms of denotative similarity (Higgins & Chaires, 1980; Higgins et al., 1977) was an attempt to circumscribe the features that determine applicability. It was assumed that a concept was used to interpret information only when the concept and the behavior had the same meaning. There are two problems with this proposal. First, assimilation effects have been found even when the priming stimuli had no denotative implications relevant to the target information. In Martin (1986, Experiment 3), for example, subjects wrote positive or negative self-referent statements (e.g., It's great to be alive vs. It's a pain to be alive) as a priming task. Then, they were asked to form an impression based on information that was ambiguous with respect to the traits *adventurous/reckless, persistent/stubborn, independent/aloof,* and *self-confident/*

egotistical. As can be seen, there are no denotative features in the priming task that relate to the ambiguities in the target paragraph. Yet, subjects assimilated their impressions toward the valence of the self-referent statements (when the priming task was interrupted). That is, subjects who had written positive self-referent statements formed more positive impressions of the target than did subjects who had written negative self-referent statements. These results could not have been obtained if applicability was determined exclusively by the denotative match between the primed concepts and the target information (see also Martin, Seta, & Crelia, 1990).

The second problem with denotative applicability as a rule for concept use is that *contrast* can occur even when the primed concepts are denotatively applicable to the target information (e.g., Lombardi et al., 1987; Martin, 1986; Martin, Seta, & Crelia, 1990; Newman & Uleman, 1990). In Martin (1986, Experiment 1), for example, subjects were asked to categorize a series of behaviors in terms of two traits. For some subjects, the traits were *adventurous* and *self-confident*. For others, the traits were *reckless* and *egotistical*. In each of these groups, some subjects were led to believe that they would have to categorize 8 behaviors, whereas others were led to believe that they would have to categorize 12. All subjects were stopped after categorizing 8. Thus, subjects who had been asked to categorize 8 finished the priming task, whereas subjects who had been asked to categorize 12 did not.

Following the interruption or completion of the priming task, subjects were asked to form an impression of a target person described in terms that were ambiguous with respect to adventurousness and recklessness. It was found that subjects' impressions were assimilated toward the implications of the primed concepts when subjects had been interrupted during the priming task but were contrasted with those implications when subjects had been allowed to complete the priming task. What makes these results problematic for the feature match models is that subjects across the interrupted and completed-task conditions were exposed to the same priming stimuli and formed impressions of the same stimulus person. Thus, the applicability of the primed concepts to the target information was the same for all subjects. Yet, assimilation as well as contrast occurred.

Similar results have been obtained by Lombardi et al. (1987). They also found assimilation when a priming task was interrupted, and contrast when it was completed. However, they found contrast only for subjects who recalled the priming stimuli. When subjects did not recall the priming stimuli, even those who had completed the priming task showed assimilation. The point of these findings, for present purposes, is that both assimilation and contrast were obtained with the same degree of applicability between the primed concept and the target behavior. Such results are incompatible with a simple feature match model (see also Martin et al., 1990; Newman & Uleman, 1990).

So, the question becomes "What, other than (or in addition to) denotative

similarity, determines whether a concept will be used to interpret information?''
One answer appears to lie in subjects' awareness of the priming stimuli. In the
early priming experiments, the experimenters went to great lengths to disguise
the relation between the priming task and the target judgment. They often used
subtle, disguised priming manipulations placed in "two experiment" paradigms.
Other researchers (e.g., Bargh & Pietromonaco, 1982) presented the priming
stimuli too quickly for subjects to consciously detect. So, in a very real sense,
subjects in the initial priming experiments did not know that they were being
primed.

By comparison, the priming procedures in the more recent experiments tended to be blatant, in the sense that at least some subjects were able to recall
the priming event at the time they were forming their impressions. So, there
appears to be something about awareness of the priming event that makes subjects use the primed concepts differently than they do when they are not aware
of that event.

Models of Active Use

Two models have been developed recently that can integrate the results of the
initial priming experiments with those of the more recent experiments. One of
these is the set/reset model of Martin (1986; Martin et al., 1990); the other
is the flexible processing model of Lombardi et al. (1987). In this section, we
describe each model and then compare and contrast the two.

The Set/Reset Model.   The set/reset model is based on the assumption
that people have many sources of information that they can use at any given
time to form an impression. These include activated trait concepts, evaluative
concepts, scripts, exemplars, and other general knowledge structures. Individuals may also be experiencing global moods, specific emotions, or bodily states
such as arousal, fatigue, or hunger. They may consider previously formed judgments or attributions, general attitudes, general word knowledge, communication rules, and more. All of these kinds of information seem to play important
roles in judgments at one time or another (for a review, see Martin & Clark,
1990). However, they do not all come into play for each and every judgment.
People are selective in their use of information. What determines this selection?

According to the set/reset model, individuals seek information that appears
appropriate (or at least not inappropriate) to their current processing objectives.
For example, when individuals take seriously the goal of forming an impression, one of their goals should be to assess their genuine reaction to the target person. To reach this goal, individuals should *not* report on their current
mood, their impression of the contextual stimuli or their impression of the priming
stimuli. Neither are they to report on their impression of their neighbor, their
accountant, or what they saw on TV last night. They are not to report some

other subject's impression of the target person. Their objective is to report *their* impression of the *target*, and nothing else.

So, if individuals find themselves thinking negative thoughts that appear to be due to their exposure to negative priming stimuli, for example, then they may avoid using these thoughts in forming their impression. These thoughts pertain to the priming stimuli, and not to the target person. Hence, these thoughts do not help the individuals to fulfill their processing objective (i.e., give your impression of *the target*). What perceivers may do in such cases is search for another concept that allows them to interpret the target information, but that does not appear to have been made accessible by something other than the target. So, rather than interpret a high risk-taking behavior as reckless (which was blatantly primed), individuals may interpret this behavior as adventurous.

To account for the differences in results between the initial, subtle priming paradigms and the more recent blatant paradigms, Martin (1986) suggested that:

> when a concept is primed very subtly, individuals may not even be aware that it has been activated in them (Bargh & Pietromonaco, 1982). Consequently, when this concept comes to mind in the subsequent impression formation task they have no reason to believe that it is anything other than their own spontaneous reaction to the target. This means that they have no reason not to use the primed concept in interpreting the target information, provided that it is consistent with the implications of that information.
>
> The same may not hold true, however, when a concept is primed more blatantly. Under these conditions, individuals may associate the activation of the concept with their exposure to the priming stimuli rather than with the target stimulus. As a result, they may actually avoid using the primed concept to interpret the target information, as its use would appear to bias their independent evaluation of the target. (p. 494)

It is important to point out that the set/reset model is not limited to explaining the difference between subtle and blatant priming. The model assumes more generally that any processing objective that tells subjects not to use primed information will cause subjects to reset. Several experiments have obtained evidence for this more general view. Strack, Martin, and Schwarz (1988), for example, asked subjects two questions in the context of a survey. The questions were, "How frequently do you go out on a date?" and "How happy are you with your life as a whole?" For the sampled population (i.e., college students), happiness with dating tends to be highly correlated with happiness with life in general (Emmons & Diener, 1985). Thus, there should be a high correlation between subjects' answers to the dating question and their answers to the life satisfaction question.

For some subjects, however, the two questions were prefaced with the following introduction: "Now we are going to ask you about two aspects of your life that may be related: frequency of dating and happiness with life in general."

According to Strack et al. (1988), this introduction prompts subjects to engage the given-new communication rule (Grice, 1975). According to this rule, respondents should provide questioners with information that is new (i.e., not redundant with the information that the questioner already has).

In the context of the survey, answering the question about dating frequency allowed the subjects to assume that the questioner had the information he or she needed with regard to that topic. Hence, the subjects may have interpreted the subsequent question about "life in general" as a request for new information, that is, a request for information about aspects of their lives other than dating frequency. Consequently, subjects appeared to answer the life in general question by considering aspects of their lives other than dating (e.g., school, home, health), and thereby the correlation between the dating question and the life satisfaction question was reduced. More specifically, when the two questions were merely presented one following the other, the correlation between the two was .66. When the two were presented in the communication context, the correlation was .15 (see also Schwarz, Strack, & Mai, 1991).

According to the set/reset model, when the dating question preceded the life in general question as just another item in the survey, it was not inappropriate for subjects to answer the general question using information made accessible in answering the dating question. After all, dating frequency is a part of general life satisfaction. And, there was no processing objective to give new information. On the other hand, when the two questions were placed in a communication context, subjects' adherence to the given-new contract demanded that they avoid redundancy. Subjects were *not* to answer the life satisfaction question using information made accessible by the dating question. So, they partialled this information from their answer to the subsequent life satisfaction question (i.e., they reset), and the result was a lowered correlation between their answers to the two questions.

Another example of the operation of set/reset processes comes from research on categorization effects in person perception (e.g., Martin & Seta, 1983; Seta, Martin, & Capehart, 1979; Tajfel & Wilkes, 1963; Wedell & Parducci, 1988). In these studies, it was generally found that assimilation occurred when stimuli were rated as a unit, whereas contrast occurred when the stimuli were rated as distinct entities (Martin & Seta, 1983; Schwarz & Bless, this volume). Seta, Martin, and Capehart (1979), for example, asked subjects to indicate their liking for two target persons. These persons were depicted in terms of their responses on an attitude survey. The responses of the first person were constructed to agree with the subjects at a 50% rate, whereas the responses of the second person were constructed to agree at a 100% rate.

Because people tend to like those who agree with them (Byrne, 1971), subjects should like the second person more than the first. Seta et al. (1979) found this to be the case. However, they also found that the difference in liking for the two people depended on the way in which they were categorized. When the two were depicted as having the same major, there was no significant difference in subjects' liking for the two. When the two were depicted as having different majors, subjects liked the second person significantly more than the first. Moreover, the second person was liked significantly more when depicted as having a major different from the first than when depicted as having a major similar to the first.

According to the set/reset model, when the targets were depicted as having the same major, it was not inappropriate to use the reactions elicited by the first person in forming an impression of the second. After all, the people were similar in some ways. When the targets had different majors, however, it was inappropriate to judge the second person using reactions elicited by the first. So, subjects reset, producing contrast.

In short, any factor that makes information inconsistent with a processing objective increases the chances that subjects will not use that information. If subjects have no reason to question the usefulness of information in helping them to fulfill their processing objectives, then they use the information. Thus, information use is determined by factors in addition to accessibility and applicability. Strack, Martin, and Schwarz (1988) previously summarized these factors under the term *appropriateness* (see also Higgins, 1989). More precisely, they argued that:

> applicability and accessibility do not exhaust the list of factors that determine information use. Cues in the judgmental setting can prompt individuals into using or not using primed information. These cues include the relationship between the target and the context (Martin & Seta, 1983; Strack et al., 1985), the desire to make a context independent judgment (Kubovy, 1977; Martin, 1986), instructional sets (Leach, 1974), and communication rules. We summarize these factors under the term "appropriateness." Adoption of this notion allows one to understand how a concept can be accessible and applicable to information and yet not be used to interpret that information. (Strack et al., 1988, p. 439)

More generally, the set/reset model proposes a *sifter* metaphor of social judgment rather than (or in addition to) a category match metaphor. People sift through their thoughts and feelings and attempt to partial the relevant from the irrelevant. People do not use information simply because that information is accessible and applicable. Use of that information might violate a communication rule (Strack et al., 1988). Similarly, subjects do not use their feelings toward Person A in evaluating Person B when the two are portrayed as belonging to distinct categories (Martin & Seta, 1983). And, individuals do not use primed concepts to interpret target information if they associate the accessibility of those concepts with their exposure to the priming stimuli (Lombardi et al., 1987; Martin, 1986).

According to the model, the term *set* refers to the use of primed information in the formation of the target impression, whereas the term *reset* refers to the suppressed use of primed information and the use of independently activated information in forming an impression. Set may be the default process with resetting being most likely to occur when there are demands (either implicit or explicit) to exclude the primed information from consideration (Clore, this volume; Kubovy, 1977; Leach, 1974; Martin & Seta, 1983; Mettee, Taylor, & Friedman, 1973; Schwarz & Bless, this volume; Strack, this volume; Strack et al., 1988). Whereas a set is most likely to produce assimilation, a reset is most likely to produce contrast. The set/reset model is depicted graphically in Fig. 7.1.

It is important to keep in mind that the set/reset model does not imply that people go around second guessing each and every judgment they make. As can be seen in Fig. 7.1, the model assumes that people assess *in*appropriateness,

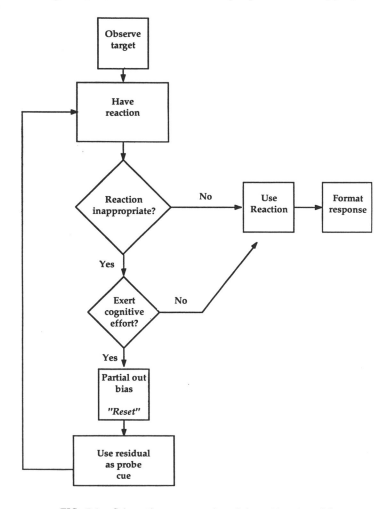

FIG. 7.1.   Schematic representation of the set/reset model.

not appropriateness. In other words, people may use the information that is most accessible to them unless some factor (e.g., instructional set, lack of fit, blatant priming) calls that use into question. Moreover, the model does not assume that the decision to use or not use information is always open to introspective awareness. In fact, in debriefing after our experiments our subjects usually deny that the manipulations influenced their judgments in any way.

Thus, the operation of set/reset processes may reflect the automatic activation of procedural knowledge (Smith & Lerner, 1986). A hypothetical reset production system might look something like:

IF attempting to assess own reaction to target, and
IF irrelevant reaction is detected,
THEN delete the irrelevant reaction and access relevant reaction.

This kind of production system could be automatically cued when subjects have the goal of forming an accurate judgment and they detect an irrelevant reaction. Though automatically activated, the execution of the production system's routine might demand the expenditure of cognitive effort (i.e., resetting appears to demand cognitive effort, Martin et al., 1990). However, the activation of the system and its role in the judgment may remain beyond the subject's awareness. In short, the model suggests that people can process information in adaptive, flexible ways, but that this more complex processing does not imply rational or conscious use of that information.

The Flexible Processing Model.   Lombardi et al. (1987) based their model on their findings that subjects who recalled the priming stimuli tended to contrast their impressions with the implications of the primed concepts, whereas subjects who did not recall the priming stimuli tended to assimilate their impressions toward the implications of the primed concepts. Lombardi et al. (1987) hypothesized that "the function of consciousness of the priming events may be to enable subjects to adopt flexible strategies in processing subsequent information relevant to those primed constructs" (p. 426). They did not speculate, however, on the nature of this processing or how it sometimes leads to contrast as opposed to assimilation. This issue was later addressed by Higgins (1989) who suggested that:

When a priming event describes a person, as in the Srull and Wyer (1979) and Higgins, Bargh, and Lombardi (1985) paradigms that have been used in many studies, subjects are provided with statements or labels describing people who possess or display a particular trait (e.g., hostility). According to the rules of language comprehension (see, e.g., Huttenlocher & Higgins, 1971), such statements should be interpreted as an instance of a person's possessing or displaying the trait to a greater extent than the average person. If such instances or exemplars are recalled later when subjects are asked to categorize the stimulus person, they may function as a high standard or reference point relative to which the stimulus person's ambiguous or vague behavior is judged. This should produce a contrast effect of the priming event on subjects' categorizations of the stimulus persons (see Higgins & Stangor, 1988). (Higgins, 1989, p. 81)

So, in a sense, what is being suggested is a variant of the feature match model. Concepts that are applicable when subjects are not aware of the priming event become too extreme to be applicable when subjects *are* aware of that event. In terms of predictions, Lombardi et al. (1987) suggested that "without consciousness of the priming events, subsequent stimuli are inevitably assimilated to the primed construct" (p. 426), whereas with consciousness, priming "may result in *either* assimilation *or* contrast effects, with the subjects' perception of the priming task as complete or incomplete, and possibly other as yet unidentified factors (e.g., aspects of the task context), determining which will occur" (p. 422).

Comparing and Contrasting the Two Models

The set/reset model and the flexible processing model are similar in a number of ways. Both grew out of experiments in which contrast was obtained when subjects completed a blatant priming task, and assimilation was obtained when subjects were interrupted during a blatant priming task. Both suggest that awareness of the priming event prompts subjects into more controlled processing. And, both suggest that factors in addition to simple applicability are necessary to account for the use of primed concepts (although Higgins' account of the effects of awareness is a modified applicability account).

There are also differences between the models, however, and in many ways these differences are more interesting than the commonalities. For example, the set/reset model suggests that awareness of the priming stimuli can cause perceivers to judge the use of the primed concepts to be inappropriate for their processing objectives. The flexible processing model suggests that awareness of the priming events makes the primed concepts seem more extreme. The set/reset model suggests that contrast to an applicable concept is a partialling process. The flexible processing model suggests that contrast is the effect of comparison to an extreme standard. The set/reset model suggests that when contrast is the result of a partialling process, the more similar the primes are to the target, the greater the contrast. The flexible processing model suggests that the more extreme the standard (i.e., the primed concept) relative to the target information, the greater the contrast.

As yet, there have been no experiments directly comparing predictions from the two models. However, there are data from a number of experiments that bear on the models' predictions. These data center on the role of extremity of the priming stimuli, the role of meta-knowledge, and the role of awareness.

The Effects of Prime Extremity.   The flexible processing model assumes that contrast results from a comparison to an extreme standard. Thus, the more extreme the standard, the more extreme the contrast. The set/reset model, on the other hand, assumes a partialling process. More specifically, the set/reset model assumes that contrast occurs when subjects partial primed information from their reaction to the target, and use the residual to generate a new reaction (See Fig. 7.2). The greater the overlap between the primed response and the target response, the more features of the target response subjects partial out. Thus, the more similar the prime is to the target, the greater the shift in judgment relative to a condition in which no partialling has occurred.

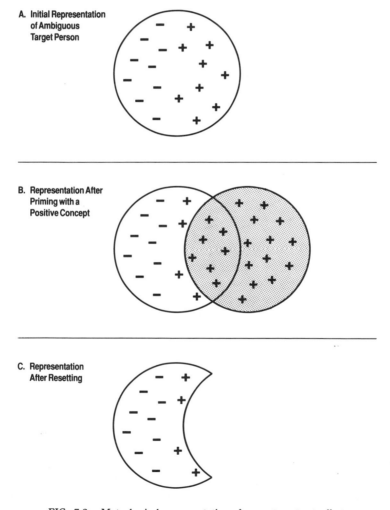

FIG. 7.2.   Metaphorical representation of a reset contrast effect.

It is likely, however, that this effect has limits. If the overlap is too great, then there may be an insufficient number of distinct target features left after partialling to generate a unique response to the target. In this case, subjects may accept the primed response, producing an assimilation. Outside of this extreme case, however, the more similar the prime and the target, the more features of the target response subjects are likely to partial out (under conditions where they partial), and the greater the contrast.

Evidence bearing on these predictions was obtained by Skowronski, Carlston, and Isham (1991, Experiment 2). They had subjects perform either a subtle priming task, a blatant priming task, or both. In addition, subjects were primed with concepts that varied in their extremity. For the subtle priming task, subjects were presented with a number of words and asked to judge the frequency of occurrence of these words. Of the 160 presented, 8 were related to the primed dimension (mental retardation), and these 8 were each presented twice. For the blatant priming task, there were 10 explicit references in the target description that the target was mentally retarded. And, it was stated that the target's IQ was between 55 and 65.

Skowronski et al. (1991) varied the extremity of the primed concepts in the subtle priming task. More specifically, some subjects received no words related to mental retardation, some (moderate prime condition) were exposed to words such as addled, plodding, slow, and dull, and some (extreme prime condition) were exposed to words such as idiot, moron, dimwit, and stupid.

Skowronski et al. (1991) found that when subjects were exposed to subtle priming only, the more extreme the prime, the greater the assimilation. When subjects received the blatant as well as the subtle priming tasks, there was contrast with a moderately extreme prime and assimilation with an extreme prime.

These results are not easily reconciled with the view that blatant primes function as a standard of comparison. If they had, then the more extreme the standard, the greater should have been the contrast. On the other hand, if resetting was occurring, then the more similar the prime and the target, the more features of the target were likely to have been partialled out when subjects attempted to remove the influence of the primes. Thus, the finding of greater contrast with the moderate than the extreme primes is consistent with the set/reset model.

The Role of Meta-Knowledge. Yzerbyt, Schadron, and Leyens (1991) also obtained evidence relevant to predictions of the flexible processing model and the set/reset model. They gave subjects non-diagnostic biographical information about a target person. Then, they informed subjects that the target was either a library archivist or a comedian, occupations shown to be associated with introversion and extraversion, respectively. Subjects were then asked to shadow a text during a dichotic listening task. The subjects heard two voices, one male and one female, each on a different channel of the head phones.

The non-shadowed channel contained a number of irrelevant nouns and adjectives, but at the end of the experiment, subjects were unable to tell what kind of information had been presented on the non-shadowed channel. Immediately after the shadowing task, however, half of the subjects were told that the information on the non-shadowed channel were answers provided by the target person in the course of an earlier interview. The remaining subjects were told nothing about the content of the non-shadowed channel. Thus, both groups of subjects had been presented with stereotypical information only, but some subjects believed that they had obtained additional, individuating information.

Subjects were then asked to indicate their impression of the target person. Yzerbyt et al. (1991) found that subjects formed impressions consistent with the stereotype when they believed they had individuating information, but not when they believed that they did not have this information. In fact, in the latter conditions, subjects' general impressions showed contrast.

These results appear difficult to interpret in terms of a standard of comparison model. The "information" and "no information" conditions were identical except for subjects' belief that individuating information had been given. There is no reason why this belief would lead to differences in subjects' ability to recall the prime (i.e., the occupation). Moreover, recall of the primes is assumed to transform the prime into an extreme standard to which the target is compared. But in this experiment, the prime is a feature of the target person. So if this feature becomes more extreme, then subjects should rate the target as more (not less) extreme in the direction of the occupation.

According to the set/reset model (see also Yzerbyt et al., 1991), on the other hand, when people wish to form accurate, unbiased impressions, they attempt to partial out inappropriate information. Stereotypical information is inappropriate, but individuated information is not. So, subjects reset when only the stereotype is provided, but set when they believe they have been provided with individuating information. In the latter case, subjects may interpret their reactions to the stereotype to be their reactions to the (nonexistent) individuating information. The result is contrast in the stereotype-only condition and assimilation in the information condition.

The Role of Awareness. According to the flexible processing model, awareness of the priming event engenders the use of communication rules. More specifically, subjects assume that the priming stimuli represent extreme exemplars of the primed concept. In comparing the ambiguously described target person with this extreme exemplar, judgment of the target shifts away from the implications of the exemplar (i.e., a contrast effect). If this comparison mechanism is operating, then subjects do not need to associate the activation of the concept with their exposure to the priming task. Having a salient, extreme standard in mind while they are forming their impression of the target should be sufficient to produce a contrast effect.

According to the set/reset model, on the other hand, awareness of the priming event leads to contrast when it leads subjects to perceive a violation of their processing objectives. Subjects cannot use their reaction to the priming stimuli if their objective is to give their reaction to the target. In other words, contrast is a function of awareness of a bias, not awareness of the priming event per se.

What would happen, then, if subjects became aware of the priming event but did not associate the increased accessibility of the concept with their exposure to the priming stimuli? According to the flexible processing model, there should still be contrast. As long as subjects recall the priming stimuli, they should see those stimuli as extreme exemplars and contrast the target impression with those exemplars. According to the set/reset model, however, subjects who recall the priming stimuli but do not associate the increased accessibility of the primed concept with their exposure to the priming stimuli have no reason to avoid the primed concepts. These concepts seem to be their response to the target and not their response to the priming stimuli. So, subjects use them and the result will be assimilation.

How can one get recall of the priming stimuli without having the subjects associate the increased accessibility of the concept with their exposure to the priming stimuli? The answer comes from work on *reality monitoring* (Johnson & Raye, 1981). Reality monitoring is the process people use in deciding whether memories initially had an external or an internal source. Johnson and Raye proposed that externally obtained knowledge has features that distinguish it from internally generated knowledge, and people can use these features to discriminate between knowledge they generated and knowledge they obtained from the environment.

More specifically, relative to internally generated knowledge, externally obtained knowledge has more information about the time and place in which the knowledge was obtained, more sensory information, and more meaningful details. Knowledge that has been internally generated, on the other hand, has more information about the cognitive operations involved or the processing that took place when the memory was established. So, generally speaking, if a memory has a high sensory component and a clear sense of place, then one can classify it as externally generated. If a memory lacks these features, then one can classify it as internally generated.

As Johnson and Raye (1981) noted, however, "it should be possible to produce confusion about the origin of an event by manipulations that cause it to have abnormally high or low values on one or more dimension, compared to typical memories of its class" (p. 72). Thus, subtle priming procedures may give rise to assimilation precisely because they give rise to externally generated thoughts that have the features of internally generated ones. The subtle procedures leave no time or place information along with the increased accessibility, and they produce no strong sensory component. Thus, "subjects have no reason to believe that the concepts that come to mind are anything other than their reaction to the target stimulus" (Martin, 1986, p. 494). On the other hand, when subjects recall the priming stimuli, there is a time and a place marker. Subjects can tell that their thoughts of recklessness, for example, come from the priming task and not from the target. So, if their objective is to give their impression of the target, then they will reject the use of the primed information.

To explore the role of reality monitoring in the use of primed information, Martin and Scott West (1991) presented subjects with a list of three word sets. The words of each set were semantically related (e.g., purple—yellow—green), but at least one letter was missing from each word. Subjects were instructed to simply fill in the missing letters.

Once subjects completed this task, they were blatantly primed with either positive or negative trait concepts, and asked to form an impression of a person described in terms that were ambiguous with respect to these concepts. Finally, subjects were presented with the original list of word sets, this time with all of the letters included, and asked to identify the letters in each word that they had filled in earlier in the experiment.

It was assumed that performance on the letter task would reflect a more general reality monitoring skill (Johnson & Raye, 1981). Thus, subjects who are better at discriminating the letters they filled in from the letters presented to them should be better at identifying whether the reactions they experience while forming their impression came from the target or from their exposure to the priming stimuli. Thus, these subjects should be able to judge the primed concept as inappropriate to forming an impression of the target and should attempt to partial out the influence of this concept (i.e., contrast). On the other hand, subjects who are not as skilled at discriminating letters they generated from letters given to them might also be poor at discriminating between their reaction to the target and their reaction to the primes. Hence, they may not see the primed response as inappropriate, and may use it in their impression. The result would be assimilation.

The results were consistent with these predictions. The impressions of subjects high in reality monitoring skills showed contrast, whereas the impressions of subjects low in reality monitoring skills showed assimilation. It is unclear how the flexible processing model could account for these results. All subjects recalled the priming stimuli. So, all subjects should have seen those stimuli as extreme exemplars and thus should have shown contrast. However, only subjects who were good at reality monitoring showed contrast.

The results are consistent with the set/reset model. Although all subjects recalled the priming stimuli, use of the primed concept would violate the processing objective "give your impression of the *target*" only for subjects who were good at discriminating what they generated from what was provided externally. For subjects low in reality monitoring, any accessible, applicable concept may seem to be their reaction to the target person. Thus, subjects with good reality monitoring skills show contrast, whereas subjects with poor reality monitoring skills show assimilation.

In sum, there is evidence favoring a partialling model over a comparison model. This does not mean, however, that comparison contrast never occurs. As noted previously, assimilation and contrast may occur through any number of processes. However, because past research has concentrated most heavily on comparison processes (Helson, 1964; Herr et al., 1983; Sherif & Hovland, 1961), it may be time to concentrate on partialling processes.

GENERAL CONCLUSIONS

The data we just reviewed suggest a two-stage model of information use (cf. Gilbert & Hixon, 1991; Kubovy, 1977; Martin, 1986; Martin et al., 1990; Strack & Martin, 1987). In the first stage, individuals retrieve their most accessible information. Then, in the second stage, they test to see if there are situational constraints to the use of this information. If no constraints are detected, then they use the information. If constraints are detected, then individuals suppress the use of this information, and access new information that they believe to be more congruent with their processing objectives. Use of the primed information in judgment produces assimilation, whereas use of the alternative information often produces contrast.

Why Does Resetting Produce Contrast?

It should be pointed out that the set/reset model is not exclusively a model of assimilation and contrast. It is a model of information use. The model addresses assimilation and contrast because these effects reflect different uses of information. In fact, the model does not assume that contrast is the inevitable outcome of resetting. There may be conditions in which people reset but produce judgments showing no effect of the prime or even a reduced assimilation effect. But if these alternative outcomes are possible, then why is contrast so often obtained in priming and social judgment research?

The answer lies, at least partially, in the theories people employ in dealing with inappropriate information (see Schul & Manzury, 1990; Strack, this volume; Wyer & Budesheim, 1987). We know, for example, that subjects do not correct for situational influences on their judgments when they do not know how to correct for those influences. The anchoring and adjustment paradigm provides a good example of this (Tversky & Kahneman, 1974). In a typical anchoring and adjustment experiment, some subjects are told that 65% of the countries of Africa belong to the U.N. Others are told that 15% of the countries of Africa belong to the U.N. Both groups of subjects are then told that the initial figure was wrong, and they are to make an estimate as to what the true percentage is. The typical result is insufficient adjustment. That is, subjects given the high anchor still make estimates higher than those given the low anchor.

One reason subjects may adjust insufficiently in the anchoring and adjustment paradigm is that they have been given insufficient information with which to adjust. How can one adjust accurately without having some idea of the degree to which the initial figure over- or under-estimates the target percentage? Moreover, the amount of adjustment that is considered sufficient can change with the situation. When the anchors are 65% and 15%, for example, an adjustment of 20% leads to insufficient adjustment. When the anchors are 65% and 35%, however, an adjustment of 20% produces an *over*-adjustment (i.e., contrast). So, without additional information, subjects have no clue as to how to move from the wrong answer to a good answer.

In the priming paradigm, on the other hand, subjects do have a clue. The clue is given by their processing objectives. In the course of forming an impression, subjects presumably attempt to interpret the target information and report on their reactions to that information. When subjects decide that the reaction they are experiencing is the result of their exposure to the priming stimuli, they may suppress the use of the primed concept and attempt to retrieve an alternate. If reset contrast is to occur, it does so at this point, with the choice of the alternate concept. So, the question becomes: How do subjects select an alternate concept?

In the case of blatant priming, two criteria must be satisfied: (a) the alternate concept must allow the person to make sense of the target information, and (b) it must not appear to have been made accessible as a result of the subject's exposure to the priming stimuli. To meet these criteria, people must select a concept that is relevant to the target information, yet distinct from the primed concept. Let us consider a specific example.

In most priming experiments, the target information is evaluatively but not descriptively ambiguous. For example, it is clear that a behavior like *never changes his mind* reflects a singleness of purpose, but it is not clear whether this behavior reflects singleness of purpose in a positive (persistent) or a negative (stubborn) way. When subjects are blatantly primed with the positive concept *persistent*, they may avoid the use of this concept in favor of an alternate. The alternate they choose must reflect singleness of purpose but must not reflect persistence. In other words, subjects must select a concept that is *descriptively related* to persistent (i.e., the concept must make sense of the behavior), but that is *evaluatively unrelated* to it (i.e., the concept must not have been made accessible by the priming task). Thus, subjects are more or less constrained to interpret the behavior as *stubborn*. The result is an evaluative contrast effect.

SUMMARY

The data we have reviewed suggests that people do not always respond with the information that is on the top of their heads. In some conditions, they make decisions about the appropriateness of using certain information. Thus, they may suppress the use of inappropriate information and seek out specific information in order to fulfill their processing objectives. So, although social perceivers may not be perfect in their processing, they may be more sophisticated than we had previously believed.

REFERENCES

Bargh, J. A., & Pietromonaco, P. (1982). Automatic information processing and social perceptions: The influence of trait information. *Journal of Personality and Social Psychology, 43*, 437–449.

Bruner, J. S. (1957). On perceptual readiness. *Psychological Review, 64*, 123–152.

Byrne, D. (1971). *The attraction paradigm.* New York: Academic Press.

Emmons, R. A., & Diener, E. (1985). Factors predicting satisfaction judgments: A comparative examination. *Social Indicators Research, 16*, 157–167.

Fiske, S. T., & Taylor, S. E. (1984). *Social Cognition.* Reading, MA: Addison-Wesley.

Gilbert, D. T., & Hixon, J. G. (1991). The trouble of thinking: Activation and application of stereotypic beliefs. *Journal of Personality and Social Psychology, 60*, 509–517.

Grice, H. P. (1975). Logic and conversation. In P. Cole & J. L. Morgan (Eds.), *Syntax and semantics: Speech acts* (Vol. 3, pp. 41–58). New York: Academic Press.

Helson, H. (1964). *Adaptation-level theory: An experimental and systematic approach to behavior.* New York: Harper & Row.

Herr, P. M. (1986). Consequences of priming: Judgment and behavior. *Journal of Personality and Social Psychology, 51*, 1106–1115.

Herr, P. M., Sherman, S. J., & Fazio, R. H. (1983). On the consequences of priming: Assimilation and contrast effects. *Journal of Experimental Social Psychology, 19*, 323–340.

Higgins, E. T. (1989). Knowledge accessibility and activation: Subjectivity and suffering from unconscious sources. In J. S. Uleman & J. A. Bargh (Eds.), *Unintended thought* (pp. 75–123). New York: Guilford Press.

Higgins, E. T., Bargh, J. A., & Lombardi, W. A. (1985). The nature of priming effects on categorization. *Journal of Experimental Psychology: Learning, Memory, and Cognition, 11*, 59–69.

Higgins, E. T., & Chaires, W. M. (1980). Accessibility of interrelational constructs: Implications for stimulus encoding and creativity. *Journal of Experimental Social Psychology, 16*, 348–361.

Higgins, E. T., & King, G. A. (1981). Accessibility of social constructs: Information-processing consequences of individual and contextual variability. In N. Castor & J. F. Kihlstrom (Eds.), *Personality, cognition, and social interaction* (pp. 69–121). Hillsdale, NJ: Lawrence Erlbaum Associates.

Higgins, E. T., Rholes, W. S., & Jones, C. R. (1977). Category accessibility and impression formation. *Journal of Personality and Social Psychology, 13*, 141–154.

Higgins, E. T., & Stangor, C. (1988). A "change-of-standard" perspective on the relations among context, judgment, and memory. *Journal of Personality and Social Psychology, 54*, 181–192.

Huttenlocher, J., & Higgins, E. T. (1971). Adjectives, comparatives, and syllogisms. *Psychological Review, 78*, 487–504.

Johnson, M. K., & Raye, C. L. (1981). Reality monitoring. *Psychological Review, 88*, 67–85.

Kubovy, M. (1977). Response availability and the apparent spontaneity of numerical choices. *Journal of Experimental Psychology: Human Perception and Performance, 3*, 359–364.

Leach, C. (1974). The importance of instructions in assessing sequential effects in impression formation. *British Journal of Social and Clinical Psychology, 13*, 151–156.

Lombardi, W. J., Higgins, E. T., & Bargh, J.A. (1987). The role of consciousness in priming effects on categorization: Assimilation versus contrast as a function of awareness of the priming task. *Personality and Social Psychology Bulletin, 13*, 411–429.

Martin, L. L. (1986). Set/reset: Use and disuse of concepts in impression formation. *Journal of Personality and Social Psychology, 51*, 493–504.

Martin, L. L., & Clark, L. F. (1990). Social cognition: Exploring the mental processes involved in human social behavior. In M. Eysenck (Ed.), *International review of cognitive psychology* (Vol. 1, pp. 265–310). Sussex, England: Wiley.

Martin, L. L., & Scott West, M. (1991, April). *Assimilation and contrast in impression formation as a function of people's ability to distinguish own vs. other's input.* Paper presented at the annual convention of the Southeastern Psychological Association, New Orleans, LA.

Martin, L. L., & Seta, J. J. (1983). Perceptions of unity and distinctiveness as determinants of attraction. *Journal of Personality and Social Psychology, 44*, 755–764.

Martin, L. L., Seta, J. J., & Crelia, R. (1990). Assimilation and contrast as a function of people's willingness and ability to expend effort in forming an impression. *Journal of Personality and Social Psychology, 59*, 27–37.

Medin, D. L. (1989). Concepts and conceptual structure. *American Psychologist, 44*, 1469–1481.

Mettee, D. R., Taylor, S. E., & Friedman, H. (1973). Affect conversion and the gain-loss like effect. *Sociometry, 36*, 505–519.

Murphy, G., & Medin, D. (1985). The role of theories in conceptual coherence. *Psychological Review, 92*, 289–316.

Newman, L. S., & Uleman, J. S. (1990). Assimilation and contrast effects in spontaneous trait inferences. *Personality and Social Psychology Bulletin, 16*, 224–240.

Schul, Y., & Manzury, F. (1990). The effects of type of encoding and strength of discounting appeal on the success of ignoring an invalid testimony. *European Journal of Social Psychology, 20*, 337–349.

Schwarz, N., Strack, F., & Mai, H. P. (1991). Assimilation and contrast effects in part-whole question sequences: A conversational logic analysis. *Public Opinion Quarterly, 55*, 3–23.

Seta, J. J., Martin, L. L., & Capehart, G. (1979). The effects of contrast and generalization on the attitude similarity-attraction relationship. *Journal of Personality and Social Psychology, 37*, 462–467.

Sherif, M., & Hovland, C. I. (1961). *Social judgment: Assimilation and contrast effects in communication and attitude change.* New Haven, CT: Yale University Press.

Skowronski, J. J., Carlston, D. E., & Isham, J. T. (1991). *Implicit versus explicit impression formation: The differing effects of overt labeling and covert priming on memory and impressions.* Manuscript submitted for review.

Smith, E. R., & Lerner, M. (1986). Development and automatism of social judgments. *Journal of Personality and Social Psychology, 50*, 246–259.

Srull, T. K., & Wyer, R. S. (1979). The role of category accessibility in the interpretation of information about persons: Some determinants and consequences. *Journal of Personality and Social Psychology, 37*, 1660–1672.

Strack, F., & Martin, L. L. (1987). Thinking, judging, and communicating: A process account of context effects in attitude surveys. In H. J. Hippler, N. Schwarz, & S. Sudman (Eds.), *Social information processing and survey methodology* (pp. 123–148). New York: Springer-Verlag.

Strack, F., Martin, L. L., & Schwarz, N. (1988). Priming and communication: Social determinants of information use in judgments of life satisfaction. *European Journal of Social Psychology, 18*, 429–442.

Strack, F., Schwarz, S., & Gschneidinger, E. (1985). Happiness and reminiscing: The role of time perspective, affect, and mode of thinking. *Journal of Personality and Social Psychology, 49*, 1460–1469.

Tajfel, H., & Wilkes, A. L. (1963). Classification and quantitative judgment. *British Journal of Psychology, 54*, 101–114.

Tversky, A. (1977). Features of similarity. *Psychological Review, 84*, 327–352.

Tversky, A., & Kahneman, D. (1974). Judgment under uncertainty: Heuristics and biases. *Science, 185*, 1124–1131.

Wedell, D. H., & Parducci, A. (1988). The category effect in social judgment: Experimental ratings of happiness. *Journal of Personality and Social Psychology, 55,* 341–356.

Wyer, R. S., & Budesheim, T. L. (1987). Person memory and judgments: The impact of information that one is told to disregard. *Journal of Personality and Social Psychology, 53,* 14–29.

Wyer, R. S., & Srull, T. K. (1980). The processing of social stimulus information: A conceptual integration. In R. Hastie, T. Ostrom, E. Ebbesen, R. Wyer, D. Hamilton, & D. Carlston (Eds.), *Person memory: The cognitive basis of social perception* (pp. 227–300). Hillsdale, NJ: Lawrence Erlbaum Associates.

Wyer, R. S., & Srull, T. K. (1981). Category accessibility: Some theoretical and empirical issues concerning the processing of social stimulus information. In E. T. Higgins & M. P. Zanna (Eds.), *Social cognition: The Ontario symposium* (Vol. 1, pp. 161–197). Hillsdale, NJ: Lawrence Erlbaum Associates.

Yzerbyt, V. Y., Schadron, G., & Leyens, J. (1991). *Social judgeability: The impact of meta-informational rules on the use of stereotypes.* Manuscript submitted for review.

Constructing Reality and Its Alternatives: An Inclusion/ Exclusion Model of Assimilation and Contrast Effects in Social Judgment

Norbert Schwarz
Zentrum für Umfragen, Methoden und Analysen, ZUMA, Mannheim, Germany

Herbert Bless
Universität Mannheim, Mannheim, Germany

That social judgment is context dependent is no news. From philosophical treatments of human reasoning (see Tatarkiewicz, 1984) and early research on attitude measurement (see Eiser, 1990, for a review) to current public opinion research (see Schwarz & Sudman, 1992) and theorizing in social cognition (cf. the contributions to this volume), students of social judgment have been fascinated by the context dependency of human thought. As numerous experimental studies and natural observations indicate, the evaluation of a target stimulus may be either assimilated or contrasted to the context in which it is presented. In this chapter, we use these terms in their most general form, speaking of an *assimilation effect* whenever the judgment reflects a positive (direct) relationship between the implications of some piece of information and the judgment, and of a *contrast effect* whenever the judgment reflects a negative (inverse) relationship of the judgment and the implications of some piece of information.

Given the generality of these definitions, it is not surprising that a host of different variables has been shown to moderate the emergence of assimilation and contrast effects (see Eiser, 1990, for a review). Moreover, there is wide agreement among researchers that assimilation and contrast effects may reflect the operation of a number of different processes, which have been conceptualized in independent, and apparently unrelated, theories. One group of theories focused on the distribution of the contextual stimuli, assuming that they influence the adaptation level (Helson, 1964), standard of comparison (e.g., Thibaut & Kelley, 1959), or scale anchor (e.g., Ostrom & Upshaw, 1968; Parducci, 1965) used in making a judgment. These models account for the frequently observed finding that evaluations of moderate stimuli are displaced away from ratings of extreme stimuli, reflecting a contrast effect. Another group of models focused on categorization processes (e.g., Herr, Sherman, & Fazio, 1983; Sherif & Hovland, 1961; Tajfel, 1959, 1981; Tajfel & Wilkes, 1963; Turner, 1987). According to these models, assimilation effects are likely to emerge when the target stimulus and the context stimuli are assigned to the same category, whereas contrast effects may emerge when they are assigned to different categories.

In this chapter we build on this previous theorizing as well as on recent research by Barsalou (1987, 1989), Herr et al. (1983), Kahneman and Miller (1986), and Martin and colleagues (Martin, 1986; Martin, Seta, & Crelia, 1990), emphasizing the role of categorization processes in the operation of numerous variables known to elicit assimilation and contrast effects. Clearly, categorization processes have been addressed in previous models, and much of what we have to say is not new. Nevertheless, focusing explicitly on the interplay of cognitive accessibility and the categorization of accessible information provides a heuristically fruitful integrative framework for the conceptualization of assimilation and contrast effects. Moreover, this focus generates numerous hypotheses that have not been tested previously and it helps to specify the conditions under which each of different processes may result in assimilation or contrast effects.

INCLUSION/EXCLUSION AND THE EMERGENCE OF ASSIMILATION AND CONTRAST EFFECTS

Briefly, we assume that individuals who are asked to form a judgment about some target stimulus first need to retrieve some cognitive representation of it. In addition, they need to determine some standard of comparison to evaluate the stimulus. As Kahneman and Miller (1986) suggested, this is frequently a representation of some "alternative" state of reality. Both the representation of *reality*, that is, of the target stimulus, and of its alternatives are, in part, context dependent. Individuals do not retrieve all knowledge that may bear on the stimulus, nor do they retrieve and use all knowledge that may potentially be relevant to constructing its alternative. Rather, they rely on the subset of potentially relevant information that is most accessible at the time of judgment (see Bodenhausen & Wyer, 1987; Higgins, 1989; Higgins & Bargh, 1987, for reviews). Accordingly, their temporary representation of the target stimulus, as well as their construction of a standard of comparison, includes information that is chronically accessible, and hence context independent, as well as information that is only temporarily accessible due to contextual influences (see Barsalou, 1989).

Whether the information that comes to mind results in assimilation or contrast effects depends on how it is *categorized*. However, the specific operation of the categorization process differs somewhat, depending on whether the information that comes to mind is *subordinate* or *superordinate* to the target category. Suppose, for example, that you are asked to evaluate a political party and a specific politician comes to mind who is a member of that party. In that case, the politician who comes to mind is subordinate to the target category. Conversely, however, you may be asked to evaluate this particular politician and his party membership may come to mind. In that case, information bearing on his party in general would be superordinate to the target category. In both cases, the impact of what comes to mind depends on categorization processes, but the specifics of these categorization processes are somewhat different. Accordingly, we discuss both cases in turn.

Subordinate Context Information and the Evaluation of Superordinate Targets

If the information that comes to mind is subordinate to the target category, it will result in an assimilation effect if it is included in the temporary representation that individuals form of the target category. Thus, thinking of a well-respected member of a political party is likely to result in more favorable evaluations of the party as a whole. This simply reflects that the evaluation of a target is based on the information that is included in the temporary representation that individuals construct of it.

Empirically, however, assimilation effects due to the inclusion of a given piece of information can only be observed if the valence of that information is more extreme than the overall valence of the representation in general. Moreover, the size of the emerging assimilation effect should depend on the amount of competing information: The more information is used in constructing a representation, the smaller should be the impact of any additional piece of information that is included in the representation.

Information that is excluded from the target category, on the other hand, may result in contrast effects, although for different, and not mutually exclusive, reasons. First, suppose that individuals exclude some positively valenced information from their representation of the target category. If so, they will base their judgment on a representation that includes less positive information than would otherwise be the case, resulting in less positive judgments. Empirically, this type of contrast effect, which we call a *subtraction effect*, can only be observed if the valence of the excluded information is more extreme than the overall valence of the representation. Such a subtraction effect does not require any assumption about a change in the standard of comparison used. Moreover, the size of subtraction effects should again depend on the amount of information that is used in constructing a temporary representation: The more information is included in the representation, the smaller should be the impact of subtracting a given piece of information.

The subtraction assumption discussed here parallels Martin's (1986; see also Martin et al., 1990) *reset* assumption, where the emergence of contrast effects is traced to the exclusion of valenced features from the representation that individuals form of an ambiguously described target. However, we do not assume that this is the only process that underlies the emergence of contrast effects, nor would we like to restrict the operation of this process to the encoding of ambiguous information that was investigated in the research by Martin and colleagues.

As a second possibility, information that is excluded from the representation of the target stimulus may come to mind when individuals construct a relevant standard of comparison, and may be used for that purpose. If the valence of this information is more extreme than the valence of other information used in constructing the standard, it results in a more extreme standard of comparison, and hence in more pronounced contrast effects. We assume that the representations of the target category and of the standard are mutually exclusive, and that the same piece of information cannot be used to represent the target and the standard against which it is evaluated. Accordingly, we propose that the exclusion of information from the representation of the target is a necessary prerequisite for its use in constructing a standard.

Moreover, extreme information that is excluded from the target category may be used to anchor the response scale, as suggested by Ostrom and Upshaw's (1968) *perspective theory* and related models, and may result in contrast effects for that reason. As an extended debate in social judgment research indicates, changes in the standard of comparison used and changes in scale anchoring are difficult to distinguish empirically (see Eiser, 1990), and we do not attempt to do so in this chapter.

Whereas the mere subtraction of information should only affect the evaluation of the target category from which this information is excluded, the use of excluded information in constructing a standard of comparison should also affect the evaluation of related stimuli, to which the standard may be relevant. For example, subtracting a highly respected politician from the representation formed of his party should result in less favorable evaluations of this particular party. Using this politician in constructing a relevant standard of comparison, on the other hand, may also affect the evaluation of other parties, or specific politicians, to which this standard may be applicable. Moreover, the size of comparison-based contrast effects should not depend on the amount of information used in constructing the representation of the target, in contrast to the subtraction effects discussed previously. Accordingly, assessments of the generalization of contrast effects across targets, and the presence or absence of set size effects, allow for a differentiation of subtraction versus comparison/anchoring-based contrast effects.

Superordinate Context Information and the Evaluation of Subordinate Targets

Similarly, context information that bears on a superordinate category will result in assimilation effects in the evaluation of a subordinate target if the target is included in the superordinate category. Thus, recalling a politician's party membership will result in more favorable evaluations when we like his party than when we dislike it. This reflects the fact that inclusion of his party membership in our cognitive representation of the target politician adds a positively evaluated feature. Moreover, his inclusion in the superordinate category does allow the derivation of other features, such as his standing on various issues, reflecting that "categorization of an object licenses inductive inferences about that object" (Smith, 1990, p. 35).

Note, however, that the inclusion process discussed here is more complex than in the case of subordinate context information and superordinate targets: We assume that inclusion of a subordinate target in a superordinate category allows the derivation of features from our knowledge about the superordinate category. These features, as well as the category membership, are then included in the temporary representation of the target, which serves as a basis of judgment. Of course, this is a key assumption of many current theories of stereotyping (see, for example, Allport, 1954; Brewer, 1988; Fiske & Neuberg, 1990; Hamilton, 1981), and we will not elaborate on this point beyond noting its compatibility with the general approach offered here.

Excluding the target from the superordinate category, on the other hand, again allows for the emergence of contrast effects. These contrast effects may again reflect that a valenced feature is subtracted from the temporary representation of the target (subtraction effect), or that information bearing on the superordinate category is used in constructing a relevant standard of comparison or scale anchor (*comparison effect*). As discussed previously, subtraction-based contrast effects should be limited to the evaluation of the specific target, whereas comparison-based contrast effects may generalize to other targets for whom the standard of comparison may be relevant.

Summary

In summary, the key assumptions of the present model hold that the inclusion of a given piece of information in the temporary representation of the target category is a necessary prerequisite for the emergence of an assimilation effect, whereas the exclusion of a given piece of information from that representation is a necessary prerequisite for the emergence of contrast effects. Whether the emerging contrast effect is limited to the evaluation of the target stimulus, or generalizes to related stimuli, depends on whether the excluded information is merely subtracted from the data base used to evaluate the target, or is used in constructing a standard of comparison, or a scale anchor, which may be applicable to related stimuli as well. In addition, we assume that the default operation is to include easily accessible information in the representation of the target category and that exclusion needs to be triggered by salient features of the task or its context, an issue to which we will return later.

The general inclusion/exclusion approach offered here provides a heuristically fruitful framework for the conceptualization of many variables that are known to moderate the emergence of assimilation and contrast effects. Before we review some of these variables in more detail, however, we report on two studies in which the inclusion or exclusion of context information was directly manipulated, using these studies to elaborate on our basic assumptions.

Direct Manipulations of Categorization:
The Varying Impact of a Politician On
Evaluations of His Party

Suppose that you are asked to provide a general evaluation of the politicians of the Christian Democratic Party of the Federal Republic of Germany. To do so, you may either retrieve a previously formed judgment from memory, or you may form a judgment on the spot (Strack & Martin, 1987). If a previously formed judgment can be retrieved, the current context is unlikely to exert much influence. Hence, we will not address this special case. If you need to form a judgment on the spot, you presumably need to retrieve some representation of the politicians of the Christian Democratic Party. Assuming some basic familiarity with German politics, this representation is likely to include some chronically accessible information, for example, that it is a conservative party, and that Chancellor Kohl is one of its prominent members. In addition to such context-independent information, the representation may include some information that only comes to mind under specific circumstances, for example, because it was needed to answer a preceding question (Schwarz & Strack, 1991a; Strack & Martin, 1987). Under which conditions this context-dependent information results in assimilation or contrast effects on your general evaluation of politicians of the Christian Democratic Party is of key interest in the present chapter.

One of the most highly regarded members of the Christian Democratic Party is Richard von Weizsäcker, who currently serves as president of the Federal Republic of Germany. He has been a member of this party for several decades, but the office of president requires that he no longer actively participate in party politics. The president, as the representative figurehead of the Federal Republic of Germany, is supposed to take a neutral stand on party issues, much as the Queen in the United Kingdom. This rendered him particularly suitable for the present experiment, in which we exploited this ambiguity of his status as a party member (Schwarz & Bless, 1990, Experiment 1).

Specifically, we asked subjects a number of political knowledge questions. In one condition, they were asked to recall the party of which "Richard von Weizsäcker has been a member for more than 20 years." Answering "Christian Democratic Party" should make it more likely that the highly respected Richard von Weizsäcker is included in the temporary representation that subjects form of *politicians of the Christian Democratic Party* when they are later asked to evaluate this group. Accordingly, it was expected that they would evaluate the Christian Democratic Party more favorably when they were asked the party membership question than when they were not.

The data supported this hypothesis, as shown in the first row of Table 8.1. Specifically, including Richard von Weizsäcker in the category increased the evaluation of Christian Democratic politicians as a group, relative to a condition in which no question about Richard von Weizsäcker was asked.

In another condition of the same study, however, subjects were asked which office Richard von Weizsäcker holds "that sets him aside from party politics." Answering this question should exclude Richard von Weizsäcker from the category of Christian Democratic Party politicians. If so, it was expected to result in lower evaluations of Christian Democratic politicians in general. This was again the case, as shown in the first row of Table 8.1.

So far, these findings indicate that asking a preceding question increased the cognitive accessibility of the information that was used to answer it. This, in turn, increased the likelihood that this information came to mind when respondents were later asked another question to which it was relevant. How this easily accessible information affected the judgment, however, depended on whether it was included in the temporary representation that subjects formed of the target category or not. If Richard von Weizsäcker was assigned to the target category, that is, the Christian Democrats in the preceding example, he was included in the data base considered in making the general judgment. This

TABLE 8.1
Evaluation of Political Parties as a Function of the Inclusion or Exclusion
of a Highly Respected Politician

| | Preceding Question About Richard von Weizsäcker | | |
Target	Party Membership	None	Presidency
Christian Democrats	6.5	5.2	3.4
Social Democrats	6.3	6.3	6.2

Note: n = 19 to 25 per condition. 1 = unfavorable; 11 = very favorable opinion about politicians of the respective party in general. Adapted from Schwarz and Bless (1990, Experment 1).

resulted in an assimilation effect, relative to a control group in which no question about Richard von Weizsäcker was asked.

If Richard von Weizsäcker was excluded from the target category, however, a contrast effect emerged, again relative to a condition in which no question about Richard von Weizsäcker was asked. This may reflect either of two processes. On the one hand, Richard von Weizsäcker and his party membership may have been chronically accessible for some subjects who were not asked a question about him. If so, the assimilation effect would reflect that the party membership question increased the number of subjects who included Richard von Weizsäcker in their temporary representation, whereas the presidency question decreased the number of subjects who did so. In that case, the obtained contrast effect would reflect the subtraction of Richard von Weizsäcker from the data base used. On the other hand, subjects may not only have excluded Richard von Weizsäcker from their representation of politicians of the Christian Democratic Party, but may also have used him in constructing a standard of comparison, or a scale anchor, against which politicians of the Christian Democratic Party in general were evaluated.

We can distinguish both possibilities by assessing the generalization of the obtained contrast effect across different stimuli to which the standard of comparison, or the scale anchor, may be relevant. If the obtained contrast effect solely reflects the exclusion of Richard von Weizsäcker from the representation of the target category *politicians of the Christian Democratic Party*, the presidency question should only affect the evaluation of this party. If respondents used Richard von Weizsäcker in constructing a standard of comparison or a relevant scale anchor, on the other hand, the obtained contrast effect should generalize to the evaluation of politicians of other parties, such as the Social Democratic Party, as well. In this case, we may expect contrast effects to emerge in response to both questions about Richard von Weizsäcker, because the presidency as well as the party membership question should bring this respected politician to mind without allowing his inclusion in subjects' temporary representation of the target category *politicians of the Social Democratic Party*, of which he has never been a member.

To explore this possibility, other subjects of the aforementioned study (Schwarz & Bless, 1990, Experiment 1) were exposed to the same questions but were asked to provide a general evaluation of politicians of the Social Democratic Party. As shown in the second row of Table 8.1, neither of the questions about Richard von Weizsäcker affected subjects' evaluations of politicians of the Social Democratic Party. This suggests that the contrast effect obtained on the evaluation of Christian Democratic politicians reflected a subtraction effect, rather than a change in the standard of comparison, or scale anchor, used.

In summary, directly manipulating the categorization of Richard von Weizsäcker by different knowledge questions provided clear support for the emergence of assimilation effects as a function of his inclusion in respondents' representations of the target category, and for the emergence of a subtraction-based contrast effect as a function of his exclusion from the target category.

The Impact of Category Width: Scandals and Trust in Politicians

If the emergence of assimilation and contrast effects is determined by subjects' categorizations of highly accessible information, as the preceding experiment suggests, all variables that influence the inclusion or exclusion of information from a target category may be expected to moderate the impact of highly accessible information. Whereas we manipulated subjects' categorizations of context information in the previous study by means of direct questions, a particularly relevant variable in social judgment research may be the *width* of the target category. In principle, a given piece of information should be more likely to be included in a category, the wider the respective category is, but more likely to be excluded from the category, the narrower it is. The next study bears on this assumption and extends the inclusion/exclusion logic by demonstrating changes in the standard of comparison or scale anchor, as indicated by a generalization of contrast effects across different targets.

Suppose, for example, that subjects are induced to think about politicians who were involved in a specific political scandal, and are subsequently asked to evaluate the trustworthiness of politicians in general. According to the present model, the politicians involved in the scandal are members of the superordinate category *politicians* and are therefore likely to be included in subjects' temporary representations of that category. If so, subjects' evaluations of the trustworthiness of politicians in general should decrease, reflecting an assimilation effect.

Suppose, however, that subjects are not asked to evaluate the trustworthiness of politicians in general, but the trustworthiness of a specific politician, Mr. Joe Doe, who was not involved in the scandal. We may assume that in evaluating a specific person, this person makes up a category by him or herself (cf. Wyer & Srull, 1989). If so, the politicians who were involved in the scandal should not be included in subjects' temporary representations of Joe Doe. Nevertheless, the scandal-ridden politicians should be highly accessible in memory and may come to mind when subjects are asked to evaluate Joe Doe. If so, they may be used in constructing a standard against which Joe Doe is evaluated, or they may be used to anchor the response scale. In either case, Joe Doe should be evaluated as particularly trustworthy by comparison, reflecting a contrast effect. Thus, the present model predicts that thinking about politicians who were involved in a scandal may decrease judgments of the trustworthiness of politicians in general, but may increase judgments of the trustworthiness of specific exemplars of the category, provided that they were not involved in the scandal.

To test this implication of the inclusion/exclusion model, we (Schwarz & Bless, in press) asked subjects to recall the names of some politicians who were involved in a recent political scandal in West Germany, either before or after they answered the dependent variables. The scandal used in this study was the so-called "Barschel Scandal," which bears some resemblance to the Watergate scandal in the United States. All subjects were able to provide the names of at least two participants. Subsequently, some subjects were asked to evaluate the trustworthiness of politicians in the Federal Republic of Germany in general. As shown in the first row of Table 8.2, thinking about the Barschel scandal resulted in decreased judgments of the trustworthiness of German politicians in general. This assimilation effect presumably reflects that subjects included the politicians who were involved in the scandal in their representation of German politicians in general.

Other subjects, however, were asked to evaluate the trustworthiness of three specific politicians, whom pretests had shown to be not particularly trustworthy to begin with, although they were nòt involved in the scandal under study. As shown in the second row of Table 8.2, thinking about the Barschel scandal increased judgments of trustworthiness of these specific politicians. This contrast effect presumably reflects that subjects used the easily accessible politicians who were involved in the scandal in constructing a standard of comparison or a relevant scale anchor.

Note that this contrast effect cannot be accounted for on the basis of a mere subtraction process. The information that was primed by the scandal questions was presumably never part of the subjects' representations of the specific politicians they had to evaluate. Hence, the contrast effect obtained here presumably reflects the use of the recalled politicians in constructing a relevant standard of comparison or scale anchor. This information could only be used in constructing the standard, however, when it was not perceived to bear on the respective target category in the first place. As a result, we found that naming politicians who were involved in a scandal resulted in assimilation effects on the evaluation of a wide category that allowed the inclusion of these politicians. However, the same priming task resulted in contrast effects on the evaluation of specific politicians, reflecting that the primed politicians could not be included in the specific

TABLE 8.2
Evaluation of the Trustworthiness of Politicians in General and of
Three Exemplars as a Function of Thinking About a Scandal

| Target | Scandal Question | |
	Not Asked	Asked
Politicians in General	5.0	3.4
Specific Exemplars	4.9	5.6

Note: $n = 8$ per condition. 1 = not at all trustworthy; 11 = very trustworthy. Adapted from Schwarz and Bless (in press).

categories made up by those persons, and were hence available for the construction of a relevant standard or anchor.

These findings indicate that the same information may affect related judgments in opposite directions, depending on whether the respective target category invites the inclusion or the exclusion of the information that comes to mind. Accordingly, it comes as no surprise that political scandals are typically accompanied by attempts to channel the public's categorization of scandal-related information (see Ebbighausen & Neckel, 1989, for discussions of scandal management). To the extent that individual politicians, or groups of politicians, can dissociate themselves from the scandal, they may actually benefit from the misdemeanor of their peers, although the impact on the perception of the profession as a whole is likely to be negative.

Subtraction Versus Comparison: The Role of Salient Dimensions

So far, we have seen some evidence for the operation of subtraction as well as comparison or anchoring processes under exclusion conditions. Under which conditions, however, is each of these processes likely to operate? We propose that the mere accessibility of an extreme stimulus is unlikely to elicit comparison or anchoring processes, unless the stimulus brings the relevant dimension of judgment to mind. Accordingly, thinking about some stimulus only influences the evaluation of subsequent stimuli by means of comparison or anchoring processes if the stimulus is linked to the dimension of judgment. If the stimulus is thought about with regard to some other dimension, it is unlikely to be used as a standard or scale anchor. With regard to the preceding studies, this suggests that thinking about a political scandal was likely to bring the dimension of trustworthiness to mind. On the other hand, thinking about Richard von Weizsäcker's party membership or office may have been less likely to bring the evaluative dimension to mind that was relevant to subsequent judgments of the Social Democrats.

In line with this assumption, we observed in one of our studies that comparison or anchoring effects only emerged when highly accessible context-dependent information was linked to the dimension of judgment (Schwarz, Münkel, & Hippler, 1990). Specifically, we asked subjects to rate how "typically German" a number of different beverages are, namely wine, coffee, and milk. Before they made this judgment, some subjects were asked to estimate the caloric content of a glass of vodka, or of a glass of beer, respectively. Other subjects, however, were asked to estimate how frequently Germans drink vodka or beer.

Both questions should increase the accessibility of vodka or beer in memory. However, only the frequency-of-consumption question is related to the typicality dimension, whereas the caloric content question is not. If it is sufficient that an extreme stimulus comes to mind, both questions should result in contrast effects on subsequent typicality ratings. On the other hand, if the emergence of comparison or anchoring effects requires that the extreme stimulus is linked to the relevant judgmental dimension, contrast effects should only emerge when subjects estimate the frequency of consumption, but not when they estimate the caloric content.

Empirically, this was the case. Table 8.3 shows the mean ratings of the "Germanicness" of wine, coffee, and milk as a function of the preceding questions. When subjects estimated the frequency of consumption, they rated all beverages as more typically German after thinking about vodka than after thinking about beer. Estimating the caloric content of vodka or beer, on the other hand, did not affect their ratings. Accordingly, we concluded that the emergence of comparison or anchoring effects requires that the context-dependent information be linked to the relevant dimension of judgment. Otherwise, it may not be considered when individuals construct a standard of comparison or select a scale anchor.

This suggests that we may only see contrast effects that generalize across various target categories when respondents think about the excluded information with regard to the respective dimension of judgment. If the excluded information is thought about with regard to some other dimension, it may still result in contrast effects, but only by means of a subtraction process. Accordingly, the contrast effects that emerge under this condition should be limited to the evaluation of the category from which the information was excluded in the first place, as was the case in the Weizsäcker study. Such a subtraction effect could not be observed in the present study, however, because the extreme beverages were not part of the target categories to begin with. Most obviously, more research is needed to test these conjectures.

VARIABLES THAT DETERMINE INCLUSION AND EXCLUSION: CONJECTURES AND FINDINGS

If the emergence of assimilation and contrast effects is a function of categorization processes, then any variable that influences categorization can presumably elicit assimilation or contrast effects. In the following sections we review the

TABLE 8.3
Contrast Effects as a Function of the Dimension Tapped by Preceding Questions

Preceding Question	Context Stimulus	
	Vodka	Beer
Consumption	5.4	4.4
Caloric Content	4.4	4.5

Note: n = 25 to 27 per cell; 9 = "very typical." The mean of ratings of three beverages (milk, wine, and coffee) is given. Adapted from Schwarz, Münkel, and Hippler (1990).

operation of a number of different variables that have been shown to moderate the emergence of assimilation and contrast effects, emphasizing their impact on inclusion/exclusion processes.

Representativeness

One of the key variables that determines the inclusion or exclusion of information is the perceived representativeness of the information for the target category. Information that is not representative for the target category is likely to be excluded, and is therefore likely to result in contrast effects. A number of diverse studies bear on this prediction and we review only a few of them.

Temporal Distance of Events. Strack, Schwarz, and Gschneidinger (1985, Experiment 1) investigated the emergence of assimilation and contrast effects on judgments of current life-satisfaction as a function of the representativeness of specific life-events for the target category *my life now.* (See also Tversky & Griffin, 1991, for conceptual replications, and Schwarz & Strack, 1991b for a general discussion of life-satisfaction judgments.) In the Strack et al. study, some subjects were asked to think about their present life and to write down three events that were either particularly positive and pleasant or particularly negative and unpleasant. This was done under the pretext of collecting life-events for a life-event inventory, and the dependent variables, among them *happiness* and *satisfaction*, were said to be being assessed in order to "find the best response scales" for that instrument. As shown in Table 8.4, subjects who had previously been induced to think about positive aspects of their present life described themselves as happier and more satisfied with their life-as-a-whole than subjects who had been induced to think about negative aspects. Presumably, this assimilation effect reflects that subjects included the recent life-events that they thought about in their temporary representation of the target category *my life now.*

Other subjects, however, had to recall events that had occurred several years ago. These events are no longer representative for one's *life now*, but bear

TABLE 8.4
Subjective Well-Being: The Impact of Valence of Event and Extendure

	Valence of Event	
Extendure	*Positive*	*Negative*
Present	8.9	7.1
Past	7.5	8.5

Note: Mean score of happiness and satisfaction questions, range is 1 to 11, with higher values indicating reports of higher well-being. Adapted from Strack, Schwarz, and Gschneidinger (1985, Experiment 1).

on a previous period of one's life. Accordingly, they should be excluded from the target category *my life now*, and may serve as standards of comparison, resulting in contrast effects on current life-satisfaction. The data supported this prediction. Subjects who thought about negative past events reported higher current well-being than respondents who thought about positive past events, reversing the previously obtained effect of recent events.

These findings are consistent with recent research in autobiographical memory that suggests that life-events are organized in terms of life-time periods, often referred to as *extendures* (see Cohen, 1989, for a review). If the recalled event is included in the representation of the extendure that is to be evaluated, it results in assimilation effects. If it is excluded from this extendure, it is likely to trigger contrast effects. Accordingly, we may expect that future research into the construction of autobiographical extendures, and the variables that determine the boundaries of extendures, and the variables that determine the boundaries of extendures, will bear directly on the impact of previous life-events on judgments of current well-being (see Clark & Collins, in press, for a related discussion).

Consistent with the assumption that the impact of life-events on judgments of well-being depends on the boundaries used in constructing autobiographical extendures, subsequent research by Strack, Schwarz, and Nebel (1987) demonstrated that it is not the temporal distance of the event per se that moderates the use of accessible information about one's life, but rather the subjective perception of whether the event one thinks about pertains to one's current conditions of living or to a different extendure of one's life. Specifically, students were asked to describe either a positive or a negative event that they expected to occur in "five years from now." For half of the sample, a major role transition was emphasized that would occur in the meantime, namely leaving university and entering the job market. As major role transitions of this type are known to mark the boundaries of autobiographical extendures (Cohen, 1989), this manipulation should increase the probability that respondents assign the expected event to a different phase of their life. Accordingly, they should be likely to use the expected event in constructing a standard of comparison. The results supported this reasoning. When the role transition was not emphasized, subjects reported higher happiness and life-satisfaction when they had to describe positive rather than negative expectations. When the role transition *was* emphasized, this pattern was reversed, and subjects reported higher well-being after thinking about negative rather than positive future expectations. Again, these findings suggest that easily accessible information elicits assimilation effects if it is included in the temporary representation of the target category, but results in contrast effects if it is excluded from that category.

Feature Overlap. In a well-known study, Herr, Sherman, and Fazio (1983) asked subjects to rate ambiguous stimuli (e.g., a fictitious animal) in the context of moderate or extreme related stimuli. They observed assimilation effects in the ratings of ambiguous stimuli when they were presented in the context of moderate ones, but contrast effects when they were presented in the context of extreme ones. Later research by Herr (1986), using a social category, replicated these findings. Herr (1986) concluded that "to the extent that a comparison of features of the activated category and the target stimulus results in matching or overlap, a judgment of category membership should occur" (p. 1107), eliciting an assimilation effect. On the other hand, if the overlap is insufficient, thus constituting an exclusion relationship, "the priming exemplars serve as standards of comparison" (Herr, 1986, p. 1107), resulting in a contrast effect.

In a related vein, Seta, Martin, and Capehart (1979) observed assimilation effects in attractiveness ratings of two target persons, who showed differential agreement with the subject's attitudes, when the targets shared a salient feature (namely, their college major), but contrast effects when they did not, in line with the predictions of Tajfel's (1959) accentuation theory. They concluded that the probability of obtaining an assimilation effect "is increased as the perceived commonality between two individuals is increased. Further, the probability of obtaining a contrast effect is increased as the perceived commonality between two individuals is decreased" (Seta et al., 1979, p. 406), reflecting the impact of category membership (i.e., inclusion/exclusion) decisions.

Unitary Versus Composite Categories. Following Sherif and Hovland's (1961) hypothesis that the emergence of assimilation and contrast effects depends on the distance between a behavior and its referent distribution, Hilton and von Hippel (1990, Experiment 1) induced different expectations about the distribution of pathological behaviors at different hospitals. In line with research by Manis and colleagues (e.g., Manis & Paskewitz, 1984; Manis, Paskewitz, & Cotler, 1986), they observed that ambiguous behaviors were assimilated to the stereotype of the respective hospital when they were consistent with expectations, and hence representative of the behaviors associated with patients of that hospital. However the ambiguous behaviors were contrasted to the stereotype when they were inconsistent with expectations. Thus, an assimilation effect emerged when the target behavior could be included in the superordinate hospital category, whereas a contrast effect emerged when the target behavior was excluded from that category.

In a second experiment, Hilton and von Hippel (1990, Experiment 2) directly manipulated subjects' opportunities to recategorize a target behavior that was inconsistent with expectations. Specifically, they attributed all behaviors either to a random group of people whose names began with a letter in the same half of the alphabet, to a family, or to an individual, assuming that subjects would expect most consistency among the behaviors of an individual and least consistency among the behaviors shown by a random group of people. As expected, ambiguous behaviors were assimilated to the induced expectations when an individual was the alleged source of all behaviors, but were contrasted to expectations when a random group was given as the alleged source. Apparently, attributing all behaviors to the same individual ensured that the ambiguous behavior was included in the category constituted by the unambiguous behaviors, resulting in an assimilation effect. Attributing the behaviors to a diverse group of people, on the other hand, allowed the exclusion of the ambiguous behaviors, resulting in a contrast effect. As the authors note: "To the extent that recategorization is a viable alternative, the pressure to assimilate unexpected behaviors should diminish" (Hilton & von Hippel, 1990, p. 445).

In more general terms, it may be assumed that unitary categories (such as specific individuals) are less likely to allow for the inclusion of discrepant information than composite categories (such as random groups of individuals), reflecting assumptions about the higher degree of variation that may be observed in the latter case. If so, judgments of unitary target categories should be more likely to show contrast effects, whereas composite categories should be more likely to show assimilation effects.

In summary, the studies reviewed in this section indicate that the perceived representativeness of a given piece of information for the respective target category determines its inclusion in, or exclusion from, that category, and hence the emergence of assimilation or contrast effects.

Category Width

Closely related to the impact of perceived representativeness is the issue of category width. The wider a category is, the more likely it becomes that a given piece of information may be included. The study on the impact of political scandals on judgments of trustworthiness (Schwarz & Bless, 1990), reviewed previously, supported this assumption. For the domain of person perception, this suggests, for example, that information about a specific group member is likely to result in assimilation effects on the evaluation of the group in general, reflecting the inclusion relationship constituted by group membership. Such an assimilation effect should not be obtained, on the other hand, if the individual member is so distinct from the group that he or she is excluded from the category, or if the individual member is assigned to a different category (see Rothbart & John, 1985), as discussed previously in the context of the Herr et al. (1983) and Hilton and von Hippel (1990) studies.

On the other hand, thinking about an individual should be likely to result in contrast effects on the evaluation of other individuals, reflecting that an individual person is likely to make up a category by him- or herself, constituting an exclusion relationship. Assimilation effects would only be predicted if some higher-order category is identified to which both individuals can be assigned, and if this higher-order category serves as a basis of judgment (see Fiske & Neuberg, 1990).

According to the present model, any variable that influences category width should also influence the emergence of assimilation and contrast effects. Whereas the preceding examples reflected the nature of the respective category itself, category width may also be influenced by individual difference variables, such as the degree of differentiation at which the respective content domain is represented in the judge's knowledge system. Theoretically, more differentiated knowledge systems are composed of a larger set of more specific categories than less differentiated knowledge systems. For example, Rosch, Mervis, Gray, Johnson, and Boes-Braem (1976) observed that experts identified objects at a lower level of abstraction than novices, reflecting a shift in the level of basic categories. Whereas a novice may, for example, identify all airplanes as *airplanes*, an airplane mechanic in their study distinguished between many types of different airplanes, reflecting the use of more, and more narrowly defined, categories in the domain of his expertise. The use of more specific categories, however, implies that a given piece of information may only be included in the representation of one specific category, but may be excluded from many others. Accordingly, we may expect contrast effects to be more likely to emerge in judgments made by experts than in judgments made by novices.

Another variable that is likely to influence category width is an individual's affective state at the time of judgment. In several studies, individuals in an elated mood were found to use wider categories than individuals in a depressed mood (see Isen, 1987; Schwarz, 1990, for reviews). For example, items that were not generally considered good exemplars of a category (e.g., *cane* as a member of the category *clothing*) were more likely to be assigned to that category by individuals in an elated rather than a nonmanipulated mood (Isen & Daubman, 1984). This suggests that the emergence of assimilation effects may be more likely under elated moods, whereas the emergence of contrast effects may be more likely under depressed moods. To our knowledge, data bearing on the impact of moods and expert status are not yet available.

Presentation and Judgment Order

So far, we have considered variables that are inherent to the presented information, such as the primed information's representativeness for the target category or the perceived inclusiveness of the target category itself. However, the categorization of stimuli may also be affected by more fortuitous aspects of the experimental procedures used, such as the order in which stimuli are presented or judgments are assessed.

For example, Wedell, Parducci, and Geiselman (1987) asked subjects to rate the attractiveness of faces that were either presented successively or in pairs. When the faces were presented successively, the same face was rated more favorably when presented in the context of less attractive faces, reflecting a contrast effect. When the faces were presented in pairs, however, the same face was rated less favorably when presented simultaneously with a less attractive face, reflecting an assimilation effect. The authors traced this assimilation effect to "a failure to separate the individual stimulus from other stimuli that are simultaneously present" (Wedell et al., 1987, p. 231). Apparently, the use of a successive or simultaneous presentation format influenced the categorization of the stimuli, mediating the emergence of assimilation and contrast effects.

In a similar vein, Martin and Seta (1983) observed the emergence of assimilation and contrast effects in an experiment conducted in the context of Byrne's (1971) similarity-attraction paradigm. Specifically, subjects learned that one target person agreed with them on three issues, whereas a second target person agreed with them on six issues. Paralleling the Wedell et al. (1987) findings, an assimilation effect in subjects' evaluations of the target persons emerged when they provided their ratings after information about *both* targets had been presented, whereas a contrast effect emerged when the first target was rated before information about the second target was presented. Martin and Seta concluded that the timing of the judgment influenced the *perceived relatedness* of the stimuli, moderating the emergence of assimilation and contrast effects.

In combination, these studies illustrate that assimilation effects are likely to be obtained when the stimuli are perceived as a unit, whereas contrast effects are likely to emerge when they are perceived as distinct entities (Martin & Seta, 1983; Seta et al., 1979), again reflecting the impact of categorization processes.

Deliberate Exclusion

The variables reviewed so far were likely to influence subjects' assessments of whether the primed information belonged to the target category or not. Sometimes, however, subjects do not *use* information that comes to mind despite the fact that it seems to belong to the target category. This is the case when individuals are aware of the potential influence of the primes, or when conversational norms prohibit the use of information that has already been provided. In both cases, the easily accessible information is excluded, resulting in contrast effects.

Awareness of External Influences. As Martin and Clark (1990) noted in a review of the priming literature, the usually observed assimilation effect of concept priming on the interpretation of ambiguous information may be "most likely to occur when subjects are unaware of the priming stimuli or, at least, are unaware that their exposure to these stimuli may influence their impression of the target person" (p. 274). For example, Lombardi, Higgins, and Bargh (1987) reported that trait priming only resulted in assimilation effects when subjects were not aware of the priming episode. When subjects were aware of the primes, as assessed by their ability to recall them, contrast effects were observed. In a related study, Strack, Schwarz, Bless, Kübler, and Wänke (1990) observed that reminding subjects of the priming episode reversed the usually obtained assimilation effect, resulting in contrast.

As Higgins (1989) noted, "One interpretation of these findings is that subjects who recalled the priming events used the events to form a standard that subsequently functioned as a reference point for judging the stimulus person" (p. 92). This interpretation is nicely compatible with the present approach. Presumably, being aware that a trait comes to mind because it was introduced as part of another task prohibits that this trait is used to characterize the target person. Nevertheless, the behaviors that served as primes are highly accessible and may be used in constructing a standard of comparison or scale anchor.

As an alternative account, Martin et al. (1990; see also Martin, 1986) suggested that individuals may try to avoid an undue influence of the primed information by using other concepts that are applicable to the ambiguous information, yet distinct in their implications. In our reading, this account predicts the absence of assimilation effects, relative to a no-priming control group, when subjects are aware of the primes. However, it does not necessarily predict a contrast effect relative to a no-priming control group, unless one assumes that the concepts that subjects turn to are not only distinct, but opposite in implications to the primed concepts. Unfortunately, no-priming conditions were not included in the Martin et al. (1990) studies, which compared the impact of positive and negative primes under conditions of different processing motivation or processing load (an issue to which we will return later). More interestingly, the Higgins (1989) and Martin et al. (1990) accounts make differential predictions for evaluations based on unambiguous descriptions. If contrast effects are driven by the use of distinct concepts at the encoding stage, as suggested by Martin and colleagues, they should be restricted to evaluations of ambiguously described targets, which allow the application of different concepts. If contrast effects are due to the use of primes in the construction of a standard, as Higgins (1989) suggested, they should generalize to unambiguous targets as well, provided that the standard is applicable. To our knowledge, data bearing on these differential predictions are not yet available.

The Impact of Conversational Norms. Another variable that may prompt individuals to deliberately exclude easily accessible information is the operation of conversational norms that prohibit redundancy. Specifically, one of the principles that govern the conduct of conversation in everyday life (Grice, 1975) requests speakers to make their contribution just as informative as is required for the purpose of the conversation, but not more informative than is required. In particular, speakers are not supposed to be redundant or provide information that the respondent already has. In psycholinguistics, this principle, known as the *given-new contract*, emphasizes that speakers should provide new information rather than information that has already been given (Clark, 1985; Haviland & Clark, 1974). As Strack and Martin (1987; see also Strack & Schwarz, in press) pointed out, following related suggestions by Bradburn (1982) and Tourangeau (1984), this principle may be applied to the emergence of question order effects in psychological measurement. Specifically, they suggested that respondents may deliberately disregard information that they have already provided in response to a previous question, when answering a subsequent one. The next study illustrates how this conversational process mediates the emergence of assimilation and contrast effects by determining the inclusion or exclusion of previously provided information (see also Strack, Martin, & Schwarz, 1988; Strack, Schwarz, & Wänke, 1991).

In this study (Schwarz, Strack, & Mai, 1991), we asked a sample of German adults to report their marital satisfaction as well as their general life-satisfaction. As expected, the correlation between ratings of "happiness with marriage" and "happiness with life-as-a-whole" depended on the order in which both questions were asked, replicating previous findings by Strack et al. (1988). If the general happiness question preceded the marital satisfaction question, both questions were moderately correlated, $r = .32$. If the question order was reversed, this correlation increased to $r = .67$. This reflects that respondents included information that they had used to answer the marital satisfaction question in the temporary representation on which they based their evaluation of their life in general, resulting in an assimilation effect. Accordingly, happily married respondents reported higher, and unhappily married respondents lower, mean general life-satisfaction when the marital satisfaction preceded the general one than when it did not.

Not so, however, when both questions were explicitly placed in the same conversational context, thus evoking the norm of non-redundancy. This was accomplished by a joint lead-in to both questions that read,

Now we would like to learn about two areas of life that may be important for people's overall well-being:
a) happiness with marriage
b) happiness with life in general.

Subsequently, both happiness questions were asked in the specific-general order. In that case, the correlation of both measures dropped from the previously obtained $r = .67$, under this order condition, to $r = .18$, again replicating previous findings by Strack et al. (1988). This suggests that respondents deliberately ignored information that they had already provided in response to a specific question when making a subsequent general judgment, despite the fact that it was easily accessible in memory. This exclusion process presumably reflects that the specific and the general questions were explicitly assigned to the same conversational context, thus evoking the application of conversational norms that prohibit redundancy. In that case, respondents apparently interpreted the general question as if it referred to aspects of their life that they had not yet reported on. In line with this interpretation, a condition in which respondents were explicitly asked how satisfied they were with "other aspects" of their life, "aside from their relationship," yielded a nearly identical correlation of $r = .20$.

More importantly, however, respondents who were induced to disregard their marriage in evaluating their life-as-a-whole reported higher life-satisfaction when they were unhappily married, and lower life-satisfaction when they were happily married, than respondents who were not induced to exclude this information. Thus, contrast effects were obtained when conversational norms elicited the exclusion of the primed information, whereas assimilation effects were obtained when the activated information was included, as discussed previously.

In a related study, Ottati, Riggle, Wyer, Schwarz, and Kuklinski (1989) asked respondents to report their agreement with general and specific political statements. For example, a general statement would read, "Citizens should have the right to speak freely in public." In one condition, this general statement was preceded by a specific statement that pertained to a favorable or unfavorable group. For example, "The Parent–Teachers Association (or the Ku Klux Klan, respectively) should have the right to speak freely in public."

As expected, respondents expressed a more favorable attitude toward the general statement if it was preceded by a specific one that pertained to a favorable, rather than to an unfavorable, group. However, this assimilation effect was only obtained when the items were separated by eight filler items. If the items were presented immediately adjacent to one another, a contrast effect emerged. The latter finding presumably reflects the exclusion of the primed information as a function of conversational norms and/or awareness of the priming episode.

In addition to illustrating the operation of inclusion and exclusion processes as a function of conversational norms and awareness of the priming episode, the findings reviewed in this section draw attention the frequent neglect of conversational principles in social cognition research. According to mainstream social cognition theorizing (see Higgins & Bargh, 1987, for a review), the use of information is solely determined by its cognitive accessibility and its applicability to the judgment at hand. As the aforementioned findings illustrate, however, easily accessible information that is clearly applicable to the judgment at hand may not be used in making a judgment if its repeated use would violate the conversational norm of non-redundancy (see Martin & Clark, 1990; Strack et al., 1988; Strack & Schwarz, in press, for more detailed discussions). Thus, social cognition research needs to pay attention to the social context in which a judgment is made, in addition to the determinants of accessibility and applicability (see the contributions in Schwarz & Strack, 1991c).

THE INCLUSION/EXCLUSION MODEL

In summary, the inclusion/exclusion model assumes that assimilation and contrast effects are a function of categorization processes, as shown in Fig. 8.1.

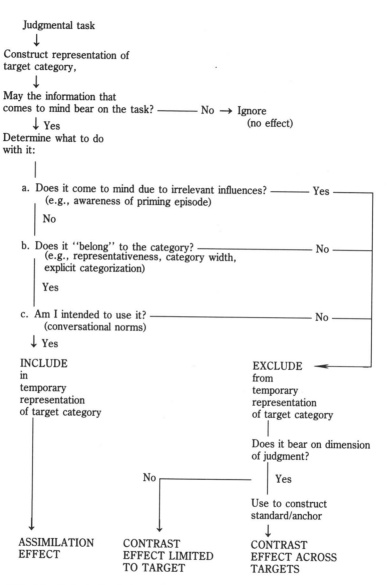

Judgmental task
↓
Construct representation of
target category,
↓
May the information that
comes to mind bear on the task? ———— No → Ignore
      ↓ Yes   (no effect)
Determine what to do
with it:

a. Does it come to mind due to irrelevant influences? ———— Yes ————
    (e.g., awareness of priming episode)

    No

b. Does it "belong" to the category? ———————————— No ————
    (e.g., representativeness, category width,
    explicit categorization)

    Yes

c. Am I intended to use it? ———————————————— No ————
    (conversational norms)

  ↓ Yes

INCLUDE   EXCLUDE ←———
in   from
temporary   temporary
representation   representation
of target category   of target category

                           Does it bear on dimension
                           of judgment?

         No ┌————————— │ Yes

                           Use to construct
                           standard/anchor
                           ↓

ASSIMILATION   CONTRAST   CONTRAST
EFFECT   EFFECT LIMITED   EFFECT ACROSS
                    TO TARGET   TARGETS

FIG. 8.1. Inclusion/exclusion and the emergence of assimilation and contrast
effects.

When asked to make a judgment, the individual has to retrieve information that bears on the task. If information comes to mind that is clearly unrelated to the task, it is ignored and does not influence the judgment. Information that appears as potentially relevant to the task may result in assimilation or in contrast effects, depending on whether it is included in, or excluded from, the temporary representation that the individual forms of the target category. We assume that the default operation is to include apparently relevant information, whereas exclusion operations need to be triggered by salient features of the judgmental task or of the communicative context in which the judgment is made. These salient features relate to three general decisions that need to be made with regard to the information that comes to mind:

1. The individual needs to decide if the information that comes to mind bears on the target category or not. Variables such as the width of the target category or the perceived representativeness of the primed information will determine categorization at this stage.

2. The individual needs to determine if the information that comes to mind reflects the impact of some irrelevant factor, such as a priming task. If so, the information will be disregarded, constituting an exclusion relationship.

3. Conversational norms may prohibit the repeated use of information that has already been provided earlier, even if that information does seem generally relevant to the judgment at hand.

In general, assimilation effects are predicted to emerge whenever the information that comes to mind is included in the temporary representation that respondents form of the target category. Empirically, however, this can only be observed if the context-dependent information is more extreme than the context-independent information. In addition, the size of the assimilation effect should be an inverse function of the amount of competing information: The more information is represented in the construction of the target category, the smaller should be the impact on including any additional piece of information.

Conversely, contrast effects are predicted to emerge whenever the information that comes to mind is excluded from the target category. This may either reflect the operation of a subtraction process, or the operation of a change in the standard of comparison or scale anchor. These possibilities can be distinguished by assessing the generalization of the emerging contrast effect across related targets, as well as the impact of competing information.

Contrast effects that are based on a subtraction process should be limited to evaluations of the category from which the information is subtracted, whereas contrast effects that are based on changes in the standard of comparison or scale anchor should generalize to evaluations of other targets along the same dimension of judgment. We propose that the latter possibility requires that the excluded information was thought about with regard to the relevant dimension of judgment. If the excluded information was thought about with regard to some other dimension, any emerging contrast effects should merely reflect a subtraction process and should hence be limited to the target category from which the information is excluded.

Moreover, the size of subtraction-based contrast effects should be an inverse function of the amount of competing information that is represented in the construction of the target category: The more information is included in the temporary representation of the target category, the smaller should be the impact of subtracting any given piece of information from that representation. Empirically, subtraction effects can only be observed if the subtracted information is more extreme than other information included in the temporary representation.

Similarly, the model implies that the impact of using a given piece of information in constructing a standard or scale anchor should be an inverse function of the amount of other information: The more information is used in constructing a standard, the smaller should be the effect of using any additional piece of information in doing so. Moreover, comparison-based contrast effects can only be observed empirically if the implications of the excluded information are more extreme than the implications of other information used to construct a standard. To our knowledge, data bearing on these implications are not yet available, although the predictions are clearly testable.[1]

The assumption that the default operation is to include information that comes to mind, whereas exclusion operations need to be triggered by salient features of the task or its communicative context, has additional important implications for the predictions generated by the model. First, it suggests that assimilation effects should generally be more likely to be obtained than contrast effects, reflecting that the latter require the presence of salient cues that trigger exclusion operations. Second, it implies that the emergence of contrast effects requires extra processing steps, and more effort, than the emergence of assimilation effects. Accordingly, reaction-time studies should indicate that judgmental processes that result in contrast effects take more time than judgmental processes that result in assimilation effects. Moreover, competing tasks that tax subjects' processing capacities may be likely to interfere with exclusion operations, and may hence undermine the emergence of contrast effects, but facilitate the emergence of assimilation effects. Similarly, we may expect that variables that reduce an individual's motivation to invest in processing effort will also

---

[1]It is interesting to note that the same logic predicts that assimilation effects may also emerge as a function of changes in the construction of the standard under some restricted conditions. Suppose that the implications of excluded information are less extreme than the implications of other information used in constructing a standard. If so, using the excluded information in constructing a standard would result in a less extreme standard and hence in less pronounced contrast effects. Given that the available evidence is restricted to the exclusion of extreme information, we will not further address this possibility.

interfere with the emergence of contrast effects, but will facilitate the emergence of assimilation effects.

These assumptions received considerable support in research on Martin's (1986) set/reset model. Specifically, Martin et al. (1990) reported three experiments in which awareness of the priming episode resulted in contrast effects when subjects were motivated and able to process the information in sufficient detail. When subjects were distracted (Experiment 1) or unmotivated (Experiments 2 and 3), however, assimilation effects emerged, suggesting that inclusion represents the default option that is used under suboptimal processing conditions, whereas exclusion requires additional processing effort. Compatible with this assumption, Bodenhausen (1990) observed in a study on circadian variations in stereotyping that ''night people'' exhibited greater stereotypic bias when tested in the morning rather than at night, whereas ''morning people'' exhibited greater stereotypic bias when tested at night rather than in the morning. Apparently, forming a judgment at a nonoptimal time of day decreased subjects' processing efforts and facilitated the emergence of assimilation effects.

These findings suggest that assimilation effects should be more likely to be obtained the less relevant the judgment is to the individual's current goals, the higher the need for closure, and the lower the fear of invalidity (Kruglanski, 1980, 1990). By the same token, an individual's affective state at the time of judgment may be expected to moderate the emergence of assimilation and contrast. As a growing body of literature indicates, individuals in an elated mood seem less motivated to invest considerable processing effort than individuals in a neutral or mildly depressed mood (see Schwarz, 1990; Schwarz, Bless, & Bohner, 1991). Accordingly, individuals in an elated mood may be less likely to engage in the extra processing effort required by exclusion operations, thus undermining the emergence of contrast effects, despite the presence of other conditions that should be likely to elicit exclusion operations.

Finally, it is worth noting that the present analysis lends itself to research on stereotyping. Although the present chapter focused primarily on the impact of subordinate information on the evaluation of superordinate categories, the logic offered here can be extended to capture the conditions under which superordinate information results in assimilation or contrast effects in the evaluation of subordinate categories, as outlined in the introduction. Elaborating on this issue, however, is beyond the scope of this chapter.

Most certainly, future research will uncover additional variables that are likely to influence the inclusion or exclusion of highly accessible information from the cognitive construction of the target category. We hope that this research will support the heuristic usefulness of the general inclusion/exclusion framework offered here, which holds that the impact of easily accessible information is a function of whether it is included in or excluded from the temporary representations that individuals construct of the target category and its alternatives.

REFERENCES

Allport, G. W. (1954). *The nature of prejudice*. Reading, MA: Addison-Wesley.

Barsalou, L. W. (1987). The instability of graded structure: Implications for the nature of concepts. In U. Neisser (Ed.), *Concepts and conceptual development: Ecological and intellectual factors in categorization* (pp. 101–140). Cambridge, England: Cambridge University Press.

Barsalou, L. W. (1989). Intraconcept similarity and its implications for interconcept similarity. In S. Vosniadou & A. Ortony (Eds.), *Similarity and analogical reasoning* (pp. 76–121). Cambridge, England: Cambridge University Press.

Bodenhausen, G. V. (1990). Stereotypes as judgmental heuristics: Evidence of circadian variations in discrimination. *Psychological Science, 1*, 319–322.

Bodenhausen, G. V., & Wyer, R. S. (1987). Social cognition and social reality: Information acquisition and use in the laboratory and the real world. In H. J. Hippler, N. Schwarz, & S. Sudman (Eds.), *Social information processing and survey methodology* (pp. 6–41). New York: Springer-Verlag.

Bradburn, N. (1982). Question wording effects in surveys. In R. Hogarth (Ed.), *Question framing and response consistency* (pp. 65–76). San Francisco: Jossey-Bass.

Brewer, M. B. (1988). A dual process model of impression formation. In T. K. Srull & R. S. Wyer (Eds.), *Advances in social cognition: Vol. 1. A dual process model of impression formation* (pp. 1–36). Hillsdale, NJ: Lawrence Erlbaum Associates.

Byrne, D. (1971). *The attraction paradigm*. New York: Academic Press.

Clark, H. H. (1985). Language use and language users. In G. Lindzey & E. Aronson (Eds.), *Handbook of social psychology* (Vol. 2, pp. 179–232). New York: Random House.

Clark, L. F., & Collins, J. E. (in press). Memories of the past and judgments of the present. In N. Schwarz & S. Sudman (Eds.), *Autobiographical memory and the validity of retrospective reports*. New York: Sringer-Verlag.

Cohen, G. (1989). *Memory in the real world*. Hillsdale, NJ: Lawrence Erlbaum Associates.

Ebbighausen, R., & Neckel, S. (Eds.). (1989). *Anatomie des politischen Skandals* [The anatomy of political scandals]. Frankfurt: Suhrkamp.

Eiser, J. R. (1990). *Social judgment*. London: Open University Press.

Fiske, S. T., & Neuberg, S. L. (1990). A continuum of impression formation, from category-based to individuating processes: Influences of information and motivation on attention and interpretation. In M. Zanna (Ed.), *Advances in experimental social psychology* (Vol. 23, pp. 1–74). New York: Academic Press.

Grice, H. P. (1975). Logic and conversation. In P. Cole & J. L. Morgan (Eds.), *Syntax and semantics: Vol. 3. Speech acts* (pp. 41–58). New York: Academic Press.

Hamilton, D. L. (Ed.). (1981). *Cognitive processes in stereotyping and intergroup behavior*. Hillsdale, NJ: Lawrence Erlbaum Associates.

Haviland, S. E., & Clark, H. H. (1974). What's new? Acquiring new information as a process of comprehension. *Journal of Verbal Learning and Verbal Behavior, 13*, 512–521.

Helson, H. (1964). *Adaptation-level theory*. New York: Harper & Row.

Herr, P. M. (1986). Consequences of priming: Judgment and behavior. *Journal of Personality and Social Psychology, 51*, 1106–1115.

Herr, P. M., Sherman, S. J., & Fazio, R. H. (1983). On the consequences of priming: Assimilation and contrast effects. *Journal of Experimental Social Psychology, 19*, 323–340.

Higgins, E. T. (1989). Knowledge accessibility and activation: Subjectivity and suffering from unconscious sources. In J. S. Uleman & J. A. Bargh (Eds.), *Unintended thought* (pp. 75–123). New York: Guilford Press.

Higgins, E. T., & Bargh, J. A. (1987). Social cognition and social perception. *Annual Review of Psychology, 38*, 369–425.

Hilton, J. L., & von Hippel, W. (1990). The role of consistency in the judgment of stereotype-relevant behaviors. *Personality and Social Psychology Bulletin, 16*, 430–448.

Isen, A. M. (1987). Positive affect, cognitive processes, and social behavior. In L. Berkowitz (Ed.), *Advances in experimental social psychology* (Vol. 20, pp. 203–253). New York: Academic Press.

Isen, A. M., & Daubman, K. A. (1984). The influence of affect on categorization. *Journal of Personality and Social Psychology, 47,* 1206–1217.

Kahneman, D., & Miller, D. (1986). Norm theory: Comparing reality to its alternatives. *Psychological Review, 93,* 136–153.

Kruglanski, A. W. (1980). Lay epistemo-logic—process and contents: Another look at attribution theory. *Psychological Review, 87,* 70–87.

Kruglanski, A. W. (1990). Motivations for judging and knowing: Implications for causal attributions. In E. T. Higgins & R. M. Sorrentino (Eds.), *Handbook of motivation and cognition: Foundations of social behavior* (Vol. 2, pp. 333–368). New York: Guilford Press.

Lombardi, W. J., Higgins, E. T., & Bargh, J. A. (1987). The role of consciousness in priming effects on categorization: Assimilation and contrast as a function of awareness of the priming task. *Personality and Social Psychology Bulletin, 13,* 411–429.

Manis, M., & Paskewitz, J. (1984). Judging psychopathology: Expectation and contrast. *Journal of Experimental Social Psychology, 20,* 217–230.

Manis, M., Paskewitz, J., & Cotler, S. (1986). Stereotypes and social judgment. *Journal of Personality and Social Psychology, 50,* 461–473.

Martin, L. L. (1986). Set/reset: Use and disuse of concepts in impression formation. *Journal of Personality and Social Psychology, 51,* 493–504.

Martin, L. L., & Clark, L. F. (1990). Social cognition: Exploring the mental processes involved in human social interaction. In M. W. Eysenck (Ed.), *Cognitive psychology: An international review* (pp. 265–310). Chichester: Wiley.

Martin, L. L., & Seta, J. J. (1983). Perceptions of unity and distinctiveness as determinants of attraction. *Journal of Personality and Social Psychology, 44,* 755–764.

Martin, L. L., Seta, J. J., & Crelia, R. A. (1990). Assimilation and contrast as a function of people's willingness to expend effort in forming an impression. *Journal of Personality and Social Psychology, 59,* 27–37.

Ostrom, T. M., & Upshaw, H. S. (1968). Psychological perspective and attitude change. In A. C. Greenwald, T. C. Brock, & T. M. Ostrom (Eds.), *Psychological foundations of attitudes* (pp. 217–242). New York: Academic Press.

Ottati, V. C., Riggle, E. J., Wyer, R. S., Schwarz, N., & Kuklinski, J. (1989). The cognitive and affective bases of opinion survey responses. *Journal of Personality and Social Psychology, 57,* 404–415.

Parducci, A. (1965). Category judgments: A range-frequency model. *Psychological Review, 72,* 407–418.

Rosch, E., Mervis, C. B., Gray, W. D., Johnson, D. M., & Boes-Braem, P. (1976). Basic objects in natural categories. *Cognitive Psychology, 8,* 382–439.

Rothbart, M., & John, O. P. (1985). Social categorization and behavioral episodes: A cognitive analysis of the effects of intergroup contact. *Journal of Social Issues, 41,* 81–104.

Schwarz, N. (1990). Feelings as information: Informational and motivational functions of affective states. In E. T. Higgins & R. M. Sorrentino (Eds.), *Handbook of motivation and cognition: Foundations of social behavior* (Vol. 2, pp. 527–561). New York: Guilford Press.

Schwarz, N., & Bless, H. (1990, April). *Ein Inklusions/Exklusions-Modell von Assimilations-und Kontrasteffekten in der sozialen Urteilsbildung* [An inclusion/exclusion model of assimilation and contrast effects in social judgment]. Tagung experimentell arbeitender Psychologen, Regensburg, FRG.

Schwarz, N., & Bless, H. (in press). Scandals and the public's trust in politicians: Assimilation and contrast effects. *Personality and Social Psychology Bulletin.*

Schwarz, N., Bless, H., & Bohner, G. (1991). Mood and persuasion: Affective states influence the processing of persuasive communications. In M. Zanna (Ed.), *Advances in experimental social psychology* (Vol. 24, pp. 161–199). New York: Academic Press.

Schwarz, N., Münkel, T., & Hippler, H. J. (1990). What determines a "perspective"? Contrast effects as a function of the dimension tapped by preceding questions. *European Journal of Social Psychology, 20,* 357–361.

Schwarz, N., & Strack, F. (1991a). Context effects in attitude surveys: Applying cognitive theory to social research. In W. Stroebe & M. Hewstone (Eds.), *European Review of Social Psychology* (Vol. 2, pp. 31–50). Chichester: Wiley.

Schwarz, N., & Strack, F. (1991b). Evaluating one's life: A judgment model of subjective well-being. In F. Strack, M. Argyle, & N. Schwarz (Eds.), *Subjective well-being* (pp. 55–71). Oxford: Pergamon.

Schwarz, N., & Strack, F. (Eds.). (1991c). Social cognition and communication: Human judgment in its social context [Special issue]. *Social Cognition, 9,* 1–125.

Schwarz, N., Strack, F., & Mai, H. P. (1991). Assimilation and contrast effects in part-whole question sequences: A conversational logic analysis. *Public Opinion Quarterly, 55,* 3–23.

Schwarz, N., & Sudman, S. (Eds.). (1992). *Context effects in social and psychological research.* New York: Springer-Verlag.

Seta, J. J., Martin, L. L, & Capehart, G. (1979). Effects of contrast and assimilation on the attitude similarity-attraction relationship. *Journal of Personality and Social Psychology, 37,* 462–467.

Sherif, M., & Hovland, C. I. (1961). *Social judgment: Assimilation and contrast effects in communication and attitude change.* New Haven, CT: Yale University Press.

Smith, E. E. (1990). Categorization: In D. N. Osherson & E. E. Smith (Eds.), *Thinking: An invitation to cognitive science* (Vol. 3, pp. 33–54). Cambridge, MA: MIT Press.

Strack, F., & Martin, L. (1987). Thinking, judging, and communicating: A process account of context effects in attitude surveys. In H. J. Hippler, N. Schwarz, & S. Sudman (Eds.), *Social information processing and survey methodology* (pp. 123–148). New York: Springer-Verlag.

Strack, F., Martin, L. L., & Schwarz, N. (1988). Priming and communication: The social determinants of information use in judgments of life-satisfaction. *European Journal of Social Psychology, 18,* 429–442.

Strack, F., & Schwarz, N. (in press). Implicit cooperation: The case of standardized questioning. In G. Semin & F. Fiedler (Eds.), *Social cognition and language.* Beverly Hills, CA: Sage.

Strack, F., Schwarz, N., Bless, H., Kübler, A., & Wänke, M. (1990). *Remember the priming episode!* Manuscript submitted for publication.

Strack, F., Schwarz, N., & Gschneidinger, E. (1985). Happiness and reminiscing: The role of time perspective, mood, and mode of thinking. *Journal of Personality and Social Psychology, 49,* 1460–1469.

Strack, F., Schwarz, N., & Nebel, A. (1987, March). *Thinking about your life: Affective and evaluative consequences.* Paper presented at the conference on "Ruminations, Self-Relevant Cognitions, and Stress." Memphis State University, Memphis, TN.

Strack, F., Schwarz, N., & Wänke, M. (1991). Semantic and pragmatic aspects of context effects in social and psychological research. *Social Cognition, 9,* 111–125.

Tajfel, H. (1959). Quantitative judgment in social perception. *British Journal of Psychology, 50,* 16–29.

Tajfel, H. (1981). Cognitive aspects of prejudice. *Journal of Social Issues, 25,* 79–97.

Tajfel, H., & Wilkes, A. L. (1963). Classification and quantitative judgment. *British Journal of Psychology, 54,* 101–114.

Tatarkiewicz, W. (1984). Über das Glück [On happiness]. Stuttgart: Klett-Cotta.

Thibaut, J. W., & Kelley, H. H. (1959). *The social psychology of groups.* New York: Wiley.

Tourangeau, R. (1984). Cognitive science and survey methods: A cognitive perspective. In T. Jabine, M. Straf, J. Tanur, & R. Tourangeau (Eds.), *Cognitive aspects of survey methodology: Building a bridge between disciplines* (pp. 73–100). Washington, DC: National Academy Press.

Turner, J. C. (1987). *Rediscovering the social group. A self-categorization theory.* Oxford, England: Blackwell.

Tversky, A., & Griffin, D. (1991). On the dynamics of hedonic experience: Endowment and contrast in judgments of well-being. In F. Strack, M. Argyle, & N. Schwarz (Eds.), *Subjective well-being* (pp. 108–118). Oxford: Pergamon.

Wedell, D. H., Parducci, A., & Geiselman, R. E. (1987). A formal analysis of ratings of physical attractiveness: Successive contast and simultaneous assimilation. *Journal of Experimental Social Psychology, 23*, 230–249.

Wyer, R. S., & Srull, T. K. (1989). *Memory and cognition in its social context.* Hillsdale, NJ: Lawrence Erlbaum Associates.

III

*Toward Theoretical
Integration*

The Different Routes to Social Judgments: Experiential versus Informational Strategies

Fritz Strack
Max-Planck-Institut für psychologische Forschung
[Max Planck Institute for Psychological Research], München, Germany

The psychological processes that underlie judgments of persons and situations are at the core of social cognition. If we understand how social judgments are generated, we have learned about those underlying processes, and about how people construe (e.g., Carlston, 1980) and evaluate (e.g., Fiske & Pavelchak, 1986) their social environment. More importantly, armed with such knowledge, we can better predict how people will behave (cf. Fazio, 1986). The benefits of explaining how people arrive at a judgment extend well beyond an understanding of the specific subject matter of that judgment; indeed, a comprehensive model of human judgment delineates the processes that mediate between the social environment and its effects on human thoughts, emotions, and actions.

Judgments, however, are not necessarily social in nature. In fact, the mental representation of our physical world is to a large degree the result of judgments that were formed at some previous time. We have to decide whether a tree is tall, whether a chair is heavy, or whether a car is fast, and the results of such judgments are likely to remain in memory while their informational basis may be lost (Wyer & Srull, 1989). The way such simple judgments of physical objects are formed may provide a useful analogy for understanding the genesis of more complicated judgments in the social realm.

The present chapter integrates findings from diverse areas of cognitive social and experimental psychology into a conceptual framework of human judgment; the judgment of the relative length of two lines will serve as a starting point.

Centrally, it is argued in this chapter that the solution of most judgment tasks can be reached via different psychological routes. In addition, it is suggested that under certain conditions, judges may engage in corrective strategies by using specific remedies. It is shown that the principles that guide such simple physical judgment tasks are closely related to those that have been described in such theoretical and research contexts as attribution theory, judgmental heuristics, mood as information, perseverance of impressions, priming, assimilation and contrast effects, implicit memory, and perhaps some others. In addition to its integrative function, the suggested framework makes some unique predictions, tests of which may eventually afford deeper insights into the psychological processes that underlie human judgment.

JUDGMENT AND PERCEPTION IN PHYSICAL AND SOCIAL SETTINGS

To identify some basic processes of social judgment, it is useful to look at a simple physical judgment task; in the present example the task is to decide which of two line segments is longer, as depicted in Fig. 9.1. To solve this task, the judge may use relevant target information (i.e., information about the longitudinal extension) that is provided, conduct a simple computational operation and decide that line *a* is longer than line *b*.

However, changing certain aspects of the task may substantially increase the cognitive effort necessary to arrive at an answer; for example, if the target information is provided in different units of measurement. Assume that the length of line *a* is described as 5.6 cm and that of line *b* as 2.1 inches. To solve this task by using the relevant target information, more cognitive capacity and/or time will be required. However, situational, motivational, or capacity constraints may preclude the allocation of these resources. Under such suboptimal circumstances, the judge may decide not to use the target information, but rather to base the judgment on the sensory experience that is elicited by the stimulus itself. Line *a* appears to be somewhat longer than line *b* and, without any computations or conscious inferences, the perception of length may serve as basis of judgment leading to the same decision. In the present example, this transfor-

a) *2.2 inches* b) *2.1 inches*

Which line is longer?

[ ] line a)
[ ] line b)
[ ] same length

FIG. 9.1. Physical judgment task A.

mation of a computational task into a perceptual one resulted in a significant simplification, because the perceptual experience could be simply "read off" without capacity-consuming computations.

There are circumstances, however, under which a distinct perceptual experience that has been elicited will not be used as the basis of the judgment. This is the case if the experience is not representative for the target of the judgment; for example, if the perception of length is determined by factors other than the actual length of the stimulus. Figure 9.2 depicts a variant of the task for which this is true. In this figure, the perception of length is influenced by features unrelated to the actual length of the lines (i.e., the specific configuration of arrow heads from the Muller-Lyer Illusion), and is therefore not representative for the judgment target.

In the case of such an extraneous influence, judgments may be corrected. Often, perceptual experiences cannot be altered by conscious strategies. Then, a correction can only be accomplished by either rejecting the experience as a basis of the judgment (and by relying on the target information), or by merely adjusting one's overt response. For both types of correction, however, a judge must be aware of having been influenced by irrelevant cues. For adjustments on the response scale, it is additionally necessary to know the direction of the influence, in order to compensate for the presumed influence by changing the response in the opposite direction (cf. Nisbett & Wilson, 1977). Whenever we are not aware of such extraneous influences, we will not question the representativeness of the experience and will use it as a valid basis of the judgment. Thus, persons who are not knowledgeable about visual illusions will base their judgments on the appearance of length, whereas students after their first course in perception may not use their visual experience as valid evidence.

The central characteristics of the described judgment situation are symbolically depicted in Fig. 9.3. The person is exposed to a stimulus event (the two lines and the additional information) and is given a particular task (a decision about which line is longer). The task and the situational context in which it has to be performed determine the processing objectives, and those in turn define whether a subjective experience or target information will serve as a basis, and if target information is to be used *which* target information is relevant for the

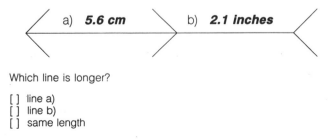

Which line is longer?

[ ] line a)
[ ] line b)
[ ] same length

FIG. 9.2. Physical judgment task B.

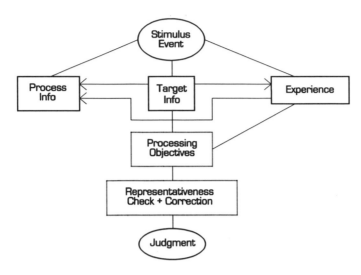

FIG. 9.3. Graphic depiction of the model.

goal of the task. The judgment may be corrected by recomputation or adjustment if judges are aware (or remember) that certain cues were eliciting a specific
experience (or activating specific information[1]). In the present framework, this
type of information is called *process information*.

Most important in this conceptualization are the notions that: (a) judges may
choose different psychological routes to arrive at a solution to the task and, (b)
they may correct their judgment for nonrepresentativeness.

Before attempting to apply the current framework to social judgments, a conceptual clarification is necessary. In the previous section, I argued that physical
judgments can often be generated either by engaging in computational activities
or by relying on perceptual experiences. The question arises of whether a similar option exists in the realm of social judgments. Judging by the labels, *social
perception, interpersonal perception*, and *self-perception* seem to be processes of
perception, not of computation. However, what is denoted by "perception"
is not the same as in physical perception. In a recently published book by
E. E. Jones (1990), entitled *Interpersonal Perception, perceiving* people is defined
to be "synonymous with making sense of their behavior, and this activity involves finding the cause or causes of that behavior" (p. 39). This definition of
perception, however, contrasts with *perception* taken as immediate experience.
Interpersonal perception is instead the result of elaborate computational processes. The same holds for Bem's (1972) self-perception theory in which *perception*
refers to the possibility that attitudes are inferred from one's own behavior.

Given the above understanding of *perception*, one might argue that *social perception* or *self-perception* are misnomers. In any case, the question arises whether

---

[1]This possibility was not addressed in the previous example.

the analogy between physical and social judgments can be maintained. Is there a perceptual route to social judgments that may result in a cognitive simplification, just like in physical judgments?

This seems unlikely if one considers that the attributes of social judgments are not directly observable but must be inferred. However, there appears to be an alternative way in which perceptual processes may become relevant in social judgments. These processes may generate experiences in the form of intero- and proprioception (Pennebaker, Gonder-Frederick, Cox, & Hoover, 1985). While experiences elicited by physical perception are transmitted by the sensory systems making contact with the external world (visual, acoustic, haptic, gustatory, olfactory), interoception may be based on sensations that are transmitted by sensory systems that record physical states of the person (e.g., autonomically controlled activities like visceral responses, unspecific arousal, blood temperature, heart rate, or centrally controlled activities such as peripheral muscle contractions). Experiences triggered by internal sensory cues may influence behaviors (cf. Pennebaker et al., 1985) and judgments.

Thus, the interoceptive experience[2] of hunger (for a discussion of the different internal cues, cf. Logue, 1991) not only influences our eating behavior but may also affect judgments of food. The experience of fatigue not only influences our sleeping behavior, but may also affect judgments of how interesting a book or a lecture is (Damrad-Frye & Laird, 1989). Best studied, however, are influences of emotional "feelings" (cf. Schwarz, 1990; Schwarz & Clore, 1988) that can be understood as *affective* experiences.

Clore convincingly argued (this volume; Clore & Parrot, 1991; see also Laird & Bresler, 1990; Schwarz, Bless, et al., 1991) that feelings are not necessarily emotional in nature. He pointed out that there may be feelings of familiarity, boredom, expectation, and even of knowing. But if it is not their valence, what makes feelings distinct from thought? In the present conceptualization, it is their perceptual (i.e., sensation-based) character. Phenomenal experiences—feelings forming a subset—are distinct from propositional thought because they have a sensory component such as the visual perception of the length of a line in the previous example (for a similar perspective, see Buck, 1985).

Visual experiences can also be *simulated* if a person engages in visual imagery (see Farah, 1988, for some neurological evidence). If the content is evaluative in nature (e.g., a negative or positive autobiographical event), visual imagery typically elicits congruent affect while non-visual, propositional thinking leads to the activation of evaluative propositions. Depending on whether they are based on evaluative propositions or on affective experience, subsequent judgments may be influenced in opposite directions (Strack, Schwarz, & Gschneidinger, 1985). Affective experiences entail intero- and proprioceptive components (cf.

---

[2]Of course, external cues like the sight or smell of food may contribute to the experience of hunger. In fact, interindividual differences have been found to play an important role in determining the relative weight of internal vs. external cues for the emotional experience (MacArthur, Solomon, & Jaffee, 1980).

Darwin, 1872; Ekman, Levenson, & Friesen, 1983; James, 1890; Laird, 1974; Martin, Harlow, & Strack, in press; Strack, Martin, & Stepper, 1988; Zillmann & Bryant, 1974), such as autonomic arousal and peripheral muscle activity. *Nonemotional feelings* (Clore, this volume) such as familiarity, boredom, or expectation, are nonaffective experiences that may also have a sensory component. The feeling of *expectation*, for instance, has been found to be increased if people generate a visual image of the outcome (e.g., Carroll, 1978; Strack, 1983). Boredom may be based on experienced fatigue or expended effort to attend (Damrad-Frye & Laird, 1989) and familiarity may be based on the experienced *fluency of perception* (cf. Jacoby & Dallas, 1981).

A FRAMEWORK FOR JUDGMENTS

Although the following discussion focuses on judgments of social targets, the features of the proposed model apply to physical judgments as well. The present framework comprises two components: (a) an *exposure phase*, in which the person confronts an external stimulus that has certain psychological effects, and (b) a *judgment phase* in which the person performs the judgmental task. Both phases are clearly interdependent and can occur simultaneously rather than in succession. Furthermore, elements of the judgment task often determine aspects of the situation to which people will attend, and the encoding of these aspects into memory (for a more complete account, see Wyer & Srull, 1989).

The Exposure Phase

Let us start with a simplified social situation of being exposed to a specific social event. For example, the judge encounters another person asking for help, as did subjects in Darley and Batson's (1973) experimental study of helping behavior.

What are the psychological concomitants of this situation? First, the judge will encode information about the target person in this particular situational context. This information could consist of cues such as verbal or nonverbal behavior from the target, and its interpretation could depend on the judge's goal in the situation (Wyer, Srull, Gordon, & Hartwick, 1982). The information will be semantically categorized and the subsequent accessibility of the activated category will be increased (Higgins, Rholes, & Jones, 1977; Srull & Wyer, 1979, 1980). In the present model, the categorized information is called *target information*. For example, both the target's explicit request for help and outward signs of need will be encoded and stored in memory.

Second, exposure to an event might evoke a specific subjective *experience* in the judge. In the present example, the observer of the person in need may well experience empathy, shock, fear, sadness, embarrassment, or repulsion (cf. Schaller & Cialdini, 1990). Experiences may be elicited at different stages of the information processing sequence. Affect, for instance, can be elicited at different depths of encoding (cf. Lazarus, 1982; Zajonc, 1980). Moreover, some experiences are automatic reactions to sensory input (cf. Lang, Bradley, & Cuthbert, 1990); others are the outcome of more complex cognitive processes (e.g., Lazarus, 1984). No matter what its form or specific origin, an experienced sensation can be viewed as a concomitant or a result of an underlying psychological process.

Finally, judges might note that certain thoughts or emotions occur in a specific context. Rather than simply noting this co-occurrence, they might elaborate and interpret aspects of the context as causal determinants of these psychological consequences. To return to our helping situation, the sight of the helpless person may remind the judge of some similar situation, or create feelings of depression or anxiety. This information about one's experienced psychological processes is called *episodic process information* or *process information*. That is, it may be conceived of as an episodic tag that is appended to the process of thinking about something and experiencing a sensation.

Of course, it must be acknowledged that people often fail to identify the true causal influences on their immediate experiences. They also fail to reconstruct experiences veridically after the fact. These failures occur because people do not have immediate, introspective access to their psychological processes and must rely on theory-based inferences instead (Nisbett & Wilson, 1977). Similarly, they often misidentify the sources of a psychological process when they attempt to reconstruct an influence retrospectively (Johnson, 1988).[3] Thus, observers of the emergency incident may recall incorrectly that the target person elicited empathy in them or may erroneously assume that the particular affect was caused by a previous negative experience.

To summarize, there are three distinct consequences of exposure to an event that may come into play in the genesis of social judgments: (a) target information that is encoded by activating semantic categories, (b) experiences that are elicited by the event or exist for other reasons at the time the event occurs, and (c) information about (a) and (b) that is encoded in relation to the event.

The Judgment Phase

During or some time after exposure to a social situation, a person is often asked to form a specific judgment. In our previous example, the judgment is an assessment of the target's need for help. Typically, the judgment is generated and communicated as part of a particular task that is defined on both semantic

---

[3]These shortcomings, however, are not problematic for the model under consideration, for whether experiences are accurately construed—at the moment or retrospectively—does not change the influence of sensations per se in the judgment process.

and procedural dimensions. Processing objectives control the translation of task requirements into specific cognitive operations. It is also important to note that processing objectives of unrelated cognitive tasks may influence subsequent judgments (Lingle & Ostrom, 1979).

Judgments Based on Target Information.

Judgments Based on Target Information. In a typical judgment task, a person must decide if or to what degree a particular attribute fits a target. The attribute's meaning determines the class of target information to be retrieved or generated for the judgment. For example, if a judgment concerns how helpless a target person is, the judge must recall information about the attribute *helplessness*. Similarly, if one's task is to report one's liking for the target person, one might search for information that refers to *liking* (for a more complete account, see Wyer & Srull, 1989).

It is hardly earthshaking that people required to make a judgment on a certain dimension are willing and able to retrieve relevant information. However, because it is impossible to engage in an exhaustive search of *all* relevant information stored in memory, the outcome of a search will be influenced by the relative accessibility of the relevant information. Of course, prior use will influence the accessibility of that relevant information (cf. Wyer & Srull, 1989). Suppose, for example, that instead of receiving instructions to give a talk on the Good Samaritan (Darley & Batson, 1973), the judge had just left a Red Cross instruction in which relevant information about helping was activated. This information will subsequently be more accessible for interpreting the ambiguous emergency situation. Thus, in essence, the cognitive consequences of a preceding task will influence a subsequent judgment (e.g., Lingle & Ostrom, 1979; Srull & Wyer, 1979, 1980).

One example of the effect of context accessibility is a study in which we (Strack et al., 1985) had subjects engage in an autobiographical memory task. More precisely, they listed either positive or negative events from their recent past. In an ostensibly unrelated subsequent task, subjects later reported about their happiness and satisfaction with life in general. We assumed that the selective activation of either positive or negative information would increase its accessibility and thus influence subsequent judgments in the same direction. Results clearly supported this hypothesis: Subjects who had previously been induced to ponder recent positive events judged themselves to be happier and more satisfied with their life in general than did subjects who had thought about recent negative events. Thus, the processing objectives of the ostensibly unrelated preceding task (i.e., retrieving either positive or negative autobiographical events from memory) influenced the outcome of the judgment task that followed.

A series of studies by Lee Ross and his colleagues (e.g., Ross, Lepper, Strack, & Steinmetz, 1977) demonstrated how specific processing objectives may determine probability judgments. Subjects used clinical case study information to explain either why a target person with psychological problems would commit suicide, or alternatively, volunteer for the Peace Corps. Subsequently, subjects judged the probability that the target person would actually perform these critical behaviors in the future and held the event that they had explained far more likely to occur. Clearly, the first explanation task required the subjects to focus on different types of information, and this information influenced subsequent judgments of probability. This study, like Strack et al.'s (1985), demonstrated that the activation of concepts in the performance of one task can influence judgments made when performing a subsequent task, provided that those concepts are relevant.

Judgments Based on Elicited Experiences. Judgments can also be affected by task characteristics and requirements that are not content-specific (for a related position, cf. Kruglanski, 1990). For example, a task can be so complicated, or the target so obscure and ambiguous that the generation of a judgment requires considerable cognitive effort. Distraction or time pressure can also render the judgment task more difficult. Such complicating circumstances often induce people to simplify the basis of their judgments. This is particularly true if judges are not sufficiently motivated to spend the necessary cognitive effort. Such a simplification might be realized by taking recourse to experiences that are based on one's bodily sensations.

Why do such experiences simplify the judgment task? There are two reasons. Once experiences are elicited, they are immediately accessible to the individual. That is, we have direct introspective access to them; they can be "read" like an internal meter, and no inferences are necessary to determine their nature. Typically, we need not engage in extensive inferential processes to decide whether we are feeling good or bad, whether we are experiencing pain or arousal, whether we are expending effort, or whether we are experiencing an auditory or visual image.

Second, subjective experiences simplify the judgment task because they can be brought to bear on the judgment without capacity-consuming computations. Judgmental heuristics (Kahneman, Slovic, & Tversky, 1982) can be used to connect experiences with the topic of the judgment in a simple correlational manner, if the type of experience is relevant for the attribute of the judgment task. Positive or negative affect, for example, can be used to make positive or negative evaluative judgments (e.g., Richman & Petty, 1991; Schwarz & Clore, 1983; Schwarz, Strack, Kommer, & Wagner, 1987; Strack et al., 1985). The experienced vividness of a mental image, or the consequent ease with which certain contents can be brought to mind, can serve as the basis for judgments of frequency or probability (Carroll, 1978; Sherman, Cialdini, Schwartzman, & Reynolds, 1985; Strack, 1983). The experience of familiarity may be used for judgments of previous occurrence (Mandler, 1980) or for judgments of fame (Jacoby, Woloshyn, & Kelley, 1989).

It is interesting to speculate whether subjects are aware of the functional role of their experiences with respect to judgments. That is, do they draw a conscious inference on the basis of their experiences? On the one hand, people do not seem to have introspective knowledge about how they generate experience-based judgments. Otherwise, some of the judgmental heuristics (Kahneman et al., 1982) could have been discovered via mere introspection. The immediacy of the phenomenal experience seems to be automatically transferred to the attribute of the judgment such that people may experience an intuitive sense of happiness with their lives, of the likelihood of a certain outcome, or of their familiarity with a particular face.

On the other hand, it is obviously possible to discount experiences and to control for their influence on judgments (Cooper, Zanna, & Taves, 1978; Jacoby, Kelley, Brown, & Jasechko, 1989; Schwarz & Clore, 1983). This discounting may imply a dissociation between the experience and the judgment. Of course, such a correction does not necessarily require introspective access to the judgment generation. Instead, it may be based solely on a theory-guided assumption that a potentially distorting influence may be operating. These and other correction processes will be discussed in a later section of this chapter.

One great advantage of judgments that are based on phenomenal experiences is that they often require less cognitive capacity than judgments based on information. Unlike experiences, target information must either be connected with general knowledge to draw an inference or be integrated with different pieces of information to form a global judgment (Fiske & Pavelchak, 1986). Certainly, other cognitive shortcuts are also available (Chaiken, 1987; Petty & Cacioppo, 1986), but reliance on experiences practically guarantees simpler judgments.

Experimental examples come from several sources. In numerous studies on judgmental heuristics, Tversky and Kahneman (1973) demonstrated that the ease with which people can bring a certain content to mind often influences judgments of frequency or probability. For example, subjects overestimated the number of women's names amid men's names if the women's names were associated with another characteristic that served as a retrieval cue. In the case of one experiment, the characteristic was the targets' prominence, and more women's names referred to famous personalities than did men's. According to the authors, the salient characteristic of fame facilitated the recall of women's names, and subjects consequently overestimated the frequency of those names.

Jacoby, Kelley, Brown, & Jasechko (1989) also demonstrated that processing effort and fame are heuristically related in the reverse direction. They used judgments of fame as a dependent variable and varied the prior exposure to nonfamous names. After a delay, subjects judged names to which they had previously been exposed to be more famous than novel names. The authors argued that the experience of greater perceptual fluency influences the judgment of fame (see also Jacoby & Dallas, 1981).

In the present framework, the experienced effort necessary to complete a cognitive task determines people's experience of the ease or difficulty of that task. Not only does the experience of effort serve as a basis of frequency judgments, but it also influences judgments about one's own personality. Schwarz, Bless, et al. (1991) had subjects recall either 6 or 12 behaviors of their own that exemplified high or low assertiveness. Although it was relatively easy to come up with 6 behavioral instances, it was more difficult to generate 12. Subsequent self-ratings of assertiveness were influenced by the ease with which these instances could be brought to mind. As expected, subjects asked to recall 6 assertive behaviors (low effort) judged themselves to be more assertive than subjects asked to generate 12 behaviors (high effort). The authors concluded that subjective experiences like the ease of retrieval may function as a source of information that enters into the judgment.

Other experiments illustrate that affective experiences influence judgments of well-being (e.g., Schwarz & Clore, 1983; Strack et al., 1985), as well as of judgments of funniness (Strack, Martin, & Stepper, 1988). Often, however, the nature of the judgment task precludes the use of affect as the basis of the judgment; this may have very important practical consequences. For example, if experimental subjects are asked to report their present mood state (e.g., as checks in studies that manipulate mood as an independent variable) they may base their answer on their current affective experience. However, if they are asked about the effect a particular manipulation has had on their mood (another measure used as a manipulation check), it is not sufficient to read off current affect. Unless the impact of the mood manipulation is rather dramatic or salient, judgments of impact (see also Silka, 1988) that are based on affective experiences require that people have spontaneously encoded their affective state prior to a mood manipulation, and that they compare it to the affect they experienced after the manipulation.

Of course, the described procedure is quite complex and the requirements for implementing it (e.g., the encoding of the affect before the manipulation) are rarely fulfilled. Therefore, respondents are likely to resort to other information. For example, they base their response on target information about the experimental influence and infer its impact on the basis of general knowledge about psychological processes (Nisbett & Wilson, 1977). A series of studies by Strack, Schwarz, and Nebel (1990b) support this possibility. In these studies, subjects were exposed to positive or negative information, generated it, or recalled positive or negative events from the past. In addition, experimental procedures varied such that a *vivid* mode of thinking elicited affect while a *pallid* mode of thinking did not. After exposure to these conditions, subjects reported both their mood state and how the experimental manipulation had changed their mood. Consistent with Nisbett and Wilson's (1977) findings, we expected that subjects would be more likely to directly experience their current mood state at the time of judgment than the *change* that had occurred as a function of the manipulation. To answer the change question, subjects would therefore have to rely on intuitive psychological theories that explain how certain events influence experienced affect. We assumed that such theories would be more likely to focus solely on the valence of a thought content than on the interaction of the valence with the mode of thinking. More simply put, a theory-based judgment should result in a main effect of valence whereas an experience-based judgment should show the more complicated interaction of valence with the mode of thinking.

The results supported this prediction. Mood *state* measures were very sensitive to the rather subtle mode of thinking manipulation. Thus, whether the event was positive or negative influenced people's reported affect only if they imagined the event in a vivid fashion but not when they were induced to think about the event in an abstract manner. Judgments reflecting how the event had *changed* their mood, however, depended only on the valence of the event. That is, regardless whether they had been instructed to think vividly or abstractly, subjects indicated that positive events had improved their mood whereas negative events had a deteriorating effect. Apparently, people do not use their affective experiences to answer mood change questions. Rather, they draw inferences on the basis of the potential influence and theoretical knowledge (cf. Wilson, Laser, & Stone, 1982).

If this hypothesis is correct, then subjects should apply the same strategy in answering a question when the experience of current affect is inaccessible. This is the case when subjects try to assess the affective *state* of a third person. To test this idea, we conducted an interpersonal simulation in which subjects were provided with the "authentic" stimulus material of an ostensible participant in the Strack et al. (1985) study (Experiment 3). Depending on the conditions, they received the original subject's instructions to recall either a positive or a negative event and describe the event in either a vivid or abstract fashion. Subjects were provided with the event the original participant had ostensibly recalled and were asked to answer the subsequent questions in the same way as the original participant.

As expected, subjects in the interpersonal simulation study who had to assess the other person's mood state showed the same pattern of results as subjects who had to report their own mood change. In both cases, the judgments were a function only of the valence of the event (and not of the more subtle mode of thinking manipulations). As there exists no immediate access to the other person's phenomenal experience, these results support the contention that in both cases judgments were based on general theories.

In a more general sense, these findings show that the type and the target of a question may determine whether an answer will be based on the respondent's present experience or on computations based on specific and general information. The results also demonstrate that answers may greatly differ depending on which strategy is used.

Representativeness Check

Once information has been activated or experiences have been elicited, judges may check to determine if such information or experiences are appropriate. This stage is hereafter called the *representativeness check*. As an example, let us assume a person evaluating her life on the basis of relevant autobiographical information that she recalls. Let us further assume that she recalls a particular life event from the very distant past. In this case, although the activated information is relevant for the judgment (it is, after all, an event of her life), it may not be representative of the target of the judgment (it is an event from the distant past that may not reflect her current life experience). As a consequence, a correction may be called for.

Alternatively, suppose our judge's affective experience and not the information she retrieves becomes the basis of the evaluation of her life. At the same time, let us further assume that she becomes aware that this affective experience has been caused by a transient influence that is entirely unrelated to the quality of her life—such as current weather conditions (Schwarz & Clore, 1983). Under these circumstances, the judge may consider the experience as irrelevant for the judgment and she may recompute the judgment or adjust the response.

These examples illustrate two aspects of representativeness: (a) the similarity of information with respect to the target of the judgment, to be called *content representativeness*, and (b) the degree to which the event that produced the outcome (an experience or the accessibility of target information) is in itself relevant for the judgment, to be called *process representativeness*. The present use of the term *representativeness* is similar to that employed by Kahneman and Tversky (1972). That is, an event is representative to "the degree to which it is (i) similar in essential properties to its parent population and (ii) reflects the salient features of the process by which it is generated" (p. 431). Thus, *content* and *process* are both components of representativeness and have similar antecedents and consequences.

In the proposed framework, it is assumed that representativeness is the default option in the formation of judgments. That is, information or subjective experiences will be considered representative until proven nonrepresentative. More precisely, as long as the representativeness check is not negative, the activated information or the elicited experience will serve as a basis of the judgment and will influence that judgment in the direction of its semantic, evaluative, or heuristic implications.

What are the effects of representativeness for the judgment? Representative information or experiences will influence the judgment in the direction of their semantic or affective implications and lead to an assimilation[4] effect. Nonrepresentative information, on the other hand, will decrease the likelihood that information or an experience will be the basis of the judgment, and assimilation effects will be eliminated.

The effects of a representativeness check hinge on a number of factors. First, the *determinants* of representativeness must be considered. Second, attention must be directed toward the *conditions* of a representativeness check. Third,

---

[4]In this chapter, *assimilation* and *contrast* are used to refer to the *direction* of an influence and not to a specific psychological process.

possible *corrections* on the part of the judge must be taken into account if the outcome of the check is nonrepresentativeness.

Determinants of Representativeness.

Determinants of Representativeness. What are the determinants of representativeness? Let us first consider content representativeness and briefly address the assimilation-contrast literature.

There is ample evidence that similarity on the dimension of judgment is a determinant of the outcome of a representativeness check. Herr, Sherman, and Fazio (1983), for example, found that for judgments of animals' ferocity, the more extreme a previously exposed exemplar was on the relevant dimension of judgment, the less likely was there an assimilation effect. That is, a fox was judged to be more ferocious if the subjects had previously been exposed to a wolf (a moderate exemplar), but less ferocious if subjects had previously been exposed to a tiger (an extreme exemplar). In a more recent study, Herr (1986) conceptually replicated this finding for the dimension "hostility," and demonstrated that judgments had behavioral consequences in interactions with targets. These findings suggest that exposure caused subjects' internal representations of targets to change, rather than merely producing a change in how subjects use the response scale (cf. Ostrom & Upshaw, 1968).

Content representativeness is not only determined by similarity or difference on the relevant dimension of judgment; it can also be determined by superordinate classification on a peripheral dimension that leads to a more general categorization of the target as being *same* or *different* with respect to the activated information. A rather arbitrary ingroup/outgroup classification might have this effect (cf. Tajfel, 1970). A different time period to which an event belongs may serve as another example. In a series of studies (Strack et al., 1985; Strack, Schwarz, & Nebel, 1990a) we had subjects generate life events that belonged to either the distant past, the present, or the future, and then, after generating these items, report their well-being. Assimilation effect on judgments of well-being were only found for present but not for future or past events.

Episodic cues may even trigger such a superimposed classification. For example, Martin (1986) found that if the exposure episode is distinct from the judgment episode, it is less likely that activated information influences subsequent judgments in the direction of their semantic content. In several studies, Martin obtained contrast effects on judgments of an ambiguously described person if the priming episode was completed and thus distinct from the judgment phase of the experiment. Conversely, he found assimilation if the subjects were merely interrupted in the priming activity such that the subsequent judgment belonged to the same experimental episode.

Another type of content representativeness depends on the intention of the communicator. In deciding what information to bring to bear in making a judgment, it is not sufficient to rely solely on the semantic features of the task. It is also important to infer the questioner's intention on the basis of such pragmatic considerations as Gricean rules of conversation (Grice, 1975). Thus, if a person is asked to judge the well-being of his family, the target of his judgment may not be sufficiently defined by the semantic meaning of the word. For example, should *family* include one's parents, one's brothers and sisters or only relatives who live in the same house? The respondent can sometimes infer the intended meaning of the question by applying normative rules of communication. For example, one of those rules (i.e., the Gricean *maxim of quantity*) requires the respondent to convey information that the questioner does not already have (Clark & Haviland, 1977). By applying this rule, the respondent can conclude that the questioner does not want information that the recipient has already provided. Thus, in the previous example, the respondent would infer that the questioner's intended meaning of *family* does not include members who have previously been targets of the same judgment. Therefore, if the respondent is asked to report his family's well-being after reporting his wife's, he will infer that *family* is not intended to include his wife, and will exclude her from consideration in reporting this judgment.

Conversants make use of the Gricean principles of communication in natural conversations. In standardized judgment situations like surveys or experiments, however, this may occur only when the questions being asked are presumed to be episodically related (cf. Strack, 1991). More precisely, such a perception can be manipulated to separate priming effects from effects that are based on a conversational inference. In fact, one would expect that a category activated by a preceding question would produce an assimilation effect unless the interpretation of the intended meaning requires that the activated aspect be precluded from the judgment.

A set of studies provide a test of this hypothesis (Schwarz, Strack, & Mai, 1991; Strack, Martin, & Schwarz, 1988; Strack, Schwarz, & Wänke, 1991). Briefly, a preceding judgment task can serve one of two functions (Strack, 1991; Strack & Schwarz, in press), each exerting a distinct effect on a respondent's judgment. The first function is a priming function, whereby a preceding question activates information that is a relevant basis for a subsequent judgment. For example, a task requiring a judgment of a respondent's happiness with dating activates information about one specific life domain. This information may in turn influence the respondent's judgment about happiness with life in general. An assimilation effect thus occurs in the sense that the correlation between the specific and the general happiness questions is higher when the specific question precedes the more general one.

The second function is an informative function whereby completion of the preceding judgment task informs the respondent about what the questioner already knows. This informative function allows the respondent to apply conversational rules to infer the questioner's communicative intention. In this case, the respondent knows that the questioner is already informed about happiness with dating and can infer that the questioner views this specific domain as irrelevant to judgments about general happiness. Thus, the activated information should not be the basis of the subsequent judgment, and no assimilation effect should be observed.

Whether the priming or the informative function operates depends on the presumed episodic relationship between the two tasks. In fact, a central independent variable of the above studies involved a manipulation of just such a perception. In two studies (Schwarz, Strack et al., 1991; Strack, Martin, & Schwarz, 1988), question order was varied such that the judgment task that activated the specific content either preceded or followed the more general one.

The results were very consistent: Asking a specific question prior to a more general question yielded an assimilation effect. Respondents who reported happiness with romantic relationships provided more positive judgments of happiness and satisfaction with life in general than did respondents who reported happiness with the specific (romantic) domain. This relationship did not obtain when the general question was asked before the more specific one. These results suggest that the specific judgment task did indeed activate the content that became the basis for answers to the more general question.

However, this priming influence was eliminated if the two tasks were presumed to be episodically related. More specifically, the correlation between subjects' responses to the two questions was reduced to zero when they read a lead-in that mentioned that two questions would be asked about their lives; in short, the assimilation effect was completely eliminated in this condition. Similar results were also obtained by Ottati, Riggle, Wyer, Schwarz, and Kuklinski (1989). These authors found that respondents expressed a more positive attitude toward the general issue of free speech if a preceding question about free speech referred to a specific positively evaluated group (e.g., the American Civil Liberties Union) than if it referred to a negatively evaluated group (e.g., the American Nazi Party). However, this assimilation effect was found only when the related questions were separated in the questionnaire. If the specific question immediately preceded the general question, a contrast effect was obtained such that positive content led to a more negative general attitude and vice versa.

In a related study (Strack, Schwarz, & Wänke, 1991), the targets of the judgment were semantically similar (*happiness* and *satisfaction* with life in general), and their order was not varied. For the outlined reasons, it was assumed that the correlation between the answers would be lower when the judgment tasks were episodically related (a box was drawn around the two questions) than when they were episodically unrelated (questions were parts of different surveys). The results clearly supported this prediction.

Taken together, these findings suggest that, on the one hand, preceding judgments may serve a priming function by activating semantic information, increasing the likelihood that this information may serve as the basis of the judgment. On the other hand, a preceding question may inform the respondent about the intended meaning of a question and thereby decrease the likelihood that the activated information will be the basis of the judgment.

In many situations, the intended meaning will be automatically activated at the time of exposure. For example, if the specific communication situation activates certain concepts that are associated with idiosyncratic aspects of the communicator, inferences are not necessary for the interpretation of the intended meaning. The increased accessibility of the particular concept will be sufficient to account for the effect. For example, if a doctor asks whether a patient is allergic to any drugs, the respondents will spontaneously think of pharmaceuticals and not of narcotics.

In other situations, however, respondents must use the rules of conversation (see Grice, 1975) to examine activated semantic information and divine the communicator's intention. In the studies we conducted, respondents were required to keep track of their previous contributions and to infer the communicator's intended meaning on the basis of semantic content and a presumed episodic relationship between the two judgment tasks.

Thus, content representativeness is determined by specific similarity on the focal dimension of judgment, or by a more generalized distinctiveness that results either from superordinate classification on a peripheral dimension or from episodic cues. Alternatively, content representativeness may be determined by the match of a question's semantic content with the communicator's presumed intention.

Process representativeness, on the other hand, is determined by the degree to which the cause of an elicited experience or activated information is by itself relevant to a judgment. Let us assume, to use a study by Jacoby, Woloshyn, and Kelley (1989), that a person bases judgments of fame on the experience of perceptual fluency or familiarity as she reads the names. At the same time, she becomes aware that these experiences are caused by prior exposure to the stimulus. If the cause (prior exposure) is by itself not relevant information for judgments of fame, the experience is not representative and the respondent will not base her judgment on that experience. However, if the prior exposure to the name had occurred through a headline of a newspaper (i.e., a cause that is by itself relevant information for judgments of fame), the elicited experience would continue to be a basis of the judgment.

Similarly, if an experience of effort is attributed to an irrelevant cause, like music being played during the task to recall either 6 or 12 behavioral episodes, then self-ascriptions of the trait that is implied by these behaviors should not be based on the nonrepresentative experience of recall effort. This was the case in the study conducted by Schwarz, Bless, et al. (1991). However, if subjects had been aware that the experienced effort was affected by a variable that was by itself associated with the trait, the judgment would still be based on the experience.

Finally, if an experience of affect is caused by the transient weather situation (see Schwarz & Clore, 1983), these atmospheric conditions are not relevant for judgments of happiness with life in general. Again, in this case, the experience of affect is not representative, and if the subject is aware of this fact, it is unlikely to serve as the basis of happiness judgments. However, if it had been a constant climate that was responsible for subjects' mood states, the affective experience would have been representative because the cause is relevant information to the judgment.

Conditions of the Representativeness Check.

Conditions of the Representativeness Check.   Some determinants of both content and process representativeness have been described. The question remains, however, under what conditions judges actually engage in a representativeness check. In the present model, this check is viewed as an additional cognitive activity that requires cognitive capacity. It follows that if capacity is diminished at the time of judgment formation, representativeness checks will be less likely, and assimilation effects will consequently be more likely. More concretely, this occurs when people encounter such suboptimal conditions as distraction, time pressure, or other situations in which attention is diverted from the judgment task.

There is evidence for such mechanisms for both content and process representativeness. In a recent series of studies, Martin, Seta, and Crelia (1990) found that in a standard priming task, assimilation effects on trait inferences were more likely when judges were distracted, did not expect their responses to be checked individually, or were low in "need for cognition." Thus, both situational and motivational factors reduced cognitive capacity and caused activated information to serve as a basis for subjects' judgments; in short, these factors produced assimilation effects.

In a different theoretical context, Strack, Erber, and Wicklund (1982) found that time pressure exerted similar effects. Subjects exposed to information about a person showed stronger assimilation effects when they were put under time pressure in the judgment situation. More specifically, subjects were exposed to a picture of a target and to information implying that the target was either a moderately active or moderately passive person. Regardless of the content, subjects showed stronger assimilation effects toward the implications of this information when they were put under time pressure to make their judgments.

These two sets of studies support the assumption of the present model that when cognitive capacity at the time of judgment is diminished by situational or by motivational factors, people are less likely to detect nonrepresentativeness with respect to both content and process. Evidence has also been provided for similar influences on conversational inferences. Martin and Harlow (in press) found that subjects were less likely to observe the Gricean maxim of quantity if their cognitive capacity was reduced either by situational or motivational determinants. In line with our previous reasoning, their results suggested that subjects in those conditions were less likely to encode or retrieve their previous contributions and use them to infer another's communicative intention.

Process representativeness, however, involves an additional requirement: The judge must remember the supposed cause of an influence on a judgment. This requires that an event at the time of exposure leaves an episodic trace that can be detected and used at judgment time.

It follows that a decreased cognitive capacity at the time of exposure should prevent the causal episode from being encoded and remembered at the time of judgment. Jacoby and his collaborators provided evidence in support of this claim. In one of their studies of exposure and judgments of fame, Jacoby, Kelley, Brown, and Jasechko (1989) used a short time delay between exposure and judgment and had some subjects read the names under conditions of divided attention. The fame effect only obtained under the divided attention condition. This suggests that when subjects devoted full attention to the exposure situation, they remembered having seen a particular name before. That is, although previous exposures did influence their experience of fluency, subjects were able to correct for this influence in making judgments.

Judges can compensate for such memory deficits if they are reminded of the episode of influence at the time of judgment. This was also demonstrated by Jacoby and colleagues (Jacoby, Kelley, et al., 1989). In their study, the influence of exposure on judgments of fame was reduced if the subjects were required to remember whether or not the name was presented before.

In a more direct fashion, we (Strack, Schwarz, Bless, Kübler, & Wänke, 1991) found that the typical assimilation effect on subsequent judgments disappeared for some subjects when we reminded them of the priming episode. Moreover, the results suggested a contrast effect (see also Lombardi, Higgins, & Bargh, 1987).

In summary, these findings support the thesis that checking both content and process representativeness consumes cognitive capacity and that such checks are less likely under suboptimal judgment conditions. By default, the activated information and the elicited experience will influence judgments in the direction of their semantic, evaluative, or heuristic implications. In the case of process representativeness, it is additionally important that the episodic information about the eliciting event is remembered at the time of judgment. Again, this is less likely if judges are distracted at the time of encoding, and more likely if the judgment situation directs their attention toward the encoding episode.

Corrections for Nonrepresentativeness. What can judges do if they have engaged in a representativeness check and the outcome is negative? That is, how do they respond if the content is recognized to be dissimilar either on the judgmental or on a peripheral dimension, or if the causing event is by itself not relevant for the judgment?

It is important to note that neither the accessibility of information nor the particular experience can be undone if they are considered to be nonrepresentative. Therefore, correction attempts cannot be directed at these aspects of judgment generation and must be accomplished in alternative ways. These are described in turn.

The first possibility is that judges try to ignore the activated content (see also Wyer & Budesheim, 1987; Wyer & Unverzagt, 1985) or the elicited experience. Most clearly, Kubovy (1977) was able to show that subjects who were asked to spontaneously generate a one-digit number did not use the number that was suggested by the experimenter as an example. In the previously described study by Schwarz and Clore (1983), the influence of the elicited affect on judgments of well-being was eliminated if subjects' attention was directed toward the current weather (germane to current affect, but irrelevant to judgments about general happiness with life). This suggests that they did not use affect as a basis of their well-being judgments, focusing instead on information about their lives.

Similarly, the positive correlation between subjects' responses to an initial specific question (happiness with dating) and a subsequent general question of related content (happiness with life in general) was reduced if the semantic content was qualified by pragmatic considerations (Schwarz, Strack, & Mai, 1991; Strack, Martin, & Schwarz, 1988; Strack & Schwarz, in press). This suggests that the respondents did not use the activated specific information if it did not seem relevant to their particular informational needs.

These examples illustrate that—under certain circumstances—people are able to ignore information or experiences if they are not representative. Instead, they may rely on different available information. However, other findings suggest that this is not always the case. An example is provided by research on the phenomenon of perseverance (e.g., Ross, Lepper, & Hubbard, 1975; Ross et al., 1977). In the typical experimental situation, subjects formed an impression on the basis of some information. Subsequently, they learned that the information was not a reliable basis for inferences. How can judges correct their impressions by ignoring information that has already been integrated into their impressions? Results showed that they cannot. Even discredited information continued to exert effects on subjects' judgments. Can such erroneous judgments ever be corrected?

An applied study by Hatvany and Strack (1980) suggests they can. In this research, we moved the perseverance paradigm from the laboratory to the courtroom. In a simulated trial, student jurors listened to videotaped eyewitness evidence clearly suggesting that the plaintiff was either guilty or innocent. At the end, this information was discredited when the witness admitted she was wrong and regretted the misidentification. In this courtroom situation, there was no perseverance effect. Moreover, when the discredited testimony was originally against the defendant, the correction resulted in a rebound effect. Jurors under those conditions found the defendant less guilty than jurors who had not seen the evidence at all.

Why is this the case? As Schul and Manzury (1990) pointed out, it is likely that natural settings like courtroom situations provide explicit rules about how information must be corrected. For example, the principle that when the evidence is doubtful, the ambiguity should be resolved by giving the benefit of doubt to the defendant provides a clear prescription about how the judgment should be modified.

Such correction rules may also originate from people's desire to be unprejudiced. Evidence comes from a courtroom study by Shaffer and Case (1982), in which some of the subject jurors received information subtly implying that the defendant was homosexual. This information had no effect on verdict ratings by highly dogmatic jurors. However, for subjects who were low in dogmatism, a rebound effect was observed. That is, subjects judged the defendant in a more lenient fashion if the defendant was a homosexual than if he was a heterosexual. This suggests that judges corrected for a possible influence of the stereotype (see also Devine, 1989). Like in the Hatvany and Strack (1980) study, they overadjusted their response.

This suggests a second vehicle for correcting judgments if it is impossible to filter out the nonrepresentative influences. People can apply norms, rules, or theories to adjust their response for the effect of the pernicious influence (cf. Jacoby & Kelley, 1987; Wyer & Srull, 1989). It is important, however, that judges have such rules at the ready; otherwise, they would not know how to alter their responses. Such a theory-based adjustment (see also Wyer & Budesheim, 1987), however, will not necessarily change an internal representation; it may exert its corrective effects solely at the response level.

In a diploma thesis, Almut Kübler tested this notion in a classic perseverance paradigm in which subjects explained an outcome they knew to be entirely hypothetical. One condition was a conceptual replication of the original experimental situation (e.g., Ross et al., 1977) in which subjects estimated the probability of an occurrence. In a second condition, subjects were alerted to the fact that explaining an event might affect subsequent assessments of its probability, although they were provided with no specific information as to the direction of the influence. In a third condition, subjects received additional specific information about the direction of the influence; that is, the subjects were informed that explaining an event would make the event appear more likely than it really is.

The original perseverance effect was replicated under conditions in which subjects received no information about the possible influence. It was also observed when subjects received a nonspecific alert about the possible influence. Only when subjects received specific information about the direction of influence of explaining the event did they correct their judgments to eliminate perseverance effects. This suggests that it is not enough to know that a correction on the response scale is required; it is also necessary to know how to correct. Further, unlike explanations for an event, response scale adjustments are not related to changes in the internal representation of the target. More specifically, the perseverance effect should affect both probability judgments and other variables that are conceptually related to the explained outcome. Thus, a subject who explains why a person provides nursing care for a relative should judge the target to be emotionally more stable and have a more fulfilled life than would a subject who explains the target's hypothetical suicide. A mere adjustment of the response, however, should not alter the internal representation of the target and therefore should not affect variables that are conceptually related. This was the case. While explaining why the target person would provide nursing care for a relative affected both the subjective expectancy for this event and assessments of the target person's emotional stability and the fulfillment of her life, the correction was only obtained on the focal dimension, that is, for the probability judgments.

Judges can choose to forgo useless or misleading information. They can adjust their responses—if not internal representations—in light of information about nonrepresentativeness. They also have a third option: They can make different use of the nonrepresentative information. More specifically, they can use such information not as a basis for judgments, but as a standard of comparison. Judgments thereby acquire a comparative, relative quality, yielding a contrast effect.

Results of the previously described study by Herr et al. (1983) suggest that extreme exemplars (in their case, ferocious animals) will be used as a standard of comparison and lead to judgments of lower ferocity. Similarly, findings from a study by Strack et al. (1985) suggest that positive or negative life events that are removed in time serve as standards for evaluating one's present life. Here again, judgments were influenced in the opposite direction from the implications of the content, and produced a contrast effect.

It is important to recall, however, that a contrast effect by itself is not yet diagnostic of the underlying mechanisms that produced it. It is true that if the nonrepresentative information enters into the judgment as a standard of comparison, a contrast effect will occur; extreme or distinct information yields contrasting judgments.

But both a theory-based adjustment and disuse of the information may also produce contrast effects. This is hardly a given, but it cannot be ruled out, for the amount of adjustment depends on the theory or rule that is applied. As suggested by the previously described courtroom study (Hatvany & Strack, 1980), some rules yield overcorrections. Similarly, an attempt to ignore nonrepresentative information may cause judges to focus on information about distinctive features of the target—features that are not shared with the target—and this may lead to a judgmental contrast.

CONCLUDING REMARKS

The purpose of this chapter was to demonstrate that the solution to one and the same judgment task may be reached via different psychological routes.

Activated target information and elicited subjective experiences have been identified as the main sources of input for judgment genesis. Conditions have been specified under which one or the other is likely to serve as a judgmental basis, and correctional strategies have been described that may operate on both types of input as a function of their representativeness. These mechanisms have been integrated into a unifying conceptual framework in an attempt to merge divergent research perspectives with the potential benefit of generating new insights into the dynamics of human judgment formation.

Predictions concerning the relationship of the various elements are obvious benefits of the present integrative approach. This may be apparent for the understanding of assimilation vs. contrast effects (cf. Schwarz & Bless, this volume) where the type of input and its representativeness in combination with the situational and motivational conditions under which a correction has to be executed allow specific predictions about the direction of a particular influence. Moreover, the type of correction permits conclusions about the resulting internal representation of the target. As our evidence suggests, certain types of corrections may not undo specific cognitive consequences of judgment generation and subsequent decisions may be unaffected by the previous correction.

Finally, the model highlights the role of subjective experiences. Whether they are affective or not, experiences are part of the grain of social and nonsocial judgments (cf. Clore, this volume). Most importantly, they serve a simplifying function. Although their role in judgment formation has been frequently demonstrated, the very nature of experiences is insufficiently explored. What makes them distinct from "mere thought"? Why does experiencing "feel" different from thinking? What are the determinants of the phenomenal quality of an experience? It appears that such questions must be answered next to move forward in our understanding of human judgment.

ACKNOWLEDGMENTS

I would like to thank Roy Baumeister, Axel Bühler, Jerry Clore, Don Dulany, Peter Gollwitzer, Claudia Woodward Halvorson, Bettina Hannover, Alan Lambert, Kerstin Matthias, Norbert Schwarz, Bob Wyer, and the editors of this volume for valuable comments on an earlier draft of this chapter. Thanks also go to the members of the University of Illinois Social Cognition Group for stimulating discussions and numerous suggestions and to Marti Hope Gonzales who provided invaluable help in editing the manuscript. Writing of this chapter was partly supported by a Heisenberg-Fellowship from the Deutsche Forschungsgemeinschaft.

REFERENCES

Bem, D. J. (1972). Self-perception theory. In L. Berkowitz (Ed.), *Advances in experimental social psychology* (Vol. 6, pp. 1–62). New York: Academic Press.

Buck, R. (1985). Prime theory: An integrated view of motivation and emotion. *Psychological Review, 92*, 389–413.

Carlston, D. E. (1980). The recall and use of traits and events in social inference processes. *Journal of Experimental Social Psychology, 16*, 303–328.

Carroll, J. S. (1978). The effect of imagining an event on expectations for the event: An interpretation in terms of the availability heuristic. *Journal of Experimental Social Psychology, 14*, 88–96.

Chaiken, S. (1987). The heuristic model of persuasion. In M. P. Zanna, J. M. Olson, & C. P. Herman (Eds.), *Social influence: The Ontario symposium* (Vol. 5, pp. 3–39). Hillsdale, NJ: Lawrence Erlbaum Associates.

Clark, H. H., & Haviland, S. E. (1977). Comprehension and the given-new contract. In R. O. Freedle (Ed.), *Discourse production and comprehension* (pp. 1–40). Norwood, NJ: Ablex.

Clore, G. L., & Parrott, W. G. (1991). Moods and their vicissitudes: Thoughts and feelings as information. In J. Forgas (Ed.), *Emotion and social judgment* (pp. 107–123). Oxford: Pergamon.

Cooper, J., Zanna, M. P., & Taves, P. A. (1978). Arousal as a necessary condition for attitude change following induced compliance. *Journal of Personality and Social Psychology, 36*, 1101–1106.

Damrad-Frye, R., & Laird, J. D. (1989). The experience of boredom: The role of self-perception of attention. *Journal of Personality and Social Psychology, 57*, 315–320.

Darley, J. M., & Batson, C. D. (1973). From Jerusalem to Jericho: A study of situational and dispositional variables in helping behavior. *Journal of Personality and Social Psychology, 27*, 100–108.

Darwin, C. R. (1872). *The expression of emotions in man and animals.* London: John Murray.

Devine, P. G. (1989). Stereotypes and prejudice: Their automatic and controlled components. *Journal of Personality and Social Psychology, 56*, 5–18.

Ekman, P., Levenson, R. W., & Friesen, W. V. (1983). Automatic nervous system activity distinguishes among emotions. *Science, 221*, 1208–1210.

Farah, M. J. (1988). Is visual imagery really visual? Overlooked evidence from neuropsychology. *Psychological Review, 95*, 307–317.

Fazio, R. H. (1986). How do attitudes guide behavior? In R. M. Sorrentino & E. T. Higgins (Eds.), *Handbook of motivation and cognition. Foundations of social behavior* (pp. 204–243). New York: Guilford Press.

Fiske, S. T., & Pavelchak, M. A. (1986). Category-based vs. piecemeal-based affective responses: Developments in schema-triggered affect. In R. M. Sorrentino & E. T. Higgins (Eds.), *Handbook of motivation and cognition. Foundations of social behavior* (pp. 167–203). New York: Guilford Press.

Grice, H. P. (1975). Logic and conservation. In P. Cole & J. L. Morgan (Eds.), *Syntax and semantics 3: Speech acts* (pp. 41–58). New York: Academic Press.

Hatvany, N., & Strack, F. (1980). The impact of a discredited key witness. *Journal of Applied Social Psychology, 10*, 490–509.

Herr, P. M. (1986). Consequences of priming: Judgment and behavior. *Journal of Personality and Social Psychology, 51*, 1106–1115.

Herr, P. M., Sherman, S. J., & Fazio, R. H. (1983). On the consequences of priming: Assimilation and contrast effects. *Journal of Experimental Social Psychology, 19*, 323–340.

Higgins, E. T., Rholes, W. S., & Jones, C. R. (1977). Category accessibility and impression formation. *Journal of Personality and Social Psychology, 13*, 141–154.

Jacoby, L. L., & Dallas, M. (1981). On the relationship between autobiographical memory and perceptual learning. *Journal of Experimental Psychology: General, 110*, 306–340.

Jacoby, L. L., & Kelley, C. M. (1987). Unconscious influences of memory for a prior event. *Personality and Social Psychology Bulletin, 13*, 314–336.

Jacoby, L. L., Kelley, C. M., Brown, J., & Jasechko, J. (1989). Becoming famous overnight: Limits on the ability to avoid unconscious influences of the past. *Journal of Personality and Social Psychology, 56*, 326–338.

Jacoby, L. L., Woloshyn, V., & Kelley, C. M. (1989). Becoming famous without being recognized: Unconscious influences of memory produced by dividing attention. *Journal of Experimental Psychology: General, 118*, 115–125.

James, W. (1890). *The principles of psychology*. New York: Holt.

Johnson, M. K. (1988). Discriminating the origin of information. In T. F. Oltmanns & B. A. Maher (Eds.), *Delusional beliefs: Interdisciplinary perspectives* (pp. 34–65). New York: Wiley.

Jones, E. E. (1990). *Interpersonal perception*. New York: Freeman.

Kahneman, D., Slovic, P., & Tversky, A. (Eds.). (1982). *Judgment under uncertainty: Heuristics and biases*. New York: Cambridge University Press.

Kahneman, D., & Tversky, A. (1972). Subjective probability: A judgment of representativeness. *Cognitive Psychology, 3*, 430–454.

Kruglanski, A. W. (1990). Motivations for judging and knowing: Implications for causal attribution. In E. T. Higgins & R. M. Sorrentino (Eds.), *Handbook of motivation and cognition: Foundations of social behavior* (Vol. 2, pp. 333–368). New York: Guilford Press.

Kubovy, M. (1977). Response availability and the apparent availability of numerical choices. *Journal of Experimental Psychology: Human Perception and Performance, 3*, 359–364.

Laird, J. D. (1974). Self-attribution of emotion: The effects of expressive behavior on the quality of emotional experience. *Journal of Personality and Social Psychology, 29*, 475–486.

Laird, J. D., & Bresler, C. (1990). William James and the mechanisms of emotional experience. *Personality and Social Psychology Bulletin, 16*, 636–651.

Lang, P. J., Bradley, M. M., & Cuthbert, B. N. (1990). Emotion, attention, and the startle reflex. *Psychological Review, 97*, 377–395.

Lazarus, R. (1982). Thoughts on the relations between emotion and cognition. *American Psychologist, 37*, 1019–1024.

Lazarus, R. S. (1984). On the primacy of cognition. *American Psychologist, 39*, 124–129.

Lingle, J. H., & Ostrom, T. M. (1979). Retrieval selectivity in memory-based impression judgments. *Journal of Personality and Social Psychology, 37*, 180–194.

Logue, A. W. (1991). *The psychology of eating and drinking* (2nd ed.). New York: Freeman.

Lombardi, W. J., Higgins, T. E., & Bargh, J. A. (1987). The role of consciousness in priming effects on categorization: Assimilation vs. contrast as a function of awareness of the priming task. *Personality and Social Psychology Bulletin, 13*, 411–429.

MacArthur, L. A., Solomon, M. R., & Jaffee, R. H. (1980). Weight and sex differences in emotional responsiveness to proprioceptive and pictoral stimuli. *Journal of Personality and Social Psychology, 39*, 308–319.

Mandler, G. (1980). Recognizing: The judgment of previous occurrence. *Psychological Review, 87*, 252–271.

Martin, L. L. (1986). Set/reset: The use and disuse of concepts in impression formation. *Journal of Personality and Social Psychology, 51*, 493–504.

Martin, L. L., & Harlow, T. F. (in press). Basking and brooding: The motivating effects of filter questions in surveys. In N. Schwarz & S. Sudman (Eds.), *Context effects in social and psychological research*. New York: Springer-Verlag.

Martin, L. L., Harlow, T. F., & Strack, F. (in press). The role of one's own bodily sensations in the evaluation of social events. *Personality and Social Psychology Bulletin*.

Martin, L. L., Seta, J. J., & Crelia, R. (1990). Assimilation and contrast as a function of people's willingness and ability to expend effort in forming an impression. *Journal of Personality and Social Psychology, 59*, 27–37.

Nisbett, R. E., & Wilson, T. D. (1977). Telling more than we can know: Verbal reports on mental processes. *Psychological Review, 84*, 231–259.

Ostrom, T. M., & Upshaw, H. S. (1968). Psychological perspective and attitude change. In A. G. Greenwald, T. C. Brook, & T. M. Ostrom (Eds.), *Psychological foundations of attitudes* (pp. 217–242). New York: Academic Press.

Ottati, V. C., Riggle, E., Wyer, R. S., Schwarz, N., & Kuklinski, J. (1989). Cognitive and affective bases of opinion survey responses. *Journal of Personality and Social Psychology, 57*, 404–415.

Pennebaker, J. W., Gonder-Frederick, L., Cox, D. J., & Hoover, C. W. (1985). The perception of general vs. specific visceral activity and the regulation of health-related behavior. In E. S. Katkin & S. B. Manuck (Eds.), *Advances in behavioral medicine* (Vol. 1, pp. 165–198). Greenwich, CT: JAI Press.

Petty, R. E., & Cacioppo, J. T. (1986). The elaboration-likelihood model of persuasion. In L. Berkowitz (Ed.), *Advances in experimental social psychology* (Vol. 19, pp. 123–205). Orlando, FL: Academic Press.

Richman, S. A., & Petty, R. E. (1991, May). *The influence of a positive mood on persuasion under high and low elaboration likelihood.* Paper presented at the 63rd Annual Meeting of the Midwestern Psychological Association, Chicago.

Ross, L., Lepper, M. R., & Hubbard, M. (1975). Perseverance in self-perception and social perception: Biased attribution in the debriefing paradigm. *Journal of Personality and Social Psychology, 32,* 880–892.

Ross, L., Lepper, M., Strack, F., & Steinmetz, J. L. (1977). Social explanation and social expectation: The effects of real and hypothetical explanations upon subjective likelihood. *Journal of Personality and Social Psychology, 35,* 817–829.

Schaller, M., & Cialdini, R. B. (1990). Happiness, sadness, and helping: A motivational integration. In E. T. Higgins & R. M. Sorrentino (Eds.), *Handbook of motivation and cognition* (Vol. 2, pp. 265–296). New York: Guilford Press.

Schul, Y., & Manzury, F. (1990). The effects of type of encoding and strength of discounting appeal on the success of ignoring an invalid testimony. *European Journal of Social Psychology, 20,* 337–349.

Schwarz, N. (1990). Feelings as information: Informational and motivational functions of affective states. In E. T. Higgins & R. M. Sorrentino (Eds.), *Handbook of motivation and cognition: Foundations of social behavior* (Vol. 2, pp. 527–561). New York: Guilford Press.

Schwarz, N., Bless, H., Strack, F., Klumpp, G., Rittenauer-Schatka, H., & Simons, A. (1991). Ease of retrieval as information: Another look at the availability heuristic. *Journal of Personality and Social Psychology, 61,* 195–202.

Schwarz, N., & Clore, G. L. (1983). Mood, misattribution, and judgments of well-being: Informative and directive functions of affective states. *Journal of Personality and Social Psychology, 45,* 513–523.

Schwarz, N., & Clore, G. L. (1988). How do I feel about it? Informative functions of affective states. In K. Fiedler & J. Forgas (Eds.), *Affect, cognition, and social behavior* (pp. 44–62). Toronto: Hogrefe.

Schwarz, N., Strack, F., Kommer, D., & Wagner, D. (1987). Soccer, rooms, and the quality of your life: Further evidence on informative functions of affective states. *European Journal of Social Psychology, 17,* 69–79.

Schwarz, N., Strack, F., & Mai, H. P. (1991). Assimilation and contrast effects in part-whole question sequences: A conversational-logic analysis. *Public Opinion Quarterly, 55,* 3–23.

Shaffer, D. R., & Case, T. (1982). On the decision to testify in one's own behalf: Effects of withheld evidence, defendant's sexual preferences, and juror dogmatism on juridic decisions. *Journal of Personality and Social Psychology, 42,* 335–346.

Sherman, S. J., Cialdini, R. B., Schwartzman, D. F., & Reynolds, K. D. (1985). Imagining can heighten or lower the perceived likelihood of contracting a disease: The mediating effects of ease of imagery. *Personality and Social Psychology Bulletin, 11,* 118–127.

Silka, L. (1988). *Intuitive judgments of change.* New York: Springer-Verlag.

Srull, T. K., & Wyer, R. S. (1979). The role of category accessibility in the interpretation of information about persons: Some determinants and implications. *Journal of Personality and Social Psychology, 37,* 1660–1672.

Srull, T. K., & Wyer, R. S. (1980). Category accessibility and social perception: Some implications for the study of person memory and interpersonal judgments. *Journal of Personality and Social Psychology, 38,* 841–856.

Strack, F. (1983). *Experimentelle untersuchungen zum einfluß bildhafter vorstellungen auf die subjektive wahrscheinlichkeit sozialer ereignisse* [Experimental studies concerning the influence of visual representations on subjective probabilities of social events]. Unpublished doctoral dissertation, Universität Mannheim.

Strack, F. (1991). Order effects in survey research: Activative and informative functions of preceding questions. In N. Schwarz & S. Sudman (Eds.), *Context effects in social and psychological research.* New York: Springer-Verlag.

Strack, F., Erber, R., & Wicklund, R. (1982). Effects of salience and time pressure on ratings of social causality. *Journal of Experimental Social Psychology, 18,* 581–594.

Strack, F., Martin, L. L., & Schwarz, N. (1988). Priming and communication: Social determinants of information use in judgments of life satisfaction. *European Journal of Social Psychology, 18,* 429–442.

Strack, F., Martin, L., & Stepper, S. (1988). Inhibiting and facilitating conditions of the human smile: A non-obtrusive test of the facial-feedback hypothesis. *Journal of Personality and Social Psychology, 53,* 768–777.

Strack, F., & Schwarz, N. (in press). Communicative influences in standardized question situations: The case of implicit collaboration. In K. Fiedler & G. Semin (Eds.), *Language and social cognition.* Newbury Park, CA: Sage.

Strack, F., Schwarz, N., Bless, H., Kübler, A., & Wänke, M. (1991). *Awareness of the influence as precondition for judgmental correction.* Manuscript submitted for review.

Strack, F., Schwarz, N., & Gschneidinger, E. (1985). Happiness and reminiscing: The role of time perspective, affect, and mode of thinking. *Journal of Personality and Social Psychology, 49,* 1460–1469.

Strack, F., Schwarz, N., & Nebel, A. (1990a, June). *Happiness and anticipating the future: Affective and cognitive consequences.* Paper presented at the General Meeting of the European Association of Experimental Social Psychology, Budapest, Hungary.

Strack, F., Schwarz, N., & Nebel, A. (1990b, April). *Stimmungsbericht vs. stimmungsurteil* [Mood report versus mood judgment]. Paper presented at the 32. Tagung experimentell arbeitender Psychologen in Regensburg, Germany.

Strack, F., Schwarz, N., & Wänke, M. (1991). Semantic and pragmatic aspects of context effects in social and psychological research. *Social Cognition, 9,* 111–125.

Tajfel, H. (1970). Experiments in intergroup discrimination. *Scientific American, 223,* 96–102.

Tversky, A., & Kahneman, D. (1973). Availability: A heuristic for judging frequency and probability. *Cognitive Psychology, 4,* 207–232.

Wilson, T. D., Laser, P. S., & Stone, J. I. (1982). Judging the predictors of one's own mood: Accuracy and the use of shared theories. *Journal of Experimental Social Psychology, 18,* 537–556.

Wyer, R. S., & Budesheim, T. L. (1987). Person memory and judgments: The impact of information that one is told to disregard. *Journal of Personality and Social Psychology, 53,* 14–29.

Wyer, R. S., & Srull, T. K. (1989). *Memory and cognition in its social context.* Hillsdale, NJ: Lawrence Erlbaum Associates.

Wyer, R. S., Srull, T. K., Gordon, S. E., & Hartwick, J. (1982). The effects of taking a perspective on the recall of prose material. *Journal of Personality and Social Psychology, 43,* 674–688.

Wyer, R. S., & Unverzagt, W. H. (1985). The effects of instructions to disregard information on its subsequent recall and use in making judgments. *Journal of Personality and Social Psychology, 48,* 533–549.

Zajonc, R. B. (1980). Feeling and thinking: Preferences need no inferences. *American Psychologist, 35,* 151–175.

Zillmann, D., & Bryant, J. (1974). Effect of residual excitation on the emotional response provocation and delayed aggressive behavior. *Journal of Personality and Social Psychology, 30,* 782–791.

The Role of Beliefs and Feelings in Guiding Behavior: The Mismatch Model

Murray G. Millar
University of Nevada, Las Vegas

Abraham Tesser
University of Georgia

> *Le coeur a ses raisons que la raison ne connâit point* [The heart has its reasons which reason knows nothing of].
>
> —B. Pascal

The study of attitudes has occupied a central position in social psychology from its inception. A key assumption of this work is that attitudes are powerful directors of behavior (Allport, 1954). Yet the predictive relationship between attitudes and behavior has been a continuing source of controversy. Even early studies by Lapiere (1934) examining the relationship between racial attitudes and behavior, and by Corey (1937) examining the relationship between attitudes about cheating and behavior, questioned the relationship. As time passed, evidence against the relationship continued to mount. For example, Carr and Roberts (1965) found that correlations between civil rights activities and behaviors did not exceed .30, and Freeman and Ataov (1960) found correlations between cheating and cheating attitudes were below .10. Perhaps the heaviest blow to the attitude-behavior link came in the early 1970s. Wicker (1969), in an influential review, reported that in the individual studies he reviewed correlation coefficients between attitudes and behaviors rarely exceeded .30. Based on this observation, Wicker (1971) questioned whether or not it would be desirable to abandon the attitude concept. Interest in the attitude construct began to wane (Lambert, 1980).

However, by the mid 1970s, the pessimistic conclusions concerning the attitude-behavior relation began to be challenged. If the studies in Wicker's (1969) review are examined from a meta-analytic point of view, there is good evidence in *favor* of the attitude-behavior relation. Also, a number of studies conducted after Wicker's (1969) review had reported moderate relationships between attitudes and behaviors (e.g., Goodmonson & Glaudin, 1971; Ryan & Bonfield, 1975; Seligman et al., 1979). By the late 1970s, there was more optimism concerning the attitude-behavior relation (e.g., Fazio & Zanna, 1981; Schuman & Johnson, 1976) and emphasis moved away from attempting to demonstrate whether or not attitudes predict behavior to attempting to demonstrate *when* attitudes predict behavior (Zanna & Fazio, 1982). This new emphasis manifested itself in two different approaches.

Psychometric Approach

The first approach to forecasting when attitudes will predict behavior was psychometrically oriented. It focused on issues related to the measurement of the attitude and the behavior. As early as the late 1940s, problems regarding differences in the measurement specificity of attitudes and behaviors were being used to explain the lack of consistency between attitudes and behavior (e.g., Chein, 1949; Kendler & Kendler, 1949). More recently, Ajzen and Fishbein (1977) argued that a relation between attitude and behavior will be found when the measurement level of the attitude corresponds to the measurement level of the behavior. Specifically, Ajzen and Fishbein suggested that to predict behavior, the attitude and behavior must correspond on four elements: action performed; target at which the action is directed; the context in which the action is performed; and the time when the behavior is performed.

There is considerable support for this approach. For example, Heberlein and Black (1976) attempted to predict a specific behavior (use of lead-free gasoline) using four attitude scales that varied in specificity (questions about environmentalism, pollution, the benefits of lead-free gasoline, and the respondent's personal norms about using lead-free gasoline). As expected, the attitude-behavior relation increased as the correspondence between the attitude and behavioral measure increased. The general environmental questions were only weakly related to the use of lead-free gasoline ($r = .14$) whereas specific questions about personal norms were strongly related to the use of lead-free gasoline ($r = .54$). In a conceptually similar study, Davidson and Jaccard (1979) demonstrated that specific birth control behaviors were best predicted by specific attitude measures. These studies showed that if you make the attitude measure specific you can predict specific behavior. Weigel and Newman (1976), on the other hand, demonstrated that general environmental behaviors were best predicted by general attitude measures.

The psychometric approach has yielded strong attitude-behavior correlations and has dealt with important measurement issues. However, it is not very exciting from a psychological point of view. Its solution to the attitude-behavior problem is more like a psychometric rule of thumb than a social psychological theory about the role of attitudes in behavior.

Psychological Approach

A second approach to understanding when attitudes will predict behaviors is more psychologically oriented. Instead of just focusing on measurement issues, this approach attempts to specify psychological processes that influence the attitude's ability to predict behavior. A number of psychological processes have been found to influence the attitude-behavior relation. For example, the method of attitude formation (direct experience versus indirect experience) has been shown to affect an attitude's availability in memory and, ultimately, its ability to predict behavior (Fazio & Zanna, 1981). Also, the consistency between affective and cognitive responses in an attitude has been related to the attitude's predictive power (Norman, 1975; Rosenberg, 1960).

Thesis: The Beneficial Effects of Introspection

Within this psychological approach, the effects of introspection/reflection on the attitude-behavior relation have received considerable attention. In psychology there has been a long history of interest in introspection both as a research tool (e.g., Wundt, 1874/1904) and as a therapeutic process (e.g., Kanfer & Busemeyer, 1982). Throughout this history, a variety of sources from many distinct areas of psychology have all suggested that introspection has the capacity to clarify values, beliefs, and attitudes. In social psychology, there is solid evidence that introspection can polarize attitudes (Tesser, 1978). Many psychotherapeutic procedures have self-reflection and introspection as essential elements. For example, Rogers' (1951) therapeutic procedure was designed to allow the client to gain access to the "real" self through the use of self-reflection. Also, in the area of decision-making processes, self-reflection is often considered beneficial. For example, Janis and his colleagues proposed and found evidence that the decision-making process optimally involves consideration of all possible information through careful introspection (e.g., Hoyt & Janis, 1975; Janis, 1986; Janis & Mann, 1977).

The belief in the ability of introspection to clarify attitudes has led many researchers to predict that introspection will increase the strength of the attitude-behavior relation. That is, attitudes that are thought out and salient should be better predictors of behavior than fuzzy attitudes that are not salient.

There is considerable evidence from a variety of perspectives that introspection does increase the predictive power of attitudes. Wicklund (1982), coming from a self-awareness perspective, proposed that when a person's attention is turned inward toward his or her attitudes, values, and traits (i.e., they are self-focused), he or she will be motivated to maintain consistency between attitudes and behavior. Consistent with Wicklund's hypothesis, Pryor, Gibbons, Wicklund, Fazio, and Hood (1977) in a series of studies reported higher attitude-behavior correlations for persons inwardly focused (in the presence of a mirror) than for persons not inwardly focused (in the absence of a mirror). Using similar reasoning, Scheier, Buss, and Buss (1978) found that persons dispositionally high in self-awareness exhibit higher attitude-behavior correlations than do persons low in self-awareness.

Snyder and Swann (1976), coming from an impression-management perspective, proposed that instructing persons to think carefully about an attitude would increase the attitude's availability in memory and, consequently, the likelihood that the attitude would predict behavior. Consistent with this hypothesis, both Snyder and Swann and Snyder and Kendzierski (1982) found that requiring participants to reflect on their attitudes about affirmative action led to a substantially larger correlation between their attitudes and behavior than when there was no reflection.

Fazio, Zanna, and Cooper (1978), in their exploration of information processing differences between direct experience and indirect experience attitudes, provided evidence that introspection can increase the attitude-behavior relation. They required participants to view other people performing puzzles. One half were asked to think about how they would feel about each type of puzzle, and the other half were not given these directions. After this procedure, all of the participants were given a 15 minute play period to work on the puzzles. The attitudes of the participants who were asked to think about the puzzles were better predictors of play period behavior than were the attitudes of those not asked to think about their feelings.

Antithesis: The Harmful Effects of Introspection

However, despite the traditional belief that introspection has a beneficial and clarifying effect and the evidence supporting its ability to increase the attitude-behavior relation, there is evidence suggesting the opposite; that is, that introspection may increase confusion and actually decrease the attitude-behavior relation. In a recent set of studies, Timothy Wilson and his colleagues demonstrated that on some occasions introspection can actually lead to more confusion and nonoptimal decisions (Wilson, Lisle, & Schooler, 1989; Wilson & Schooler, 1990).

Wilson and his colleagues (e.g., Wilson & Dunn, 1986; Wilson, Dunn, Bybee, Hyman, & Rotondo, 1984; Wilson, Dunn, Kraft, & Lisle, 1989; Wilson, Kraft, & Dunn, 1989) have also amassed considerable evidence that thought prior to an assessment of an attitude actually decreases the attitude's ability to predict behavior. For example, Wilson et al. (1984) required half of their participants to analyze their reasons for liking five puzzles, and the other half were not given any instructions. The participants' attitudes expressed subsequent to this procedure were correlated with behavioral measures of liking. The correlation between attitudes and behavior in the thought group was significantly lower ($r = .17$) than in the no-instruction group ($r = .54$). Wilson, Dunn, Kraft, and Lisle (1989) explained this effect by suggesting that thinking about reasons causes people to change their minds about how they feel, but does not change their behavior. In Wilson's explanation, when people are asked to explain their feelings they feel compelled to generate reasonable-sounding answers despite the fact that they often do not know exactly the reasons for their feelings. Consequently, the reasons generated may be incorrect or only a biased subset of the actual reasons underlying their attitude. In other words, people will tend to produce reasons easiest to verbalize or most available in memory. When people are required to state their attitudes subsequent to this process they are influenced by this biased set of reasons and change their attitude in the direction of the biased sample. On the other hand, according to Wilson and his colleagues, the biased set of reasons has only a short-term effect on behavior. That is, a person's behavior is initially influenced by the biased set and then "snaps back" to the person's original position as the person's affective response reasserts itself.

A STRUCTURAL APPROACH TO SYNTHESIS: THE MISMATCH HYPOTHESIS

To this point in time, there is a long tradition in psychology that supports the beneficial clarifying effects of introspection and evidence that introspection increases the attitude-behavior relation. Yet recently Wilson produced compelling evidence that introspection may both increase confusion and decrease the attitude-behavior relation. In order to reconcile these conflicting findings within a single framework, we have proposed the mismatch hypothesis that examines the relationship between thought, attitude structure, and behavior (Millar & Tesser, 1986).

Attitude Structure and Thought

Throughout the study of attitudes the attitude construct has been conceptualized in a number of different ways (McGuire, 1986; Zanna & Rempel, 1988). Although presently there is no universally agreed upon definition of the attitude construct, attitudes are usually conceptualized as multicomponent entities (e.g., Kramer, 1949; Ostrom, 1969; Thurstone, 1928). We regard attitudes as encompassing a global evaluation based on both cognition and affect (see Tesser & Shaffer, 1990, for a similar conceptualization).

The cognitive component is generally conceived of as containing the encoding of attributes and beliefs about the attitude object. For example, the cognitive component of an attitude about a puzzle may contain the following elements: The puzzle is challenging; the puzzle is clear; the puzzle is imaginative. Alternatively, the affective component of the attitude is conceived of as containing the encoding of emotions and feelings associated with the object (Fleming, 1967). For example, the affective component of an attitude about a puzzle may contain feelings of happiness. The global evaluation is usually formed from some combination of affect and cognition. Breckler and Wiggins (1989) provided evidence that in a number of domains global evaluations are based on feelings and cognitions. For example, global evaluations about blood donations were more related to both feelings ($r = .57$) and cognitions ($r = .29$).

It was our contention that attitude reports (global evaluations) are based on whatever aspect of the attitude is salient when the report is given (Millar & Tesser, 1986). If affect is salient, then the attitude report will reflect one's feelings about the attitude object. If cognitions are salient, then one's attitude report will reflect one's beliefs about the attitude object. Thought prior to making an evaluation has the potential to make either the affective or cognitive component of the attitude salient and more important in the global evaluation. For example, Wilson's procedure of requiring persons to think about reasons for liking or disliking an object would tend to make the cognitive component of the attitudes salient, that is, beliefs about the object's attributes would be salient. Alternatively, requiring persons to think about the feelings they experience in the presence of the object would make the affective component of their attitude salient. Consequently, if the affective and cognitive components of an attitude are not in perfect evaluative agreement, it is possible for thought to produce different attitude reports about the same object.

Attitude Components and Behavior

In addition, we proposed that the decision to engage in a behavior may be based more or less on the cognitive or affective component of the attitude rather than a global evaluation (Millar & Tesser, 1986). That is, some types of behavior may be more cognitively driven and other types more affectively driven. There are probably a number of dimensions that would make either the attributes of the object or the feelings the object evokes more important in directing behavior.

For the present work we distinguished between *instrumental* and *consummatory* behaviors. Behaviors intended to accomplish a goal which is independent of the attitude object (instrumental behavior) are likely to be cognitively driven. For example, a person who performs a puzzle in order to develop analytic ability would primarily be interested in various attributes of the puzzle and how they affect analytic ability, not how the puzzle makes him or her feel. Alternatively, behaviors engaged in for their own sake (consummatory behavior), are likely to be affectively driven. For example, a person who performs a puzzle simply to please himself should be primarily interested in how the puzzle makes him feel, not in the attributes of the puzzle.

Mismatch Hypothesis

Because one's global evaluation or attitude report can be more or less influenced by the affective or cognitive component, and because behavior can be more or less driven by the affective and cognitive component, we suggested that a match between the attitude component emphasized by thought and the attitude component driving behavior would lead to a strong attitude-behavior relation, and a mismatch between components would lead to a weak attitude-behavior relation (Millar & Tesser, 1986).

When the previous literature dealing with the effects of thought on the attitude-behavior relation is reexamined within this framework, many of its apparently contradictory findings can be resolved. The reasons-analysis procedure used by Wilson and colleagues made the cognitive component of the attitude salient, producing global evaluations based on this component, whereas the puzzle-playing behavior in Wilson's free-play situation was probably a consummatory behavior (i.e., there was little instrumental value in playing the puzzles). The mismatch between the attitude component influencing the global evaluation and the component driving the behavior resulted in lower attitude-behavior correlations. Alternatively, the directions of Fazio et al. (1978) to subjects to concentrate on feelings probably made the affective component salient when the global evaluation was formed, whereas the puzzle-playing behavior remained a consummatory behavior. The match between the attitude components driving the behavior resulted in higher attitude-behavior correlations.

Comparison to Cognitization Hypothesis

Before examining the evidence supporting the mismatch hypothesis, we examine a competing hypothesis offered by Wilson and his colleagues (e.g., Wilson & Dunn, 1986; Wilson, Dunn, Kraft, & Lisle, 1989). Wilson also noted the discrepancy between his findings on the effects of thought on the attitude-behavior relation and earlier findings. He suggested that the reasons-analysis procedure used in his work created an attitude with a cognitive bias, whereas the thought procedures used in earlier work did not create such a bias, for example, the procedure used by Fazio, Zanna, and Cooper (1978) that required participants to think about how they feel. In Wilson's explanation, if thought fails to produce a cognitive bias it will also fail to change the attitude and,consequently, the attitude and behavior will remain consistent.

This explanation brings out some important differences between our understanding and Wilson's of the effects of thought on the attitude-behavior relation. Wilson's model focuses primarily on the effect of thought on affective attitudes. That is, the original attitude, to be biased by cognition, must be affective. Presumably, attitudes based on cognition would be less susceptible to obtaining a cognitive bias than attitudes based on affect. In addition, Wilson's model focuses primarily on the prediction of affectively driven behaviors. That is, except for a short time when the behavior is influenced by the cognitive bias, behavior is dependent upon the person's affect. Our model, on the other hand, proposes that thought may make salient either affective or cognitive responses to the attitude object; that is, it can create either affective or cognitively based attitudes, and that behavior may either be affectively or cognitively driven. Consequently, our model allows us to integrate the effects of thought on both affectively and cognitively based attitudes and behaviors.

TESTING THE STRUCTURE EXPLANATION

In order to provide support for this structural explanation, we first attempted to demonstrate the plausibility of the model and second, we attempted to test some of the underlying assumptions of the model concerning affective-cognitive consistency.

Plausibility Test

We performed an initial test of the mismatch hypothesis by measuring the relationship between attitudes formed after either an affective or cognitive focus procedure and behavior performed under instrumental and consummatory conditions (Millar & Tesser, 1986). It was expected that attitudes reported when affect was salient would predict consummatory behavior better than instrumental behavior and, alternatively, attitudes reported when cognition was salient would predict instrumental behavior better than consummatory behavior.

To test this hypothesis, participants were informed that the purpose of the study was to evaluate the effectiveness of five types of analytic puzzles that were designed to increase analytic ability. To create *instrumental behavior* conditions, half the participants were informed in the first set of instructions that "in this experiment you will be given the opportunity to practice with five types of analytic puzzles which may be useful in developing analytic ability. After this you will be given an analytic puzzle-solving test, to assess your analytic ability." Participants in the instrumental conditions were expected to view work on the puzzles as a way to improve their performance on the upcoming test; that is, they had a goal independent of the attitude object. To create *consum-*

matory behavior conditions the other half of the participants were given the same set of instructions except they were informed that in the second part of the experiment they would be given a test to measure their social sensitivity. Participants in the consummatory conditions were not expected to have the motive to work on the puzzles as a way to improve performance on the upcoming test; that is, they were expected to engage in the behavior for its own sake.

In the second set of directions, participants were asked to familiarize themselves with each of the five types of puzzles by attempting to solve an example of each, after which they would be required to evaluate each of the puzzles. In the *cognitive focus* condition, while they worked on each puzzle the participants were asked to "analyze WHY you feel the way you do about each type of puzzle. That is, go over in your mind what it is about each puzzle that makes you think it is likable or not." (See Wilson et al., 1984, for a similar manipulation.) Participants in the *affective focus* condition were asked to "analyze HOW you feel while performing each type of puzzle. That is, go over in your mind how you are feeling while you perform each type of puzzle."

After receiving these directions, the participants were given 5 minutes to work on examples of each type of puzzle, after which they wrote down their reasons for liking or disliking each type of puzzle or the feelings they experienced while working on each type. When they had completed writing down their reasons or feelings, they were asked to evaluate each of the puzzle types on Likert scales. Finally, all of the participants were given a 7 minute free-play period to work on any of the puzzles they desired. During this period the time they spent working on each type of puzzle was used as a behavioral measure of liking.

The results from this initial test provided strong support for the mismatch hypothesis. A measure of attitude-behavior consistency was constructed by computing for each participant the rank-order correlation between the participant's first rating of the puzzles and the amount of time spent playing with each type of puzzle. This procedure produced a correlation coefficient for each participant that was transformed to Fishers' z score and analyzed in a 2 (instrumental vs. consummatory behavior) × 2 (affective vs. cognitive focus) × 2 (male vs. female) analysis of variance (ANOVA). As expected, the only source of variation to reach significance was the predicted two-way interaction of Behavior Type × Focus of Thought, $p = .004$ (see Fig. 10.1).

Participants in the consummatory-behavior conditions had higher attitude-behavior correlations when they focused on their feelings than when they focused on the cognitive component of their attitudes ($p = .03$). Alternatively, participants in the instrumental-behavior conditions produced higher attitude-behavior correlations when they focused on their cognitions than when they focused on feelings ($p = .04$).

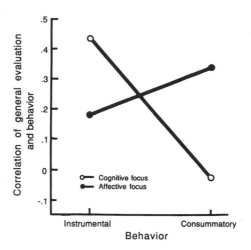

FIG. 10.1. Mean attitude-behavior correlations as a function of behavior type
and focus of thought.

The Role of Affective-Cognitive Consistency

Having obtained preliminary support for the model, a further investigation was
conducted to test the moderating role of affective-cognitive consistency in the
relationship between global evaluations and behaviors (cf. Norman, 1975; Rosenberg, 1960). From the present perspective, if the affective and cognitive components are in good evaluative agreement then thought emphasizing either
component should lead to a similar global evaluation. If this is the case, then
global evaluations should relate to consummatory or instrumental behavior in
the same manner regardless of what component is made salient by thought.
Overall, we would expect highly consistent attitudes to predict both consummatory and instrumental behavior uniformly well. On the other hand, if the cognitive and affective components are not in agreement then thought emphasizing
different components would lead to different global evaluations. Consequently,
if thought operates in the manner suggested by the model, the match and mismatch effects should occur when attitudes are characterized by low affective-
cognitive consistency and the match-mismatch effects should become attenuat-
ed when there is high affective-cognitive consistency.

Measuring Affective-Cognitive Consistency

Millar and Tesser (1989a) attempted to test this hypothesis by measuring
affective-cognitive consistency and demonstrating that the mismatch effects occur
only under low consistency. In a procedure similar to the earlier study (Millar

& Tesser, 1986), 42 female and 39 male participants were individually seated at a microcomputer and informed that the purpose of the experiment was to assess the utility of several analytic puzzles. Each participant was required to familiarize himself/herself with different types of puzzles by performing two examples of each puzzle under affective thought conditions and two examples under cognitive thought conditions. Affective and cognitive thought conditions were created using the same procedures as used in the original study (i.e., participants focused on how or why they liked the puzzles). After completing two examples under cognitive focus, the participants was asked to write down their reasons for liking or disliking each type of puzzle and to place a + after positive features and a − after negative features. After completing the two examples under affective focus, the participants were asked to write down how each type of puzzle had made them feel. Order of presentation for the affective and cognitive focus procedures was counterbalanced (affective-cognitive; cognitive-affective). By counterbalancing the order of presentation of the affective and cognitive focus procedures, participants finished this procedure with either an affective or cognitive focus salient. Immediately following the last focus manipulation (either affective or cognitive), the participants were asked to evaluate each of the five puzzle types on Likert-type scales. Note that half the participants were affectively focused prior to this evaluation and half were cognitively focused. Thus, it was expected that the overall evaluation for half the participants should be more influenced by affect and the overall evaluation for the remaining participants should be more influenced by cognition.

Following the evaluation of the puzzles, participants were allowed to play with the puzzles for 10 minutes either under the instrumental (i.e., they were informed that after the play period they would receive a test of their analytic ability) or consummatory (i.e., they were informed that they would receive a test of their social sensitivity) conditions described in the first study. During the freeplay period the amount of time that each type of puzzle was worked on was recorded and used as the primary behavioral measure.

In order to develop an index of affective-cognitive consistency for each participant, we needed to construct both a measure of cognitive liking and affective liking. A measure of cognitive liking (the cognitive component) was calculated by summing the pluses and subtracting the minuses after the reasons for liking or disliking each puzzle. For example, if a participant gave three reasons for their evaluation of the picture matching puzzle, and two were followed by plus signs and one was followed by a minus sign, the participant was given a cognitive liking score of plus one for picture matching puzzles. Affective liking (the affective component) was calculated by two raters who classified each emotion statement as positive or negative. For example, if a participant stated that picture matching made him or her feel uptight and dumb, they were given an affective liking score of minus two. An index of affective-cognitive consistency was constructed by computing the rank-order correlation of each participant's cognitive liking scores to his or her affective liking scores across the five puzzles; that is, a correlation coefficient was produced for each participant that indicated the relation between his or her affective liking and cognitive liking for the puzzles. Participants then were classified on the basis of a median split ($r = .30$), as either high or low in affective-cognitive consistency.

A measure of attitude-behavior consistency was constructed using the same procedures as the original study (i.e., the rank-order correlation of each participant's general evaluations of the puzzles to the amount of time he or she spent working on the puzzles in the free-play period was calculated). When these correlations were analyzed in a 2 (instrumental vs. consummatory behavior) × 2 (affective vs. cognitive focus prior to the initial evaluation) × 2 (high vs. low affective-cognitive consistency) ANOVA the results again provided strong support for the hypothesis examined.

The predicted three-factor interaction of Behavior Type × Focus of Thought × Affective-Cognitive Consistency was obtained, ($p = .05$). When participants were low in affective-cognitive consistency, the simple Behavior Type × Focus of Thought interaction was significant, ($p = .008$). When participants were high in affective-cognitive consistency the simple Behavior Type × Focus of Thought interaction was not significant (see Fig. 10.2).

Attitude Component Behavior Relations

The data from Millar and Tesser (1989a) also allowed us to test the relation between each of the attitude components and behavior. Recall that the present model suggested that consummatory behavior is driven by affect and instrumental behavior is driven by cognition. If this is the case, we would expect liking expressed by the cognitive component to be the better predictor of instrumental behavior and liking expressed by the affective component to be the better predictor of consummatory behavior.

To test this hypothesis, within-subject correlations between the behavior measure and both affective liking and cognitive liking measures were calculated. This procedure produced two correlation coefficients for each participant; one representing the affective liking-behavior relation and one representing the cognitive liking-behavior relation. These correlations were analyzed in a 2 (focus of thought prior to the initial evaluation) × 2 (consummatory vs. instrumental behavior) × 2 (affective-cognitive consistency) × 2 (affective vs. cognitive component) ANOVA with repeated measures assumed on the last factor.

The results provide support for the hypothesized relation between liking expressed by the attitude components (affective and cognitive) and behavior type (consummatory and instrumental). First, an effect unmediated by affective-cognitive consistency was obtained as a two-factor interaction of Behavior Type × Attitude Component ($p = .04$). Consistent with the mismatch idea, the affective component predicted consummatory behavior better than instrumental be-

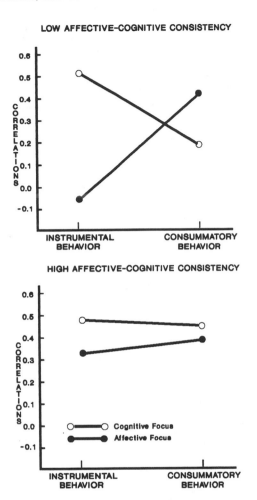

FIG. 10.2.   Mean attitude-behavior correlations as a function of behavior type, focus of thought, and affective-cognitive consistency.

havior and the cognitive component predicted instrumental behavior better than consummatory behavior. Second, the consistency hypothesis suggested that the interaction of Behavior Type × Attitude Component should be more pronounced when attitudes were low in affective-cognitive consistency than when they were high in consistency. That is, if both attitude components express similar degrees of liking then both should predict behavior equally well and the interaction should disappear. Consistent with this prediction, a marginal interaction of Behavior Type × Affective-Cognitive Consistency × Attitude Component was obtained ($p = .07$). When attitudes toward the puzzle were low in affective-cognitive consistency, the simple interaction of Behavior Type × Attitude Component was significant ($p = .005$). In contrasts when attitudes toward the puzzles were high in affective-cognitive consistency, the simple interaction of Behavior Type × Attitude Component disappeared (see Table 10.1).

In addition, several other effects emerged. Consistent with past research (Norman, 1975; Rosenberg, 1956) liking expressed by the attitude components predicted behavior better when affective-cognitive consistency was high than when affective-cognitive consistency was low ($p = .01$). Also, there was a recency effect ($p = .001$). The cognitive component predicted behavior better when cognition was focused on more recently; the affective component predicted behavior better when affect was focused on more recently.

Manipulating Consistency Through Experience

In the previous study the demonstration of the effects of affective-cognitive consistency were based on measured consistency. Consistency was not experimentally manipulated. In a second study, Millar and Tesser (1989b) attempted to manipulate consistency through the amount of experience with the attitude object. It was assumed that attitudes based on little experience would be characterized by relatively low affective-cognitive consistency compared to attitudes based on greater experience (Chaiken & Baldwin, 1981; Rosenberg, 1960, 1968).

In a procedure very similar to the previous studies, participants were asked to familiarize themselves with each of the five types of puzzles by attempting to solve examples of each type. In this study, all the participants were cognitively focused. (We used the single focus for reasons of economy.) Prior research, reviewed previously, showed that the effects of focus are symmetrical. Half the participants were given one example of each type of puzzle to complete and half were given five examples of each type of puzzle to complete. Following the completion of either one or five examples of the puzzles, the participants were asked to write down their reasons for liking or disliking each puzzle type and to evaluate their liking of each puzzle type. Then the participants were

TABLE 10.1
Means of Correlations Between Component Liking and Behavior as a Function
of Affective-Cognitive Consistency, Behavior Type, and Component Liking

	Affective-Cognitive Consistency			
	High		Low	
	Attitude Component		Attitude Component	
Type of Behavior	Affective	Cognitive	Affective	Cognitive
Instrumental	.52	.69	.35	.59
Consummatory	.57	.69	.52	.34

given 10 minutes free time with the puzzles either under instrumental or consummatory conditions. The length of time each puzzle was played with was recorded.

When affective-cognitive consistency is low (little experience) thought emphasizing the cognitive component should produce smaller attitude-behavior correlations under consummatory conditions than under instrumental conditions. However, when affective-cognitive consistency is high (more experience) thought emphasizing the cognitive component should fail to decrease the attitude-behavior correlation under consummatory conditions. In sum, since all participants have a cognitive focus, the only *functional* mismatch condition is low consistency-consummatory behavior. Both high and low consistency instrumental behavior conditions match the cognitive focus. Although the high consistency-consummatory behavior condition is operationally a mismatch, it is not functionally a mismatch: Because there is high consistency, the cognitive focus should produce a general evaluation similar to that which would have been produced by affective focus and affective focus is a match for consummatory behavior.

A measure of attitude-behavior consistency was constructed in the same manner as our previous studies by computing the rank-order correlation of each participant's first rating of the puzzles to the amount of time spent working each type of puzzle. Then this set of correlations was analyzed in a planned comparison that assigned a contrast weight of -3 to the novel attitude-consummatory behavior mean and $+1$ to each of the remaining condition means. As expected, attitude-behavior correlations were significantly smaller in the low consistency-consummatory behavior condition than in the other three conditions, $p = .01$ (see Table 10.2).

THE MISMATCH HYPOTHESIS
IN A BROADER PERSPECTIVE

The present model not only allows us to integrate previous attitude-behavior consistency literature but also has important ramifications for our understanding of the attitude construct and attitude change. In addition, the present model may have applications to other areas of study beyond attitudes.

TABLE 10.2
Means of Correlations Between General Evaluation and Behavior as a Function
of Amount of Experience and Behavior Type

Behavior Type	Experience with Puzzles	
	One Example	*Five Examples*
Instrumental	.35	.36
Consummatory	$-.24$	.33

Affective-Cognitive Distinction

One of the primary assertions of the mismatch hypothesis concerns the distinction between affective and cognitive attitudes. In general, the distinction between affect and cognition has a long and well-documented history in many areas of psychology (Hilgard, 1980). More recently, tentative theoretical and empirical support for this dichotomy was offered by Zajonc (1980, 1984), who argued that affect and cognition involve separate and partially independent systems. Also, in the study of attitudes the affective-cognitive distinction has had a long history. As we noted earlier, many theorists have conceptualized the attitude construct as containing both an affective and cognitive component (e.g., Insko & Schopler, 1967; Kramer, 1949; Smith, 1947; Zanna & Rempel, 1988). Empirical support for the affective-cognitive component distinction has been provided by Breckler (1984) and, more recently, Breckler and Wiggins (1989), who found that the affective-cognitive component distinction had discriminant validity in a number of different attitude domains (e.g., attitude toward blood donations).

However, despite this long history of recognition that attitudes contain both affective and cognitive components, most researchers have conceptualized attitudes as relatively stable and lasting unitary evaluations (e.g., Ajzen, 1984). In contrast,the present conceptualization suggests that at any particular moment one has the potential for a number of different attitudes toward an object. Some will be based on feelings toward the object and some based on beliefs about the object. In addition, the present conceptualization emphasizes the importance of immediate and changing environmental factors in determining which of the attitudes held about the object is reported. That is, different attitudes may be obtained depending on whether current environmental conditions make affect or cognition salient.

Implications. This conceptualization of the attitude construct has several important implications for both our understanding of the attitude-behavior relation and attitude change. First, because the model suggests that attitudes can be either affectively based or cognitively based it allows us to apply some of the general differences between affect and cognition to understanding these different types of attitudes. For example, Zajonc (1984) suggested that affect is more immediate, automatic, and less subject to learning than cognition. If the affective component of attitudes has these same characteristics, then the affective component should be less subject to disruption/distraction effects. As a result, we could make the prediction that over the long term affective attitudes will relate more consistently to behavior than cognitive attitudes.

Second, the mismatch model suggests that at any particular moment one has the potential for a number of different attitudes toward an object and that attitude reports are dependent on whether current environmental conditions make affect or cognition salient. This suggestion may allow us to reinterpret some instances of attitude change. It may be possible that many apparent instances of attitude change do not represent true attitude change but only shifts in emphasis from one attitude component to another (affect to cognition or cognition to affect). That is, presenting an argument may simply manipulate what is salient when the attitude is remeasured. This type of effect should occur when the original attitude measure and the type of information made salient by the argument are founded on different compounds, that is, the attitude report is based on one component in the first attitude measure and another in the second. If the affective and cognitive components of the attitude are not in perfect evaluative agreement then this will result in a different evaluation and it will appear as if attitude change has occurred.

The differential salience hypothesis we have just presented is particularly pertinent to recent work investigating the effects of informational and emotional persuasive messages on affective and cognitive attitudes (Edwards, 1990; Millar & Millar, 1990). Millar and Millar reported that informational persuasive messages change affective attitudes more than cognitive attitudes and that emotional persuasive messages change cognitive attitudes more than affective attitudes (cf. Edwards, 1990). Although Millar and Millar used a cognitive responses explanation to interpret their results, the differential salience hypothesis seems an equally likely explanation. That is, presenting an informational message to someone whose prior attitude is based on affect may simply make the cognitive component of the attitude more salient and, consequently, produce a second attitude report based on cognition, not affect. Alternatively, presenting an emotional message to someone whose prior attitude is based on cognition may simply make the affective component of the attitude more salient and, consequently, produce a second attitude report based on affect.

Within the context of the present model, one way to distinguish between true attitude change and a shift in salience would be to put the attitude object into a behavioral context that is either instrumental or consummatory. If there is real attitude change and not simply differences in what is salient, then the persuasion attempt should change both the attitude and the behavior. That is, we will be able to ascertain if the base of the attitude responsible for directing behavior has actually changed.

Instrumental–Consummatory Distinction

Another primary assertion of the mismatch hypothesis concerns behavioral goal structure. The present model suggests that behavioral goal structure is not unidimensional but instead may be divided into two categories: (a) instrumental behaviors performed to accomplish goals independent of the behavior, and (b) consummatory behaviors performed to accomplish goals dependent on the behavior. This distinction between instrumental and consummatory is echoed directly and indirectly in many other areas of social psychological study.

For example, in the study of aggression our distinction between consumma-tory and instrumental behavior is reminiscent of Feshbach's (1964) widely ac-cepted division between hostile and instrumental aggression. In hostile aggression the behavior is directed toward the objective of hurting and in instrumental ag-gression the behavior is directed toward the attainment of some outside objec-tive such as territory, money, or social status. This division is remarkably similar to our instrumental versus consummatory behavior distinction. Hostile aggres-sion could be equated with our consummatory behavior because the aggression act has no other purpose than the activity involved in performing it, that is, to hurt someone. On the other hand, instrumental aggression, as the name sug-gests, could be equated with our instrumental behavior because it is performed to accomplish a goal independent of the behavior.

This same distinction between instrumental and consummatory behaviors can also be seen in the study of prosocial behavior. A number of models (e.g., La-tane & Darley, 1970; Piliavin, Dovidio, Gartner, & Clark, 1981; Piliavin, Piliavin, & Rodin, 1975) view helping as the product of a decision-making process. Piliavin et al. (1981) proposed that people engage in a cost-reward analysis in which consequences of helping or failing to help are evaluated. If the rewards (e.g., praise) outweigh the costs (e.g., physical danger, effort, and time) the person will help and, alternatively, if the costs outweigh the rewards the person en-gages in some other behavior such as escaping the situation. However, other approaches to helping have focused more on the motivating effects of empathic concern (Batson & Coke, 1981; Batson, Fultz, & Schoenrade, 1987). For ex-ample, in altruistic helping, the person's actions are directed only at alleviating the distress of another person.

Again, these two different types of helping seem to fit into our instrumental versus consummatory behavior distinction. Piliavin et al. (1981) suggested that cost-reward helping seems to be describing an instrumental behavior because the helping act is performed to accomplish a goal independent of the behavior (e.g., to gain praise). On the other hand, the altruistic helping described by Bat-son could be equated with our consummatory behavior because the helping act has no other purpose than the activity involved in performing it, that is, to help someone (Batson & Coke, 1981).

Finally, the distinction between consummatory and instrumental behaviors can also be found in the study of interpersonal relationships. Margaret Clark and her colleagues (Clark & Mills, 1979; Clark, Mills, & Powell, 1986) distin-guished between what they call *exchange relationships* and *communal relation-ships*. In exchange relationships, the participants expect and desire strict reciprocity in their interactions; in communal relationships the participants ex-pect and desire mutual responsiveness to each other's needs. Again, these two different types of relationships seem to fit into our instrumental versus con-summatory behavior distinction. Exchange relationships would seem likely to lead to more instrumental behaviors because acts are performed toward the other person because they will be reciprocated. On the other hand, communal relationships would seem likely to lead to consummatory behaviors because the acts toward the other person have no other purpose than the activity involved in performing it, that is, the behavior is satisfying in and of itself.

Implications. To the extent that this rough mapping between our instrumental versus consummatory behavior distinction and other areas of social psychological study holds up, it may be possible to use the mismatch hypothesis as a way of integrating a variety of areas of psychology in a more abstract way. Perhaps cognitive factors will be important for instrumental behaviors and emotional factors will be important for consummatory behaviors, not only in the attitude behavioral relationship, but also in these other areas of study. Indeed, a close examination of the areas mentioned above reveals that there is already a link between the behaviors we described as consummatory and emotion. For example, there is considerable evidence that hostile aggression is primarily motivated by angry emotional responses (e.g., Berkowitz, 1983, 1988), and altruistic helping is motivated by empathic emotional responses (Batson & Coke, 1981). There are also links between behaviors we described as instrumental and cognitive responses. For example, Piliavin et al. (1981) suggested that the cost-reward type of helping is ultimately controlled by the person's thoughts. Consequently, in order to adequately integrate research findings about these behaviors we may need to know whether affect or cognition is salient during the behavioral decision and whether the person views the behavior as instrumental or consummatory.

An example of the model's integrative power can be demonstrated by examining the helping literature, where there are discrepant findings concerning the effects of the cost of the helping. There is considerable evidence to support the suggestion in Piliavin et al. (1981) that the cost of helping is central to the decision to help. For example, Clark (1976) found that people were less likely to help a blind student study as the cost of the helping increased. However, other research has found that participants will, under certain circumstances, engage in high cost/low reward helping. For example, Schroeder, Dovidio, Sibicky, Matthews, and Allen (1988) found that participants would receive painful electric shocks to help another person. Even Piliavin et al. (1981) were forced to note that in some situations people engage in "impulsive helping" where they fail to weigh costs and rewards.

This apparent contradiction can be resolved if we examine the type of conditions under which the behavioral decision was made (affective vs. cognitive) and the way in which participants viewed the helping behavior (instrumental vs. consummatory). In the 1988 study by Schroeder et al., where high cost helping occurred, participants were asked to focus on feelings of the other person (affective focus) and engage in a behavior that had few independent benefits (consummatory behavior). That is, under anonymous laboratory conditions there is little chance to receive praise or gratitude. Overall, in this study there was an affectively based decision driving a consummatory behavior. On the other hand, in Clark's (1976) study participants were not focused on feelings but were instead focused on the attributes of the person and situation (cognitive focus). That is, the participants were given considerable information about the person they were helping (e.g., the person was a good student, a first quarter senior, had recently been in an accident) and the situation (e.g., the number of miles they would need to drive to help). In addition, the helping behavior that the participants were asked to engage in had potential independent benefits (e.g., the gratitude of the blind student, recognition from a handicap association). Overall, in this study there was a cognitively based decision driving an instrumental behavior.

SUMMARY

In this chapter, we have noted that thought about one's attitude seems to have inconsistent effects on the attitude-behavior relation. In order to resolve this inconsistency we proposed that thought may make either the affective or cognitive component of the attitude more salient and, thus, more important in the formation of a general evaluation. If affect is salient, then the attitude report will reflect one's feelings about the attitude object. If cognitions are salient, then one's attitude report will reflect one's beliefs about the attitude object. In short, one's self-reported attitude will differ as a function of what is salient. We further proposed that one's behavior may be more or less affectively or cognitively driven. Consummatory behaviors, which are engaged in for their own sake, are likely to be affectively driven. On the other hand, instrumental behaviors, which are intended to accomplish a goal which is independent of the attitude object, are likely to be cognitively driven. We hypothesized that a match between the attitude component emphasized by thought and the attitude component that drives behavior would increase the attitude-behavior relation, and, alternatively, a mismatch between the attitude components would decrease the relation. After examining our evidence for these proposals and hypotheses we briefly explored some of the implications of this model for our understanding of the attitude construct and attitude change. Also, some of the implications of the model for other areas of study (e.g., aggression, altruism, and social relations) were touched on.

REFERENCES

Allport, G. W. (1954). The historical background of modern social psychology. In G. Lindzey (Ed.), *Handbook of social psychology: Theory and method* (Vol. 1, pp. 3–56). Cambridge, MA: Addison-Wesley.

Ajzen, I. (1984). Attitudes. In R. J. Corsini (Ed.), *Encyclopedia of psychology* (Vol. 1, pp. 99–100). New York: Wiley.

Ajzen, I., & Fishbein, M. (1977). Attitude-behavior relations: A theoretical analysis and review of empirical research. *Psychological Bulletin, 84*, 888–918.

Batson, C. D., & Coke, J. S. (1981). Empathy: A source of altruistic motivation for helping? In J. P. Rushton & R. M. Sorrentino (Eds.), *Altruism and helping behavior: Social, personality, and developmental perspectives* (pp. 167–187). Hillsdale, NJ: Lawrence Erlbaum Associates.

Batson, C. D., Fultz, J., & Schoenrade, P. A. (1987). Distress and empathy: Two qualitatively distinct vicarious emotions with different motivational consequences. *Journal of Personality, 55*, 19–40.

Berkowitz, L. (1983). Aversively stimulated aggression: Some parallels and differences in research with animals and humans. *American Psychologist, 38*, 1135–1144.

Berkowitz, L. (1988). Frustrations, appraisals, and aversively stimulated aggression. *Aggressive Behavior, 14*, 3–11.

Breckler, S. J. (1984). Empirical validation of affect, behavior, and cognition as distinct components of attitude. *Journal of Personality and Social Psychology, 47*, 1191–1205.

Breckler, S. J., & Wiggins, E. C. (1989). Affect versus evaluation in the structure of attitudes. *Journal of Experimental Social Psychology, 25*, 253–271.

Carr, L., & Roberts, S. O. (1965). Correlates of civil-rights participation. *Journal of Social Psychology, 67*, 259–267.

Chaiken, S., & Baldwin, M. W. (1981). Affective-cognitive consistency and the effect of salient behavioral information on the self-perception of attitudes. *Journal of Personality and Social Psychology, 41*, 1–12.

Chein, I. (1949). The problems of inconsistency: A restatement. *Journal of Social Issues, 5*, 52–61.

Clark, R. D. (1976). On the Piliavin & Piliavin model of helping behavior: Costs are in the eye of the beholder. *Journal of Applied Social Psychology, 6*, 322–328.

Clark, M. S., & Mills, J. (1979). Interpersonal attraction in exchange and communal relationships. *Journal of Personaltiy and Social Psychology, 37*, 12–24.

Clark, M. S., Mills, J., & Powell, M. C. (1986). Keeping track of needs in communal and exchange relationships. *Journal of Personaltiy and Social Psychology, 51*, 333–338.

Corey, S. M. (1937). Professed attitudes and actual behavior. *Journal of Educational Psychology, 28*, 271–280.

Davidson, A. R., & Jaccard, J. (1979). Variables that moderate the attitude-behavior relation: Results of a longitudinal survey. *Journal of Personality and Social Psychology, 37*, 1364–1376.

Edwards, K. (1990). The interplay of affect and cognition in attitude formation and change. *Journal of Personality and Social Psychology, 59*, 202–216.

Fazio, R. H., & Zanna, M. P. (1981). Direct experience and attitude behavior consistency. In L. Berkowitz (Ed.), *Advances in experimental social psychology* (Vol. 14, pp. 161–202). New York: Academic Press.

Fazio, R. H., Zanna, M. P., & Cooper, J. (1978). Direct experience and attitude-behavior consistency: An information processing analysis. *Personality and Social Psychology Bulletin, 4*, 48–52.

Feshbach, S. (1964). The function of aggression and the regulation of aggressive drive. *Psychological Review, 71*, 257–272.

Fleming, D. (1967). Attitude: The history of a concept. *Perspectives in American History, 1*, 287–365.

Freeman, L. C., & Ataov, T. (1960). Invalidity of indirect and direct measures of attitude toward cheating. *Journal of Personality, 38*, 443–447.

Goodmonson, C., & Glaudin, V. (1971). The relationship of commitment-free behavior and commitment behavior: A study of attitude toward organ transplantation. *Journal of Social Issues, 27*, 171–183.

Heberlein, T. B., & Black, J. S. (1976). Attitudinal specificity and the prediction of behavior in a field setting. *Personality and Social Psychology, 33*, 474–479.

Hilgard, E. R. (1980). The trilogy of mind: Cognition, affection, and connotation. *Journal of the History of the Behavioral Sciences, 16,* 107–117.

Hoyt, M. F., & Janis, I. L. (1975). Increasing adherence to a stressful decision via a motivational balance-sheet procedure: A field experiment. *Journal of Personality and Social Psychology, 31,* 833–839.

Insko, C. A., & Schopler, J. (1967). Triadic consistency: A statement of affective-cognitive-conotive consistency. *Psychological Review, 74,* 361–376.

Janis, I. L. (1986). Problems of international crisis management in the nuclear age. *Journal of Social Issues, 42,* 201–220.

Janis, I. L., & Mann, L. (1977). Emergency decision making: A theoretical analysis of responses to disaster warnings. *Journal of Human Stress, 3,* 35–48.

Kanfer, F. H., & Busemeyer, J. R. (1982). The use of problem-solving and decision-making in behavior therapy. *Clinical Psychology Review, 2,* 239–266.

Kendler, H. H., & Kendler, T. S. (1949). A methodological analysis of the research area of inconsistent behavior. *Journal of Social Issues, 5,* 448–456.

Kramer, B. M. (1949). Dimensions of prejudice. *Journal of Psychology, 27,* 389–451.

Lambert, J. (1980). *Social psychology.* New York: Macmillan.

Lapiere, R. (1934). Attitudes versus actions. *Social Forces, 13,* 230–237.

Latane, B., & Darley, J. (1970). *The unresponsive bystander: Why doesn't he help?* New York: Appleton-Century-Crofts.

McGuire, W. J. (1986). The vicissitudes of attitudes and similar representational constructs in twentieth century psychology. *European Journal of Social Psychology, 16,* 89–130.

Millar, M. G., & Millar, K. U. (1990). Attitude change as a function of attitude type and argument type. *Journal of Personality and Social Psychology, 59,* 217–218.

Millar, M. G., & Tesser, A. (1986). Effects of affective and cognitive focus on the attitude-behavior relation. *Journal of Personality and Social Psychology, 51,* 270–276.

Millar, M. G., & Tesser, A. (1989a). The effects of affective-cognitive consistency and thought on the attitude-behavior relation. *Journal of Experimental Social Psychology, 25,* 189–202.

Millar, M. G., & Tesser, A. (1989b). *The effects of prior experience on the attitude-behavior relation.* Unpublished manuscript.

Norman, R. (1975). Affective-cognitive consistency attitudes, conformity,and behavior. *Journal of Personality and Social Psychology, 32,* 83–91.

Ostrom, T. M. (1969). The relationship between the affective, behavioral, and cognitive components of attitude. *Journal of Experimental Social Psychology, 5,* 12–30.

Piliavin, I. M., Dovidio, J. F., Gartner, S. L., & Clark, R. D. (1981). *Emergency intervention.* New York: Academic Press.

Piliavin, I. M., Piliavin, J. A., & Rodin, J. (1975). Costs, diffusion, and the stigmatized victim. *Journal of Personality and Social Psychology, 32,* 429–438.

Pryor, J. B., Gibbons, R. X., Wicklund, R. A., Fazio, R. H., & Hood, R. (1977). Self-focused attention and self-report validity. *Journal of Personality, 45,* 514–527.

Rogers, C. R. (1951). *Client-centered therapy: Its current practice, implications, and theory.* Boston: Houghton Mifflin.

Rosenberg, M. J. (1956). Cognitive structure and attitudinal affect. *Journal of Abnormal and Social Psychology, 53,* 367–372.

Rosenberg, M. J. (1960). A structural theory of attitude dynamics. *Public Opinion Quarterly, 24,* 319–341.

Rosenberg, M. J. (1968). Hedonism, inauthenticity, and other goals toward expansion of a consistency theory. In R. P. Ableson, E. Aronson, W. J. McGuire, T. M. Newcomb, M. J., Rosenberg, & P. H. Tannenbaum (Eds.), *Theories of consistency: A sourcebook* (pp. 73–111). Chicago: Rand McNally.

Ryan, M. J., & Bonfield, E. H. (1975). The Fishbein extended model and consumer behavior. *Journal of Consumer Research, 2,* 118–136.

Scheier, M. R., Buss, A. H., & Buss, D. M. (1978). Self-consciousness, self-report of aggressiveness, and aggression. *Journal of Research in Personality, 12*, 133–140.

Schroeder, D. A., Dovidio, J. F., Sibicky, M. E., Matthews, L. L., & Allen, J. L. (1988). Empathic concern and helping behavior: Egoism or altruism? *Journal of Experimental Social Psychology, 24*, 333–353.

Schuman, H., & Johnson, M. P. (1976). Attitudes and behavior. *Annual Review of Sociology, 2*, 161–207.

Seligman, C., Kriss, M., Darley, J. M., Fazio, R. H., Becker, L. J., & Pryor, J. B. (1979). Predicting summer energy consumption from homeowners' attitudes. *Journal of Applied Social Psychology, 9*, 70–90.

Smith, M. B. (1947). The personal setting of public opinions: A study of attitudes toward Russia. *Public Opinion Quarterly, 11*, 507–523.

Snyder, M., & Kendzierski, D. (1982). Acting on one's attitudes: Procedures for linking attitude and behavior. *Journal of Experimental Social Psychology, 18*, 165–183.

Snyder, M., & Swann, W. B. (1976). When actions reflect attitudes: The politics of impression management. *Journal of Personality and Social Psychology, 34*, 1034–1042.

Tesser, A. (1978). Self-generated attitude change. In L. Berkowitz (Ed.), *Advances in Experimental Social Psychology* (Vol. 11, pp. 289–338). New York: Academic.

Tesser, A. (1978). Self-generated attitude change. In L. Berkowitz (Ed.), *Advances in Experimental Social Psychology* (Vol. 11, pp. 289–338). New York: Academic Press.

Thurstone, L. L. (1928). Attitudes can be measured. *American Journal of Sociology, 33*, 529–544.

Weigel, R. H., & Newman, L. S. (1976). Increasing attitude-behavior correspondence by broadening the scope of the behavioral measure. *Journal of Personality and Social Psychology, 33*, 793–802.

Wicker, A. W. (1969). Attitudes versus actions: The relationship of verbal and overt behavioral responses to attitude objects. *Journal of Social Issues, 25*, 41–78.

Wicker, A. W. (1971). An examination of the "other-variables" explanation of attitude-behavior inconsistency. *Journal of Personality and Social Psychology, 19*, 18–30.

Wicklund, R. A. (1982). Self-focused attention and the validity of self-reports. In M. P. Zanna, E. T. Higgins, & C. P. Herman (Eds.), *Consistency in social behavior: The Ontario Symposium* (Vol. 2, pp. 149–172). Hillsdale, NJ: Lawrence Erlbaum Associates.

Wilson, T. D., & Dunn, D. S. (1986). Disruptive effects of explaining attitudes: Moderating effects of knowledge about the attitude object, and mediating effects of affective-cognitive discrepancies. *Journal of Experimental Social Psychology, 22*, 249–263.

Wilson, T. D., Dunn, D. S., Bybee, J. A., Hyman, D. B., & Rotondo, J. A. (1984). Effects of analyzing reasons on attitude-behavior consistency. *Journal of Personality and Social Psychology, 47*, 4–16.

Wilson, T. D., Dunn, D. S., Kraft, D., & Lisle, D. J. (1989). Introspection, attitude change and attitude-behavior consistency: The disruptive effects of explaining why we feel the way we do. In L. Berkowitz (Ed.), *Advances in experimental social psychology* (Vol. 19, pp. 123–205). Orlando, FL: Academic Press.

Wilson, T. D., Kraft, D., & Dunn, D. S. (1989). Disruptive effects of explaining attitudes: The moderating effect of knowledge about the attitude object. *Journal of Experimental Social Psychology, 25*, 379–400.

Wilson, T. D., Lisle, D. J., & Schooler, J. (1989). *Some undesirable effects of self-reflection.* Unpublished manuscript, University of Virginia, Charlottesville.

Wilson, T. D., & Schooler, J. W. (1990). *Effects of self-reflection of preferences and decisions: Who agrees with the experts?* Unpublished manuscript, University of Virginia, Charlottesville.

Wundt, W. (1904). *Principles of physiological psychology* (5th ed.). New York: Macmillan. (Original work published 1874)

Zajonc, R. B. (1980). Feeling and thinking: Preferences need no inferences. *American Psychologist, 35*, 151–175.

Zajonc, R. B. (1984). On the primacy of affect. *American Psychologist, 36,* 117–123.

Zanna, M. P., & Fazio, R. H. (1982). The attitude-behavior relation: Moving toward a third generation of research. In M. P. Zanna, E. T. Higgins, & C. P. Herman (Eds.), *Consistency in Social Behavior: The Ontario Symposium* (Vol. 2, pp. 283–301). Hillsdale, NJ: Lawrence Erlbaum Associates.

Zanna, M. P., & Rempel, J. K. (1988). Attitudes: A new look at an old concept. In D. Bar-Tal & A. Kruglanski (Eds.), *The social psychology of knowledge* (pp. 315–334). New York: Cambridge University Press.

11

Impression Formation and the Modular Mind: The Associated Systems Theory

Donal E. Carlston
Purdue University

> *It is the case that well-designed systems tend to have special representations for the kinds of information they have to process frequently. These representations are designed to facilitate the kind of computations useful for this kind of information.*
>
> —J. R. Anderson (1978), p. 273

People frequently have to process information about other people, and as the preceding quotation suggests, special representations are likely to develop to handle the kinds of "computations" that are useful in doing so. The resultant impressions seemingly incorporate a wide variety of informational forms. When I think of my wife, for example, what comes to mind are warm feelings, a clear image of her appearance, memories of things we've done together, and a few terms of endearment that I use to describe her. When I think of our local senator, I recall his political identification, a host of (largely negative) trait terms, and the fact that I didn't vote for him.

The purpose of this chapter is to articulate a multi-component theory of the cognitive representation of impressions. This theory suggests that a number of different forms of person information are represented simultaneously in memory, that they are related to each other and to other cognitive structures in varying ways, and that they are differentially reflected in reported impressions, judgments, and behavior. The theory expands on other recent models that accomodate several representational forms at once (e.g., Andersen & Klatzky, 1987; Brewer, 1988; Fiske & Pavelchak, 1986; Wyer & Martin, 1986;

Wyer & Srull, 1989). Moreover, it is consistent, at least in spirit, with recent modular views of cognitive activity that characterize mental processing as a function of the joint operation of a number of partially independent systems operating in parallel (Fodor, 1983; Gazzaniga, 1985; Marshall, 1984; Sherry & Schacter, 1987).

The associated systems theory has two parts. The first is a representational model that suggests the different forms of representational content hypothesized to compose impressions, and the nature of the interrelationships among these forms. The second part is a process model, which explains how different informational content comes into existence and how it is accessed and used during judgment and interpersonal processes. After discussing these two parts of the model, this chapter discusses several implications of this approach.

THE REPRESENTATIONAL MODEL

The model discussed herein distinguishes among forms of person representation that differ systematically in (a) the kinds of attributes they represent, (b) their relationship to primary mental systems, and (c) their degree of abstraction and self/other reference.

Attributes

Past taxonomies (e.g., Beach & Wertheimer, 1961; Dornbusch, Hastorf, Richardson, Muzzy, & Vreeland, 1965; Fiske & Cox, 1979; Livesley & Bromley, 1973; Ostrom, 1975; see also Gordon, 1968, and McGuire & Padawer-Singer, 1976, for self-description taxonomies) provide some valuable suggestions regarding different forms of representation that people often incorporate into their impressions of others. Beach and Wertheimer (1961), for example, identified four major subcategories of person descriptions: (a) objective information, which includes appearance, background and other descriptive facts, (b) social interaction, encompassing the target person's behavior, the subject's reactions to the target, and others' behaviors toward the target, (c) temperament, morals and values, and (d) abilities, motivation, and interests. Fiske and Cox (1979) distinguished several different subtypes of appearance (what people look like), behavior (what they do), relationships (what one does with them), context (where one finds them), origins (how they got this way), and properties (what makes them up).

These taxonomies of public descriptions do not necessarily provide an accurate or exhaustive account of underlying cognitive representations. Public descriptions may reflect only the most accessible forms of data, reconstructions based on multiple representations, or selection of representations thought to be most responsive to the description task (see Fiske & Cox, 1979). Moreover, some forms of representation may be difficult to access under standard experimental procedures, or difficult to report using verbal labels (cf. Anderson, 1988; Zajonc, 1980). Nonetheless, these taxonomies suggest some of the kinds of person attributes that inhere in person descriptions and that a model of social representation needs to take into account. The associated systems theory incorporates many of these attributes, producing considerable overlap, though the ties to past taxonomic efforts will not be detailed here.

Mental systems

The model described in this chapter focuses on distinguishable forms of representation that vary in their relationships to various primary processing systems. These differing relationships serve to emphasize the origins of the representational forms, their characteristic features and properties, and their similarities and differences. Moreover, the relational structure among representational forms has a number of important implications for impression processes.

The Four Cornerstones. Mental representations have sometimes been viewed as internal constructs that mediate the input of external stimuli and the output of behavioral responses (Norman, 1985). It therefore stands to reason that different forms of representation should correspond to the major mental systems governing stimulus input and behavioral response. Arguably, one such system governs sensory perception, a second involves language, a third encompasses affective responding, and a fourth relates to action (or "behavior production").

The first three of these systems seem to correspond closely to the analogue (appearance), propositional (trait), and affective representational codes discussed by Fiske and Taylor (1984; see also Holyoak & Gordon, 1984). The fourth system might involve a motoric code (Norman, 1981) and/or features of episodic storage (Tulving, 1972, 1983). In the latter respect it would be somewhat related to the temporal representation which constitutes Fiske and Taylor's (1984) fourth code.

These four mental systems provide the cornerstones of the representational model. Each system is hypothesized to involve a form of representation that is a direct analogue to the inputs or outputs with which it deals. In fact, the activation of a cognitive representation may involve the re-activation of higher-level structures within the primary system that was involved in the initial perception or production of this material (Damasio, 1989a). Thus, for example, perceptual representations should involve mental images that mimic the original experience of visual perception (Kosslyn & Pomerantz, 1977; Shepard & Podgorny, 1978).

The reader may have noted that three of the cornerstones described here correspond to the cognitive, conative, and affective components of the classic tripartite definition of attitudes (e.g., Breckler, 1984; Katz & Stotland, 1959). The notion that these components represent different sources of information that can contribute to common cognitive processes is shared with recent models of attitudinal representation (e.g., Fazio, 1986; Millar & Tesser, 1986; Zanna & Rempel, 1988). The potential therefore exists to extend the associated systems model beyond the domain of person perception to other kinds of attitudinal issues. However, such extensions lie outside the scope of this chapter.

Hybrid Systems. The cognitive system is capable of doing more than merely representing information from primary input and output structures. It is also hypothesized to provide association areas where the contents of primary structures interact to produce new material with some characteristics of each contributing system (Damasio, 1989a). Likely interactions among sensory, verbal, affective, and action structures are included in the associated systems model as "hybrid" representations. *Categorizations,* for example, are here construed as a form of representation that generally combines direct perceptual data (e.g., physical appearance) with verbal encodings (e.g., trait descriptors).[1]

As shown in Fig. 11.1, the relational structure posited by associated systems theory incorporates nine different forms of person representation, reflecting the separate and combined operations of the primary mental systems discussed previously. In Fig. 11.1, forms of representation that directly correspond to the sensory, verbal, affective, and production systems are shown in the corners, and hybrid forms of representation are shown in the mediate cells, adjacent to the primary forms to which they are hypothesized to be related. Thus, this arrangement not only reflects the theorized relationship between the nine forms and the primary processing systems, but also the hypothesized degree of similarity and association among the different representational forms. Evaluations, for example, are viewed as closely related to traits and to affective responses. Various implications of these associations are detailed elsewhere in this chapter.

Specific Forms of Representation

Visual Appearance. Of all the sensory systems, the visual system is most central to the present analysis. Its characteristic form of representation, physical appearance, has been extensively researched by social psychologists (e.g., Dion, Berscheid, & Walster, 1972; Herman, Zanna, & Higgins, 1986; McArthur 1982; Secord, 1958) and incorporated into a number of models of social representation (e.g., Brewer, 1988; Lord, 1980; Swann & Miller, 1982; Wyer

---

[1]This proposal is consistent with J. R. Anderson's (1978) observation that a conjunction of internal representations can itself be an internal representation (p. 263).

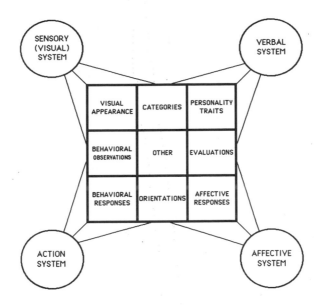

FIG. 11.1. Multiple forms of person representation.

& Srull, 1986). The nature of visual representations remain controversial, with some cognitive theorists suggesting they are stored in an *analog code* (Kosslyn & Pomerantz, 1977; Paivio, 1971; Shepard & Podgorny, 1978) and others disagreeing (J. R. Anderson, 1978; Pylyshyn, 1973, 1981).[2] The present formulation suggests that a visual image of a physical appearance is a primary component of our impressions of others.

Personality Traits. The verbal system is ideally suited for the representation of descriptive verbal labels such as personality traits, which were once considered the essential embodiment of interpersonal impressions. Impression formation was interpreted as the deduction of traits from appearance (Miller, 1970), behaviors (Jones & Davis, 1965) or other traits (Bruner, Shapiro, & Tagiuri, 1958), and impression structures were defined in terms of trait interrelationships (Rosenberg & Sedlak, 1972). Winter and Uleman (1984) suggested that trait inferences about an actor are inherent in the encoding of behavioral episodes, a view recently questioned by others (e.g., Bassili, 1989). The manner

---

[2]Debates over representational formats in cognitive psychology address the issue of representation at a somewhat different level than do models of social cognition, such as the present one. For example, J. R. Anderson (1978) argues that propositional formats are capable of representing all of the properties attributed to *picture* formats for mental imagery, calling into question the need for a distinct picture format. Even the apparent isomorphism between perception and imagination can be accomodated within a propositional model. However, from the social cognition point of view, it is the apparent properties of a visual system (such as this isomorphism) that are critically important, not the underlying representational format.

in which traits are represented cognitively has also prompted debate (e.g., Ostrom, 1987); the present view is that trait impressions are closely linked to language, so that their representation is dictated by linguistic structure and conventions (see Bromley, 1977; Livesley & Bromley, 1973). This primary form of representation is theorized to be strongly implicated in the conscious cognitive consideration of others.

Categorizations. Categorization is a widely studied form of representation involving assignment of a target person to one or more social groups. It is here characterized as a hybrid form of representation embodying elements of both the verbal and the visual (sensory) systems. Thus, when people think of Blacks or Whites or many other kinds of social groupings, they are likely to access both a descriptive label for that grouping and a visual image of characteristic group members. The visual or *pictoliteral* component of social categorization has recently been emphasized by a number of theorists (e.g., Brewer, 1988; Klatzky & Andersen, 1988). Evidence for this feature of categorizations is suggested by the speed with which people make race and gender categorizations based on visual attributes (Zarate & Smith, 1990), the vivid appearance details frequently accompanying descriptions of category prototypes (Ashmore, Del Boca, & Titus, 1984), and the ability of category labels to prime pictorial processing (Klatzky, Martin, & Kane, 1982).

Other theorists have emphasized the close link between categorical representations and ascribed traits (Cantor & Mischel, 1977), and have sometimes even wondered whether distinguishing between the two is fundamentally meaningful (Rothbart, 1988). From the current perspective, categorizations and traits differ primarily in their relative reliance on visual and verbal forms of content. This is only one of many characteristics of categorizations that have been the subject of debate (see Medin, 1989, for a review).

Behavioral Responses. A perceiver's behavioral responses to another are here hypothesized to be an important part of the perceiver's mental representation of that other. At one level, these behavioral responses embody specific acts toward others, which have become associated with them, and which are therefore likely to be initiated in their presence. At another level, these responses represent components of plans or scripts (Abelson, 1976, 1981) that have been constructed with respect to the other. And at yet another level, these actions provide informational content that can cue other forms of representation. Thus, for example, we may infer trait characteristics of another person from ways we have treated that person in the past.

The notion that our own past actions provide informational content is central to self-perception theories of attitude change (Bem, 1967). In these theories, people use their past behaviors as a source of information about their own attitudes when other, internal cues are relatively weak. Extending this logic, people may also use their own behaviors toward another person to infer other properties of that person, including traits, evaluations, category assignments (see, e.g., Higgins & McCann, 1984), or other representational forms described here.

Several models of the action system (e.g., Martindale, 1991; Shallice, 1978) are consistent with the notion that behavioral responses are represented at different interconnected levels. The lowest-level "action units" are closely linked to the motor system responsible for behavior production, whereas higher-level scripts are linked to dispositions and self-conceptions. Similarly, in the associated systems model, responses are viewed as closely related to both the action (or *behavior production*) system and to general goals and orientations regarding the other. Additionally, as shown in Fig. 11.1, response information is here viewed as closely related to other forms of episodic representation (i.e., observations of others) with which it shares temporal and context organization.

Behavioral Observations. Behavioral observations can be construed as a subset of entries in episodic memory (Tulving, 1972, 1983), though the existence of such a separate memory store is in dispute in cognitive psychology (McKoon, Ratcliff, & Dell, 1986). In keeping with Tulving's conception, behavioral observations are here characterized as products of direct perception that strongly implicate the perceiver. For this reason, such observational representations are depicted in Fig. 11.1 between the direct representations of the perceptual system (visual appearance) and the action system (behavioral responses). Indeed, observations of others' behaviors are ordinarily likely to be intermeshed both with perceptions of their appearance and with episodic representation of one's own role in ongoing events (see Conway, 1990). This comingling of perception and interaction has been described as one of the features that distinguishes social from non-social cognition (Ostrom, 1984).

Affective Responses. In the past decade, a number of theorists have emphasized the importance of affective responses to the understanding of social cognitions (Isen, 1984; Zajonc, 1980). Bower (1981) explicitly suggested that affects can be viewed as constructs that are linked to other forms of representation within a general associative network. In the current approach, affective responses are treated as a form of information that is copied into the associative structure linked to a given individual. Affect is thus retrievable in the same way that other forms of representation are, and it can contribute, along with other kinds of information, to a variety of responses to an individual. (See Clore & Parrott, in press, and Schwarz & Clore, 1988, for a similar view.) Research has demonstrated that affect can influence people's liking for others (Gouaux, 1971; Griffitt, 1970; Griffitt & Veitch, 1971) as well as their trait impressions (Erber, in press; Forgas & Bower, 1987) and memories (e.g., Bower, Monteiro, & Gilligan, 1978). These effects might be even stronger were the target individual actually the source of the affect, which is seldom true in these studies (Schwarz & Clore, 1988; see Isen, 1984, for a review).

It is often suggested that affective information tends to degrade more slowly than other forms of representation (e.g., Zajonc, 1980). However, it also seems that the visceral experience associated with positive or negative experiences diminishes fairly rapidly. We can all attest that we lose both the joy of having a manuscript accepted, and the irritation of having one rejected, long before the events themselves fade from memory. It is possible that affective responses actually degrade rather quickly, but that we preserve such information in a more cognitive form (e.g., evaluations). It is also likely that we sometimes generate affect anew when we remember and ruminate about emotionally laden experiences. In general, it may be that affect is neither more nor less accessible than other forms of representation, and that its accessibility is determined by the same sorts of factors (e.g., organization, rehearsal, and perhaps interference) as retrieval of other forms of representation.

Orientations. The 3 × 3 organization depicted in Fig. 11.1 suggests the existence of a hybrid form of representation joining features of the affective and action systems. This form should represent an affectively loaded abstraction of behavioral acts. In other words, it should reflect the perceiver's general style or manner of interacting with the person being perceived (see, e.g., Fiske, 1991). These *orientations* might include prototypic behaviors enacted toward the target person as well as goals or other behavioral correlates of affect (e.g., approach and avoidance). Though not an essentially verbal form of representation, such orientations would be reflected in remarks like "I generally treat her well," or "I don't want to have anything to do with her."

The centrality of orientation to the cognitive representation of others was recently demonstrated in a series of experiments by Fiske, Haslam, and Fiske (1991). They examined the extent to which people's orientations, which they termed "relationship mode" (see Fiske, 1991) affected misidentification of others. They found that similar orientations toward others played a larger role in misidentification than did many other personal attributes, such as age and race. Fiske et al. concluded that "people represent their social world in terms of the kinds of relationships they have with others" (p. 673).

Evaluations. Evaluations represent affective reactions expressed in verbal form, producing a hybrid with characteristics superficially like those of traits. Most common of these is liking, which is frequently couched as the *likability* of the person represented, and which has been studied extensively in the literature on interpersonal attraction (Byrne, 1971). A number of other evaluative impressions that require more complex verbal descriptions (e.g., *he's a good person to have around*) might also be included here.

Many ascribed traits (e.g., *dishonest* or *friendly*) also have a strong evaluative component. A key difference between traits and evaluations is whether the ascribed characteristic is ostensibly a property only of the perceived, or whether it also inherently implicates the perceiver (as likability judgments do). The distinction between affect and evaluation has recently been emphasized by several attitude theorists. Zanna and Rempel (1988) view evaluation as a more cognitive, pro/con judgment, whereas they reserve the term *affect* for experienced feelings or emotions. Breckler and Wiggins (1989) found affect and evaluation to be less correlated for less controversial domains (e.g., comprehensive exams) than for more controversial ones (e.g., abortion), and also found them differentially related to behavior.

Other Representations. Additional forms of representation can be identified that do not fit into the eight outside cells of Fig. 11.1. Many of these are incorporated within a more exhausting taxonomy of person descriptors that has been developed using the framework outlined here (Carlston & Sparks, 1991). Included in that 5 × 5 taxonomic scheme are several kinds of information that are here lumped into the center cell.[3]

An example will help to illustrate the theoretical logic underlying the central placement of these representations. Several theorists have suggested the importance of relationship constructs in the representation of people (e.g., Baldwin, Carrell, & Lopez, 1990; Fiske & Cox, 1979). Examples would be characterizations such as *my best friend* or *my brother*. Such labels are forms of categorization, as well as of evaluation, and they incorporate elements of orientation and episodic recall, as well. They are trait-like, implicate affect, summarize behavior, and may even have a visual component (see Baldwin et al., 1990). In short, they embody elements of many of the primary and hybrid forms of representation already discussed. Their placement in the center cell is intended to emphasize these close associations with a variety of different representational forms. This is similarly true of other representations included in this center cell, such as the personal preferences of the target individual and certain kinds of biographical information.

Self-Reference and Abstraction

The arrangement of cells in Fig. 11.1 is intended to emphasize several systematic differences among the various forms of representation (see Fig. 11.2). For example, the representational forms in the top row pertain primarily to inherent

---

[3]This taxonomy includes the 9 representations described here with 16 additional kinds of person descriptors interspersed among them. The expanded scheme allows finer distinctions to be made among different content actually found in open-ended person descriptions. The underlying assumption remains the same, and each of the descriptive types is assumed to represent a unique combination of the four primary processing systems described here.

characteristics of the person being perceived, and those in the bottom row to responses of the perceiver to the target. Representations in the middle row arguably implicate both the target and the perceiver (or others).[4] These differences are relative, because all aspects of an impression to some extent implicate both the person being perceived and the perceiver whose subjective perceptions make up the representations. Nonetheless, in general, the rows differ progressively in the extent to which they pertain to characteristics of the person being perceived or of the person doing the perceiving.

The columns in Figs. 11.1 and 11.2 vary progressively in abstraction, which is another important characteristics of different kinds of person information (see Hastie & Carlston, 1980). The representational forms on the far left (appearance, observations, and own responses) are all relatively concrete, and may include details reflecting the time and place at which they were recorded. Representational forms in the center column (categorizations, relationships, orientation) are somewhat more abstract, embodying summaries of multiple instances or observations. And the forms on the far right (traits, evaluations, affect) are most abstract, reflecting fairly undetailed and nonspecific associations to the target person.[5]

THE PROCESS MODEL

J. R. Anderson (1978) argued that it is impossible to evaluate claims regarding mental representation separate from a model of the processes presumed to act on such representations. The associated systems process model is a multi-stage information processing model that emphasizes exposure to the stimulus, translation into representational forms, organizational structure, retrieval/judgment processes, and response editing.

An underlying premise of this model is that impressions of other people consist of aggregations of information represented in a variety of different forms. Information about a given individual need not assume all possible representational forms, though it may assume many different ones, depending on the pre-

---

[4]Behavioral observations describe the target, but also tend to implicate the observer, as Tulving (1972, 1983) recognized in defining episodic memory. Relationship descriptors (e.g., *my brother*) similarly pertain to the perceiver as well as the perceived. Finally, evaluations (e.g., *I like her*) are explicitly subjective, and are therefore informative with regard to both perceiver and perceived.

[5]It should be noted that some variation in abstraction and self/other reference can occur within, as well as between, different forms of representation. Categorizations, for example, can vary from the concretely visual (e.g., *she's a blond bombshell*) to trait-like abstraction (e.g., *she's a genius*). At the extremes, such category descriptions may be difficult to differentiate from appearances and traits, respectively. In fact, for reasons to be described later, few overt descriptors are likely to be pure reflections of one and only one form of representation. The characteristics described here are thus generalities that pertain to ideal types of each representation.

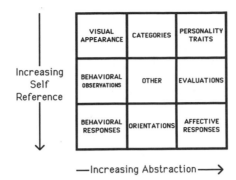

FIG. 11.2. Basic dimensions of person representation.

cise experiences of the perceiver. These different forms of information may have redundant or conflicting implications. In either case, it is the total aggregation of information, here represented as an associative network, that funnels and ultimately determines the individual's responses. The following account is intended to provide an overview of this perspective and of the kinds of factors that influence the formation and utilization of these multi-representational aggregations.

Exposure

A major determinant of the manner in which people represent stimuli about other people is undoubtedly the manner in which those stimuli are represented in the environment. In other words, the nature of people's impressions should differ in important ways depending on whether they are formed during face-to-face interactions or verbal (telephone, letter, computer) contacts, from descriptions of traits or episodes, in emotionally neutral or emotionally charged contexts, and so on. Such contextual factors have been explored in other areas of social psychology (e.g., DePaulo, Rosenthal, Green, & Rosenkrantz, 1982; Gilovich, 1987; Maxwell, Cook, & Burr, 1985), but have not been systematically related to the representation of impressions.

It is hypothesized that people's impressions are likely to initially consist of representations that are isomorphic to the information encountered. This does not mean that information is copied into representations accurately, but rather that the form of the representation will reflect features of the modality in which it is processed (see Nairne, 1990). However, this isomorphism principle must be modified slightly depending on whether the stimulus is experienced first hand or described by others.

First-Hand Exposure. When observations are made first hand, the nature of the observations should determine the initial form of representation. Thus, for example, when Jim first observes Dora (or her photograph), his impression should consist of an internal representation of her appearance. If he sees her kiss a baby, his impression should also include an episodic representation of that event. In other words, each of the primary processing systems is hypothesized to produce a characteristic form of representation. Direct observation by itself will initially produce forms of representation that are characteristically associated with the perceptual system (primarily appearance and behavior observation, and perhaps some kinds of appearance-based categorization). Similarly, action toward a person will produce representations relating to response production (primarily responses, but sometimes also orientations and behavior observations). Affective state should produce affective representations (primarily affect, but also some kinds of evaluations and orientations). And rumination or communication should produce verbal representations (primarily traits, but also categorizations and evaluations).

Second-Hand Exposure. When information about a target person is learned through communications from others, the situation becomes more complicated. Technically, the act of receiving a communication is itself always an episodic event. However, it may produce a somewhat impoverished episodic trace, as when a perceiver is so completely engrossed in a book or conversation that details of the immediate physical and temporal location are unattended. Moreover, it is possible to communicate some social information in a way that closely approximates internal (especially verbal) forms of representation. Thus, for example, Jim might hear Carolyn describe Dora as a feminist (categorization), as intelligent (trait), or as likeable (evaluation). The content features of such characteristics may not much differ from the characteristics of internally generated categorizations, traits, or evaluations.

A high degree of isomorphism seems more likely for trait descriptions than for any other form of communicated description, because the verbal nature of the material matches the verbal nature of the representation.[6] Categorizations and evaluations also have strong verbal components, though they ordinarily involve nonverbal features as well, and these may be missing from the stimulus communication, and thus from the induced representation of the target person. For example, a written description of someone as a *slob* omits explicit appearance features that would ordinarily be a part of such a categorization if it were generated through first-hand observation. Second-hand exposure to appearance and behavior information may differ most from first-hand experiences, because of the difficulties inherent in fully communicating visual features and situational context (see Gilovich, 1987).

---

[6]One index of isomorphism between presented and represented information is the degree of confusion that can be created over the internal or external source of the information. As discussed later in this chapter, a lack of isomorphism allows people to detect features suggesting that material was learned rather than inferred. But isomorphic descriptions are less likely to have such distinguishing features, and are thus more likely to be misattributed to internal origins.

Exposure Frequencies. Because the form in which person information is encountered determines its initial form of representation, and because repeated encounters can contribute to the development of processing automaticity (discussed shortly), it is important to understand the rates at which different forms of representation are ordinarily encountered in the social world. These exposure frequencies will logically depend both on the nature of people's direct experiences with others and on the content of everyday communications regarding others. Of these, the descriptive content of everyday communications is likely to be more readily examined empirically. All that is needed is to extend the analysis of person descriptions to various naturalistic situations and materials (see Bromley, 1977; Rosenberg & Jones, 1972). For example, one might analyze the forms of representation characterizing conversational or literary descriptions of other people.

Obviously, functional and normative constraints will be important determinants of the kinds of information communicated in naturalistic situations. For example, it is more useful to use appearance than trait descriptors in describing an assailant to police; convention may dictate that communicators focus on privileged or idiosyncratic representational content, rather than describing attributes that are widely known (Haviland & Clark, 1974); and norms may inhibit disclosure of some kinds of evaluative or affective content to some audiences.

The frequency of different informational content in people's direct interactions with others raises more difficult issues. Initial representations formed during face-to-face interaction presumably include appearance, observations, and response information; those formed from passive observation presumably include appearance and observations, but not responses; and those formed from remote (e.g., telephone and correspondence) interactions presumably include observations and responses, but not appearance. However, there is little data regarding the relative frequency or importance of these or other kinds of impression contexts. Similarly, little is known about the specific attributes likely to be encountered in those contexts (Hastie, Park, & Weber, 1984).

Finally, exposure to various kinds of person information is not likely to be an entirely accidental process. That is, people may engage in active efforts to obtain information (Fiske & Ruscher, 1988), just as they seemingly do in the attitude realm (Cotton, 1985; Frey, 1986). One interesting possibility is the *completion hypothesis*: To fill out incomplete impressions, people may seek information relevant to those representational forms that they lack. Thus, for example, people seem to desire appearance information about previously unseen "acquaintances,"[7] they try to interact with celebrities whom they know in more remote ways, they seek to define their relationships with regular acquaintances, they infer the traits of people they observe, and so on. Although such behaviors

---

[7]Graduate students, for example, often seem fascinated by photos of "famous" psychologists taken at one or another convention. Textbook publishers seem to have decided in recent years that such photos hold a similar fascination for undergraduates.

are explicable in a variety of ways, they may reflect a need to round out incomplete impressions.

Elaborations

Aspects of an impression that are initially stored in one representational form may be elaborated into other forms. For example, appearance information often precipitates categorization processes (Klatzky, 1984; Zarate & Smith, 1990); affective reactions (Zajonc, 1980), observed behaviors (Jones & Davis, 1965; Winter & Uleman, 1984), and social categorizations (Zarate & Smith, 1990) often lead to trait inferences; trait or behavioral information may stimulate a mental image of a person's appearance (Paivio, 1971).

The Process of Elaboration. To elaborate information about a particular person in new ways, the perceiver must draw on an existing store of knowledge about the relationships among different representations. This knowledge resides within conceptual social memory, which Hastie and Carlston (1980) defined as encompassing "referential and relational 'definitions' of all important social concepts, events and generic individuals" (p. 14) and "procedures that generate inferences from abstract representations" (p. 26).

Included among these are the behavior-trait and trait-trait relationships commonly dealt with by attribution (e.g., Jones & Davis, 1965) and implicit personality (e.g., Rosenberg & Sedlak, 1972) models (see also Schneider, 1973). But presumably also included are linkages between behavior and affect, categorization and evaluation, appearance and orientation, and so on. Elaboration involves the use of such linkages to generate new representations from the particulars known about an individual.

Influences On Elaboration. Although in principle any of the nine representational forms can be used to generate any other representation, certain kinds of elaborations may be more likely than others. The kinds of elaboration that are most likely are hypothesized to depend on the nature of the perceiver's involvement with the target individual. Specifically, as illustrated in Fig. 11.3 verbal elaborations should generally result from verbal activities (e.g., thinking or communicating about people), affective elaborations from affective involvements (emotional experiences), and behavioral elaborations from actual or planned interactions. Some forms of hybrid representation may result from the engagement of several primary systems at once.

These effects of involvement may sometimes reflect the "pull" of the environment, which can require the perceiver to make a verbal, affective or behavioral response. An example is the formation of verbal representations while describing the target to another person. Involvement effects may also sometimes result from the "push" of specific objectives or intentions of the per-

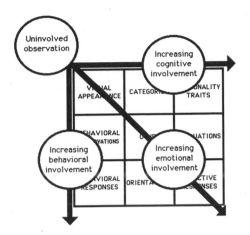

FIG. 11.3. Effects of involvement on representation.

ceiver. For example, sexual interest may increase the likelihood of strong affective and behavioral responses to a target.

When elaborations are not directed toward a particular response (by a judgment question, for example), they seem likely to involve forms of representation that are closely related to each other (as shown in Fig. 11.1). Adjacent forms of representation generally implicate the same primary systems, and share certain morphological features. Therefore, if one representation is already salient, some of the ingredients necessary for the generation of the other will already be activated. For example, because evaluation and affect both involve the affective system, either should readily cue generation of the other. Similarly, categorizations should readily cue appearance and trait representations, behavioral responses should cue orientations and observations, and so on.

Automatic Elaborations. When a stimulus prompts the same mental activity on enough occasions, that activity can become automatic (J. R. Anderson, 1982; Smith, 1989). Automaticism causes the activity to occur reliably in the presence of the stimulus, and to execute without conscious intent or attention (Bargh, 1984; Schneider & Shiffrin, 1977). In this manner, repeated generation of one representational form from another can ultimately produce automatic *procedures* that accomplish the elaboration without conscious involvement. Theorists have suggested that procedures exist to automatically prompt behavioral (Langer, Blank, & Chanowitz, 1978), categorical (Zarate & Smith, 1990), trait (Winter & Uleman, 1984), and affective (Clark & Isen, 1982; Zajonc, 1980) responses. (Though each of these suggestions has its critics; e.g., Bargh, 1984; Bassili, 1989; Gilbert & Hixon, 1991; Lazarus, 1982.)

In principle, a given individual might develop procedures to automatically handle virtually any kind of elaboration. For example, the appearance of a friend might come to automatically produce a positive affective response; one's own negative behaviors toward another might lead to negative evaluations of that individual; or categorizing someone might unintentionally influence behaviors toward that person. Automatic elaborations may also be precipitated by particular representational combinations: For example, when I advise (behavior production) an undergraduate (categorization) who is not a student of mine (relationship) and that person responds positively (observed behavior), it makes me feel good (affect).

Not all potential elaborations are as likely as others. To become automatized, an elaboration should have been repeated many times in the past (Bargh, 1984; Smith, 1989). The likelihood that this will be true for any particular kind of elaboration presumably depends on a number of factors that are likely to differ from individual to individual. For example, it logically depends on the frequency and nature of an individual's past exposure to, and involvements with, people like the stimulus person.[8] As discussed earlier (and illustrated in Fig. 11.3), different kinds of involvement are hypothesized to favor different kinds of elaborations, and thus ultimately to influence the kinds of elaborations that become automatized. For example, frequent interaction with people like the target increases the likelihood that particular behavioral responses will have been emitted often enough to have become automatic; repeated cognitive engagement increases the likelihood that particular verbal responses will have become automatic; and so on.

The development of automatized elaborations is also favored by factors that cause greater consistency in the encoding of the precipitating representation, in the elaborations precipitated, or in the generation of particular elaborations from particular stimuli. For example, automatic elaborations may be more likely from attributes that are relatively unambiguous (e.g., gender), to attributes that are more abstract and less complex (e.g., traits and affect), and by individuals who chronically elaborate targets in particular ways (see Bargh & Thein, 1985).

Many different kinds of responses may be made consistently enough in certain settings or for certain groups of people to achieve a degree of proceduralization. For example, consistent patterns of behavioral response are likely among people interacting in prescribed roles;[9] and consistent elaborations with regard to intelligence are likely within academic settings. Overall, however, it is unclear how frequently representational elaborations become automatized.

---

[8]Who is similar to the stimulus person depends, of course, on how that person is currently represented. Thus, if the perceiver's current impression consists of a categorical representation, the nature of past involvements with other members of the same category will determine the likelihood of various kinds of representational elaborations.

[9]Because routine in-role behaviors can become at least partially automatic, people may be less consciously involved in the production of such behaviors (Kitayama & Burnstein, 1988; Langer et al., 1978). This lack of cognitive mediation may explain why even positive in-role contact between races often fails to change racial attitudes (Cook, 1978).

Research on automatic trait inference remains inconclusive (Bassili, 1989; Uleman & Bargh, 1989). Evidence regarding the automatic generation of category and trait representations from ethnic appearance is discussed in the next section.

Automatic Activation of Stereotypes. A number of researchers (Devine, 1989; Dovidio, Evans, & Tyler, 1986; Fiske & Neuberg, 1989) have recently argued that stereotypes are automatically activated upon observation of a category member. Stereotypes are defined as the traits associated with a particular categorical group. From the present perspective, activation of a stereotype therefore involves the generation of a categorical representation from appearance information, and then the generation of stereotypical traits from the categorization.[10] To become automatic, these two elaborations (appearance to category and category to traits) must have been repeated frequently in the past. Appearance to category elaborations might become proceduralized for target groups that have been encountered frequently and categorized consistently, and category to trait elaborations might become proceduralized for people who utilize the stereotype regularly.[11]

Evidence on these possibilities is provided by an ingenious study by Gilbert and Hixon (1991) in which subjects completed word fragments presented by either a Caucasian or an Asian research assistant. Some of these fragments could be completed with traits common to the cultural stereotype of Asians (e.g., *shy* and *polite*).[12] Subjects who were not cognitively busy generated more stereotypical trait terms while observing an Asian than a Caucasian experimenter, whereas cognitively busy subjects did not. This suggests that capacity was necessary for the trait elaboration to occur, meaning that the stereotypical trait terms were not generated automatically.

Whether physical appearance led to automatic generation of the *Asian* category representation is unclear. Cognitively busy subjects were able to identify the experimenter's race on a subsequent questionnaire, but this response could have been generated at that time from recalled appearance information. A sec-

---

[10]Mediation through a categorical representation is assumed here because the culturally learned associations tend to be between the category representation and the stereotypical traits, rather than directly from appearance features to stereotypical traits. There may be exceptions, such as the stereotypical association between lightness of skin and intelligence among Blacks. In general, however, categorical identification is presumed to precede ascription of stereotypical attributes (Ashmore & Del Boca, 1979; Lingle, Altom, & Medin, 1984).

[11]It is unclear whether automatization can occur among people who are aware of the stereotype but have not practiced it, as Devine (1989) has suggested. In general, repetition of the relevant elaborations would seem necessary for them to become automatic. However, recent research (Logan & Klapp, 1991) does suggest that even without practice, familiarization with a rule can increase the automaticity of responding.

[12]Unfortunately, the other stereotypical attributes included a category term (*Nip*), an appearance descriptor (*short*) and a random associate (*rice*), making the present interpretation of these results a little overly simplistic.

ond experiment found that the cognitively busy subjects failed to give stereo-typic ratings to the Asian experimenter on a later impression task, under condi-tions where non-busy subjects did, which might suggest absence of the categorical representation. These subjects listened to an audio recording of the experimenter talking about herself just prior to the impression task, so if a cate-gorical representation existed, there should have been ample time to retrieve it and to derive stereotypical traits from it.

These results imply that subjects did not automatically generate trait represen-tations, and may not have even automatically generated category representa-tions, from available appearance information. Possibly, the University of Texas students had not had enough experience interacting with Asians, or stereotyping them, for these elaborations to have become automatized. Other studies (e.g., Brewer, 1988) suggest that automatic appearance to category elaborations do occur for gender categories (see also Bem, 1981), with which most non-Asians presumably have more experience. Theorists (e.g., Fiske, 1989) have argued that the next step, category to trait elaboration, is less likely to be automatic.

Organization

Although different forms of representation are here viewed as directly linked to different primary processing systems, the representations themselves are presumed to be interconnected within a single associative structure. Regard-less of form, specific information about a person is represented as a node[13] that is linked directly to the node representing that person, as well as to other specific information of the same or different form. A sample impression structure is shown in Fig. 11.4.

The notion that different forms of representation may be linked within a com-mon connectionist structure is not new. Theorists have suggested such link-ages between affect and episodic memories (Bower, 1981), categorical and propositional representations (Brewer, 1988), attitudes and behaviors (Fazio, Chen, McDonel, & Sherman, 1982), and episodic memories and traits (Carl-ston & Skowronski, 1986). Associative network models have incorporated diverse forms of representation within both the person perception (Wyer & Carl-ston, 1979) and attitude (see Fazio, 1989) realms. Moreover, neural network models (e.g., Grossberg, 1988; Rumelhart & McClelland, 1982, 1986) assume massive interconnections among separate systems dealing with sensory, seman-tic, episodic, action and affective processing (see Martindale, 1991).

---

[13]Actually, in many current connectionist models (e.g., Grossberg, 1988; McClelland & Rumel-hart, 1985), concepts are not represented by simple nodes but rather by patterns of activation of feature nodes. In the associated systems theory, these featural components are important primari-ly in discussing differences between representational forms, particularly as they relate to issues regarding elaboration and confusion among representations. Less molecular issues are more easily understood by allowing molar concepts to be represented as single nodes (Martindale, 1991).

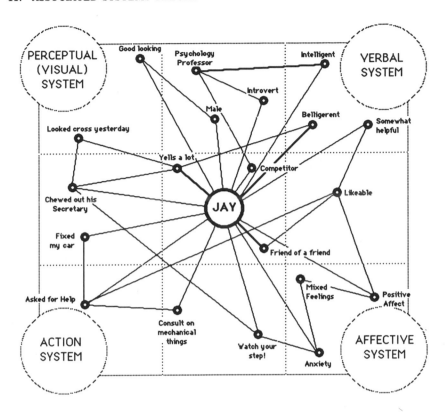

FIG. 11.4. Sample representational network. (Although described here verbally, many of these representations would not be stored in verbal form.)

The rules governing the formation, strengthening, and use of connective linkages (generally called *associative pathways*) are assumed to be fundamentally the same regardless of the form of information involved. However, different forms of representation are distinguished by the strength of their linkages to the primary processing systems, and coincidentally, to other forms of representation (see Fig. 11.1). One implication of these linkages is that particular forms of representation are likely to emerge from the engagement of the primary systems to which they are most closely related. A second is that various outputs (e.g., verbal communications, affective and behavioral responses) will tend to be most influenced by more strongly associated forms of representation. A third implication is that each form of representation will ordinarily be most closely associated with other forms of representation that share linkages with the same primary processing systems. Although there may be exceptions where more distant forms of representation have become closely linked through past use, strength of association should generally reflect morphological similarity (which is represented by proximity in Fig. 11.1).

Retrieval

In the associated systems theory, the retrieval of information from an impression structure is modeled with the spreading activation metaphor (see Anderson & Bower, 1973/1979; Carlston & Skowronski, 1986; Wyer & Carlston, 1979). In free recall about an individual, for example, excitation would begin at the node representing that person and spread to associated concept nodes through connecting pathways. In the associated systems model, those associated concepts include items reflecting all of the different forms of representation. When enough excitation accumulates at one of these items, either directly from the person node, or indirectly through other associated concepts, the item is retrieved.

Although the mechanisms that make up the spreading activation metaphor may be familiar to most readers, several nuances merit elaboration. First, the accessibility of a concept is a function of (a) the strength of pathways linking it directly or indirectly with activated concepts, and (b) the concept's level of activation prior to initiation of the search. Pathway strength (representing strength of association) is a function of the recency and frequency with which the pathway has been used (Higgins, Bargh, & Lombardi, 1985). In the present model, pathways from a person node are strengthened each time specific attributes of that individual are retrieved. Additionally, pathways between different representational contents are strengthened each time they are thought of concurrently, as when one (e.g., physical appearance) leads to generation of another (e.g., a categorization).

A concept's level of activation prior to memory search can be affected by recent cognitive activities involving that concept or (more speculatively) primary systems relating to that concept. Thus the impressions that we retrieve of a given individual may differ, depending on momentary variations in the accessibility of different component representations. (For similar arguments regarding attitudes, see Fazio et al., 1982; Feldman & Lynch, 1988).

Second, activation may ordinarily spread through the associative structure from more than one seminal site. A variety of concepts are likely to be activated at any time, and excitation presumably emanates from all of these active sites during retrieval processes. The flow of excitation from multiple sources may be analogous to the expanding and overlapping ripples caused when a handful of stones are thrown into a pond. The movement (or *excitation*) of anything on the surface of the pond will be inversely proportional to its combined distance from all of the stones' points of entry. Similarly, the concepts most likely to be stimulated in memory, and thus retrieved, will be those that are most closely associated with all other activated concepts (Miller & Read, in press). This implies that retrieval of information about a person will vary depending on the nature of other currently accessible material.

When sufficient excitation converges on a construct, and that construct becomes activated, several changes occur in the system. For one, the newly activated construct becomes a source of activation capable of stimulating other constructs with which it is associated. At the same time, other concepts that were in competition with the activated one are likely to be inhibited (Carlston & Skowronski, 1986; Grossberg, 1988). Though still controversial, the *lateral inhibition* of competing concepts has been suggested by numerous theorists (Grossberg, 1988; Hoffman & Ison, 1980; Neely, 1976; Roediger & Neely, 1982) to deal with problems of excessive "noise" within purely excitatory systems.

Consider an observer being approached from a distance by a barely recognizable woman. In a purely excitatory system, this observer would be endlessly bombarded with memories of different acquaintances whose appearances are sufficiently similar to be activated by the approaching woman. Even as the woman is recognized as a specific individual, these memories of other possible acquaintances would presumably continue to be excited both by aspects of the woman's appearance, and by the return of activation previously passed along to other associated memories. However, inhibitory mechanisms allow for the suppression of these irrelevant memories as soon as the woman is correctly identified, so that excitation can proceed instead to the attributes associated with this one person.

One implication of the notion of lateral inhibition is that retrieval of any form of representation is most likely to diminish retrieval of other alternate concepts of that same form. Thus, for example, interpretation of a behavior in terms of one trait dimension seems to reduce recognition of alternative trait implications (Carlston, 1980a; see also Higgins, Rholes, & Jones, 1977; Smith, 1989); interpreting an ambiguous picture in one way interferes with alternate perceptions (Leeper, 1935); categorizing a person in one way makes alternative categorizations less likely (Zarate & Smith, 1990); and so on. Inhibition seems to spread primarily to morphically similar, alternative associates to the seminal stimulus. Therefore, for example, retrieving a prior categorization of an individual is more likely to inhibit retrieval of other categorizations than retrieval of previously observed behaviors, inferred traits, or other non-categorical representations.

A final nuance is that retrieval is probably directed by some kind of executive system (e.g., Hastie & Carlston, 1980), possibly consisting of processing goals and procedures (e.g., Wyer & Srull, 1989), combined with mechanisms allowing for the directed spread of excitation and inhibition (e.g., Rumelhart & McClelland, 1986). Substantial directedness may be introduced into retrieval simply by the duration with which material is held in working memory, since such activated constructs determine the nodes from which excitation subsequently emanates. Possibly additional direction can be attained by strategically or randomly activating different memory contexts, like tossing a handful of stones into a particular section of the pond, to see what will emerge. For example, in trying to recall something about former Vice-President Spiro Agnew, I might resort to sampling political concepts associated with that general era (Nixon, Watergate, Vietnam), hoping that the resultant excitation will converge on some piece of information that I will recognize as relevant to my processing goal.

Memory and Judgment

When people need to retrieve information about a target individual, they do so by accessing the network of associations relating to that individual. As detailed in the previous section, excitation spreads through this network from the activated person node to associated concepts in a process that continues until the perceiver retrieves information satisfying the task at hand. In responding to a trait inquiry, for example, a perceiver may search memory until able to retrieve either a prior trait inference or another form of representation that can be translated into a trait inference (Carlston, 1980b; Lingle & Ostrom, 1979).

Ebbesen and Allen (1979) suggested that in making trait inferences, people ordinarily search for relevant trait representations first, before retrieving and evaluating potentially relevant observational memories. The associated systems approach suggests that reliance on these different forms of representation should generally depend on associative strengths and levels of activation, as well as on relevance. Therefore, when non-trait representations are more closely associated with a target individual, or are already highly accessible, they should be used in preference to trait representations, even though the traits are more directly relevant (Carlston & Skowronski, 1986, 1988).

The Judgment Process.   When the information retrieved by a perceiver fails to precisely match the form of representation required, the retrieved information must somehow be elaborated. As discussed earlier, such elaboration can often be achieved through reference to generic inter-representational associations stored in conceptual social memory. Carlston and Skowronski (1988, see also 1986) suggested that this process involves the importation of associations between generic representations into the impression structure for a specific individual. For example, if Dave was known to have stolen money, the conceptual link between *stealing things* and *dishonesty* could be used to generate an indirect association between Dave and dishonesty. The judgment of Dave's honesty would then involve the spread of excitation through this elaborated structure until the existence of the association can be verified.

Judgment can thus involve essentially the same mechanisms as retrieval. In both, excitation spreads through the associative structure until information is encountered that satisfies task demands. Moreover, in both processes the structure involved is an elaborated one that involves both representations of a specific person and associations imported from conceptual social memory. If the information retrieved was already directly associated with the actor, the retrieval would be characterized as a *memory*, whereas if this direct association did not previously exist, the retrieval would be characterized as an *inference*.

Other inference processes are also described in the literature, involving consciously applied heuristics, attribution, or integration rules (Hastie & Carlston, 1980; for a broader review see Sherman & Corty, 1984). Many of these processes appear to take some time and effort, and may occur after an initial associative inference (or "valuation process"; N. H. Anderson, 1974) has already occurred (cf. Gilbert, Pelham, & Krull, 1988). Consequently, such processes may be less likely (and associative retrieval may play an even larger role) when people lack the time or motivation to engage in such effortful, secondary inference processes. Moreover, these other forms of inference-making may evolve toward a simple associationistic retrieval process as the steps involved become proceduralized through repetition. That is, after a rule has been applied repeatedly, its constituent steps should become more automatic, so that they progress quickly and outside of conscious awareness, as though the instigating stimulus were directly associated with the product inference.

Memory Reconstruction and Bias. The retrieval of information about a person involves activation of a network of representations, some of which are observational, but some of which are affective or inferential. Any or all of these associated representations can provide information pertinent to the task at hand. For example, research suggests that memories for specific events can be shaped by salient appearance (Miller, 1988), category (Sagar & Schofield, 1980), trait (Hastie & Kumar, 1979), affect (Laird, Wagener, Halal, & Szegda, 1982), evaluation (Hartwick, 1979), and orientation (Harvey, Yarkin, Lightner, & Town, 1980) information. This "contamination" between different representations might be viewed as the inevitable product of a system that "reconstructs" memories from all available information (see, for example, Loftus & Palmer, 1974).

On the other hand, critics (e.g., Alba & Hasher, 1983) have suggested that memory for events is often quite accurate, and that reconstructive biases may be the exception, rather than the rule. A key consideration might be the availability of special features that distinguish different kinds of representations (Johnson, Raye, Foley, & Foley, 1981). Representations that share morphological features should be more difficult to distinguish, and therefore more likely to foster reconstructive distortions.

For example, behavioral observations, appearance, and categorizations are all imbued with imagery, which should increase their confusability. Consistent with this logic, Katz, Silvern, and Coulter (1990) recently found that people's recognition of the appearance of stereotypic figures was affected by both attributed behaviors and by gender categorization. Confusion of closely related forms of representation might also contribute to other social psychological phenomena: for example, people's inability to recognize the appearance of members of other racial categories (Malpass & Kravitz, 1969), or to distinguish the observed behaviors of others from their own contributions to a project (Thompson & Kelley, 1981).

Even more distantly related forms of representation may be confused or combined when people lack motivation to make distinctions. For example, in relating behavioral anecdotes to friends, there may be no reason to sort out episodic detail from trait inferences, evaluations, and other accessible associations. It may only be in certain kinds of formal memory or judgment tasks that people are called on to discriminate one form of representation from another.

Affect and Behavior

Like memory and judgment, the recognition of people, generation of emotional responses, and production of behavioral acts are also retrieval-based tasks (though the retrievals may be less intentional or conscious than for memory or judgment). One strength of the associated systems model is that all of these activities are viewed as products of the same basic retrieval mechanisms, operating on the same representational structure. This makes explicit some of the relationships between cognition and behavior that are uncertain in many other models of social cognition (see Landman & Manis, 1983).

Although they are products of the same representational structure, memory, judgment, emotion, and behavior are hypothesized to differ in the forms of representation on which they most depend. Verbal judgment tasks should depend primarily on verbal information, recognition should depend primarily on appearance information, emotion should depend primarily on affective information, and action should depend primarily on response information. In other words, each primary system should draw primarily on its correspondent form of representation.[14]

In addition, closely related forms of representation may tend to play a special role. For example, actions toward a target person should tend to be influenced by representations of the target's behavior and of the actor's orientation toward the target. Similarly, affective responses should tend to be influenced both by orientation toward, and evaluations of, the target person. Other forms of representation may influence each activity as well, if they are either strongly associated with the target or already in a state of activation. In other words, the influence of each form of representation should be determinable by the same sorts of structural considerations that determine information retrieval in memory and judgment tasks.

---

[14]Moreover, each form of representation should primarily reflect past operations of that same system.

Response Editing

Activation of a representation does not automatically produce an overt response. The perceiver must still decide whether to express or enact the retrieved representation, or whether instead to alter or suppress it. This *editing* (Holyoak & Gordon, 1984; Tourangeau & Rasinski, 1988) is a secondary process that constrains output so that it does not simply reflect the accessibility of representations.

Editing processes are often hypothesized to involve self-presentational concerns, including, for example, a reluctance to report negative thoughts and feelings about others, events that reflect badly on oneself, or judgments that may be too extreme. In the same vein, people may modify their actions in response to social norms or other strategic considerations. Additionally, people may edit accessed material that is viewed as irrelevant or non-responsive to current task demands.

Editing requires cognitive capacity, and is not always entirely successful, particularly when the associations underlying the response are well-learned and automatic, and the perceiver is less than vigilant in monitoring the system. In such cases, the associations composing the impression structure may completely dictate a person's response. But to the extent that a person is actively engaged in responding, the relationship between memory structure and output may be indirect and imperfect. The existence of editing processes can therefore complicate the task of assessing representational structure.

SOME IMPLICATIONS OF THE ASSOCIATED SYSTEMS THEORY

The formulation described here has implications for research on a variety of issues, including impression formation, attitudes, and personal relationships. Exhaustive treatment of these issues is beyond the scope of this chapter. However, speculations about a few will serve to highlight features of the model not yet discussed.

Individual Differences

People may differ in the extent to which they characteristically rely on different forms of representation. For example, some people may tend to emphasize verbal forms of representation, some may emphasize visual forms, some affective, and some action (see Anshel & Ortiz, 1986). These emphases could involve either a greater likelihood that representations of this type will be generated in response to stimulus situations, or a greater likelihood that such representations will be retrieved and utilized when generating later responses. Rough estimates of people's tendencies to generate or utilize different representations might be provided by existing individual difference measures. Examples include measures related to visual imagery (the Vividness of Visual Imagery Questionnaire; Marks, 1973, 1989), verbal cognition (the Need for Cognition scale; Cacioppo & Petty, 1982), behavioral responses (the Private Self-Consciousness scale; Fenigstein, Scheier, & Buss, 1975) and affective intensity (Larsen & Diener, 1987), sensitivity (Katkin, 1985) or style (Ehrlich & Lipsey, 1969).

However, all of these are essentially self-report measures, and people may be rather poor at estimating their own reliance on different forms of representation (see, e.g., Nisbett & Wilson, 1977; Wilson & Nisbett, 1978; but see also Katkin, 1985; Smith & Miller, 1978). It may therefore be preferable to develop representational preference indexes based on more direct evidence. One possibility is to assess the frequency with which people use different representational forms in open-ended descriptions (see, for example, Fiske & Ruscher, 1989; McGuire & Padawer-Singer, 1976).[15] Perhaps such measures would allow people's impressional styles to be classified as primarily *observational* (emphasizing visual representations), *categorical* (emphasizing categorizations), *analytic* (emphasizing trait representations), *judgmental* (emphasizing evaluations), *emotional* (emphasizing affect), or *reactive* (emphasizing behavioral responses).

Alternatively, individual differences may tend to be more global, reflecting, for example, preferences for abstract versus concrete representations, or self-referent (affective/behavioral) versus external sources of information. Examples of the latter difference may be found in Snyder's work on self-monitoring (e.g., Snyder, 1987), Laird's work on emotional experience (e.g., Laird & Bresler, 1990), and work on self-consciousness (e.g., Fenigstein et al., 1975). Another possibility is that people differ less in the particular forms of representation they use than in the extent to which they retrieve and utilize more than one form of representation. Such *representational complexity* might be related to measures of cognitive complexity (Crockett, 1965) or self-complexity (Linville, 1987).

Although the possibility of individual differences in representational preference is intriguing, and supported by some data (Anshel & Ortiz, 1986), it ought not to be overstated. In general, the associated systems model suggests that impressions will be multi-modal, reflecting the combined operations of several different representational systems. Moreover, the forms of representation that tend to be emphasized should depend largely on situational factors discussed previously, such as stimulus exposure, nature of involvement, task demands,

---

[15]However, for reasons discussed in a later section, such measures may be suspect, and more novel methods may be necessary.

and so on. Individual difference factors may therefore have limited room to operate.

Priming of Representational Systems

Specific informational content can be primed so it is more accessible and more likely to influence inference processes (e.g., Higgins & King, 1981; Sedikides & Skowronski, 1991). The present analysis suggests the possibility that entire representational systems might be similarly primed, increasing the likelihood that available information in that form will be generated or retrieved during information processing. Thus, for example, if an individual is primed with emotional material this may serve to increase the accessibility of affective responses toward people subsequently encountered or thought about. Similarly, if an individual has been thinking about people in general, this may serve to make verbal concepts related to any single individual more accessible. Or, if an individual has been reminiscing about old times, this may serve to prime observational memories regarding others. The individual differences discussed in the preceding section might thus be construed as chronically heightened states of activation for entire systems of representation.

This form of generalized *priming* must be distinguished from the priming of specific material regarding a particular individual. Elsewhere in this chapter it has already been suggested that: (a) different kinds of involvement tend to engage different processing systems (see Fig. 11.2), influencing the kinds of representations that are generated or retrieved, and (b) the recent activation of any information about a person will increase the subsequent accessibility of that material. The possibility discussed here is that the priming of a system using material unrelated to a particular individual may increase the accessibility of similarly represented material about that individual.

While this notion of priming entire representational systems is intriguing, it may also be unrealistic. Most evidence on priming suggests that the effects are limited to closely associated content. For example, verbal primes influence responding only for semantically related material, not for unrelated material that happens to also be verbal (Higgins, Rholes, & Jones, 1977). Additionally, an argument can be made that the activation of a representational system for one purpose might actually interfere with the utilization of that same system for other purposes. For example, although physical movements ordinarily aid in the memorization of action phrases, this benefit is lost when subjects also engage in distracting uses of the action system (Englekamp, 1991). It may be that each representational system has capacity limitations that preclude simultaneous activation of too many unrelated representations. Along these lines, it would be interesting to see if one could experimentally disrupt subjects' reliance on appearance representations by having them make judgments of one person while viewing slides of another, or inhibit their utilization of affective information by simultaneously subjecting them to a physiologically arousing task (as in Zillman, Katcher, & Milavsky, 1972).

Measurement Issues

It is tempting to assess the accessibility of different representational forms using free association (e.g., McGuire & McGuire, in press), open-ended description (Fiske & Cox, 1979), or person-comparison tasks (Kelly, 1955). Using any of the available taxonomies, researchers might assess the availability of different representations under different conditions (e.g., Park, 1986; Peevers & Secord, 1973). However, such procedures may not be suitable for distinguishing among representational forms (cf. Carlston, in press) unless care is taken to reduce editing processes.

Potential problems include the possibility that people will interpret the descriptive task as calling for one or another kind of information, which they may then obligingly generate from their actual representations (Feldman & Lynch, 1988; Tourangeau & Rasinski, 1988). Other forms of distortion may be introduced by contamination among different representational forms. For example, observational descriptions may be colored by previous trait inferences (Carlston, 1980a), and reports of affective responses may be biased by other available forms of representation (Schwarz, Strack, Kommer, & Wagner, 1987). Additional problems are introduced by researchers' over-reliance on verbal stimuli and questionnaires, and their under-emphasis of behaviorally and affectively engaging situations (Holyoak & Gordon, 1984; Ostrom, 1984). As a consequence, the representations revealed in subjects' written responses are more likely to reflect the upper than the lower rows of Fig. 11.1. To capture the complexity of people's representations, it may be necessary to devise paradigms and materials that more fully engage behavioral and affective, as well as cognitive, systems.

Inter-Representational Consistency

The different representations making up a perceiver's impression of another person may have similar or dissimilar implications for judgments or activities. In considering factors that influence congruence between different representational forms, it is useful to distinguish between two cases. First, when one form of representation is generated on the basis of another, the two will ordinarily be congruent. This is true, for example, when trait inference processes are based on recalled behaviors (Hastie & Park, 1986), and when behavioral responses (e.g., voting for a candidate) are based on salient evaluations (cf. Fazio & Williams, 1986).

Second, when two forms of representation already exist in memory, their congruence will depend on various historical factors. One such factor is the amount of experience the perceiver has had with the target, which relates to the frequency with which different representations are likely to have been retrieved and associated in the past. Such experience can increase congruence (Fazio et al., 1982; Fazio, Powell, & Herr, 1983), especially when congruent representations existed in the first place. This is often the case, for example, when people freely interact, so that their behavioral, affective and cognitive representations are in harmony. On the other hand, when divergent representations exist, increased experience might lead to diminished congruence. This would logically occur when the perceiver's activities selectively activate or strengthen one form of representation, without requiring reconciliation with other forms. Examples would be impression formation processes among subjects exposed to incongruent stimuli (Hastie & Kumar, 1979), and biased rumination among subjects trying to rationalize their attitudes (e.g., Wilson, Dunn, Bybee, Hyman, & Rotondo, 1984).

The implications of congruence or incongruence in different forms of representation are unclear. Logically, incongruent representations might lead to greater response uncertainty or inconsistency. Moreover, a case could be made that either consistency or inconsistency would lead to response polarization, the latter having been demonstrated in the attitude realm (Katz & Hass, 1988). It is likely that the precise effects of both consistency and inconsistency will depend on the particular kinds of representations involved, the nature of associations among them, and the kind of response being made (e.g., verbal, behavioral, or affective).

Rumination

The effects of thought, or *rumination*, on representational structures has been given considerable attention recently (Millar & Tesser, 1986, 1989; Tesser & Leone, 1977; Uleman & Bargh, 1989). From the current point of view, the primary effects of rumination should be the selective strengthening of associations between representations that are simultaneously generated or activated in the process, and the strengthening of representational features that are central to the representations activated.

Strengthening of Associations. Rumination should strengthen the association between a person concept and those representations that are retrieved and rehearsed in the process. The particular forms of representation that benefit from ruminative strengthening are likely to vary depending on such factors as: (a) individual preferences for various kinds of rumination, and (b) situational influences that favor particular kinds of rumination. Because individual differences have already been discussed, this section emphasizes situational influences.

Different kinds of mental tasks should favor ruminations involving different representational forms. For example, anticipated communication (Cohen, 1961) or rational analysis (Wilson et al., 1984) should precipitate verbal thought, which will tend to involve traits, categorizations, and evaluations. Anticipated interaction (Devine, Sedikides, & Fuhrman, 1989) or behavior prediction (e.g., Griffin, Dunning, & Ross, 1990) should focus attention more on behaviorally related representations, including observation, responses, and orientations. Casual daydreaming might implicate visual forms of representation, including appearance, categorization, and observations. And romantic reflection or obsessional hatred should activate affectively related representations, such as affect, evaluations, and orientations. The effect of such ruminations, in each case, should be to strengthen the association between the person concept and the particular representations involved, increasing the likelihood that activation of the person node will lead to activation of that representation in the future. When rumination involves several different forms of representation at once (e.g., thinking about behaviors that hurt our feelings), the effect should be to reinforce the pathways between the different representations retrieved, as well as between those representations and the person concept.

Strengthening of Features.   Rumination rarely results in the exhaustive retrieval of a representation, with all its associated features. When we visualize people, we see a generic or idealized image that omits many relevant features (Kosslyn, 1981). When we retrieve a behavioral episode, we seemingly recall only the most salient features of the act or context. Even recalled affect presumably omits some of the specific somatic features involved in the initial affective response. In fact, casual rumination may often involve a kind of mental base-touching, by which we "check in" with representations just long enough to derive needed meaning. For just an instant we become vaguely aware of a person's appearance, or some situation we observed them in, or our feelings toward them. This fleeting awareness presumably involves activation of the most accessible features of the most accessible representations. Its consequence may be that representations ultimately degrade into their most prominent characteristics.

An introspection will illustrate. I had a teacher in seventh grade who used to throw erasers at students to get their attention. When I think of this teacher, I briefly get a mental image of such an episode, which at this point encapsules my entire impression of him. The image includes the classroom, which by now is pretty generic, except that my location within it remains clear, along with the location of the door and the blackboard. I can't identify the target of the erasers (could it have been me?) or the teacher's features, though I know he was male. The observational memory has been retained, possibly because it so well summarizes my impression of this teacher that I touched base with it whenever I thought of him. However, this representation is now just a caricature of what it must once have been.

Mental base-touching presumably increases the likelihood that a particular representation will be retrieved in the future. It is unclear whether it also introduces more distortion or degradation than would otherwise occur. For example, suppose that two people observe someone rob a bank, and that one (who comes forward as a witness) retrieves an image of the robber's appearance regularly over the ensuing months, whereas the other does so less often. Presumably the witness will be more likely to recognize the bank robber in the future than the other person, due to rehearsal of the mental image. But is the witness also more likely to misidentify people who look somewhat similar to the robber, due to selective enhancement of the robber's most salient features? Suggestive evidence is provided by Schooler and Engstler-Schooler (1990), who found that verbalizing an appearance description can impair subsequent recognition of the described face.

CONCLUSIONS

Multi-modal models of cognitive processes are becoming more common. Researchers are beginning to compare and consider the contributions of sensory, verbal, motor, and affect processes on learning and memory (e.g., Davis & Hathaway, 1986; Noller, 1985). Multi-modalism is also evident in recent models of cognitive function, which propose that the mind is divided into a wide variety of processors or modules, each of which performs a very specific function (e.g., Fodor, 1983; Garfield, 1987; Gazzaniga, 1985; Marshall, 1984). Damasio's (1989b) neurological model of representation posits a multi-modal architecture in which "memories" for object and event features are "recorded in the same neural ensembles in which they occur during perception" (p. 129). Integrated memories for such entities are achieved through the simultaneous activation of multiple primary sites by *convergence zones* at varying levels, including anterior association cortices responsible for more complex events.

Although the constructs involved in my associated systems model are somewhat more molar, an analogous system is postulated. Impressions are distributed memories which retain the character of the different mental structures in which their features were first represented. Low-level convergence zones provide additional ("hybrid") representational forms, which possess attributes similar to those of the primary sites that they integrate. Higher-level convergence zones are responsible for the retrieval and integration of different representational forms during judgment and behavior processes.

Multi-modalism is also becoming prominent in the social cognition literature. Medin's (1988) commentary on Brewer's (1988) multi-modal model reflects this view:

> Another strong point of Brewer's model is that she entertains the ideas that there are multiple types of representation at different stages of processing and at different levels of abstraction. It may not matter so much whether or not her conjectures

are correct as it does that they serve to help free one from the normal default assumption that there is basically a single type of processing yielding a single form of representation. The idea of multiple representation and processing types appears to be gaining currency in the area of social cognition, and I do not mean to imply that Brewer should be given exclusive credit for the general idea. The idea of multiple representation and processing types does stand in contrast to most of the research on the categorization of natural objects which assumes (incorrectly I think) that people are relentlessly doing the same thing (e.g., abstracting prototypes) more or less all the time. (pp. 120–121)

The associated systems model attempts an even more ambitious integration, combining a variety of different representational forms within a single associative structure. Admittedly, it reflects many conjectures that may ultimately prove incorrect. In the meantime, it is offered as a potentially useful perspective on the many different ways that people perceive, consider, and remember each other.

ACKNOWLEDGMENTS

The author expresses his appreciation to Leslie Clark, Reid Hastie, Mark McDaniel, John Skowronski, Eliot Smith, Cheri Sparks, Robert S. Wyer, Jr., and the editors of this volume for their helpful comments regarding associated systems theory, this chapter, or both.

REFERENCES

Abelson, R. P. (1976). Script processing in attitude formation and decision-making. In J. S. Carroll & J. W. Payne (Eds.), *Cognition and social behavior* (pp. 33–46). Hillsdale, NJ: Lawrence Erlbaum Associates.

Abelson, R. P. (1981). The psychological status of the script concept. *American Psychologist, 36,* 715–729.

Alba, J. W., & Hasher, L. (1983). Is memory schematic? *Psychological Bulletin, 93,* 203–231.

Andersen, S. M., & Klatzky, R. L. (1987). Traits and social stereotypes: Levels of categorization in person perception. *Journal of Personality and Social Psychology, 53,* 235–246.

Anderson, J. R. (1978). Arguments concerning representations for mental imagery. *Psychological Review, 85,* 249–277.

Anderson, J. R. (1982). Acquisition of cognitive skill. *Psychological Review, 89,* 369–406.

Anderson, J. R., & Bower, G. H. (1979). *Human associative memory.* Hillsdale, NJ: Lawrence Erlbaum Associates. (Originally published 1973)

Anderson, N. H. (1974). Information integration theory: A brief survey. In D. H. Krantz, R. C. Atkinson, R. D. Luce, & P. Suppes (Eds.), *Contemporary developments in mathematical psychology* (Vol. 2, pp. 236–305). San Francisco: Freeman.

Anderson, N. H. (1988). A functional approach to person cognition. In T. K. Srull & R. S. Wyer, Jr. (Eds.), *Advances in social cognition: A dual process model of impression formation* (Vol. 1, pp. 37–51). Hillsdale, NJ: Lawrence Erlbaum Associates.

Anshel, M. H., & Ortiz, M. (1986). Effect of coding strategies on movement extent as a function of cognitive style. *Perceptual and Motor Skills, 63,* 1311–1317.

Ashmore, R. D., & Del Boca, F. K. (1979). Sex stereotypes and implicit personality theory: Toward a cognitive-social psychological conceptualization. *Sex Roles, 5,* 219–248.

Ashmore, R. D., Del Boca, F. K., & Titus, D. (1984, August). *Types of women and men: Yours, mine, and ours.* Paper presented at the annual meeting of the American Psychological Association, Toronto.

Baldwin, M. W., Carrell, S. E., & Lopez, D. F. (1990). My advisor and the Pope are watching me from the back of my mind. *Journal of Experimental Social Psychology, 26,* 435–454.

Bargh, J. A. (1984). Automatic and conscious processing of social information. In R. S. Wyer & T. K. Srull (Eds.), *Handbook of social cognition* (Vol. 3, pp. 1–43). Hillsdale, NJ: Lawrence Erlbaum Associates.

Bargh, J. A., & Thein, R. D. (1985). Individual construct accessibility, person memory, and the recall-judgment link: The case of information overload. *Journal of Personality and Social Psychology, 49,* 1129–1146.

Bassili, J. N. (1989). Traits as action categories versus traits as person attributes in social cognition. In J. N. Bassili (Ed.), *On-line cognition in person perception* (pp. 61–89). Hillsdale, NJ: Lawrence Erlbaum Associates.

Beach, L., & Wertheimer, M. (1961). A free-response approach to the study of person cognition. *Journal of Abnormal and Social Psychology, 62,* 367–374.

Bem, D. J. (1967). Self-perception: An alternative interpretation of cognitive dissonance phenomena. *Psychological Review, 74,* 183–200.

Bem, S. L. (1981). Gender schema theory: A cognitive account of sex typing. *Psychological Review, 88,* 354–364.

Bower, G. H. (1981). Mood and memory. *American Psychologist, 36,* 129–148.

Bower, G. H., Monteiro, K. P., & Gilligan, S. G. (1978). Emotional mood as a context for learning and recall. *Journal of Verbal Learning and Verbal Behavior, 17,* 573–585.

Breckler, S. J. (1984). Empirical validation of affect, behavior, and cognition as distinct components of attitude. *Journal of Personality and Social Psychology, 47,* 1191–1205.

Breckler, S. J., & Wiggins, E. C. (1989). Affect versus evaluation in the structure of attitudes. *Journal of Experimental Social Psychology, 25,* 253–271.

Brewer, M. (1988). A dual process model of impression formation. In T. K. Srull & R. S. Wyer (Eds.), *Advances in social cognition: A dual process model of impression formation* (Vol. 1, pp. 1–36). Hillsdale, NJ: Lawrence Erlbaum Associates.

Bromley, D. B. (1977). *Personality description in ordinary language.* London: Wiley.

Bruner, J. S., Shapiro, D., & Tagiuri, R. (1958). The meaning of traits in isolation and in combination. In R. Tagiuri & L. Petrullo (Eds.), *Person perception and interpersonal behavior* (pp. 277–288). Stanford: Stanford University Press.

Byrne, D. (1971). *The attraction paradigm.* New York: Academic Press.

Cacioppo, J. T., & Petty, R. E. (1982). The need for cognition. *Journal of Personality and Social Psychology, 42*(1), 116–131.

Cantor, N., & Mischel, W. (1977). Traits as prototypes: Effects on recognition memory. *Journal of Personality and Social Psychology, 35,* 38–48.

Carlston, D. E. (1980a). Events, inferences and impression formation. In R. Hastie, T. Ostrom, E. Ebbesen, R. Wyer, D. Hamilton, & D. Carlston (Eds.), *Person memory: The cognitive basis of social perception* (pp. 89–119). Hillsdale, NJ: Lawrence Erlbaum Associates.

Carlston, D. E. (1980b). The recall and use of traits and events in social inference processes. *Journal of Experimental Social Psychology, 16,* 303–328.

Carlston, D. E. (1991). Free association and the representation of complex cognitive structures. In T. K. Srull & R. S. Wyer, Jr. (Eds.), *Advances in social cognition* (Vol. 4, pp. 87–96). Hillsdale, NJ: Lawrence Erlbaum Associates.

Carlston, D. E., & Skowronski, J. J. (1986). Trait memory and behavior memory: The effects of alternative pathways on impression judgment response times. *Journal of Personality and Social Psychology, 50,* 5–13.

Carlston, D. E., & Skowronski, J. J. (1988). *Trait memory and behavior memory II: The effects of conceptual social knowledge on impression judgment response times.* Unpublished manuscript, University of Iowa, Iowa City.

Carlston, D. E., & Sparks, C. (1991). *A theory-based taxonomy for classifying person descriptors.* Unpublished manuscript, Purdue University, West Lafayette, IN.

Clark, M. S., & Isen, A. M. (1982). Toward understanding the relationship between feeling states and social behavior. In A. Hastorf & A. Isen (Eds.), *Cognitive social psychology* (pp. 73–108). New York: Elsevier North-Holland.

Clore, G. L., & Parrott, W. G. (in press). Moods and their vicissitudes: Thoughts and feelings as information. In J. Forgas (Ed.), *Emotion and social judgment.* Oxford: Pergamon Press.

Cohen, A. R. (1961). Cognitive tuning as a factor affecting impression formation. *Journal of Personality, 29,* 235–245.

Conway, M. A. (1990). Associations between autobiographical memories and concepts. *Journal of Experimental Psychology: Learning, Memory, and Cognition, 16,* 799–812.

Cook, S. W. (1978). Interpersonal and attitudinal outcomes in cooperating interracial groups. *Journal of Research and Development in Education, 12,* 97–113.

Cotton, J. L. (1985). Cognitive dissonance in selective exposure. In D. Zillmann & J. Bryant (Eds.), *Selective exposure to communication* (pp. 11–33). Hillsdale, NJ: Lawrence Erlbaum Associates.

Crockett, W. H. (1965). Cognitive complexity and impression formation. In B. A. Maher (Ed.), *Progress in experimental personality research* (Vol. 2, pp. 47–90). New York: Academic Press.

Damasio, A. R. (1989a). The brain binds entities and events by multiregional activation from convergence zones. *Neural Computation, 1,* 123–132.

Damasio, A. R. (1989b). Time-locked multiregional retroactivation: A systems-level proposal for the neural substrates of recall and recognition. *Cognition, 33,* 25–62.

Davis, A. J., & Hathaway, B. K. (1986). The effects of visual, verbal, and motor elaborations on preschool children's recall and comprehension of prose. *Reading Psychology, 7,* 231–248.

DePaulo, B. M., Rosenthal, R., Green, C. R., and Rosenkrantz, J. (1982). Diagnosing deceptive and mixed messages from verbal and nonverbal cues. *Journal of Experimental Social Psychology, 18,* 433–446.

Devine, P. G. (1989). Stereotypes and prejudice: Their automatic and controlled components. *Journal of Personality and Social Psychology, 56,* 5–18.

Devine, P. G., Sedikides, C., & Fuhrman, R. W. (1989). Goals in social information processing: The case of anticipated interaction. *Journal of Personality and Social Psychology, 56,* 680–690.

Dion, K. K., Berscheid, E., & Walster, E. (1972). What is beautiful is good. *Journal of Personality and Social Psychology, 24,* 285–290.

Dornbusch, S. M., Hastorf, A. H., Richardson, S. A., Muzzy, R. E., & Vreeland, R. S. (1965). The Perceiver and the perceived: Their relative influence on the categories of interpersonal cognition. *Journal of Personality and Social Psychology, 1,* 434–440.

Dovidio, J. F., Evans, N. E., & Tyler, R. B. (1986). Racial stereotypes: The contents of their cognitive representations. *Journal of Experimental Social Psychology, 22,* 22–37.

Ebbesen, E. B., & Allen, R. B. (1979). Cognitive processes in implicit personality trait inferences. *Journal of Personality and Social Psychology, 37,* 471–488.

Ehrlich, H. J., & Lipsey, C. (1969). Affective style as a variable in person perception. *Journal of Personality, 37,* 522–540.

Englekamp, J. (1991). Memory of action events: Some implications for memory theory and for imagery. In. C. Cornoldi & M. A. McDaniel (Eds.), *Imagery and cognition* (pp. 183–219). New York: Springer-Verlag.

Erber, R. (in press). Affective and semantic priming: Effects of mood on category accessibility and inference. *Journal of Experimental Social Psychology.*

Fazio, R. H. (1986). How do attitudes guide behavior? In R. M. Sorrentino & E. T. Higgins (Eds.), *The handbook of motivation and cognition: Foundations of social behavior* (pp. 204–243). New York: Guilford Press.

Fazio, R. H. (1989). On the power and functionality of attitudes: The role of attitude accessibility. In A. R. Pratkanis, S. J. Breckler, & A. G. Greenwald (Eds.), *Attitude structure and function* (pp. 153–179). Hillsdale, NJ: Lawrence Erlbaum Associates.

Fazio, R. H., Chen, J., McDonel, E. C., & Sherman, S. J. (1982). Attitude accessibility, attitude-behavior consistency, and the strength of the object-evaluation association. *Journal of Experimental Social Psychology, 18*, 339–357.

Fazio, R. H., Powell, M. C., & Herr, P. M. (1983). Toward a process model of the attitude-behavior relation: Accessing one's attitude upon more observation of the attitude object. *Journal of Personality and Social Psychology, 44*, 723–735.

Fazio, R. H., & Williams, C. J. (1986). Attitude accessibility as a moderator of the attitude-perception and attitude-behavior relations: An investigation of the 1984 Presidential election. *Journal of Personality and Social Psychology, 51*, 505–514.

Feldman, J. M., & Lynch, J. G. (1988). Self-generated validity and other effects of measurement on belief, attitude, intention and behavior. *Journal of Applied Psychology, 73*, 421–435.

Fenigstein, A., Scheier, M. F., & Buss, A. H. (1975). Public and private self-consciousness: Assessment and theory. *Journal of Consulting and Clinical Psychology, 43*, 522–527.

Fiske, A. P. (1991). *Structures of social life: The four elementary forms of human relations*. New York: The Free Press.

Fiske, A. P., Haslam, N., & Fiske, S. T. (1991). Confusing one person with another: What errors reveal about the elementary forms of social relations. *Journal of Personality and Social Psychology, 60*, 656–674.

Fiske, S. T. (1989). Examining the role of intent: Toward understanding its role in stereotyping and prejudice. In J. S. Uleman & J. A. Bargh (Eds.), *Unintended thought* (pp. 253–286). New York: Guilford Press.

Fiske, S. T., & Cox, M. G. (1979). Person concepts: The effect of target familiarity and descriptive purpose on the process of describing others. *Journal of Personality, 47*, 136–161.

Fiske, S. T., & Neuberg, S. L. (1989). A continuum model of impression formation, from category-based to individuating processes: Influences of information and motivation on attention and interpretation. In M. P. Zanna (Ed.), *Advances in experimental social psychology* (Vol. 23, pp. 1–74). New York: Academic Press.

Fiske, S. T., & Pavelchak, M. A. (1986). Category-based vs. piecemeal-based affective responses: Developments in schema-triggered affect. In R. M. Sorrentino & E. T. Higgins (Eds.), *Handbook of motivation and cognition* (pp. 167–203). New York: Guilford Press.

Fiske, S. T., & Ruscher, J. B. (1989). On-line processes in category-based and individuating impressions: Some basic principles and methodological reflections. In J. N. Bassili (Ed.), *On-line cognition in person perception* (pp. 141–176). Hillsdale, NJ: Lawrence Erlbaum Associates.

Fiske, S. T., & Taylor, S. E. (1984). *Social cognition*. Reading, MA: Addison-Wesley.

Fodor, J. A. (1983). *The modularity of mind*. Cambridge, MA: MIT Press.

Forgas, J. P., & Bower, G. H. (1987). Mood effects of person-perception judgments. *Journal of Personality and Social Psychology, 53*, 53–60.

Frey, D. (1986). Recent research on selective exposure to information. *Advances in Experimental Social Psychology, 19*, 41–80.

Garfield, J. L. (1987). *Modularity in knowledge representation and natural-language understanding*. Cambridge, MA: MIT Press.

Gazzaniga, M. (1985). *The social brain*. New York: Basic Books.

Gilbert, D. T. & Hixon, J. G. (1991). The trouble of thinking: Activation and application of stereotypic beliefs. *Journal of Personality and Social Psychology, 60*, 509–517.

Gilbert, D. T., Pelham, B. W., & Krull, D. S. (1988). On cognitive busyness: When person perceivers meet persons perceived. *Journal of Personality and Social Psychology, 54*, 733–740.

Gilovich, T. (1987). Secondhand information and social judgment. *Journal of Experimental Social Psychology, 23,* 59–74.

Gordon, C. (1968). Self conceptions: Configurations of content. In C. Gordon & K. J. Gergen (Eds.), *The self in social interaction: Classic and contemporary perspectives* (Vol. 1, pp. 115–136). New York: Wiley.

Gouaux, C. (1971). Induced affective states and interpersonal attraction. *Journal of Personality and Social Psychology, 20,* 37–43.

Griffin, D. W., Dunning, D., & Ross, L. (1990). The role of construal processes in overconfident predictions about the self and others. *Journal of Personality and Social Psychology, 59,* 1128–1139.

Griffitt, W. (1970). Environmental effects on interpersonal affective behavior: Ambient effective temperature and attraction. *Journal of Personality and Social Psychology, 15,* 240–244.

Griffitt, W., & Veitch, R. (1971). Hot and crowded: Influences of population density and temperature on interpersonal affective behavior. *Journal of Personality and Social Psychology, 17,* 92–98.

Grossberg, S. (1988). Nonlinear neural networks: Principles, mechanisms, and architectures. *Neural Networks, 1,* 17–62.

Hartwick, J. (1979). Memory for trait information: A signal detection analysis. *Journal of Experimental Social Psychology, 15,* 533–552.

Harvey, J. H., Yarkin, K. L., Lightner, J. M., & Town, J. P. (1980). Unsolicited interpretation and recall of interpersonal events. *Journal of Personality and Social Psychology, 38,* 551–568.

Hastie, R., & Carlston, D. E. (1980). Theoretical issues in person memory. In R. Hastie, T. Ostrom, E. Ebbesen, R. Wyer, D. Hamilton, & D. Carlston (Eds.), *Person memory: The cognitive basis of social perception* (pp. 1–53). Hillsdale, NJ: Lawrence Erlbaum Associates.

Hastie, R., & Kumar, P. A. (1979). Person memory: Personality traits as organizing principles in memory for behaviors. *Journal of Personality and Social Psychology, 37,* 25–38.

Hastie, R., & Park, B. (1986). The relationship between memory and judgment depends on whether the judgment task is memory-based or on-line. *Psychological Review, 93,* 258–268.

Hastie, R., Park, B., & Weber, R. (1984). Social Memory. In R. S. Wyer, Jr. & T. K. Srull (Eds.), *Handbook of social cognition* (Vol. 2, pp. 151–212). Hillsdale, NJ: Lawrence Erlbaum Associates.

Haviland, S. E., & Clark, H. H. (1974). What's new? Acquiring new information as a process in comprehension. *Journal of Verbal Learning and Verbal Behavior, 13,* 512–521.

Herman, C. P., Zanna, M. P., & Higgins, E. T. (1986). *Physical appearance, stigma, and social behavior: The Ontario Symposium* (Vol. 3). Hillsdale, NJ: Lawrence Erlbaum Associates.

Higgins, E. T., Bargh, J. A., & Lombardi, W. (1985). The nature of priming effects on categorization. *Journal of Experimental Psychology: Learning, Memory, and Cognition, 11,* 59–69.

Higgins, E. T., & King, G. A. (1981). Accessibility of social constructs: Information processing consequences of individual and contextual variability. In N. Cantor & J. F. Kihlstrom (Eds.), *Personality, cognition, and social interaction* (pp. 69–122). Hillsdale, NJ: Lawrence Erlbaum Associates.

Higgins, E. T., & McCann, C. D. (1984). Social encoding and subsequent attitudes, impressions and memory: "Context-driven" and motivational aspects of processing. *Journal of Personality and Social Psychology, 47,* 26–39.

Higgins, E. T., Rholes, W. S., & Jones, C. R. (1977). Category accessibility and impression formation. *Journal of Experimental Social Psychology, 13,* 141–154.

Hoffman, H. S., & Ison, J. R. (1980). Reflex modification in the domain of startle: I. Some empirical findings and their implications for how the nervous system processes sensory input. *Psychological Review, 87,* 175–189.

Holyoak, K. J., & Gordon, P. C. (1984). Information processing and social cognition. In R. S. Wyer & T. K. Srull (Eds.), *Handbook of social cognition* (Vol. 1, pp. 39–70). Hillsdale, NJ: Lawrence Erlbaum Associates.

Isen, A. M. (1984). Affect, cognition, and social behavior. In R. S. Wyer & T. K. Srull (Eds.), *Handbook of social cognition* (Vol. 3, pp. 179–236). Hillsdale, NJ: Lawrence Erlbaum Associates.

Johnson, M. K., Raye, C. L., Foley, H. J., & Foley, M. A. (1981). Cognitive operations and decision bias in reality monitoring. *American Journal of Psychology, 94*, 37–64.

Jones, E. E., & Davis, K. E. (1965). From acts to dispositions: The attributional process in person perception. In L. Berkowitz (Ed.), *Advances in experimental social psychology* (Vol. 2, pp. 220–266). New York: Academic Press.

Katkin, E. S. (1985). Blood, sweat, and tears: Individual differences in autonomic self-perception. *Psychophysiology, 18*, 252–267.

Katz, D., & Stotland, E. (1959). A preliminary statement to a theory of attitude structure and change. In S. Koch (Ed.), *Psychology: A study of a science* (Vol. 3, pp. 423–475). New York: McGraw-Hill.

Katz, I., & Hass, R. G. (1988). Racial ambivalence and American value conflict: Correlational and priming studies of dual cognitive structures. *Journal of Personality and Social Psychology, 55*, 893–905.

Katz, P. A., Silvern, L., & Coulter, D. K. (1990). Gender processing and person perception. *Social Cognition, 8*, 186–202.

Kelly, G. A. (1955). *The psychology of personal constructs*. New York: Norton.

Kitayama, S., & Burnstein, E. (1988). Automaticity in conversations: A reexamination of the mindlessness hypothesis. *Journal of Personality and Social Psychology, 54*, 219–224.

Klatzky, R. L. (1984). Visual memory: Definitions and functions. In R. Wyer & T. Srull (Eds.), *Handbook of social cognition* (Vol. 2, pp. 233–270). Hillsdale, NJ: Lawrence Erlbaum Associates.

Klatzky, R. L., & Andersen, S. M. (1988). Category-specificity effects in social typing and personalization. In T. K. Srull & R. S. Wyer, Jr. (Eds.), *Advances in social cognition: A dual process model of impression formation* (Vol. 1, pp. 91–101). Hillsdale, NJ: Lawrence Erlbaum Associates.

Klatzky, R. L., Martin, G. L., & Kane, R. A. (1982). Semantic interpretation effects on memory for faces. *Memory and Cognition, 10*, 195–206.

Kosslyn, S. M. (1981). The medium and the message in mental imagery: A theory. *Psychological Review, 88*, 46–66.

Kosslyn, S. M., & Pomerantz, J. R. (1977). Imagery, propositions and the form of internal representations. *Cognitive Psychology, 9*, 52–76.

Laird, J. D., & Bresler, C. (1990). Centennial celebration of The Principles of Psychology. *Personality and Social Psychology Bulletin, 16*, 636–651.

Laird, J. D., Wagener, J. J., Halal, M., & Szegda, M. (1982). Remembering what you feel: The effects of emotion on memory. *Journal of Personality and Social Psychology, 42*, 646–657.

Landman, J., & Manis, M. (1983). Social cognition: Some historical and theoretical perspectives. In L. Berkowitz (Ed.), *Advances in experimental social psychology* (Vol. 16, pp. 40–125). Orlando, FL: Academic Press.

Langer, E., Blank, A., & Chanowitz, B. (1978). The mindlessness of ostensibly thoughtful action: The role of "placibic" information in interpersonal interaction. *Journal of Personality and Social Psychology, 36*, 635–642.

Larsen, R. J., & Diener, E. (1987). Affect intensity as an individual difference characteristic: A review. *Journal of Research in Personality, 21*, 1–39.

Lazarus, R. S. (1982). Thoughts on the relations between emotion and cognition. *American Psychologist, 37*, 1019–1024.

Leeper, R. W. (1935). A study of the neglected portion of the field of learning: The development of sensory organization. *Journal of Genetic Psychology, 46*, 41–75.

Lingle, J. H., Altom, M., & Medin, D. L. (1984). Of cabbages and kings: Assessing the extendability of natural object concept models to social things. In R. S. Wyer & T. K. Srull (Eds.), *Handbook of social cognition* (Vol. 1, pp. 71–117). Hillsdale, NJ: Lawrence Erlbaum Associates.

Lingle, J. H., & Ostrom, T. M. (1979). Retrieval selectivity in memory-based impression judgments. *Journal of Personality and Social Psychology, 37*, 180–194.

Linville, P. W. (1987). Self-complexity as a cognitive buffer against stress-related illness and depression. *Journal of Personality and Social Psychology, 52*, 663–676.

Livesley, W. J., & Bromley, D. B. (1973). *Person perception in childhood and adolescence*. London: Wiley.

Loftus, E. F., & Palmer, J. C. (1974). Reconstruction of automobile destruction: An example of the interaction between language and memory. *Journal of Verbal Learning and Verbal Behavior, 13*, 585–589.

Logan, G. D., & Klapp, S. T. (1991). Automatizing alphabet arithmetic: I. Is extended practice necessary to produce automaticity? *Journal of Experimental Psychology: Learning, Memory, and Cognition, 17*, 179–195.

Lord, C. G. (1980). Schemas and images as memory aids: Two modes of processing social information. *Journal of Personality and Social Psychology, 38*, 257–269.

Malpass, R. S., & Kravitz, J. (1969). Recognition for faces of own and other race. *Journal of Personality and Social Psychology, 13*, 330–334.

Marks, D. F. (1973). Imagery differences and eye movements in the recall of pictures. *Perception and Psychophysics, 14*, 407–412.

Marks, D. F. (1989). Bibliography of research utilizing the Vividness of Visual Imagery Questionnaire. *Perceptual and Motor Skills, 69*, 707–718.

Marshall, J. C. (1984). Multiple perspectives on modularity. *Cognition, 17*, 209–242.

Martindale, C. (1991). *Cognitive psychology: A neural-network approach*. Pacific Grove, CA: Brooks/Cole.

Maxwell, G. M., Cook, M. W., and Burr, R. (1985). The encoding and decoding of liking from behavioral cues in both auditory and visual channels. *Journal of Nonverbal Behavior, 9*, 239–263.

McArthur, L.Z. (1982). Judging a book by its cover: A cognitive analysis of the relationship between physical appearance and stereotyping. In A. Hastorf & A. Isen (Eds.), *Cognitive social psychology* (pp. 149–211). New York: Elsevier North Holland.

McClelland, J. L., & Rumelhart, E. E. (1985). Distributed memory and the representation of general and specific information. *Journal of Experimental Psychology: General, 114*, 159–188.

McGuire, W. J., & McGuire, C. V. (1991). The content, structure, and operation of thought systems. In T. K. Srull & R. S. Wyer, Jr. (Eds.), *Advances in social cognition: A dual process model of impression formation* (Vol. 4, pp. 1–78). Hillsdale, NJ: Lawrence Erlbaum Associates.

McGuire, W. J., & Padawer-Singer, A. (1976). Trait salience in the spontaneous self-concept. *Journal of Personality and Social Psychology, 33*, 743–754.

McKoon, G., Ratcliff, R., & Dell, G. S. (1986). Observations: A critical evaluation of the semantic-episodic distinction. *Journal of Experimental Psychology: Learning, Memory, and Cognition, 12*, 295–306.

Medin, D. L. (1988). Social categorization: Structures, processes, and purposes. In T. K. Srull & R. S. Wyer, Jr. (Eds.), *Advances in social cognition: A dual process model of impression formation* (Vol. 1, pp. 119–126). Hillsdale, NJ: Lawrence Erlbaum Associates.

Medin, D. L. (1989). Concepts and conceptual structure. *American Psychologist, 44*, 1469–1481.

Millar, M. G., & Tesser, A. (1986). Effects of affective and cognitive focus on the attitude-behavior relation. *Journal of Personality and Social Psychology, 51*, 270–276.

Millar, M. G. & Tesser, A. (1989). The effects of affective-cognitive consistency and thought on the attitude-behavior relation. *Journal of Experimental Social Psychology, 25*, 189–202.

Miller, A. (1970). Role of physical attractiveness in impression formation. *Psychonomic Science, 19*, 241–243.

Miller, C. T. (1988). Categorization and the physical attractiveness stereotype. *Social Cognition, 6*, 231–251.

Miller, L. C., & Read, S. J. (in press). On the coherence of mental models of persons and relationships: A knowledge structure approach. In G. J. O. Fletcher & F. Fincham (Eds.), *Cognition in close relationships*. Hillsdale, NJ: Lawrence Erlbaum Associates.

Nairne, J. S. (1990). A feature model of immediate memory. *Memory & Cognition, 18*, 251–269.

Neely, J. H. (1976). Semantic priming and retrieval from lexical memory: Evidence for facilitatory and inhibitory processes. *Memory and Cognition, 4*, 648–654.

Nisbett, R. E., & Wilson, T. D. (1977). Telling more than we can know: Verbal reports on mental processes. *Psychological Review, 84*, 231–259.

Noller, P. (1985). Video primacy: A further look. *Journal of Nonverbal Behavior, 9*, 28–47.

Norman, D. A. (1981). Categorization of action slips. *Psychological Review, 88*, 1–15.

Norman, D. A. (1985). Human information processing: the conventional view. In A. M. Aitkenhead & J. M. Slack (Eds.), *Issues in cognitive modeling* (pp. 309–336). Hillsdale, NJ: Lawrence Erlbaum Associates.

Ostrom, T. M. (1975, August). *Cognitive representation of impressions*. Paper presented at the meeting of the American Psychological Association, Chicago, IL.

Ostrom, T. M. (1984). The sovereignty of social cognition. In R. S. Wyer & T. K. Srull (Eds.), *Handbook of Social Cognition* (Vol. 1, pp. 1–38). Hillsdale, NJ: Lawrence Erlbaum Associates.

Ostrom, T. M. (1987). Bipolar survey items: An information processing perspective. In H. J. Hippler, N. Schwarz, & N. Sudman (Eds.), *Social information processing and survey methodology* (pp. 71–85). New York: Springer-Verlag.

Paivio, A. (1971). *Imagery and verbal processes*. New York: Holt, Rinehart & Winston.

Park, B. (1986). A method for studying the development of impressions of real people. *Journal of Personality and Social Psychology, 51*, 907–917.

Peevers, B. H., & Secord, P. F. (1973). Developmental changes in attribution of descriptive concepts to persons. *Journal of Personality and Social Psychology, 27*, 120–128.

Pylyshyn, Z. W. (1973). What the mind's eye tells the mind brain: a critique of mental imagery. *Psychological Bulletin, 80*, 1–24.

Pylyshyn, Z. W. (1981). The imagery debate: Analogue media versus tacit knowledge. *Psychological Review, 88*, 16–45.

Roediger, H. L., III, & Neely, J. H. (1982). Retrieval blocks in episodic and semantic memory. *Canadian Journal of Psychology, 36*, 213–242.

Rosenberg, S., & Jones, R. A. (1972). A method for investigating and representing a person's implicit theory of personality: Theodore Dreiser's view of people. *Journal of Personality and Social Psychology, 22*, 372–386.

Rosenberg, S., & Sedlak, A. (1972). Structural representations of implicit personality theory. In L. Berkowitz (Ed.), *Advances in experimental social psychology* (Vol. 10, pp. 235–297). New York: Academic Press.

Rothbart, M. (1988). Categorization and impression formation: Capturing the mind's flexibility. In T. K. Srull & R. S. Wyer, Jr. (Eds.), *Advances in social cognition: A dual process model of impression formation* (Vol. 1, pp. 139–144). Hillsdale, NJ: Lawrence Erlbaum Associates.

Rumelhart, D. E., & McClelland, J. L. (1982). An interactive activation model of context effects in letter perception: Part 2. The contextual enhancement effect and some tests and extensions of the model. *Psychological Review, 89*, 60–94.

Rumelhart, D. E., & McClelland, J. L. (Eds.). (1986). *Parallel distributed processing* (Vol. 1). Cambridge, MA: MIT Press.

Sagar, H. A., & Schofield, J. W. (1980). Racial and behavioral cues in black and white children's perceptions of ambiguously aggressive acts. *Journal of Personality and Social Psychology, 39*, 590–598.

Schneider, D. J. (1973). Implicit personality theory: A review. *Psychological Bulletin, 79*, 294–309.

Schneider, W., & Shiffrin, R. M. (1977). Controlled and automatic human information processing: I. Detection, research and attention. *Psychological Review, 84*, 1–66.

Schooler, J. W., & Engstler-Schooler, T. Y. (1990). Verbal overshadowing of visual memories: Some things are better left unsaid. *Cognitive Psychology, 22*, 36–71.

Schwarz, N., & Clore, G. L. (1988). How do I feel about it? The informative function of affective states. In K. Fiedler & J. Forgas (Eds.), *Affect, cognition and social behavior* (pp. 44–62). Toronto: Hogrefe International.

Schwarz, N., Strack, F., Kommer, D., & Wagner, D. (1987). Soccer, rooms, and the quality of your life: Mood effects on judgments of satisfaction with life in general and with specific life domains. *European Journal of Social Psychology, 17*, 69–79.

Secord, P. F. (1958). Facial features and inference processes in interpersonal perception. In R. Tagiuri & L. Petrullo (Eds.), *Person perception and interpersonal behavior* (pp. 300–315). Stanford, CA: Stanford University Press.

Sedikides, C., & Skowronski, J. J. (1991). The law of cognitive structure activation. *Psychological Inquiry, 2*, 169–184.

Shallice, T. (1978). The dominant action system: An information-processing approach to consciousness. In K. S. Pope & J. L. Singer (Eds.), *The stream of consciousness: Scientific investigations into the flow of human experience* (pp. 117–157). New York: Plenum.

Shepard, R. N., & Podgorny, P. (1978). Cognitive processes that resemble perceptual processes. In E. Rosch & B. Lloyd (Eds.), *Cognition and categorization* (pp. 189–237). Hillsdale, NJ: Lawrence Erlbaum Associates.

Sherman, S. J., & Corty, E. (1984). Cognitive heuristics. In R. S. Wyer, Jr. & T. K. Srull (Eds.), *Handbook of social cognition* (Vol. 1, pp. 189–286). Hillsdale, NJ: Lawrence Erlbaum Associates.

Sherry, D. F., & Schacter, D. L. (1987). The evolution of multiple memory systems. *Psychological Review, 94*, 439–454.

Smith, E. R. (1989). Procedural efficiency: General and specific components and effects on social judgment. *Journal of Experimental Social Psychology, 25*, 500–523.

Smith, E. R., & Miller, F. D. (1978). Limits on perception of cognitive processes: A reply to Nisbett and Wilson. *Psychological Review, 85*, 355–362.

Snyder, M. (1987). *Public appearances: Private realities*. New York: Freeman.

Swann, W. B., & Miller, L. C. (1982). Why never forgetting a face matters: Visual imagery and social memory. *Journal of Personality and Social Psychology, 43*, 475–480.

Tesser, A., & Leone, C. (1977). Cognitive schemas and thought as determinants of attitude change. *Journal of Experimental Social Psychology, 13*, 340–356.

Thompson, S. C., & Kelley, J. J. (1981). Judgments of responsibility for activities in close relationships. *Journal of Personality and Social Psychology, 41*, 469–477.

Tourangeau, R., & Rasinski, K. A. (1988). Cognitive processes underlying context effects in attitude measurement. *Psychological Bulletin, 103*, 299–314.

Tulving, E. (1972). Episodic and semantic memory. In E. Tulving & W. Donaldson (Eds.), *Organization and memory* (pp. 381–403). New York: Academic Press.

Tulving, E. (1983). *Elements of episodic memory*. Oxford: Clarendon Press.

Uleman, J. S., & Bargh, J. A. (Eds.). (1989). *Unintended thought* (pp. 253–286). New York: Guilford.

Wilson, T. D., Dunn, D. S., Bybee, J. A., Hyman, D. B., & Rotondo, J. A. (1984). Effects of analyzing reasons on attitude-behavior consistency. *Journal of Personality and Social Psychology, 47*, 5–16.

Wilson, T. D., & Nisbett, R. E. (1978). The accuracy of verbal reports about the effects of stimuli on evaluations and behavior. *Social Psychology, 41*, 118–131.

Winter, L., & Uleman, J. S. (1984). When are social judgments made? Evidence for the spontaneousness of trait inferences. *Journal of Personality and Social Psychology, 47*, 237–252.

Wyer, R. S., & Carlston, D. E. (1979). *Social cognition, inference, and attribution*. Hillsdale, NJ: Lawrence Erlbaum Associates.

Wyer, R. S., & Martin, L. L. (1986). Person memory: The role of traits, group stereotypes and specific behaviors in the cognitive representation of persons. *Journal of Personality and Social Psychology, 50*, 661–675.

Wyer, R. S., & Srull, T. K. (1986). Human cognition in its social context. *Psychological Review, 93*, 322–359.

Wyer, R. S., & Srull, T. K. (1989). *Memory and cognition in its social context*. Hillsdale, NJ: Lawrence Erlbaum Associates.

Zajonc, R. B. (1980). Feeling and thinking: Preferences need no inferences. *American Psychologist, 35*, 151–175.

Zanna, M. P., & Rempel, J. K. (1988). Attitudes: A new look at an old concept. In D. Bar-Tal & A. Kruglanski (Eds.), *The social psychology of knowledge* (pp. 315–344). New York: Cambridge University Press.

Zarate, M. A., & Smith, E. R. (1990). Person categorization and stereotyping. *Social Cognition, 8,* 161–185.

Zillmann, D., Katcher, A. H., & Milavsky, B. (1972). Excitation transfer from physical exercise to subsequent aggressive behavior. *Journal of Experimental Social Psychology, 8,* 247–259.

Author Index

Subject Index

A

Accessibility; *see also* priming
  attitude construction, effects on, 41–42
  person perception, effects on, 14–19,
    41–42, 196–198
  of representations of persons, 327–328
  and subjective judgments, 70–73
Affect; *see* mood
Affective-cognitive consistency
  and attitude–behavior relation, 54–60,
    281–291
  and instrumental and consummatory be-
    haviors, 282–284, 288–290, 293–296
  and interpersonal relationships, 293–296
  mismatch model, 281–296
  and reasons analysis, 51–52
Anchoring and adjustment; *see* change of
    standard effect
Assimilation and contrast effects
  and categorization, 218–241
    awareness of external influences, role of,
      234–235
    into categories of different widths,
      225–227, 232–233
    communication norms, role of, 235–237
    order effects in experiments, role of,
      233–234
    representativeness, role of, 229–232
    salient dimensions, role of, 227–228

    into superordinate or subordinate
      categories, 219–225
  change of standard effect, 218
  and chronic accessibility, 222–225
  in life satisfaction judgments, 201–202,
    229–232, 236–237
  in person perception, 4–14, 70–73, 90–92,
    196–212, 218–241
    flexible processing model, 205–206
    inclusion-exclusion model, 218–241
    person memory model, 4–14
    set-reset model, 200–205, 212–213
Associated systems model, 302–331
Attention; *see* cognitive capacity
Attitude
  and affective-cognitive consistency, 51–60,
    281–296
  change; *see also* attitude stability
    and attitude strength, 49–51
    and attitude structure, 51–52, 281–282
    and context effects, 48–53
    and latitude of acceptance, 48–49
    and mere thought, 43–44, 281–282
    and reasons analysis, 44–47, 283
  construction of, 39–47; *see also* construc-
    tivism
    and accessibility, 41–42
    and context effects in surveys, 40–41
    and latitude of acceptance, 48–49
    from mood, 42–43

355